URBAN EXCESS AND THE LAW:

Capital, Culture and Desire

Christopher Stanley, LLB, PhD, Barrister
Quintin Hogg Research Fellow in Law and Social Theory
University of Westminster, London

Cavendish Publishing Limited

First published in Great Britain 1996 by Cavendish Publishing Limited, The Glass House, Wharton Street, London WC1X 9PX.

Telephone: 0171-278 8000 Facsimile: 0171-278 8080

British Library Cataloguing in Publication Data

A catalogue record for this book is available from the British Library

ISBN 1-85941-209-2

Printed and bound in Great Britain by

Biddles Ltd, Guildford and King's Lynn

DEDICATION

In memory of my father, Brian Stanley, gone too soon

PREFACE

In retrospect this book is a preliminary consideration of the relationship between law, ethics and politics. It was only toward the conclusion of the book that this fact became apparent to me. I am now aware that this book is an opening into a line of inquiry quite different to the one which I had originally intended to pursue. The original line of inquiry informing the essays which constitute this book was one in which I intended to interrogate the relationship between the processes of postmodernisation and the organisation and application of various levels of regulation. The book would therefore have been a particular intervention, a sociology of law. Specifically it would have been a sociology of law couched in terms of the politics of postmodernism as a politics of representation and an examination of the laws of representation. Some of this material survives but the context in which it is worked through has altered. I am now aware that I was embarking upon a larger project, not revising the sociology of law but attempting a statement of possibilities in terms of the relationship between ethics and politics articulated as justice and community. A transition has occurred, as Ari Hirvonen would put it, from an interest in postmodern culture ('Who cares!') to my concern for the expression of justice in the communities of the city ('Who cares?')

This latter concern can be considered in terms of proximity and distance within communities of selves and the mechanisms employed to structure relationships along particular lines of association, obligation and solidarity. These mechanisms are laws which are generated both internally within communities and externally through the processes of the state. A governing tenet of this book, as bell hooks has written, has become the quest for a more generous sense of space and a more compassionate sense of justice. This statement emphasises the relationship between space and ethics and assumes that possibilities remain in the becoming of an alternative humanistically orientated replacement discourse; that there is space left in the city in which justice can be retrieved. If the city is inhabited by 'strangers to ourselves' then a configuration of justice which enables identity must be a justice which protects the space of the other, that other who is the stranger or the refugee denied representation. This is a configuration of justice which does not seek to represent the other but respects the unrepresentability of the other. It is a justice which is operative within a community of others and therefore a justice of multiplicity and difference.

The question 'Who cares?' might be framed as 'Who comes after the Subject?' Poststructuralist analysis has involved variations in the deconstruction of the subject (including the legal subject). The question 'Who comes after the Subject?' raises important issues of identity, agency and community. These issues are central not only to many contemporary accounts within social and cultural theory but more importantly to everyday existence in the city: Who am I? Who should I respect? Where do I belong? I realise now that the ideas contained in this book were circling around these concerns and that, in part, it is a response to the crisis of politics in an anti-political age. This is a preliminary exercise which prepares the ground for further excavations in an explicitly ethical and political context moving toward an intervention in an evolving postmodern jurisprudence.

The original line of inquiry involved the excavation of connections between the processes of cultural change and legal relations in the context of political economy. Specifically the relationship between postmodernisation and regulation became central, with particular emphasis placed upon materialist relations in terms of commodification and consumption, reproduction and simulation. It became apparent that this form of inquiry could not avoid more general considerations regarding the relationship between capital, culture and desire in terms of the tension between legitimation, governmentality and the consequences of deregulation and excess. The structure of this book was modified accordingly into two sections representing the tension identified as existing between regulation and deregulation. In the context of this book the terms 'regulation' and 'deregulation' should be interpreted as meaning, at different points in the text, both strategic ideological imperatives and broader psychological and political consequences in terms of the philosophy and practice of legitimation and governmentality. Prior to elaborating upon the structure of the book it is useful, at this juncture, to reveal some of the other influences and anxieties in operation in its production and organisation.

In addition to the principal relationship between regulation and deregulation and the interrogation of the effects of the tensions inherent between these organisational strategies, the book is also balanced between a number of other broadly defined oppositions and relations: the relationship between order and disorder, the concepts of being within and being without and of being orientated and disorientated. These oppositions and relations might, on occasion, appear to be artificial and contrived but at least serve to juxtapose particular forces and tensions into a relatively coherent series of practices. I do not seek to deny the complexity of the everyday of the city and reject reductionist arguments such as those presented by David Harvey (1990) in his critique of Jean-Francois Lyotard (1984). These oppositions and the ways in which they are deployed can be understood in terms of spatial analysis.

It has been suggested that within modernity an understanding and organisation of time was central and that within postmodernity it is an understanding and organisation of space that is central (Foucault (1986a)). Despite the limitations of this broad perception it is possible to develop it in terms of a law of space and space of law within the contemporary urban sphere. Throughout this book the urban environment is an important element or arena of analysis. The postmodern city – megalopolis – ensures that there is a boundary between the natural world and the material world. The natural world becomes a site of escape or dissent, the world of the theme park and the dispossessed convoy. Nature is mythologised or tamed and the distinctions between the urban and rural, which were established in antiquity and mass produced through the industrial processes of modernisation, are accentuated. The city is bounded for reasons of security and surveillance. The city is the location of the Law and the communities of the city are sites in the expression of justice and identity. The city is the location of the matrix of forces which determine identity, the arena of regulatory strategies ranging from coercion to seduction and the location in which an excess of reality and meaning enables the affirmative reconfiguration of identity, desire, ethics and belonging.

Because I live in a distinct locality within a global city (Stoke Newington, London)

I draw upon my experience in terms of the tensions and effects within particular regulatory rationales. These experiences are translated through theorisation into the oppositions which operate throughout the text. I hope that in the process I do not flatten the intensity of the experiences of negotiating the everyday, but identify actual processes which are in operation and which generate the simulation and banality which constitutes much of the everyday and which is violently encoded into the experiences of regulated bodies. The city is therefore an important site-sight within the ensuing analysis which might be described as a contribution to an examination of the regulation of urbanisation. There is nothing strikingly original in utilising the city as a point of analysis or the experience of urbanisation upon a political, economic and psychological level fitting into a lineage that commences with the psychoanalysis of Sigmund Freud, the cultural theory of Walter Benjamin and the sociology of Georg Simmel. However, the oppositions and relations which I work within and the relationship between postmodernisation and regulation which I interrogate enable me to identify the significance of excess in the postmodern city. The simple identification from the physical sciences that if a force is operative then a counter-force is produced suggests that the forces operative in the city in terms of regulation, order, colonisation and territorialisation generate the counter-forces of deregulation, disorder, de-colonisation and de-territorialisation. It is a suggestion of this book, following Gilles Deleuze, that the process of simultaneous fragmentation and coalescing between regulatory strategies and structures in the local communities or habitus of the global city, produces unintended, random and subversive effects which I identify in terms of excess and dissent. The postmodern city is a site of both governability and ungovernability. This book sets out to confront what are identified as a series of consequences which this tension produces in a transition from the maintenance of order and the classification of that which constitutes the 'within' to the eruption of disorder and the disruption of that which constitutes the 'without'. A strategic deregulatory initiative, as pursued within neo-liberal ideology, has social effects. Some of these are examined in the course of this book and have been studied elsewhere (see for example the collection edited by Ian Taylor (1990)). However, the principal contribution of this book is to relate political economy to legal relations and psychoanalytic perspectives through the discourses of postmodernisation and spatiality.

The 'within' and the 'without' can be understood in economic, social and political terms in addition to being a psychoanalytic response to the forces of cultural production. The figure of the out-law becomes relevant as a figure occupying a particular space without-law in contrast to the sublimated figure of the within-law. To be an out-law is to occupy the territory of transgression, the territory which defines the jurisdiction of the Law. To an extent the actions of the out-law are failed attempts at incursions of the domain of Law and represent a Freudian psychoanalytic paradox (that the Law generates the desire to transgress). They are nevertheless necessary in terms of the activation of a discourse of dissent. It is a contention of this book, following Maurice Blanchot, that transgression re-interpreted does not necessarily affirm the Law but rather as a nomadic and spontaneous experiment in the articulation of desire ruptures the domain of the Law and 'carries away the Law'. In spatial terms there is no 'without' in the contemporary urban sphere but there are disturbances 'within' creating cracks and interstices in the repressive and repressing edifices of the city. These interstitial or liminal spaces might be conceived in sociological terms as the distinction between 'wild zones' and 'tame zones' (discussed by Scott Lash and John Urry (1993)) but this interpretation invests in static and paradigmatic assumptions. What is significant about these alternative spaces is their random configuration and transient existence premised upon particular practices, what Michel Foucault describes as *heterotopias* (Foucault (1986a)). Spaces can be used, abused, neglected and re-cycled but they are not places in the sense that a house is not a home (a statement contained in the problematic art installation *House* by Rachel Whiteread). This book examines the consequences of the simultaneous implosion and explosion of regulatory strategies which enable the identification of disordered spaces of excess and dissent (the trading floor, cyberspace, the industrial wilderness, the bedroom as dungeon) within the urban sphere as possible spaces of community and justice, of identity and belonging. It is the task of future inquiry to examine the translation from space to place in terms of community and justice along the fissures of the postmodern city.

The force of bell hooks' statement rests in both its committed humanism (in the broadest sense) and its context as a preface to a work which relates theory to practice, charged with the understanding that contemporary societies and cultures are marked by extremes of violence and intolerance even though masked by banality and apparent equivalence. In framing this book between two statements describing the extremities of post-urbanisation in terms of satiation and refusal (a letter by Sarah Schulman and a note by Jonathan Miller) it is hoped that the reader will understand the nature of the quest which I have appropriated from bell hooks. Sarah Schulman's letter is located as an opening to the Introduction of the book. Jonathan Miller's note is located as an opening to the Conclusion. The former is a description of the consequences of an excess of regulation in terms of the production of detritus, dispossessed and disenfranchised souls and the maintenance of order through coercion. The latter is a description of the consequences of excess through the unintended effects of deregulation and the production of detritus which can be utilised, appropriated and inverted in an affirmative expression of possibility within the city. These two clippings, which I stumbled upon, describe despair and hope and reflect my anxieties and aspirations which the text in between perhaps loses on occasion but which it struggles to convey. There is perhaps too much ventured in this book. Certainly there is a commitment to disorientation and reorientation; to becoming lost in a territory that was thought familiar and to discover it again through a different route and with fresh insight. The remainder of this preface provides an initial point of departure.

★

Urban Excess and the Law is divided into two parts. The first part is concerned with the relationship between the processes of postmodernisation and the maintenance of order through regulatory strategies. The second part is concerned with the relationship between deregulation and the production of disorder through excess. In the first part capital, culture and desire are interrogated as repressive elements and in the second part they are utilised as potential elements of resistance in the becoming of the with-out law and the space of *heterotopia* as a potential place of community and justice.

Chapter One of the book serves as an Introduction and describes the principal themes. In addition the Introduction considers a number of problematic terms which are used throughout the book. The themes of the book are developed through a series of juxtapositions in an exercise in disorientation. Since the book is not a specific contribution to the sociology of law but rather seeks to inhabit territory between a number of intellectual areas (social theory, cultural studies, urban sociology, critical legal studies, criminology) the scope of the book will perhaps be disorientating on occasion. An important issue at stake in the book is that disorientation followed by reorientation is a beneficial exercise in the development of a critical perspective and ethical position regarding the relationship between postmodernisation, urbanisation and regulation. The Introduction serves as an exercise in disorientation through juxtaposition. Sarah Schulman's letter is juxtaposed with an examination of *The Condition of Postmodernity* by David Harvey (1989), one of the first accounts in English to fuse postmodern theory with political economy. I follow the criticism of Harvey proposed by Meaghan Morris (1992) specifically Harvey's appropriation of *The Postmodern Condition* by Jean-Francois Lyotard (1984). Harvey's interpretation of Lyotard sacrifices the complexities of postmodernity upon the altar of Marxist political economy. In the process, Harvey ignores the clarion call which Lyotard issues at the end of his essay 'What is Postmodernism?':

> Under the general demand for slackening and for appeasement, we can hear the mutterings of the desire for a return to terror, for the realisation of the fantasy to seize reality. The answer is: Let us wage war on totality; let us be witnesses to the unrepresentable; let us activate the differences and save the honour of the name (Lyotard (1984) p 82).

David Harvey's contribution is important because he relates postmodern theory to political economy and in that sense he asks 'Who cares?' However, he is wrong to dismiss Jean-Francois Lyotard of 'Who cares!' because Lyotard's contribution respects the domain of political economy but urges for an understanding of the relationship between economic and cultural processes on a more subtle and complex level that Harvey is not prepared to pursue. Therefore, Lyotard is dismissed and Harvey reduces a politics or justice of difference to all that constitutes the same. Harvey is politically committed but is not prepared to enunciate an ethical dimension within his work since Marx dismissed ethics. In his analysis of metanarratives and narratives of dissensus Lyotard pursues the relationship between politics and ethics. It is a relationship which I pursue in terms of the tension between regulation and deregulation. If Harvey commits an injustice to Lyotard then I commit an injustice to Goodrich. In the closing moments of *The Languages of Law: From Logics of Memory to Nomadic Masks* (1990) Peter Goodrich offers a powerful opening into a consideration of the laws of representation and movement. His discussion of David Walliker's art installation *The Contract*, which I pursue, considers Jean-Jacques Rousseau 'working off the record … outwith the law'. I do not follow Goodrich's thesis regarding the aesthetic dimension of law but develop his discussion of *The Contract* as a starting point into the territory which the essays in this book traverse. In addition, Harvey and Goodrich, in their very different accounts, are concerned with the laws of space and the space of law, specifically the operation of law in the urban sphere. The Introduction stresses the importance of the spatial dynamic and the postmodern city as megalopolis, a theme developed in Part I.

Part I of the book is divided into three chapters which provide an analysis in the conceptualisation of the problems of regulation in contemporary urban culture. The analysis considers how particular elements in the contemporary crisis of regulation can be interrogated utilising a framework of postmodern theory. The analysis is based on the proposition that contemporary urban culture is subject to an inflation or excess of regulatory strategies resulting from a crisis of legitimation pursuant upon the development of consumerism. This crisis is manifested as a struggle in the maintenance of order and the replication of a continuous series of what Fredric Jameson calls 'last minute salvage operations' as the processes of urbanisation move from the mode of production to the mode of reproduction. The sources of legitimation identifiable within modernity understood as the metanarrative and expressed as a governmentality within a political economy of domination, exploitation and subordination have been transformed through the sovereignty of consumption and signification. Governmentality within postmodernity is operative as the insidious satiation and manufacture of desire in the absence of metanarrative certainty. Regulation is reliant upon the delegation of legitimation to individuals as specialists in multiple deregulatory strategies. This tendency contains the possibility of the activation of resistance through the alienation of desire in deregulated spaces of refusal, spaces identified within urban culture as a result of the excesses of urban culture.

Chapter Two (Regulation and Urban Culture: Defining Elements) is divided into two sections. The first section (Variations upon Postmodernism) introduces the principal configurations of postmodernity specifically in terms of the transition in the mode of production. It also serves as an incomplete map of the postmodern urban sphere and how the terrain of contemporary urban culture might be approached (Megalopolis: An Emptiness Filled With Signs). The second section (Sources of Order) engages with the issue of the tension between regulation and deregulation in the maintenance of order and the production of disorder through an analysis of the related themes of legitimation, culture and regulation.

Chapter Three (Regulation and Urban Order: Determining Forces) is concerned with a process of retrieval in an examination of the forces of affluence, anomie and alienation. These forces are considered as the principal sources in the erosion of legitimation and the crisis of regulation. These are the forces or conditions which determine cultures for action and are therefore operative in the construction of identity. It is suggested that the accentuation of these forces serve as the central determinants in the emancipation through de-colonisation of emergent spaces of resistance through refusal (Megalopolis: Tears in the Fabric).

Chapter Four (Speculations on the Disorder of Capital) serves as a bridge between the previous expository and theoretical chapters and Part II of the book. This chapter examines the specific issues of relations of capital and the processes of postmodernisation within a central arena (the capital markets). Chapter Four is divided into two sections. The first section (The Symbolic Laws of Capital) examines the transition in the nature of finance capital in a political economy of reproduction. The tension existing between competing regulatory regimes suggests that the culture of consumption into which capitalism has developed is an order where capital itself has transmuted into a sign system devoid of reality of meaning and value and is therefore, in terms of legitimation, a deregulated order. The second section (Panic! Coke-Blip Capitalism) explores some of the consequences in this development of capitalism. Specifically the impact of 'the symbolic laws of capital' upon the physical structure of the city and individual attitudes toward regulation and legitimation is assessed. This section is in the form of a case study of the financial markets of the City of London between 1984–1989. This was a period in which financial transactions were deregulated under the ideological imperative of the neo-liberal 'enterprise culture ethos' which was a principal tenet of the prevailing political administration. If capital ceased to convey meaning and value in the sense of being attached to transferable commodities then the attitudes of practitioners now encouraged to become 'enterprising' and self-regulating ensured that there was a regulatory void into which 'deviant' or anomic activity flourished. The fracturing of the previously stable, if fragile, hegemony engendered an indeterminacy in normative values accentuated by regulatory confusion: an economy of transgression. The analysis concludes with an interrogation of the concepts of the 'wild zone' and the 'tame zone' through a comparison between transgressive behaviour in the financial markets of the City of London (a culture of affluence) and in the East End of London which has similarly been subject to deregulation (a culture of urban deprivation). Simple distinctions such as 'tame' and 'wild' in urban sociological discourse are far more complex than initially perceived when considered in terms of violence and banality when the forces of affluence, anomie and alienation are the principal determinants of power relations and deregulation is adopted as the strategic regulatory initiative.

Part II consists of an exercise in the theory and practice of excess (The Laws of Desire) illustrated and supplemented by Three Stories in Urban Excess. Chapter Five provides a framework of analysis regarding an approach to the conceptualisation of the problems and possibilities resulting from the deregulation of urban culture. This framework utilises contemporary social, cultural and psychoanalytic theory. This theoretical exercise is then applied in the form of a series of narratives of dissent (Three Stories in Urban Excess) interrogating the possibility of resistance through excess. Chapter Five serves as an introductory intervention as to how particular representations of excess (developed within the narratives of dissent as the psychotic-pathological, the asocial and the sexual) articulated within 'subversive' or alternative social theory and psychoanalytic practice can be affirmatively utilised in the formation of patterns of resistance. Building upon the effects of the determining forces examined in Part I and developing the idea of implosion and rupture of order through regulatory excess, I propose an analysis of a post-regulatory urban culture.

Chapter Five is divided into four related sections. In maintaining an affirmative expression of possibility each section examines that which lies beyond or between the constant of the external forces of the contemporary urban order. I move from the ordered zone within-law to the disordered zone without-law. The analysis does not seek to identify that which is beyond (there is no beyond within megalopolis) but rather to approach the spaces of refusal constituted through excess. These are the spaces which at the moment of their recognition deny presence. But they 'constitute' violent and random de-determined possibilities in the activation of nomadic fields of alternative governmentality within which identity, desire, justice and community might be affirmatively re-configured. Each of the four sections of the chapter deals with a different aspect of excess. The first aspect is the politic-poetics of representation. Politics in the postmodern is a politics of representation. In the absence of metanarrative as ideology what is left is the trace of ideology and belief through the organisation of signs. The source of the image of the political disappears leaving only the processes of representation of the political. This can be described as a crisis of nomination if the naming of emergent signs is a regulatory goal. To be unrepresentable and in excess of the limits of representation-nomination assumes a dual prospect of being refused but also a freedom in the expression of an unencumbered identity. The second aspect is the body. If the 'punitive archipelago' of the postmodern city is constituted by a repressing body politic then the force of this repression is operative upon the body of the individual through the body of law. The manipulation, adaptation and destruction of the body as the principal site in the articulation of desire determines that its location as a site of power relations attains a resonance in the 'processes' of spatial and temporal disorder when all other sites in the expression of desire have been neutralised by external forces. This idea is pursued through an examination of three bodies: the body of self, the body politic and the body-without-organs. The third aspect is the concept of transgression. Transgression is the practice through which a boundary is constituted. In one interpretation transgression is what Law desires. This does not deny the importance of transgression in continuously challenging the inscription of externally determined boundaries. However, I argue that transgression can be alternatively interpreted as an affirmative function 'toward transcendence' in the erosion of the norm. The moment and movement of transgression as experiment simultaneously causes a limit to arise but is also the moment which releases the spores of the phantasm and the nomad. The limit is not destroyed but rather it is ruptured and the Law carried away. The final aspect is therefore the figure of the phantasm. Desire represents lack: how are we to interpret this statement in an affluent-satiated urban culture where the primary regulatory mode is the structuring of the expectation that desire will be fulfilled? Phantasy is a *mis-en-scène* of desire, both a setting out of lack (of what is absent) and a representation of satisfaction (of what is present). The affirmation of a lack (expressed as refusal) becomes a moment in the deregulation of the representation of desire. As a political moment of opposition, phantasy encapsulates the unrepresentable, the body-without-organs and affirmative transgression. The movement of the phantasm is the movement of a nomadic and de-structured or rhizomic governmentality affording alternative possibilities in justice and community.

Three Stories in Urban Excess supplement and illustrate the operation of the theoretical perspective suggested in Chapter Five. These narratives of dissent each tell stories of particular moments of excess in the postmodern city and reflect experiences 'off the record', 'moonlighting' activities 'out with the law'. They are offered as a palliative to the ordered and violent banality of contemporary consumer culture; but they must remain random and disordered if they are to maintain their force as affective mutterings of discord which disrupt the 'moving equilibrium' of external hegemonic conflict. These stories reflect activities within, and the interstitial and liminal. They are 'dangerous' stories because they relate the violent instability of de-determined desire, desires which have not yet been spoken and nominated, located and ordered. These are stories which in my act of locating them immediately constitutes them as failures because they reflect the lack of the Law. But as deregulated moments within deregulated spaces they can be interpreted as affirmations of that which remains possible, alternative configurations of identity and governmentality. These localised and transitory moments demonstrate the possibility of rupturing the fabric of the punitive archipelago of megalopolis, constant incursions and struggles out with an equally destabilised and dangerous and despotic nomadic law of movement, a conflict in terms of affirmative and negative discontinuity.

The first story (Chapter Six) is the most obvious failure in terms of an affirmative transgression. It serves, in part, as a supplement to the themes of Part I (Speculations on the Disorder of Capital) in that it is an analysis of a representation (*American Psycho*) of the violent tyranny of consumption. It also serves as the most violent example of a consequence of the shattering of the relationship between identity and consumption (the refusal or excess of desire) and the retrieval of the 'pre-modern' instincts toward sacrifice and catharsis. In its depiction of violence against others the protagonist of *American Psycho* attempts to affirm and define, through existential angst and *ressentiment*, his fractured identity as an other to the order which has produced him through the satiation of his desire.

The second story (Chapter Seven) confronts activities which have been classified as deviant within contemporary British society. The narrative operates on two levels. First, it identifies the limitations of a social policy orientated criminology. In explaining deviancy in the absence of a 'subcultural career' model, criminologists offer inadequate explanations of the social effects of deregulatory ideology in the areas of (white-collar crime), computer hacking, joyriding and raving. Second, these 'problems of deviance' within contemporary urban youth culture are activities performed in the absence of affluence. They can be interpreted as activities in a refusal of consumption and manifestations of a de-determined collectivity of desire through the utilisation of the techniques of appropriation and inversion.

The techniques of appropriation and inversion are significant in the final story of urban excess (Chapter Eight). Here the disordered body and the construction of desire through sexuality are central. The activity of sado-masochism can be interpreted as a narrative of dissensus in that it is operative as a non-referential sexual practice which does not rely upon external models of order and governance and inverts stabilised conceptions of sexual relations. The case of *R v Brown* illustrates the desire of the Law to regulate sexuality (to achieve docile bodies) and the impossibility of Law to recognise any other desires but its own, even when bought within its gaze and appropriating the techniques of the Law. As a *mis-en-scène* of desire, sado-masochism is the expression of an alternative governmentality where individual desire-identity is reliant upon the desire-identity of an other. The desire within sado-masochistic sexual practice is premised upon lack but it is the affirmative celebration of this lack (the absence of penetration) which suggests sado-masochism as a possible source of alternative configurations of ethical responsibility and solidarity.

The Conclusion (Chapter Nine) develops the discussion regarding the relationship between law, desire and violence through an examination of the later work of Michel Foucault utilising the critique offered by John Rajchman (1991). Central to Foucault's late work was the question of the relationship between desire-identity and community-obligation. The Conclusion also offers a review of some of the problems which have arisen through an analysis of the possibility of resistance through the exploitation of excess, principally the potential falling toward apocalypticism and fascism. The Conclusion is prefaced by an extract from the notes which accompany Jonathan Miller's scrapbook of photographs, images of 'stuff seized from the edge of the officially visible'. The Three Stories of Urban Excess can be understood as 'stories at the edge of the officially visible'. Miller's notes on these images suggests their potentiality ('that I might do something with them'). It is a similar idea to the one which I pursue in this book. In locating sites of potentiality through rejection (the social effects of free market policies) or through the identification of activities and spaces occurring in the interstitial spaces between competing regulatory strategies (alternative sources of legitimation) the book offers an affirmative response to the question of politics in an anti-political age through the utilisation of chaos and indeterminacy in an expression of the potential of alternative configurations of identity and desire, justice and community in the space of the *heterotopia*.

ACKNOWLEDGMENTS

> This is an intervention. A message from that space in the margin that is a site of creativity and power, that inclusive space where we recover ourselves, where we move in solidarity to erase the category coloniser/colonised. Marginality is the space of resistance. Enter that space. Let us meet there (hooks (1990) p 152).

I wish to thank a number of people who have been important either directly or indirectly in the formulation and production of this book. These are some of the people I would desire to meet in the marginal space. Rolando Gaete provided good humour and paganism on Lesvos and afterwards in *The Magpie and Stump* where he was joined by Sam Whimster who boosted my confidence when the black dog barked. Colin Perrin was a constant source of intellectual provocation and provided a critical gaze. Peter Fitzpatrick and the Postgraduate Group on Law and Social Theory at the University of Kent at Canterbury provided an amenable space in which to discuss some of the issues confronted in my research. Ari Hirvonen gave me the possibility of refuge in addition to a sense of poetry. Anne Bottomley provided the initial intellectual spur. Peter Goodrich has consistently demonstrated a condition of possibility. Lee Sheridan, Margaret Sheridan, David Staton and Clive Unsworth kept me supplied with gin, cigarettes and much else beside. Lynne Williams provided the space in which I could play with the monster in the box. Without her tolerance and enthusiasm beyond the call of duty my indolence and desire to fall toward un-working would have overwhelmed me. For which my love is inadequate.

I have presented papers relating to this book at a number of seminars and conferences: *Critical Legal Conference*, University of Staffordshire, 1992; *Colloquium of the International Association for the Semiotics of Law*, Lesvos, 1992, Jerusalem, 1993, Bordeaux, 1994; *Sex-Theory-Law Conference*, University of Keele, 1993; *Polycentric Law*, University of Helsinki, 1993 and 1994; *Manchester Institute for Law and Popular Culture*, Manchester, 1993; *Boundaries Seminar*, University of Kent, 1993; *Journal of Law and Society Seminar*, Cardiff, 1994; *Private Licence and Public Order Seminar,* London Guildhall University, 1994; Institute for Legal Science B, University of Copenhagen, 1995; *City, Nation, World*, 2nd Theory, Culture & Society Conference, Berlin, 1995. I am grateful to all those who have offered advice and criticism and to the University of Kent at Canterbury and the British Council for funding my participation at these events.

Christopher Stanley
Stoke Newington
September 1995

CONTENTS

URBAN EXCESS AND THE LAW

CAPITAL, CULTURE AND DESIRE

Preface — *iii*
Acknowledgments — *xiii*

1 INTRODUCTION: DISORIENTATION *CONTRA* HARVEY AND *VIA* GOODRICH — 1
David Harvey, *The Condition of Postmodernity* — 1
Possibilities on the Other Side of Harvey — 5
Peter Goodrich, *The Languages of Law* — 11
Out-With the Law: Strategies in Critique — 16

PART I

2 REGULATION AND URBAN CULTURE: DEFINING ELEMENTS — 21
Problems of Definition — 21
Variations upon Postmodernism — 25
1 Postmodernity — 27
2 Postmodernisation — 28
3 Postindustrialism — 29
Megalopolis: An Emptiness Filled With Signs — 30
Sources of Order — 35
1 Legitimation — 35
2 Culture — 37
3 Regulation — 42

3 REGULATION AND URBAN ORDER: DETERMINING FORCES — 45
Affluence: — 45
1 An Urban Culture of Consumption — 45
2 An Urban Economy of Transgression — 47
Anomie: — 48
1 Access To and Absence of Means — 48
2 Excessive Abstract Fantasies — 50
Alienation: — 56
1 Market Transformations — 56
2 Accelerated Sclerosis — 59
Megalopolis: Tears in the Fabric — 61

4 SPECULATIONS ON THE DISORDER OF CAPITAL — 69
The Territory and Tyranny of Money — 69
1 The Symbolic Laws of Capital — 72
(a) From Finance Capital to Panic Money — 72
(b) Old City and New City — 80

2 Panic! Coke-Blip Capitalism 87
(a) Money Crime and State Crime 87
(b) Tame Zones and Wild Zones 99

PART II

5 DEREGULATION AND URBAN EXCESS: THE LAWS OF DESIRE 105
Excess, Critique and the Limit: Introduction 105
1 The Politic-Poetics of the Unrepresentable 108
2 Disciplined Body to Body-Without-Organs 112
3 Transgression as Affirmation 117
4 Law, Desire and the Phantasm 121

6 THREE STORIES IN URBAN EXCESS: *AMERICAN PSYCHO* 127
American Psycho, Visual Culture and Genre 127
'This is Not an Exit' 132
'Abandon All Hope Ye Who Enter Here' 134
The Aesthetics of Violence 136
Sacrifice and Catharsis 138

7 THREE STORIES IN URBAN EXCESS: YOUTH CULTURES 145
Narratives of Dissent in the Wild Zone 145
Definition and Deconstruction of Events 156
Individuals, Groups and Subcultures 159
Techniques of Appropriation and Inversion 162
Excess, Movement and Spatial Disorganisation 164

8 THREE STORIES IN URBAN EXCESS: *R v BROWN* 169
Sado-Masochism and the Law 169
From Operation Spanner to *R v Brown* 171
Interpretations and Diversions 174
The Common Law and a Remembrance of Times Past 178
Techniques of Appropriation and Inversion 181

9 CONCLUSION: REORIENTATION 191

Bibliography *199*
Index *215*

CHAPTER ONE

INTRODUCTION: DISORIENTATION *CONTRA* HARVEY AND *VIA* GOODRICH

New York is death.

They have closed all public schools, all walk-in clinics and pharmacies in city hospitals; eliminated conductors from the subways at night, and are eliminating half of the VD and HIV testing centres. They are shutting off 10% of the street lights, cutting back on street cleaning and eliminating housing inspection.

Yesterday, 7000 city workers were laid off. The arts budget has been cut by 56%. I have one to three acquaintances who die every week.

Tompkins Square Park was put under police occupation at a cost of 100,000 dollars per day to keep the homeless out. Now the park is closed for the entire summer. They only let you in if you are going to play basketball or walk your dog. This requires about fifty policemen to maintain. They have knocked down the bandshell and taken out all the benches and the chess tables because people sleep on them. There are police officers in every coffee shop and in every store. They stand on every corner.

If I bump into a friend on the corner, and we have a conversation, it takes place in front of the police.

ACT-UP has requested emergency disaster relief from the UN.

My personal goal is not to fall apart and to live intact throughout the nineties.

It is virtually impossible to set a goal higher than this right now (Sarah Schulman, letter of 19 June 1991).

DAVID HARVEY, *THE CONDITION OF POSTMODERNITY*

In *The Condition of Postmodernity* David Harvey states his 'Argument' in four paragraphs. It is an achievement enviable in its certainty. I utilise this 'achievement' as a starting point in a process of disorientation on two levels. First, regarding the wonder of the moment of alterity. Second, as a point of departure in which Harvey's work is utilised in a positioning of my own. My centre established through his margin:

> There has been a sea-change in cultural as well as in political-economic practices since around 1972.
>
> This sea change is bound up with the emergence of new dominant ways in which we experience space and time.
>
> While simultaneity in the shifting dimensions of time and space is no proof of necessary or causal connection, strong *a priori* grounds can be adduced for the proposition that there is a sole kind of necessary relation between the rise of postmodernist cultural forms, the emergence of more flexible modes of capital accumulation, and a new round of 'time-space compression' in the organisation of capitalism.

> But these changes, when set against the basic rules of capitalistic accumulation, appear more as shifts in surface appearance rather than as signs of the emergence of some entirely new postcapitalist or even postindustrial society (Harvey (1989) p vii).

Alternatively ... New York is death ...

The encounter with an alien taxonomy can be both comic and wondrous, antagonistic and humiliating. I confront another's certainty in an image of the world far removed from what had previously been perceived as real. The centre is relocated and you find that you are elsewhere. My confrontation with Harvey and therefore my point of departure is based upon his erasure of difference and his sovereignty of completeness upon an ideological premise. But as Meaghan Morris comments, what is wonderful about the moment of alterity is that we apprehend in an 'exotic' system of the thought 'the limitation of our own' (Morris (1992) p 253; see also Morris (1993)). The critical and cultural practices that Harvey reduces to the same may constitute a world of difference to me, but they also set practical limits to my everyday world. My encounter with Harvey forces me to confront the tensions and paradoxes inherent in my view of the contemporary and the stories that I desire to tell about it. But there are many ways of telling and using stories. My dispute with Harvey enables me to offer an alternative story via Peter Goodrich, and in the process commence telling a third story.

I am alarmed by Harvey's reduction of the fragmented, ephemeral and chaotic condition of the contemporary into an equation between 'time-space compression and flexible accumulation'. Harvey analyses postmodernity by first rewriting as 'the same' all the differences that for him constitute it as a topic for debate in the first place. This allows him to state: 'If there is a meta-theory with which to embrace all these gyrations of postmodern thinking and cultural production, then why should we not deploy it?' (Harvey (1989) p 337). This statement flattens the complexity of the power relations Harvey is confronting and constitutes the phenomena they claim to describe. As Morris comments: 'Harvey's discourse on place is itself a little mired in theoretical nostalgia' (Morris (1993) p 43). Counter this with Jean-Francois Lyotard's postmodern clarion call and certainty or completeness is immediately vanquished:

> The answer is: Let us wage a war on totality; let us be witness to the unrepresentable; let us activate the differences and save the honour of the name.'(Lyotard (1984) p 82).

It is possible to commence from the position that there is no meta-theory and that there are good reasons why we should not pretend that there is. What Harvey appropriates is a partial reading of Lyotard. Harvey undertakes an *Inquiry* into the origins of cultural change. He is impressed by the pace and variety of change in advanced societies and accepts a version of the modernity-postmodernity distinction. Harvey concludes that recent transformations are 'certainly within the grasp of historical materialist enquiry, even capable of theorisation by way of the metanarrative of capitalist development that Marx proposed' (Harvey (1989) p 328). Harvey's problem is his attempt to make the phenomenon fit the framework capped by the announcement that the framework fits the phenomenon.

Lyotard undertakes a *Report* on knowledge. He challenges the framework and explores the phenomenon. Harvey never confronts Lyotard's thesis about postmodern knowledge. Instead he treats Lyotard's work as a symptom of the postmodern condition, using fragments of Lyotard's discourse to create an image of a complete postmodernism. Lyotard's 'grand narrative' and 'metadiscourse' merge in Harvey's 'meta-theory', and the 'specifity' that Lyotard accords to 'language games' is converted by Harvey into a 'fetishism' of 'impenetrable', 'opaque otherness' (Harvey (1989) p 117). 'Meta-theory' and 'otherness' represent major stakes for Harvey's critique of postmodernism - a defence of a totalising ideology and an attack on particularism. Lyotard *becomes* The Postmodern Condition through which Harvey constructs his economically determinist version.

In spatial terms Harvey desires structure. His language regularly attests to a form of grounding. It is a language which continually sets depth, radicality and foundation against the airy insubstantiality or miasmatic opacity of the cultural. He writes of the 'perverse base' which place-bound identity provides, and of 'the invariant elements and relations that Marx defined as fundamental to any capitalist mode of production' which are 'omnipresent beneath all the surface froth and evanescence, the fragmentations and disruptions, so characteristic of present political economy'. The proliferating epiphenomenality of the postmodern is imaged as 'froth and evanescence', an opaque world of unfathomable differences (Harvey (1989) pp 188; 179), which Lyotard, for Harvey, has unwisely invested in.

But, where is Lyotard and what stories does *he* desire to tell? Harvey gives us only his particular reading of the anxiety that Lyotard arouses and misses completely the sarcasm of Lyotard's text. For example, Harvey cites the following passage in which Lyotard becomes the arch postmodernist who accommodates art to capitalism: 'Eclecticism is the degree zero of contemporary general culture: one listens to reggae, watches a western, eats McDonald's food for lunch and local cuisine for dinner, wears Paris perfume in Tokyo and 'retro' clothes in Hong Kong' (Harvey (1989) p 87 citing Lyotard (1984) p 76). What Harvey fails to include (I will not impute intent) is Lyotard's statement following this extracted passage, which is preceded by a semi-colon and not by a full stop: 'Knowledge is a matter for TV games. It is easy to find a public for eclectic works' (Lyotard (1984) p 76). Ironically, Harvey reflects Lyotard's concern with contemporary 'anything goes' culture but Lyotard becomes the celebrant of that culture in Harvey's reading. This identification enables Harvey to confront a particular definition of postmodernism *competitive* with his own. Lyotard's contempt for 'TV games' disappears in Harvey's quotation just as the similarity between the two is dismissed. Harvey presents a partial representation of Lyotard.

This issue of representation locks Harvey's text into a theory of representation which is reductive and not productive of social experience. It is a text which cannot tell the difference. What Harvey is left with, after the failure of his deployment of the materialist critique in comprehending the ephemeral and the nostalgic, is ambivalence. This leaves Harvey with a space, alien to a totalising ideological analysis. It is this space that constitutes the postmodern. Harvey finds refuge in an 'other space' which is the site of production of 'othering' tropes in response to images because the interpretation of this space depends on denying its own status – *like theirs* – as representation, as material production, as 'image'. Harvey is compelled to install his discourse in the endless circuit of its own specularity - 'oscillating between desire and hostility' for that 'other space', its 'mirror image' (Morris (1992) p 271). Harvey is confined as the theorist of the 'gigantic pincer of the dialectic' which means that he is confined to a wasteground in which postmodernism becomes a privileged non-space, where he constantly desires to affirm the possibility of value, though this value can never be articulated in forms which are not simultaneously alienated into one or other of particular vested aestheticisms.

Foucault (1986a) has a term for an 'other space' – *heterotopia*. Foucault's 'other spaces' are to be found elsewhere in contemporary social and cultural theory. In Maffesoli (1991a) they are 'lived spaces'. In hooks (1991) they are 'margins'. In Jardine (1985) they are maps of spaces to be explored . In Deleuze and Guattari (1986) they are 'constellations or networks of nomadology'. In Certeau they are spaces of 'being in between' (Certeau (1988) p 41). Massey comments:

> In debates around identity the terminology of space, location, positionality and place figures prominently. Homi Bhaba, in discussions of cultural identity, argues for a 'third space'. Jameson, faced with what he sees as the global confusion of postmodern times, the 'disorientation of saturated space', calls for an exercise in cognitive mapping. And Laclau, in his own very different reflections on the 'new revolution of our time', uses the terms 'temporal' and 'spatial' as the major differentiations between ways of conceptualising systems of social relations (Massey (1993) p 141).

David Harvey, thinking of an 'impossible' space, relates this to the postmodern sense of 'incongruous space' (Harvey (1989) p 48). For Foucault, 'other' does not mean 'impossible'. Utopia is a placeless place; heterotopias are *real* places, social countersites which may juxtapose *incompatible* spaces. Between utopia and heterotopia, states Foucault, there exists 'a sort of mixed, joint experience' – the mirror. It is utopian since 'I see myself there where I am not, in an unreal virtual space that opens up behind the surface.' But the mirror does exist in reality, where it exerts 'a sort of counteraction' on my own position; gazing back at myself, I 'reconstitute myself there where I am' (Foucault (1986a) p 24). Harvey's reflection does not appear in this mirror.

Harvey acknowledges a 'radical edge' to what he calls postmodernism's stress on the 'multiple forms of otherness'. He also wants to see postmodernism as 'mimetic of the social, economic and political practices in society' (Harvey (1989) p 113), again putting cultural practice outside social relations. He next wants to say that postmodernism is *not* 'solely mimetic', but 'an aesthetic intervention in politics, economy and social life in its own right' (Harvey (1989) p 114). But he has no way of differentiating aesthetic interventions, no way of explaining how they relate to other kinds of actions, and no way of theorising the 'conjoining of mimesis and aesthetic intervention' (Harvey (1989) p 115) that he asserts but cannot explain. It is this failure that allows a different voice to speak another story about another space.

POSSIBILITIES ON THE OTHER SIDE OF HARVEY

> The imaginary landscape of an inquiry is not without value, even if it is without rigour. It restores what was earlier called 'popular culture', but it does so in order to transform what was represented as the matrix-force of history into a mobile infinity of tactics ... The landscape that represents these phenomena is an imaginary mode and thus has an overall corrective and therapeutic value in resisting their reduction by a lateral examination. It at least assures their presence as ghosts (Certeau (1988) pp 41-42).

I am left with a disjuncture and an apparent dysfunctional series of interventions. The intention is to interpret the space which is other to Harvey but to do so without the threat of colonisation. In not deploying a meta-theory I am able to articulate the process of simultaneous rupture and suture between discourses and the fragmentation and cohesion between the dominant forms of cultural existence. The postmodern is not a state of fragmentation but rather of the peculiar persistence to the 'dominant' institutional narratives and structures of the modern which are invariably represented as homogeneous and without contradiction. This is one of the more alarming oversights of the commentators and a partial excuse for Harvey's position. It is necessary to interrogate the persistence of the modern through the opportunities provided in the glimpses of the postmodern: the definition of the centre by the determination of the margin. The postmodern in this version becomes the intermediary of subtle, subaltern and alternative voices telling other stories. The activation and interrogation of these other voices occurs in the spaces in between, the interstices and the spaces of otherness and liminality. These are the countersites to the colonised spaces of the contemporary of metanarrative fatigue which constitutes the fragile structures of the everyday of ordered existence. These are the voices which speak of a more generous sense of space and a more compassionate sense of justice.

A glimpse of the 'other' side can only be made available through the deployment of an impression or the creation of an ambience which conveys something of the nature of the disorder in the contemporary from which dominant strategic interests and forces constantly strive to construct order so as to reproduce and reconstruct themselves. The metaphor becomes the principal mechanism through which experience can be articulated. It is the spatial metaphor as opposed to the temporal metaphor which is persistent within contemporary theory: 'It is space not time that hides consequences from us' (Berger (1984)). Whilst the metaphor serves as a device for translating experience, spatial relations are power relations representing particular interests. What must be examined is the mutual translation between geographical and metaphorical space and the nullification of the significance in philosophical and political terms of absolute space. It is not space per se which expresses power but the thoroughly naturalised absolute conception of space that developed with capitalism and which expresses a specific tyranny of power. The spatial metaphor must be approached as one of complexity. It is a complexity which can be demonstrated in the metaphor of the central determinant in the organisation of contemporary power relations, the metaphor of the impossible map of megalopolis as the postmodern city. The urban is both the material form and geography of megalopolis and simultaneously the real and representable, imagined and represented, a broad definition, an encompassing and combinatorial social spatiality which is a grounded metaphor, a concrete abstraction and a social hieroglyph.

In its everyday details, its mixed histories, languages and cultures and its elaborate evidence of global tendencies and local distinctions, the figure of the city, as both a real and an imaginary space, provides a map for interpreting the experiences and theories of the everyday. But the map with its implicit dependence upon the survey of a stable terrain, fixed referents and measurement, seems to contradict the palpable flux and fluidity of metropolitan life and cosmopolitan movement: maps are full of references and indications but they are not peopled. A preliminary orientation does not exhaust reality. The city plan is a rationalisation of space and time and permits us to grasp an outline – some sort of location – but not the contexts, cultures, histories, languages, experiences, desires and hopes that course though the urban body as the cognitive map of the mental life of the metropolitan. The latter pierce the topography and spill over the edges of the map.

Beyond the edges and abstract one-dimensional indications are encountered the space of the vibrant, everyday world and its challenge of complexity. Here movement is along invisible grids and networks where emotional energies and the imaginary flow, and where the continual slippage of sense maintains the promise of meaning. This is the gendered city, the city of ethnicities, the territories of different social groups, shifting centres and peripheries. The city is both a fixed object of design and simultaneously plastic and historical: the site of transitory events, movements and memories. This is the experience of the city as both space of conflict and space of discourse. Here both thought and everyday activities move in the realm of uncertainty. The linearity of epistemology and ontology breaks down as we orbit in a perpetual paradox: we bestow sense yet we can never be certain in our proclamations. The idea of cultural complexity weakens earlier schemata and paradigms; it destabilises and decentres previous theories and sociologies. The narrow arrow of linear progress is replaced by an open spiral of hybrid cultures and contaminations. The city suggests creative disorder, an instructive confusion and disorientation, an interloping space in which imagination conveys you in every direction, even toward the previously unthought. Here dissonance and interrogation lie between situated and disembodied knowledges and the location of theory is disturbed. This is a city incapable of being mapped (Chambers (1993) p 190):

> A map can tell me how to find a place. When I get there, following the map faithfully, the place is not the place of my imagination. Maps, growing ever more real, are much less true (Winterson, 1989: p 81).

Heidegger (1971) translated *ethos* as 'the place where one lives or dwells.' The spatial and topographical metaphor assumes further relevance on the level of belonging. The issue in ontological terms is the struggle between the internal-nomadic and the external-symbolic. The urban is both the experience of the surface fusion of identity organised around the privileged voice and stable subjectivity of the external, and the failure to mask the dislocation of the intellectual subject of the internal: dislodging the inertia of the I. As Chambers writes:

> It leads to the release of diverse voices, an encounter with an 'other' side, an unfolding of the self, and negates the possibility of reducing diversity to the identical. Knowledge takes a holiday, a sabbatical, from the traditional ideas of truth and scholarship as unitary and transcendental entities. Against the virility of a self-assured, strong thought, it proposes a weaker, but more extensive, mode of thinking that is contaminated, transgressive, multi-directional and transitive (Chambers (1993) p 190).

★

On the basis of a partial critique of Harvey and an introduction to the complex fabric of the city, it is possible to state four principal themes within this work. These provide an intimation of the informing criteria through which this work operates:

- The theme of postmodernity operating as a potential site of critique not of the imminence of the present but as a parallel intermediate position from which to analyse, through disjuncture, the persistence of the 'dominant' institutional narratives and structures of the modern which appear in percipient fragmentation. The postmodern as a particular frame of analysis articulates other histories, nuances and narratives that combine in constituting the present. These are analysed in terms of the relationship between order and disorder, repression and resistance, regulation and deregulation, the hierarchical and the linear, the external and the internal and the dominant and the subordinate.
- The theme of space constituting relations of power within the urban. It is tempting to become trapped by the oppositions of space and non-space, self and other, which so often circulate in contemporary critical discourse. What is important to determine is the ambivalence and intersubjectivity between apparent oppositional forces. This allows the possibility of suggesting that there exist spaces which are yet to be colonised by competing narrative regimes, spaces which exist or are yet to exist and which are in between the real and the imaginary. These are spaces which exist beyond the border but which do not form a determinate presence: 'A boundary is not that at which something stops, but, as the Greeks recognised, the boundary is that from which something begins its presencing' (Heidegger (1971) p 154). This is the realm of the interstice or intersubjectivity: *heterotopia*.[1]

---

1 Feminist theorists in particular have been trying to find a new space and a new language with which to describe this space, while hoping to avoid the subjection of that space and the colonisation of that language by the old imperatives of male domination. I was encouraged by Alice Jardine's concept of *Gynesis*: 'a map of new spaces yet to be explored' (Jardine (1985) p 52). But when someone starts to talk about new spaces, new territories, new languages, without quite being able to describe them, they are arguing as much through image and metaphor as they are through evidence and logic. A point made eloquently by Robert Hewison ((1993) pp 248-253). I have made a claim for the value of image and metaphor as devices to capture the spirit, convey the ambience. It is necessary that the dry discourse of reason begins to run with the less channelled streams of the imagination. However, this work is 'constructed' through a sequence of images which are not arbitrarily chosen. As with the problem of the fixation with the metaphor of fragmentation which has been falsely attributed to the postmodern, the metaphor of the fracture or the interstice similarly points to the interruption of the smooth surface of reproduction. It is a gap which opens out towards the identification of new territory, to be occupied by new forms. If then, we were to step back and trace all these fractures and faultlines, it may be possible to see a new pattern, a new network emerge. Somewhere between Jameson's 'cognitive mapping' and Jardine's 'map of new spaces yet to be explored', the idea hardens that there is somewhere to go, that it is possible to move forward.

- The theme of the tension between spaces of conflict and spaces of discourse. The resilience of the structures and narratives of the modern is articulated in the postmodern within hegemonic patterns of tension. This issue is developed in terms of regulation as a specific attitude of governmentality in the form of the colonisation of, and the struggle for, the determination of everyday experience and existence in the construction of meaning and reality. Colonisation involves the control and possession of territory by an external force. Decolonisation is the process of recognising and dislodging relations of control and possession. Decolonisation is an element in resistance to repression and involves the articulation of alternative moments and places of desire.
- The former point is related to the form of the relationship between ethics-ethos in the contemporary. This is not explicitly a work of ethics but does engage with problems regarding the representation of meaning and value (particularly as applied to desire) in the articulation of an ethical strategy for surviving the contemporary. An intimation of this ethical position can be provided through the image of refusal. The postmodern has been classified as an era of refusal (Kearney (1991)). There is the refusal of the metanarrative and the refusal of the modern subject of truth; also the subject that is refused and can refuse and become other.[2] Throughout this work the refusal of the contemporary is interrogated both so as to be able to reflect back onto the dominant narratives and institutions of the modern and also in relation to the idea that it is possible to move forward – between boundaries – and that there is somewhere to go. To follow a narrative framework regarding ethics, it is possible to suggest an ethics prefaced upon a multiplicity of narratives and as an ethical responsibility to listen to other narratives, to be witness to the narratives of the unrepresented or misrepresented in the form articulating narratives of dissensus (see further Lyotard (1985) pp 93-100). In terms of locale, following Heidegger, this 'ethics' occurs in an arena of discourse as opposed to an arena of conflict. To be ethical would be, in a simple sense, to inhabit an open space, a space without limit to narrative form in which there is constant interpretation of the voice-image-story of the other, bearing constant witness to the other. As Lyotard writes:

  > And I wanted to say this too – Well, we say to ourselves (who, 'we'?), well, at least in the ghetto we shall go on. As far as it is possible. Thinking, writing, is, in our sense to bear witness for the secret timbre. That this witnessing should make up an oeuvre and that this oeuvre might be able, in a few cases, at the price of the worst misunderstanding, of the worst contempt, to be placed on the circuits of the mediated megalopolis, is inevitable, but what is also inevitable, is that the oeuvre promoted in this way be undone again, deconstructed, made redundant, deterritorialised, by the work of thinking some more, and by the bewildering encounter with a material (with the help not of god or the devil but of chance). Let us at least bear witness, and again, and for no one, to thinking as disaster, nomadism, difference and redundancy' (Lyotard (1991) p 203).

2 Goodrich (1990) analyses this image of refusal through a reading of the circulation of contracts in Thomas Pynchon's *The Crying of Lot 49* (1967): 'The refused may also, however, refuse. It may form its own network of communication, and it is largely in the name of the other, of that which remains, that the heroine Oedipa pursues the signs and clues, the marks or traces, the dross outside the contractual network, as indices of an underground postal network' (Goodrich (1990) p 175).

★

A concern with other perspectives, other stories and other spaces draws upon established vocabulary but establishes trajectories of interests and desires that are neither determined or captured by the systems in which they develop. In this sense we partake in an exercise of disorientation, we all become nomads, migrating across a system that is too vast to be our own, but in which we are fully involved, translating and transforming bits and elements into local instances of sense which become habitable as though 'they were a space borrowed for a moment by a transient, an immigrant, a nomad' (Chambers (1993) p 193).

This is an engagement with the ephemeral and the contingent in spaces of continual movement between regulation and deregulation, order and disorder, within and without. The spatial metaphor does not imply new space – the heterotopia is possible – but a counter-site identified from within the disorder and excess of the urban and at the margins of that order or causing the margins of that space as a determined order to become apparent in the very de-determination or decolonisation of that space as the disordered space of otherness. To be 'on the margin' can imply exclusion from the centre, but the margin of the social, political and economic also binds the periphery to the centre. In this way 'margins' become signifiers of everything 'centres' deny or repress. The margins serve as the condition of possibility for all social and cultural entities. In the centre of modernity entrenched groups (hegemonic strategic interests) inflate their opinions and rights to ostensibly universal proportions. But in the contemporary, given the struggle for the universal between competing dominant reference groups, everything is on the margin. As Michel de Certeau notes 'there is no way out, the fact remains that we are *foreigners* on the inside – *but there is no outside*' (Certeau (1988) pp 13-14). The limit must be constantly approached, contested and explored for the possibility of articulating the multiplicity and plurality of discourses without becoming subject to the particular or becoming trapped within the realm of specificity. We must follow Georg Simmel and all become *nomads* (Gilles Deleuze) or *strangers* (Julia Kristeva). As bell hooks writes:

> I am located in the margin. I make a definitive distinction between that marginality which is imposed by oppressive structures and that marginality one chooses as a site of resistance - as a location of radical openness and possibility. This site of resistance is continually formed in that segregated culture of opposition that is our critical response to domination. We come to this space through suffering and pain, through struggle. We know struggle to be that which pleasures, delights, and fulfils desire. We are transformed, individually, collectively, as we make radical creative space which affirms and sustains our subjectivity, which gives us a new location from which to articulate our sense of the world (hooks (1991) p 153).

Which returns us to the desperation articulated in Sarah Schulman's letter of 19 June 1991: New York is death (sentiments expanded upon in Mike Davis' analysis of Los Angeles *City of Quartz: Excavating the Future in Los Angeles* (Davis (1990)). It has become tempting for some theorists (notably Jean Baudrillard) to revel in a critique of the sign that is simply a deceptive surface and appearance which mystifies the manifestation of an underlying reality: the alienation of the human condition achieved through hyper-conformity in the excess of individuality ('Who cares!'). But this reduction to a hidden value denies the ontological reality of signs and appearances. It denies that there are sites of sense and meaning. It is a tension inherent in contemporary critiques of existence in urban culture and one which, in Part I of this book, is utilised regarding the problems inherent in the regulation of that culture (retrieving the concepts of affluence, anomie and alienation) with specific reference to the political economy of reproduction and consumption. The analysis suggests the possibility that the excess of consumption provokes a refusal of consumption and therefore a condition of disalienation through the implosion of capitalist accumulation.

It is necessary to follow the pessimistic logic of Baudrillard's argument so as to keep under view the naive assumption that it is possible to move forward when, perhaps, there is no more space left. It is a delicate balance and one where Sarah Schulman's statement arrives as a stark reminder of a reality. The everyday as terrifying and banal, a continuous struggle for orientation in terms of meaning and value. Sarah Schulman encapsulates a potential response of refusal, the social effects of the political imperative of deregulation. Here is a description of the condition in which the ethical dilemma of the contemporary – the responsibility to listen to and be witness to the other – is at its most clear, articulated against the backdrop of the pinnacle/nadir of the modernist-capitalist enterprise: New York.[3] The question becomes, what is the function of critique in these circumstances, where we are all *foreign bodies* surviving at the limit of a centre and not at a margin, always awaiting the arrival of the *post* ('Who cares?').

It is possible to venture an interpretation that critique can be equated with clarity. In Kant and later in Marx the process of critique serves to render explicit what otherwise would remain implicit. The word 'process' implies an active participation and it is this participation that Foucault's reading of Kant develops. Foucault's interpretation of critique becomes 'the art of not being governed' (Foucault (1990)). Critique becomes the movement through which the subject discovers a truth by an exercise in the art of voluntary insubordination and of thoughtful disobedience. This becomes a twist on the Kantian definition of 'Enlightenment' when individuals have the courage to follow their own reason in public *and* in private (Kant only advocates a private use of reason and a public obedience). It is a courage which Foucault interprets as the Nietzschean injunction of the *will to know* (Miller (1993) p 303). This interpretation can be related to Lyotard's injunction to become a witness to the unrepresentable and in the activation of difference in the defence of an increasingly complex and fragile heterogeneity from the forces of homogenisation (Lyotard (1988) p 73). Critique becomes an attitude, cynical but also affirmative, a demonstration of courage and a radical acceptance of the

3 It is a sentiment expressed elsewhere:

> Perhaps having become illiterate in the pursuit of self-hood, our horizon is simple. We should learn to read again. Start with Auden: 'We must learn to love one another or die'. If we don't, what can we look forward to? London already looks like Los Angeles just as Beverley Hills is as razor-wire defended as the white suburbs of Johannesburg and Ridley Scott's *Blade Runner* – conceived as science-fiction, then looking like an advert – now looks like a documentary. Parts of Manchester, Glasgow or Birmingham double for the outer circles of Hell. Forget the ban on *A Clockwork Orange*. Alex and his droogs appear weekly on *Crimewatch* (Bracewell and Evans (1993)).

vulnerability of the other. Within the frame of ethics sketched before, critique becomes both an incredulity toward metanarratives and, in the exercise of incredulity, to place oneself on the 'outside' of the established parameters of reason, even if that includes placing morality, rights and justice into a maelstrom of uncertainty so as to re-establish meaning and value.

To consider the terms that are accorded so high a political value in the contemporary – autonomy, fulfilment, responsibility, choice – from this perspective is to question whether they mark a kind of culmination of ethical evolution. But, this does not imply that we should subject these terms to critique. We should rather examine the ways in which these ideals of the self are bound up with a profoundly ambiguous set of relations between individuals and political power. Critique becomes a tool of analysis in an understanding of the processes of power in the construction and utilisation of subjectivity: to identify the centre, the margin must be operative: 'The point of critique is not justification but a different way of feeling: another sensibility' (Deleuze (1983). This is the sensibility of the without-law in the individual demonstration of insubordination and disobedience (the art of the ungovernable). Therefore, an element in the process of critique is an understanding of desire as a manifestation of this resistance to self-incurred tutelage. If one searches for the meaning of desire within a humanistically orientated replacement discourse (one that liberates desire whilst maintaining a respect for the demand of the other – the affirmation of lack), then the process of critique must occur in a political economy that offers far-from-equilibrium conditions in which both order and disorder are produced in the sense of engaging in the activity of dispute and refusal in the articulation of desire, as a moment of individual understanding of self and others.

PETER GOODRICH, *THE LANGUAGES OF LAW*

The other text which I utilise in this introductory tour of the critical terrain encompassed by this book exhibits anxieties similar to my own. As opposed to the feeling of alienation which developed during the reading of *The Condition of Postmodernity* by David Harvey, I experienced a feeling of sympathetic familiarity when reading *The Languages of Law: From Logics of Memory to Nomadic Masks* by Peter Goodrich. Goodrich proposes a thesis which returns to the study of the art of law. In the wake of the fragmentation of modernist and contractarian notions of society and law, of meaning and rule, the remaining source of interrogation becomes the study of the representations of legality. This thesis requires that we look at specific images and trace not simply the law of our vision but equally the presuppositions of the images themselves. Goodrich considers these are images of a law that has broken down and been reconstituted into more powerful and arbitrary forms: '[I]t is a law of masks, of nomadic moveable signs that territoristically invade the intensive zones of everyday life' (Goodrich (1990) p 11). Regulation becomes a matter of moving the signs and of controlling the avenues in the circulation of images. As Paul Virilio notes: 'One of the fundamental tasks of the State is to striate the space over which it reigns, or to utilise smooth spaces as a means of communication in the service of striated space' (Virilio (1986) pp 14;4). This is a moveable law whose central concern is the law of movement, a law of spatialisation organised in a conflict between colonisation-decolonisation-recolonisation. This is a nomadic law which reflects the laws of capital *in flight* and which renders into confusion and crisis the centralisation of governmentality in an attempt to vanquish nomadism and to control migration. Another tension appears, the paradoxical function of disappearing capital in the implosion of the system of regulation. If the space of the margin is momentary and contingent, the space of centre is dangerously static, rendered immobile through its very imperative of spatial governance: a state of sclerotic acceleration.

Harvey and Goodrich are both commentators on the laws of space and the spaces of law. Harvey persists in the economic determination of a modernist 'time-space compression'. Goodrich pursues a narrative of movement, a governance of intensive spaces and of a movement that no longer moves but is merely a movement of the modes of transmission. Goodrich achieves an internal configuration within his text. Harvey's survey is a static or *specular* text, diagnostic and distanced, in which significant differences can be perceived only against a background of sameness. Goodrich activates differences and dares ask of the narratives of the contemporary, who is it that speaks, who is speaking? Whereas Harvey conforms to the implicit rationalism of his meta-theory (Marxism) which circumscribes the world from the outside, as an external thing, Goodrich attempts to thaw out the frozen image and to give voice to the inside and asks troublesome questions in the process: Where are we? According to what law? At what cost? In what history? In whose speech? Goodrich's strategy is to read the inner body, 'the body that lives and feels through the law' (Goodrich (1990) p 259) and he has the courage to adopt a style which adheres to the cultural form in which his intervention takes place. It is a style of resistance to the imaginary and frozen images of logical schemata:

> The postmodern condition is one of resistance, one in which tables are to be turned and rather than being on track, linked in, connected to the exchange and remembered by the authorities, we turn to look at the image of ourselves that the system presents. It is after all essentially the ambition of ghosts to be seen and of the dead to be remembered: for the living it is a matter of letting the body remember and then of putting the ghost to rest (Goodrich (1990) p 300).

Goodrich is concerned with the three part nature of the image (sign): the interpretation of the image, the value of the image and the circulation of the image. In terms of legal discourse his project is one which attempts to understand the image of law (the iconography of symbolic authority) as re-represented image. In his discussion of the contractarian tradition, his agenda of resistance and sensibility becomes one which attempts to interrupt the transmission of the image or to figure that the image is elsewhere. His commentary on David Walliker's art installation *The Contract* demonstrates his critical agenda regarding postmodern law and provides a site of intervention.

The installation represents the allegorical movement of Rousseau's social contract. A tomb is built to celebrate the author of the first modernist contract, a consensual and democratic agreement between equals. The state removes the remains of the author from the tomb and rests them in the Pantheon in the centre of Paris. An empty tomb remains: 'In death he has been moved outside the contract; he is no longer there, no longer held to his word or bound to the agreement' (Goodrich (1990) p 319). The contract has been negotiated, interpreted to death, supplemented – interrupted in the *post*. The empty tomb becomes a utopia, a fictional place celebrating the myth of democracy which the contract purported to establish between the People and the State. As Goodrich states:

> Rousseau is not there. Rousseau has slipped away. Jean-Jacques is no longer around; even his tomb is empty
>
> ... the artist has depicted Rousseau as 'moonlighting':
>
> Far from remaining in the frame or staying within the contract, Rousseau has found alternative employment: that Rousseau is moonlighting means that he is now working off the record, both erasing the contract and working on the outside, in the black economy, *outwith the law*. In the imagery of the postmodern, working off the record suggests erasure of the tape, free play in a world made strange, a glimpse of knowledge on the outside (Goodrich (1990) p 323 (*my emphasis*)).

It is not within the scope of this book to supplement Goodrich's particular examination of the contractarian tradition and the conclusions he draws out into a frame of postmodern law premised upon semiology. Goodrich, in his commentary upon Pierre Legendre, points us towards the primacy of the poetic over rationality. 'To begin again, to create, is the most pressing task of critical reason as applied to contemporary law' (Goodrich (1990) p 296). This is where Goodrich leaves us, taking us to the edge and showing us what is possible, given such an inversion and displacement as a strategy of critique. His summons that the law should recognise itself as always and already a deep structure of the erotic body subject to the gestures, the actions, the manipulations, the betrayals, the desires and the demotic of everyday life – that we read the inner body that lives and feels through the world of law – is a unique psychoanalytic account of the symbolic legal order. Perhaps that is all there is to say and the rest is silence, Goodrich situating the sympathetic reader in the position of Samuel Beckett's protagonist Krapp:

> *Pause.*
>
> Here I end this reel. Box – (*pause*) – three, spool – (*pause*) – five. (*Pause*) Perhaps my best years are gone. When there was a chance of happiness. But I wouldn't want them back. Not with the fire in me now. No, I wouldn't want them back.
>
> KRAPP *notionless staring before him. The tape runs on in silence* (Beckett (1959) p 20).

There is an ambivalence within Goodrich's text, an ambivalence between the certainty of the passed (the unity of the metanarrative), and the uncertainty of the present (the multiplicity of narratives). It is an ambivalence, consequent upon the knowledge of the breach of the contract – that the letter never arrived at its destination although placed in the ordinary course of the *post*[4] – which is simultaneously emancipating in its relinquishment of origin and unnerving in its very nostalgia for the loss of origin. It is the sudden awareness of the erasure of origin which provokes a nostalgia for origin, even if that origin is in the form of the tyranny, the shackles of subjection to a contract which never arrived but, nevertheless, contracts the individual to an external authority masquerading as democracy complete with the consequential violence of obligation and bond. It is a nostalgia which is seductive when placed against the gobbet of the contemporary which Sarah Schulman's letter provides.

'The tape runs on in silence suggesting free play in a world made strange'. If Jean-Jacques is not in his tomb, then where has he gone? (Which mask is he wearing, if any?) There is an empty space as one of the fathers of the authority of modernity absents himself. Goodrich suggests that he is working on the outside, in the black economy, out-with the law, working off-the-record. But what might this mean? It is a question which haunts Part II of this book.

Working off-the-record, being out-with the law. If Part I of this book is concerned with being *within* the law in terms of the precarious maintenance of order in the urban through regulation, then Part II of this book is concerned with being *without* the law, or out-with the law, or the existence of the without-law. The spatial metaphor becomes the cultural terrain of the interstice or the borderzone. The countersite of complexity represents the turmoil of the everyday where we are all foreigners operating along established lines and networks, subject to established forces and representations but constantly forcing the fracture of those certainties or being subject to the fracture of those certainties. This is the arena, the experience and the moment of decolonisation which is always the territory of recolonisation. It is a territory of conflict and tension, discourse and cohesion from within and without.

It would be convenient to lapse into the graphic and seductive language of urban terrorism, asphalt sociopaths, ghetto warfare and inverse surveillance mechanisms: '[I]n which the city is at once endless text always promising meaning but ultimately offering hints and signs of a possible and final reality' (Davis (1990) p 67). In part, this sentiment is clear in Sarah Schulman's letter. But that would be to fall prey to the old myths: there are no barricades left, there are no borders between 'them' and 'us'. There are only a series of disputed borders. The hard edge is no longer political ideology but the far more insidious rule of nationalism and ethnicity. More significantly, such a language of

4 I draw here upon Goodrich's reading of Jacques Derrida in his essay *Contractions* (Goodrich (1990) pp 149-170). However, if a psychoanalytic interpretation were to be adopted it is possible to state, after Slavoj Zizek (1992), *Why Does A Letter Always Arrive At Its Destination?* Zizek adopts a Lacanian perspective in his reading of Derrida which presupposes the traditional teleological trajectory with a preordained goal (Zizek (1992) p 12). However, it is Derrida's teleological interpretation of Rousseau that enables the metaphor of the letter, delivered from the modern to postmodern and subject to interruption, to operate so powerfully.

describing also falls prey to the ghettoisation and, therefore, the disempowerment, of other voices within an opaque otherness, the specificity of this or that language game.[5]

There is a politics here but it is a politics related to the ethical position presented earlier. It is a politics of resistance which takes account of the inevitability of the economics of the market and the superiority of external control mechanisms. It is a politics which contests the realities of political economy and the circumstances of global power. It is a politics which intervenes at a very dark point but whose aim is the establishment of a humanistically determined replacement discourse of multiplicity, difference and otherness. It must be a politics operative as a resistance of the most subtle countervailing level of activity in the deployment of power. As Goodrich comments:

> The marks of politics in the discourse of critique are neither familiar nor obvious: they do not relate directly to a specific content or programme but rather to an ethics; they do not belong directly to a given tradition but rather to a necessarily ambiguous and potentially subversive place or space ... they do not share the organisational framework or umbrella of previous or pluvious movements but stand rather for a critique of organisational or managerial forms of rationality. The politics of reason is not simply a local politics; it is oppositional, fragmentary, and frequently obscure. It remains in many respects a politics of style and is in consequence resistant to normative forms of analysis. (Goodrich (1993) p 422).

It is dangerous to evoke the notion of resistance precisely because of the threat of identification, nomination and colonisation. One interpretation of resistance, in the context in which the word is utilised in this book, can be given in a comment made by Ernesto Laclau and Chantal Mouffe: 'The discourse of radical democracy is no longer the discourse of the universal ... it has been replaced by a polyphony of voices, each of which constructs its own irreducible identity' (Laclau and Mouffe (1985) pp 191-192). A polyphony of voices and the construction of identity stand as central elements in this political strategy of resistance to the forces of repression and order through consumption. The polyphony of voices can be equated in terms of identity with a multiplicity of narratives and the ethics of a responsibility to listen to the narratives of others.[6] In so doing we undertake the construction of our identity in relation to others and not in relation to an external authority of a metanarrative. The formation of identity takes place in an intimate arena where what is recognised is the multiplicity of identities available to the individual. This recognition of commingling identities can only occur in an arena of discourse. It is an arena forged through conflict and refusal in the establishment of

5 This is David Harvey's criticism of the 'postmodern politics' of Lyotard and Derrida. Harvey's point is that, within his reading, these theorists neglect the determining economic dynamic of capitalist power relations and therefore they are not able to convincingly restructure such power relations so as to privilege 'the voice of the other' (Harvey (1989) pp 113-118).

6 'Our lives are both the texts that we create, and texts created by the laws of others' (Douzinas, Warrington with McVeigh (1991) p13). Here, Douzinas, Warrington and McVeigh point to the importance of the establishment of a new narrative coherence premised upon the second order narratives eliding with the narratives of dissensus which evolve in the vacated space of the metanarrative of the modern. We must vanquish the narrative myths of justice, ethics, morality and have recourse to a responsibility to our own narratives (short stories) and the narratives of others, listening to other voices, being witnesses to other representations: this would be justice.

deterritorialised space. It is an arena characterised by the provisional, the hybrid and the local: a community of plurality. Laclau and Mouffe echo the earlier sentiments of Hannah Arendt. Arendt underlines the unforeseen, the indeterminate and the innovative. She argues that political action rests on a necessary tension with a non-sense that queries the processes of reduction. This leaves an open space, an indeterminacy. As Chambers notes: 'In that opening, and beyond that abstract ideology of a uniformity stamped with the seals of tradition, nation, race and religion we are destined to live in ... a border condition' (Chambers (1993) p 17).

At this level resistance becomes a local activity. Local in this context means unconcerted action which coalesces into an articulation of refusal by more than one. It is necessarily undetermined action; action which does not betray its motive or causation in any accessible way. There are therefore multiple points of resistance. Identity must be continually assumed and immediately called into question. It is a politics-poetics of schizoanalysis (Perez (1990). In terms of the formation of Nietzsche's 'communities of virtue' (Nietztsche (1911) p 134) or bell hooks's 'communities of resistance' (hooks (1991) p 149) the concern is with those contingent elements of resistance whose differential unity is expressed through the arbitrary and random sensibilities of individual desire.[7]

OUT-WITH THE LAW: STRATEGIES IN CRITIQUE

A further series of elements in the process of critique becomes the identification of those differential sources and strategies of resistance which escape the imperative of colonisation and order:

- The nature of representation in terms of the process of regulation through technologies of nomination. Lyotard urges us to be witnesses to the unrepresentable. The incredulity toward metanarratives which this declaration demands requires an exploration of the nature of representation. The project, in terms of resistance, becomes one of interrogation of the nature of the interpretation of the representation and the process of its transmission. The task then becomes to interrupt this process and to scramble the channels of transmission. In narrative terms the process involves the recovery of the fractured molecular plot within an ordered molar narrative. This recovery affords a glimpse of the elements, which breaks up the sterile circle of repetition which constitutes the production of desire.

  The emergence of multiple forms of representation, at increasing levels of circulation, results in the erosion of the force of a particular form of representation to

7 Which returns us to the central definition of Enlightenment as articulated by Kant: 'Enlightenment is man's exit from his self-incurred tutelage. Tutelage is man's inability to make use of his understanding without direction from another. Self-incurred is this tutelage when its cause lies not in lack of reason but in lack of resolution and courage to use it without direction from another. Dare to know! "Have courage to use your own reason!" – that is the motto of enlightenment' (Kant (1963) p 3). As Foucault interprets this statement the stress is placed on courage as a precursor to Nietzsche's injunction to discover the meaning of your own life.

frame the boundaries required in the delimination of order. The sign (the delineating mechanism in the articulation of form) as an element in the communicative system of the transmission of authority (which equates a narrative structure to every signification) is transformed. The function of the sign shifts from framing the universal to framing the particular. These signs, which initially served as determining narrative systems, become transformed into non-signifying signs or the fourth order of simulacra. In this final diachronic stage the sign no longer has any relation to reality and is pure simulacrum (Baudrillard (1983a) p 11). A conflict between signs emerges in the struggle for signification. But at this stage, the sign is merely an empty device of delineation and therefore what emerges as the principal device of signification is not the sign itself but the process of naming – the signification of authority – which is achieved, in terms of meaning and reality, through that sign. The naming of emergent signs and the simultaneous determination of legitimating narratives and their classification becomes a conflict of signification between new and existing dominant orders of authority. The power to name serves to destabilise existing symbolic hierarchies and produces classifications in accordance with particular interests. In terms of representations – what has been named – it follows that there is no single representation, only multiple representations, each with its own legitimating signification.

- The question of value in the process of interpretation becomes one of identification and recognition. The process in the delimination of order through nomination between competing regimes of non-signifying signs becomes temporarily interrupted and a space of interpretation is made available. Through the deployment of the interpretation of that which has been previously classified as the unrepresented or the unrepresentable, it is possible to enter a space of post-signification. The unrepresented and the unrepresentable attest to the force of excess. The identification of the excess of representation or of that which refuses classification within the schema of the logical order of signification, becomes a political moment of resistance. But it is a resistance which is only precariously available because the process of the identification of the excess is also the moment of immediate nomination or determination through the process of classification. The excess must move along the linear of nomadic de-classification as opposed to the hierarchical of governmental reclassification.

The project becomes one in which the order of the image is vanquished through the interruption of its transmission and for a moment is replaced with the disordered image of an unrepresentable practice or subject. To recognise the moment of this image is to turn the seducing mirror of the 'real' back upon itself and therefore to neutralise the totalising force of its fragile unity. This process of interruption by the unconstituted order of the unrepresentable becomes an element in the agenda of the politics of resistance in the articulation of the aesthetics/ethics of excess. The imagined homogeneity of an order of signification in conflict is temporarily replaced by the real heterogeneity of the disorder of signification in desire.

The operative in this project is the without-law. At the moment when the process of the maintenance of order has entered a stage of accelerated sclerosis through the hyperinflation of regulatory strategies (the conflict in the signification of order), that which was repressed as the unrepresentable becomes no longer part of the equation and becomes the refused, the expelled, the disappeared. But that which is refused may also *refuse* and form its own transverse network within the margins of governmentality. This network can be equated in spatial terms with the emergence of deterritorialised space through the elision of subgroupings in the process of withdrawal from the freneticism of the schizophrenic repetition of the desire of the external order for determination through classification. This is the moment of transgression. The moment of transgression can only be supplementary but constitutes the condition of possibility from within the stagnant order of repression in which all emotions are repressed, except the excitement of movement toward or along the line of transgression which carries away the Law.[8] Here, the inside and the outside join to form an undecidable play of perpetual displacement: the schizo-space of the heterotopia.

- Within this schema of resistance the idea of the local was introduced. Here local means either the community or that which attaches to the private realm of the individual. In utilising the spatial metaphor and the laws of movement in the operation of governmentality, it is important to be reminded of the centrality of the figure of the body. As Fredric Jameson following Henri Lefebvre states, in order to recover the sites of resistance:

> [A] new kind of spatial imagination capable of confronting the past in a new way and reading its less tangible secrets off the template of its spatial structures – body, cosmos, city, as all those marked the more intangible organisation of cultural and libidinal economies and linguistic form (Jameson (1991) pp 364-365).

If a space of resistance is to become operative then it will reflect individual desires in the formation of identity. The identification of this space of desire will also determine how relations of power and discipline are inscribed into the apparently innocent spatiality of social life and how human geographies become filled with politics and ideology. The space of desire is the space of the body as subject. The body exists in space and must either submit to the determination of desire by the external order, or demonstrate the possibility of the expression of de-determined desire through spatial and temporal displacement, in the process of the interruption of fixed power relations. The irreducibility of the body in the social scheme of order means that it is from this site of deregulated and disordered power relations that resistance in the activation of desire is situated. It is at this site that the power of the gaze is most piercing in its capture of the moment of expression of transgression as that of the movement of desire.

- 'Transgression is an act which involves the limit' (Foucault (1977a) p 33). In this sense transgression refers to the incessant crossing and recrossing of a line which

8 In using the term 'excess' to denote what is being simultatively assessed it is only possible to evoke an impression (the ambience) of that which necessarily can never be perfectly imaged or named: the unrepresentable. Through this limitation the site of excess – the arena of the event of a transgression – remains fluid as a site of the perpetual potential for opposition and resistance.

immediately redraws itself only to be crossed again. It is a political activity without apparent reference or determination, a perpetual revolution and displacement, made and unmade by that excess which transgresses it:

> Limit and transgression depend on each other for whatever density of being they possess: a limit could not exist if it were absolutely uncrossable and, reciprocally, transgression would be pointless if it merely crossed a limit composed of illusions and shadows (Foucault (1977a) p 34).

The possibility of transgression as a site of resistance is its nature as a indeterminate space that is not yet fixed. As a space of resistance within desire it is of the positive of disorder ('Nothing is negative in transgression'), operative against the negativity of the determined desire of order.

Here is where the out-laws are: not with-out law but simultaneously within and without. Transgression measures the opening at the heart of the limit and traces the flashing line that causes the limit to arise. It establishes the space of order and the space of disorder. Whilst order desires transgression it is wrong to consider that desire is repressed because it is order that constitutes both desire and the lack on which it is based. Where there is desire the power relation is present. It is a power relation that is multiple, immanent and affirmative and plays with the simultaneous possibility that transgression is both the basis of legitimacy and carries away this legitimacy, representing the line of flight toward alternative spatiality: that which is beyond the limit of the name in the territory of radical subjectivity and counter-hegemonic resistance. This is the space where we recover ourselves.

★

In the course of this introductory exercise in disorientation I have presented two series of elements. The first series is concerned with the latent priorities which inform the ensuing work in terms of repression (the site of critique, the utilisation of spatial relations, the tension in regulatory rationale, the formation of an ethical strategy). The second series is concerned with specific ideas which inform the ensuing work in terms of resistance (the translation of the sign, the excess of representation, the irreducible body, the space of transgression). These elements have been presented within the frame of an introduction which seeks both to disorientate in the sense of providing an initial survey of the ensuing territory, and to de-centre in the very process of this cartographic achievement. Since this book is about repression and resistance, order and disorder within the urban sphere, this introduction has provided a partial examination of the theoretical ambience of that experience which is also the ambience of its critique. In identifying the prevalent forces and counterforces, whether through the texts of others (David Harvey and Peter Goodrich) or through the elliptical slippage between themes encompassing ideas couched in inevitably alienating terminology, it may have been possible to provide a glimpse of what is possible.

This Introductory essay commenced with Sarah Schulman's letter of 19 June 1991. In a short statement simultaneously encompassing repression and resistance, Sarah Schulman provides a haunting evocation of the experiences with which this book struggles. She encapsulates the scale of the struggle. There are no more revolutions:

there are only the intermittent terrorist/territoristic/touristic interventions in and of others in defence of a complex and fragile heterogeneity. There is only the positive left, the ability to say: 'NO'. It begins on and against the 'ground' of space-time, the ground of both the irreducible multiplicity and the constancy of instability, the ground that presents the 'given' which encompasses the moment of compulsion and the moment of transition: we inhabit megalopolis to the extent that we declare it uninhabitable. To provide an ethically grounded and politically responsive solution to the dilemma of providing an opening into a community of difference and desire is the theme of this book.

CHAPTER TWO

REGULATION AND URBAN CULTURE: DEFINING ELEMENTS

> We have always had a sad vision of the masses (alienated), a sad vision of the unconscious (repressed). Upon our entire philosophy lies the heavy weight of these sad correlations. If only for the sake of change, it would be interesting to conceive of the masses, the object-masses, as possessing a delusive, illusive, allusive strategy, corresponding to an unconscious that is finally ironic, joyous and seductive (Baudrillard (1990) p 99).

> The decision makers, however, attempt to manage these clouds of sociality according to input/output matrices, following a logic which implies that their elements are commensurable and that the whole is determinable. They allocate our lives for the growth of power ... The application of this criterion to all our games necessarily entails a certain level of terror, whether soft or hard: be operational (that is, commensurable) or disappear (Lyotard (1984) p xxiv).

PROBLEMS OF DEFINITION

The principal concern of this chapter is a theoretical account of the mechanisms of repression operative within contemporary urban culture. The chapter identifies both the resilience of repressive techniques and the tension operative between regulatory strategies expressed in the form of patterns of discontinuity as a consequence of the development of political economy.

The content of this account is organised around issues of definition. The process of describing the postmodern has emphasised the discontinuous and fragmentary elements of contemporary experience. Strategies of describing are predominantly tautological given the indeterminacy of the critical vocabulary available and the avoidance of totalisation and systematisation. In addition particular strands of postmodern theorisation avoid the issue of the resilience of the narratives and institutions of the modern. If it is accepted that postmodernism is a condition of uncertainty and an illustration of paradoxes, tensions and contradictions within contemporary existence, then the too ready application of labels to these contradictory positions has only served as an unhelpful device of mystification, part of the distinction games of the interpretative community.[1] Accounts of the 'culture' of contemporary urbanisation determined by free market economics forces us to focus on the impact on and influence of the

1 The phrase 'interpretative community' denotes that section of society involved in the interpretation and dissemination of knowledge in the form of information. Specifically in this context I use it with regard to the 'academic community' where postmodernism has become an intellectual discourse deprived of its actuality. I am of course conscious of the fact that in embarking upon an analysis of urban culture in this form I cannot escape my position as a member of such an interpretative community. However, I use this note to point to the relevance of tendencies identified within contemporary existence – one which is ever on the edge of postmodernism – which may have travelled unnoticed, until recently, and which serve – within this theoretical framework of analysis – to identify strategies and agendas for action.

individual consciousness, which might be read, and with which this work is partially engaged, as 'narcissism'. This does not allow us to escape the puzzle of how contemporary social relations are now lived and experienced at the level of social formation. Rather it serves to illuminate the tragic consequence of fragmentation and disjuncture as a result of repressive strategies of regulatory control in operation through the final stages of capitalism: the death of the social. It is a conundrum that might be stated thus: either the final triumph of the logic of capitalism or the end of capitalism and its history and the commencement of a posthistorical period.

The competing discourses and rhetorics of description (metanarratives or legitimising myths)[2] of the modern are the subject of postmodern interrogation. There is agreement that the contemporary is far more complex than before and that it is no longer sufficient to theorise power as an expression of a singular dimension of oppression (Keith and Pile (1993) p 1).

Here I interpret some of the problematic phrases which analyses of postmodernism have given rise to. I do this so as to convey a spirit of the condition of the individual confronted with the forces of contemporary urban culture through an examination of the forces that produce and mould this culture as an order of excess. The individual is the legislative guerrilla on the margins of the centre, struggling for the possibility of transgression in an expression of an emancipated desire, unshackled from the chains of consumption and a subject produced by the excess of tensions between regulatory strategies.

Postmodern theory is preoccupied with questions of L-law. The law of the father and desire in psychoanalytic versions; the law of the other in ethical and religious versions; the law of power and discipline in political versions; the laws of mapping of places and knowledges in spatial and post-epistemological versions (Douzinas,

2 The term 'metanarrative' emanates from the work of Jean-Francois Lyotard (1984, 1992). I use it here interchangeably with the term 'legitimising myth'. Although metanarrative does not necessarily mean ideology in the context in which Lyotard developed it, it does however refer to a break with any science of narrative, hence its mythological nature and ideological structure as an assumption. The metanarrative's function is that of legitimation. The metanarrative serves to sanction activities ('first order discursive practices') within a broader and totalising metadiscourse of legitimation, whilst withholding it from others. In so doing the metanarrative functions not just as selective filter but also as an epistemological framework without which 'man' – the subject of history – is decentred and the 'universe' is committed to a new dark age in which chaos theory supersedes rationality. Thus the metanarrative staves off the Nietzschean prediction of the eternal return from the dialectics of Enlightenment. The metanarrative is 'meta' in the sense that it operates as a privileging discourse (domain of language use) capable of situating, characterising and evaluating all other discourses, but not of itself infected by the historicity and contingency which render first-order discourses potentially distorted and in need of legitimation (Wakefield (1990) pp 22-23). A metanarrative claims to be the story that can reveal the meaning of all stories. Its 'metanarrative' status comes from the fact that it relates the many narratives of culture so as to reveal the singular truth inherent in them. The principal metanarrative form I am concerned with in this work is capitalism masquerading as liberalism. Here I use capitalism as a moment of political economy within a legitimating schema of the democratic state (capitalism as told by the state). Capitalism as a particular claim to truth exists in this form, and many others. In this form capitalism becomes the primary economic determinant in the formation of culture (see further Harvey (1989) and my comments on Harvey in the Introduction to this work) and the motive of legitimation as applied regulation. The term 'legitimising myth' is a more concrete phrase available in the rhetoric of description which prevailing ideologies exhibit (perhaps more accurately, remaining ideologies). See further on narrative structures the section on 'Culture' in this chapter.

Warrington, McVeigh (1991) p ix). The stories around these laws are small-scale, provisional and open. The contagious appearances of urban reality coexist with other elements, traces and stories constituting the hidden and forgotten arenas and economies that, although unrepresented, survive and proliferate beneath and between the shadows of the urban image created through the power relations of capital. There may be an absence in the direction of critique – these stories are only heard as muttered babbling – but there is a unity in the opposition to the tall-tales of the modern. This exercise is another short story, a comment in the margin dealing where the struggle for survival is at its most dangerous and intense. Here the laws are articulated as a nomadic governmentality or as the moment of the figure of the transpolitical.[3]

The tension between Law as metanarrative and law as gossip is represented in the simultaneous play between forces of repression and forces of resistance signified in the matrix of affluence (consumption and production), anomie (absence of law and the gratification of desire) and alienation (the fourth order of simulacra as applied to the organisation of social space and interaction in terms of social activity). These words – affluence, anomie, alienation – are 'old' words, words coined in the modern which now appear to have little relevance to the patterns of order in the postmodern. They are words received heavy with meaning, forged in the factories of the 'old' disciplines of economics, sociology and political science. But they are words which when re-defined within the terminology of postmodern discourse still have a validity and ought to be retrieved, saved from their fate as part of a redundant vocabulary of modernist opposition. They are words operating within the sphere of the law of excess, a law which speaks of mesmerising gratification, which can never be satisfied but which is always within sight, in the grip of the gaze. For it is through excess, and the desire of the law itself, that opposition to the forces of repression which pervades every aspect of the everyday becomes a potentially liberating phenomenon, for capitalism involves not only repression but also new forms of existence and previously unattainable forms of emancipation (Chambers (1990) p 66; Certeau (1988) pp 13-14). This tension has been described by Gillian Rose:

> There is heteronomy at the heart of autonomy: the *hetero nomos* – the other, unknowable, law – is precisely the *auto nomos* – the law of the person. The formal law, 'necessary' to our self-consciousness, yet within which we have not 'the slightest acquaintance', utterly intimate and utterly remote, is the 'noumenal' realm of persons and property (things). The formal law which we 'revere', obeying it from no material or interested motive but sheerly because of its universal practical validity, turns out to serve a formal interest ... Theoretical reason is thereby silenced; and Practical Reason strides out of court ... (Rose (1984) p 24).

3 The nomad and the transpolitical are words which form part of a glossary of resistance. In spatial terms both words signify opposition through the linear as opposed to the dominant of the hierarchical. They are words of resistance in the political sense of denoting alternative networks or pathways towards spaces of resistance within contemporary urban culture. The nomadic subject is a disappearing subject signifying the triumph of the figure of the transpolitical in the process of hyperinflation of regulation (see further Baudrillard (1987); Deleuze and Guattari (1986)).

Regulatory rationales (strategies of control) are the key determinants meriting examination in the contemporary of urban culture because of their simultaneous erosion and perpetuation (the edge of the implosion). Analysing the networks and patterns through which control is articulated becomes central in the construction of a possibility for social change.[4] The metanarratives (legitimising myths) find expression through particular regulatory regimes which gives effect to and polices the operation of the narrative. The metanarratives of the modern in their final attempt to universalise require a configuration to sustain a regime of control. There must exist a materialisation of the regime of control in the form of norms, habits, laws, managerial tactics and accompanying regulatory networks to ensure that the unity of the process (the appropriate consistency of individual behaviours within the schema of reproduction) is coherent. 'This body of interiorized rules and social processes is called *the mode of regulation*' (Lipietz (1986) p 19; see also Aglietta (1979)). This kind of language, according to Harvey ((1989) p 122) is useful as a heuristic device. It focuses attention upon the complex interrelations, habits, political practices and cultural forms that allow a highly dynamic, and consequently unstable, capitalist system to acquire sufficient semblance of order to function coherently and through which oppositional tendencies emerge. It is possible to suggest that an excess of regulation (hyperinflation of control strategies) ensures the production of de-regulation.

Michel Foucault examined the operation of power relations and disciplines in modernity. Foucault's work analyses the mechanisms or *dispotifs* that have developed in the modern to surreptitiously reorganise the functioning of power. 'Minuscule' technical procedures serve to redistribute discursive space in order to make that space the means of a generalised 'discipline' ('surveillance'). In the contemporary of urban culture this grid of 'discipline', the fractured expression of repression as a result of the incredulity toward the totalising regime of metanarratives, is becoming clearer and more extensive in its penetration of the everyday of individual movement. Foucault added space to time in the critical sphere and developed a theory of regulation as 'governmentality' in which the governance of space is as significant as the governance of time (Foucault (1991)). As opposed to suggesting the decline or colonisation of Law in the advance of state administration, public welfarism or managerialism or juridification enhancing an administered society it is possible to suggest that Law and administrative procedure merge into a culture of regulation which is characteristic of the government of the postmodern urban sphere. Law remains autonomous (containing a 'truth' in Foucauldian terms) and is not an instrument or accessory but is an essential element in an extensive disciplinary ethos consisting of a combination of power relations and forces but in the absence of sovereignty (Foucault (1979a) p 13). Law must remain

---

4 Social change is the nearest convenient phrase which implies some element of the achievement of 'something better' in terms of justice (the possibility of a 'good life'). It is not entirely satisfactory since it carries connotation of benign social engineering or scientific planning. However it does at least signify the importance of society (community) and change in terms of active-positive resistance (revolution) and therefore, for the time being, serves it purpose.

autonomous for it is contained within a juridical system but is coeval with order which is contained within an administrative system: the combining of these systems is the mode of regulation. It can be ventured that Law's 'truth' is the justification of administrative 'rationality'.

The present work is an exercise following Henri Lefebrve (1972) and Michel de Certeau (1988) in the operation of proliferating technocratic structures which create a banal-violent order of discipline and through which individuals can organise a network of anti-discipline. It provides an initial theoretical framework for an explanation of the operation of these excessive forces and oppositional conditions in contemporary urban culture. It is a sketch – a short story – merely a preliminary version of a much needed study which would breach the existing division between the theoretical and applied laws of postmodernity.[5]

VARIATIONS UPON POSTMODERNISM

If there is a particular phrase which conveys the essence of this sketch then it is from Jean-Francois Lyotard who writes 'What affects to be a return to a pristine economic liberalism is in fact a loss of universalistic source of legitimation, and the responsibility of the legitimation of individual socialisation is thrown back on the practitioner's themselves' (Lyotard (1992) pp 49-71). The delegation of responsibility consequent upon the continuous erosion and regeneration of the narratives and structures of legitimation ensures that the individual is invested in the process of articulating personal as opposed to collective metaphors. The individual becomes the autonomous social actor *par excellence*. The individual operating within the dynamic of an interiorised order is confronted by a paradox. Within one frame of reference there is the potential to gain liberation from the repressive alien discourses of prior subordination. In the parallel frame of reference this liberation is continuously subverted through the remnants of law (now empty) and the constraints of unattainable gratification (excess) in which all is possible and nothing is achievable. Herein lies what I shall suggest is the relevance of the

5 This work complements the relatively few existing studies which attempt a similar variation of analysis, although all in very different ways. See for example the work of Harvey (1989), Crook, Pakulski and Waters (1992), Pfohl (1992) and Taylor (1990). These studies analyse contemporary existence as lived existence and utilise ideas circulating within postmodernism whilst maintaining the importance of the effect of the social-economic transition through empirical analysis. As Ian Taylor has noted regarding 'the social effects of free market policies':

> [O]ne of the most important tasks of sociology ... namely, the project of making connections, at the level of explanation, between the particular forms or objectives of economic organisation developing within particular societies and the moral character of social life obtaining within such societies. The project of 'making the connection' – between economic organisation and the moral character of social relations may be more difficult and problematic given the increasingly complex sets of social divisions that have been thrown up and accentuated by the advent of free market economic policy (and also by the apparent diminution of the nation state as the primary site of economic policy and decision making), but that is precisely the challenge that confronts any worthwhile sociological approach to the realities of 'free market societies' ((1990) p 17).

three forces of affluence, anomie and alienation. Within the construct of contemporary[6] global culture this is the schizophrenic paradigm of existence in which the margins of deviance become the centres of normativity in a potential emergence of an economy of transgression within the existent of the order of capitalism.

Theorising the arena of action is not without its problems. I have alluded to the multiplicity of labelling to which postmodern critique has given rise in its attempt to describe the existent state of available social space within this global culture. The lack of cohesion in providing a frame illustrates both the fragmentary nature of this space and the avowed distrust of the grand narratives of describing the indescribable. If responsibility for organisation is the individual's then the domestic and intimate, the provisional and small-scale 'therapeutic' critique[7] might appear to be the most applicable frame of reference. However, in attempting to operate within the boundaries of the labels currently in circulation, we realise that regarding the delegation of responsibility what is occurring is the formation of 'intermediate stage of transference' (the individual as legislature). The foundation of norms is being delegated to a multiplicity of subgroups (cultures) in which the arena of action – the site of value and meaning – becomes an important classificatory strategy in positioning the struggle and tensions endemic within contemporary urban culture.

The term urban culture is not a supplement to the labels currently in circulation within postmodern theory but is identified as the determining arena in which these labels have been identified as circulating: Megalopolis as the site of hyper or post urbanisation (following – in varying configurations – Gottmann (1961), Lyotard (1991) and Olaquiaga (1992)).

6 Within the context of this work I do not define the 'contemporary' save to relate immediate everyday experience. However I use the word to encompass the ambience of the present within advanced industrial societies. This condition of the present occurs through urbanisation and consumerism in which individuals become members of a global community where difference is apparently eradicated. Nietzsche diagnosed such alienating disembodiments in terms of a 'will to power', a masculine cultural flight from the interdependent contingencies of bodily existence itself; a flight into purified objectivity; a flight into positivism; a flight from genealogical immanence into the fetishised commodification of art posing as nature ... Nietzsche's meditation presents a brooding double to Marx's analysis of the globalisation of international capital (Pfohl (1992) p 138).

7 In deploying the phrase 'therapeutic critique' I suggest that, as opposed to analysis conducted on a 'macro' level of periodisation regarding the nature of social change with the ensuing tendency toward re-subjectification to existing imperatives, a more immediate and effective form of critique can be inscribed at the level of the radical politics of psychoanalysis. The interrogation of metanarratives becomes the radical acceptance of vulnerability. Although this chapter analyses the subject of the metanarrative (which can be identified as the limitation or partiality of the 'universal') this is achieved in part through the utilisation of the intimate/'micro' image in a metaphorical sense. Here the image is the construction of a system of order (contemporary capitalism) as a 'being' or an entity in itself with a personality. Therefore, the possibility granted in the work of Gilles Deleuze and Felix Guattari of utilising schizophrenia in the analysis of capitalism (Deleuze and Guattari (1977)). In suggesting strategies for a reinterpreted humanism (humanism without patriarchical hierarchicisation) I look for solutions not in the individual but in the culture for action in which the individual operates, assuming the socialisation of desire. It is within the institutions of that culture that the schizophrenic (Deleuze and Guattari) or the psychotic (Baudrillard) tensions become the liberating tendencies of the contemporary. In Part II of this work (Deregulation and Urban Disorder) I put forward an analysis of a radical politics of resistance premised upon de-determined individual transgressive action. There is a shift within the work from the therapeutic applied as critique to the external order of repression to the therapeutic applied as critique to the internal order of resistance.

What can be agreed upon within contemporary theory is that the phrase 'postmodern' signifies, through its prefix '*post*', that which comes after, a break or rupture with the modern which is defined in counterdistinction to it (Lyotard (1992) pp 87-95). But 'postmodernism' is more strongly based on a negation of the modern, a perceived abandonment, break with or shift away from the definitive features of the modern which makes it a relatively ill-defined term as we are only (ever) on the threshold of the alleged shift, and not in a position to regard the postmodern as a positivity (Featherstone (1991). The term is provisionally reliant upon the previous. The deployment of the phrase urban culture as a megalopolis is established through the elements of the definitions and transcends the artificiality of the break and the shift in domestic terms (the personal) which is taking place within capitalism. It also provides a lucid placement of a forum for action which is constituted on both a cultural (aesthetic) and an industrial (production) dynamic.

Following Benjamin and Simmel, the process of urbanisation produces the culture which is the determining fabric in the formation of identity in modernity. It is also the space in which the process of de-legitimation occurs, a space of crisis, indeterminacy and possibility. It is the space of the market for the exchange and consumption of the symbolic and the 'real'.[8] Without denying the pervasiveness and necessity of the aesthetic in the construction of critique, this chapter deals primarily with the sphere of exchange and consumption through those structures which determine the allocation of temporal and spatial experience (work: anomie and alienation) and which provide and deny the mechanisms for the achievement of material need (wealth: affluence). This is not to privilege economic determinants in the manner of Harvey (1989) but seeks to balance economic and socio-cultural determinants in the nature of production. The balance exists between the concerns of Part I and Part II.

★

1 Postmodernity

Postmodernity designates a transition from modernity involving the emergence of a new social totality with its own distinct organising principles. Both Lyotard (1984) and Jameson ((1984); (1991)) employ the term with regard to the periodisation of capitalism, both writing of the post-industrial and the cultural logic of late capitalism (new forms of capital circulation). Lyotard (1984) and Jean Baudrillard (1983a) inter-change the term with that of post-industrial. Lyotard writes of the computerisation of society whilst Baudrillard stresses that new forms of technology and information become central to the shift from a productive to a reproductive social order in which an economy of simulations constitute the world. An important consideration is that Lyotard and

8 According to Baudrillard (1983a) there is literally nothing left of the 'real', reality having become commodified and purely symbolic. Reality no longer has time to take on the appearance of reality. What Baudrillard contests is the reference principle of the image, according to which it appears to refer to a real world, to real objects and to produce something that is anterior to it: 'Here the real can be seen to have never existed (But 'as if you were there') without the distance that produces perspective space and our depth vision' (Baudrillard (1983a) p 50; See also Wakefield (1990) pp 132-148).

Baudrillard as philosophers both search to demolish the old paradigm of the liberal subject of Enlightenment which provided a vocabulary for articulating the aims and goals of human endeavour. Baudrillard and Lyotard might be criticised at this juncture for abandoning this certainty and investing in a polysyllabic 'technospeak' that cannot generate ideas other than those which pertain to operational efficiency. Certainly this is an accusation which can be levelled at Baudrillard. The case in respect of Lyotard is more complex. It might be argued that the removal of words like 'justice' and 'equality' and the impoverished state of the reality they refer to disappears entirely. But these words are now vacuous and empty of meaning and that it is partly within the subversive technological possibilities made available within postmodernity that alternative forms of emancipatory investment and a socialisation of desire becomes available.

2 Postmodernisation

This term refers specifically to the effects of a transition in the process of economic development on traditional social structures and values. As part of a process of periodisation and transition it refers to social developments based upon industrialisation, science and technology, the capitalist world market and urbanisation. These processes within postmodernisation have yet to be adequately theorised, being as they are trapped within bounded modernist disciplines. Baudrillard's use of the economy of simulation (the end of production) utilises the constituency of the term without naming it, for example, Baudrillard (1989); (1993a). In the field of urban studies Cooke (1988) and Zukin (1988) deploy the term in quite specific examples regarding the operation of production, consumption and the spatial organisation of urban culture (see also Featherstone (1991) p 6)

The principles underlying postmodernisation include the appeal to unadorned market relations, the erosion of the state as a source of dependence, the weakening of workplace solidarities and the elevation of the private over the public in matters of cultural and social provision (Cooke (1988) p 483). On the global level postmodernisation refers to the restructuring of socio-spatial relations by new patterns of investment and production and the structural polarity between markets and places, between forces that detach people from or anchor them to specific spaces (Zukin (1988) p 435). Cooke and Zukin follow Jameson development of a 'cultural logic of capitalism' (Jameson (1984). Within Jameson's work (as within that of Foucault) a central concern is with the elevation of space as opposed to time in the determination of cultural production (Jameson (1991) p 16). For Jameson the spatial logic of postmodern capitalism is simultaneously homogeneous and fragmented – a 'schizo-space' which has enabled the emergence of a radical political strategy of opposition which Jameson calls the aesthetic of cognitive mapping encompassing a new spatial imagination. What Jameson does not consider is that space itself is filled with politics and ideology. Whereas Jameson defines postmodernisation as a politics determined by the market this only reveals part of the equation of transition.

3 Postindustrialism

Lyotard (1984) and Baudrillard (1983a) both employ the image of the postindustrial. Lyotard's declaration of the loss of meaning and its replacement by a plurality of language games, of a loss of universalism and its replacement by localism is premised upon a thematic of science and knowledge in its social form. Baudrillard's economy of simulations stresses that the constitution of the world is one in which the distinction between the real and appearance has been erased, in which everything is part of the decentred global network and in which there is only surface and no depth. Daniel Bell (1976) accords with Baudrillard's description of a social structure dominated by the scientific and the technological as opposed to the industrial. Bell, interestingly, also prefigures a central concern of this work regarding the process of delegitimation in that the post-industrial is marked by a heightening of antimonian tendencies of desire and the instinctual which exacerbate the tensions inherent within the discourses and institutions of order and authority. This identification marks the possibility of the development of the terms affluence-anomie-alienation as analytic devices not simply of external social relations but also of internal mental processes.

A heightening of antimonian tendencies is related to the organisation of reproduction. In terms of organisation, postindustrialism occurs in the movement from Fordist to post-Fordist organisational principles. Post-Fordism relates directly to a process of transition illustrated by Cooke (1988) in his discussion of postmodernisation as an economic process in which production is disposed to customised output for markets aiming for economies of 'scope'. Post-Fordism involves the emergence of the sovereign consumer and the flexibility of production to meet consumer demands. This flexibility can only be established through a new management of time, a new organisation of space and a new allocation of capital (flexible accumulation). Demand is assessed in terms of design and the plurality of products emphasising innovation. Organisations are geared to respond to rather than regulate markets. They are seen as frameworks for learning as much as instruments of control. 'Their hierarchies are flatter and their structures more open in which planning becomes strategy and the forces of control become systems, software, corporate culture and cash' (Murray, 1988). This is an economy dominated by the multinational, in a global financial market facilitated by an information and communications network revolution (Hall, 1988a).

Urry and Lash proclaim this to be a state of 'disorganised capitalism' in which the structures of capitalism have been transformed by three simultaneous processes: of globalisation from above, of decentralisation from below, and of disintegration from within (Urry and Lash (1987); (1994), Urry (1988)). Urry and Lash propose a model of individualisation presupposed in the phenomenon of reflexivity (the significance of 'reflexive' human subjectivity). The individual as reflexive subject is sovereign and the social structures of the modern (the family, the workplace, the church) have declined in influence granted the dominance of information and communication structures. These structures are the networked flows of a cognitive reflexivity. 'That the fast frozen relations of capitalism are melting into air' encapsulates many of the ensuing consequences of the transition in contemporary urbanisation.

*

The relationship between economy, society and culture requires further analysis. It is possible to suggest that the two determining elements of modernisation are differentiation and rationalisation. The processes of transition can be analysed as the consequence of the extension of these two elements. It is further possible to suggest that the inevitable result of this extension will be tension resulting in implosion within the organisational sphere of commodification and consumption. An implosion would ensure the elements of postculture could not be subordinated to a single hierarchy of cultural values. The problem in utilising this possibility as a political or ethical moment of opposition is that the seduction of the hype will not allow us to recognise the moment when it arrives; we may stand as spectators at the spectacle of implosion.

MEGALOPOLIS: AN EMPTINESS FILLED WITH SIGNS

Postmodernity recuperates individuality. Within modernity the individual surrendered unity and coherence of identity to forms of external objective rationality. Within postmodernity individuality is excluded because change becomes a value itself. The resulting paradox is the simultaneous exclusion of the individual (as culture is negated) and the smothering of the individual (as identity becomes a value). It is a transition identified in terms of the external forms of contemporary reproduction. The dynamic that is the cultural logic of contemporary capitalism signifies the growth of a consumer society dominated by technological communication networks within a political economy of consumption. It includes the globalisation of culture through multinational capitalism and a pluralisation of control frameworks in the allocation and accumulation of capital and in the organisation of experience. As Lefebvre observed 'We are surrounded by emptiness, but it is an emptiness filled with signs.'

Postmodernity signifies the revival of 'urbanity' as a distinct concept: the centres from which the communicative networks of global capitalism and its information systems are controlled, and those from which national and international populations are surveilled, the places where hyperincomes are earned, the areas which provide the labour to service overconsumption and especially the buildings in which these activities take place, are concentrated in centralised spaces (Cooke (1988) p 486). Around these spaces are ethnic enclaves, dreadful enclosures and decaying bunkers of collective consumption, the juxtaposition of opposites expressing a heightened semiology of urbanity under capitalism. Castells (1977) describes the way in which ideology structures spaces through legitimation and communication. He follows Foucault in his description of the urban environment as one of governmentality as control.

Foucault explored the connections between knowledge, power and spatiality, and maintained that the transition from temporal to the spatial metaphors enables a discursive shift from the realm of individual consciousness to wider 'relations of power' as constitutive of social meaning. For Foucault the exercise of power through the state and other social institutions and the exercise of power inherent in social oppositions, is modelled as a spatial field described by spatial strategies and geo-strategic interests. What is central in the deployment of spatial metaphors is the realisation that space is a subject of production. To be able to utilise the fluidity of space it is important to determine the relations of spatial production in the determination of power relations. To be able to map a framework of these power relations in spatial terms, with particular reference to patterns of control within this urban arena of repression and resistance, it is necessary to interrogate the forces of fragmentation and delegation in operation in the everyday existence of the individual.

Foucault accords to the space inhabited by the physicality of the individual the status of the irreducible element in our social scheme of events, for it is in this space of individualisation that regulation is exercised:

> The body is the inscribed surface of events (traced by language and dissolved by ideas), the locus of a dissociated self (adopting the illusion of a substantial unity), and a mass in perpetual disintegration (Foucault (1977b) p 148).

The body exists in space and must either submit or create spaces of resistance. The irreducibility of the human body means that it is from this site of power relations that resistance can be mobilised in the struggle to liberate desire: a site of *becoming* (Foucault (1986)). Particular moments of becoming are the substance of Part II of this work where resistant practices are explored and where the space of the body is central.

To activate this space of becoming, which is a space of deregulated desire, it is necessary to understand the forces of spatial control in operation in contemporary urban culture, those violent micro technocratic-bureaucratic forces which constitute this as a culture of disciplinary surveillance. It may be that there is *no more space*, and that all has become colonised and subject to the gaze through the repressive order of consumption in capitalism which Baudrillard (1983a) suggests is the continuous saturation of the desire of the individual in the contemporary, the space of desire has become the ambient shopping mall where we succumb to the violent order of banality. It can be ventured that symbolic orderings of space and time provide a framework for experience through which the individual learns to survive within urban culture. As Pierre Bourdieu states:

> The reason why submission to the collective rhythms is so rigorously demanded is that the temporal forms or the spatial structures structure not only the group's representations of the world but the group itself, which orders itself in accordance with this representation (Bourdieu (1977) p 163).

Here Bourdieu arrives at a central paradox within the urban condition which Harvey describes thus:

> (Bourdieu) explains how a 'matrix of perceptions', appreciation's, and actions' can at one and the same time be put to work flexibly to 'achieve infinitely diversified tasks' while at the same time being 'in the last instance' (Engel's famous phrase) engendered out of the material experience of 'objective structures', and therefore 'out of the economic basis of the social formations in question'. The mediating link is provided by the concept of '*habitus*' – a 'durably installed generative principle of regulated improvisations' which 'produces practices' which in turn tend to reproduce the objective conditions which produced the generative principle of *habitus* in the first place' (Harvey (1989) p 219).

The trajectory of causation is obvious: habitus assumes a degree of empirically discernible regularity of material and cultural practices (the particular practices to be considered being the orders of anomie, affluence and alienation). The history of social change is captured by the history of the conceptions of space and time and the ideological uses to which those conceptions might be put. The trap within Bourdieu's concept of habitus is that of the imprisoned imagination. It is the individual desire for memory, a sense of belonging and of root which is fixed within habitus. In the moment that 'flat materialism' is threatened it becomes necessary to re-invent memory, to establish its pertinence by way of discipline and therefore to grasp it on the threshold of oblivion.

One of the characteristics of postmodernity is nostalgia (analysed in Chapter Four in its form as the economic liberalism of enterprise). But desire can also be expressed as a desire for oblivion. In the contemporary, the repressive strategies experienced in the maintenance of order through belonging are indeterminable because of the failure of the regulatory rationales of legitimation and the flight of the symbolic laws of capital to extend to this ultimate desire. The satiation of desire through consumption engenders an ultimate desire to no longer consume and therefore no longer belong to the order of consumption. It is here, I would argue, wherein lies the possibility for the identification of Foucault's heterotopias, spaces of otherness, spaces of refusal, spaces of those who no longer belong. These sites of resistance are the result of the success of the order of repression and also the sites of the last battle of politics. As Goodrich, following Paul Virilio, notes 'Asphalt becomes the political territory *par excellence* and the state a simple manager of the public course' (Goodrich (1990) p 298). Here Goodrich draws upon Paul Virilio as one of the few theorists of the politico-aesthetic of space:

> One of the fundamental tasks of the State is to striate the space over which it reigns, or to utilize smooth spaces as a means of communication in the service of striated space. It is the vital concern of every State not only to vanquish nomadism but to control migrations and, more generally, to establish a zone of rights over the entire 'exterior', over all the flows traversing the ecumenon. If it can help it, the State does not dissociate itself from a process of capture of flows of all kinds, populations, commodities or commerce, money or capital ... there is still a need for fixed paths in well-defined directions (Virilio (1986) p 14).

The holding operation of contemporary capitalism is the impossibility of organising deterritorialised space. The problem becomes one of being able to find and to utilise deterritorialised space without it becoming – in the very process of identification – a further site of repression. The desire to become 'other', one of the refused, a member of the alternative network of communication, is a desire to enter a nomadic governmentality in the organisation of identity. Through the matrix of affluence, anomie and alienation it may be possible to discern the emergence through the very processes of repression how this desire can be achieved. Through an investigation of the practice of transgression it becomes feasible to map a series of techniques in urban resistance. Either Foucault, Virilio and Deleuze and Guattari's emancipatory paradox or Baudrillard's and Bourdieu's maintenance of repressed desire. As Goodrich concludes, the narrative of movement is of a subliminal – a sublime – control, an 'ecstasy' of communication whose Law is one of structural regularities (Goodrich (1990) p 298). To 'escape' is to transcend the violent banality of the forces of the contemporary order of consumption.

The process of hyper-secularisation is the primary mode in the articulation of individuality. In the terminology of binary oppositions the urban becomes the central site of secular survival and struggle, a landscape of power, whilst the rural is transformed and becomes 'other' in a movement from agrarian centre to utopian margin (a green belt) as the spiritual site of pleasure and escape (Chambers (1990) p 58 suggests that nature only exists because there is the city, the 'natural' because there is the artificial) Nature becomes a nostalgic site and location in a mythologised 'folk' culture which is utilised by certain forces of escape as either a domain of transgression or a domain of ordered recreation; a manufactured and touristic nature.

The analogy can be played through regarding the erosion of metanarratives (collective metaphors) and the ascension of the sovereignty of narratives of the immediate and the provisional (personal metaphors). The erosion of the legitimating myths of the modern, whose collapse in the contemporary imposes desperate solutions and salvage operations, ensures that the individual becomes the central figure in the articulation of moments of responsibility, authority and order (the recuperation of identity). The disjuncture between the three realms of polity-culture-economy denies the possibility of an origin or a root. The individual is trapped in the paradox of advanced capitalist schizophrenia (Deleuze and Guattari (1977)) and becomes an element in the psychic metaphorisation of contemporary cultural space, subject to the strains and tensions of fragmented personality through being the root of legitimation in a culture of rootlessness. 'The harsh laws of capitalism, Deleuze and Guattari declare, can function only because it has infiltrated psychic life so that the unconscious is captured by macroeconomic forces' (Wyschogrod (1990) p 201)). The point has been most powerfully expressed by Baudrillard:

> The urban city is [also] a neutralised, homogenised space where indifference, the segregation of urban ghettos, and the downgrading of districts, races and certain age groups are on the increase. In short, it is the cut-up space of distinctive signs. Multiple codes assign a determinate space-time to every act and instant of everyday life ... an immense centre for marshalling and enclosure where the system reproduces itself not only economically and spatially, but also in depth by the ramifications of signs and codes, by the symbolic destruction of social relations (Baudrillard (1993a) p 77).

But the schizophrenic ethic also opens the possibility for a strategy of negotiation, producing alternative desires within the structural limits of the mode of reproduction. In this mode of (re)production, the individual is simultaneously the consumer (the affluent), the operative (the alienated) and the source of authority (the state of anomie). Under these conditions, following Baudrillard (1993a) p 78, resistance consists in saying 'I exist, I have a name, I live here, I am of the Now'. The reversal of the code according to its own logic, on its own terrain, is the possibility because it exceeds semiocracy's own non-referentiality.

Megalopolis: The coordinates have been entered. Only a glimpse of Megalopolis can be given and only the ambience of street conveyed. Harvey comments that 'The city is no longer treated as an entity malleable for broad social ends, but as a collage of spaces and people, of ephemeral events and fragmentary contacts' (Harvey (1989) p 33). The putative chain of determination of production as a material hierarchy no longer holds. Capital becomes a violent force subject to its own symbolic laws of supply and demand. This is the site of urban survival in which the emancipation of desire in the construction of identity becomes a challenge within the paradoxical conflict between the assumption of individual responsibility (legitimation) and the unattainability of continuous gratification (excess: the orgy of escalating appetites) in which all is possible and nothing is achievable.

What is at stake is the very constitution of being: the ways we perceive ourselves and others, the modes of experience that are available to us and whose sensibilities are shaped by urban exposure, the ways in which reality is deconstructed. Conflict, paradox and tension characterise the contemporary forces of the urban. These are the characteristics which enable a shift in the register and enable alternative modes of signification. The flattening of meaning is the exhaustion of certain features that we believed to be intrinsic to it – depth, linear causality, univocality – but which turned out to be dispensable when put to the test of new formations and new modes of analysis. Here the political subject is 'constructed' at the point of intersection of a multiplicity of subject-positions (Mouffe (1988) p 35).

It is inadequate to attribute to capitalism the degree of causality in the formation of culture that Harvey and Jameson propose. Megalopolis is a far more subtle arena. There is no doubt that Megalopolis is a landscape determined by capitalism but to subordinate it totally to the forces of ambient capitalism is to reduce the complexities of cultural processes and to ignore significant other forces at play in its formation. The effects of the transformation in exchange-value spreads far beyond the remit of capitalist assumptions; it enables the simultaneous glorification and seduction of consumption resulting in new experiences in the desire of satiation and transgression, new forms of living and previously inconceivable forms of liberation. To subsume this complexity of forces to a restricted materiality, as Harvey does, is to ignore the significance of cultural formations; cultural formations are in part determined by economic-material forces but they are also the sites of opposition and counter-economic forces.

Experiences from within the network of the imaginary of Megalopolis. In the contemporary confusion between appearance and reality we encounter the 'end' of false appearances and their hidden, metaphysical 'truth'. There is no longer an alternative representation or an exterior point of view. Tensions and desires remain, but they exist as differences and distinctions inside the network of Megalopolis. It is from here that criticism, anger, fear, hope, and a sense justice, and a desire for freedom and change emerge (Chambers (1990) p 57). Along the networks of Megalopolis, whether real or imaginary, run the determination of our experience, a series of contradictory inputs between simulation and transgression:

> Shown up in the light of day as stereotypes, these images cease to function as snares from the moment they are taken up by a living discourse, which remains the only space for my freedom. I know now that this city which oppressed me is imaginary; and in refusing to submit in alienation to its constraints, its fears, its ghosts I wish on the contrary to invest them with my own imagination' (Robbe-Grillet quoted in Chambers (1990) p 52).

SOURCES OF ORDER

1 Legitimation

The forces of disjuncture and rupture which can be identified in contemporary urban culture cause a proliferation of desperate legitimating strategies, or what Jameson calls 'last minute salvage operations' (Jameson (1984)). These forces can be understood in terms of the erosion of the authority of the legitimising myths of the modern consequent upon the development of networks of reproduction within contemporary urban culture resulting in the replacement of the universal by the local, the collective by the personal. This process engenders a hyperinflation of regulatory strategies. The more there is to tell the greater the desire to regulate the telling: there occurs a transition from a narrow band of *unified* legitimising discourses to a wide band of *competing* legitimising discourses.

The struggle is between the colonisation of the regimes of social practice through the fragmentation of networks involved in the communication of authority. The increasing indeterminacy of the division between the public and the private accentuates the range of legitimating strategies in operation in a desperate attempt to re-locate the parameters of control. There occurs a proliferation of regulatory agencies and mechanisms competing to authorise the (old) territory of the (new) spheres of influence. Simultaneously there is an increasing delegation of regulation to the intermediary agencies and individuals in these spheres, as the articulation of legitimation through regulatory techniques becomes fractured through over-extension. This situation will be examined regarding the position of the individual in relation to the sphere of reproduction and consumption.

Without rehearsing the much discussed differences in position between Habermas and Lyotard on the issue of legitimation (Rorty (1985); Steureman (1992)) it is possible to conclude that both the term *crisis* (Habermas) and the prefix *post* (Lyotard) suggest that legitimation is problematised at the point at which it is called into question. Habermas and Lyotard suggest a vast political problem of legitimation within the whole social order. They both point to problems which have to be confronted in the monopolisation of information by multinational corporations and financial networks in which transition cannot be achieved by peaceful evolution or by rational persuasion. However, the difference between the two appear to be regarding the conceptualisation of the mechanisms and possibilities within an interpretation of legitimation. For Habermas the crisis is ultimately liberating because the conclusion will be the triumph of the rational society defined in communicational terms of norms:

> [T]he communication of those affected, who as participators in a practical discourse test the validity claims of norms and, to the extent they accept them with reason, arrive at the conviction that in any given circumstances the proposed norms are 'right' (Habermas (1975) p 105).

For Lyotard such an assumption of norm based rationality reeks of totalising and the valorisation of conformist ideals of consensus, in which new legitimising myths replace the old. In Lyotard's interpretation of legitimation, norms are replaced by narratives and liberation resides in the erosion of the metanarratives and the retrieval of second-order narratives:

> There is, then, an incommensurability between popular narrative pragmatics, which provides immediate legitimation, and the language game known as the question of legitimacy ... Narratives ... determine criteria of competence and/or illustrate how they are to be applied. They thus define what has the right to be said and done in the culture in question, and since they are themselves a part of that culture, they are legitimated by the simple fact that they do what they do (Lyotard (1984) p 23).

Lyotard is prepared to abandon liberal politics in order to avoid universalistic philosophy and valorise the disruption of systematic order as an anarchic force. Habermas retains universalistic philosophy in order to support liberal politics against the threat of totalitarian forms of control.

A number of comments can be made on the concept of legitimation pursuant on the reading of the Habermas-Lyotard debate. First, that the informing criteria of this critique (affluence-anomie-alienation) as an interpretation of a number of oppositional narratives within modernisation has both a potentially liberating and repressive strategic consequence.

Second, that the liberal politics in Habermas is a utopian narrative, once a conscious expression of desire, now only a trace from the remnants of the previous and as such a dangerous and transfigured memory finding expression in the distorted legitimating practices of the present. Lyotard's work avoids the conservative consequence of pre-modern and counter-Enlightenment views. As Steureman comments:

> [Habermas] wants to develop the modernity project as the rational discussion and redemption of the notions of truth, justice and freedom. Habermas calls for more philosophy, for a rational discussion of values and norms. But Lyotard also asks what is the meaning of truth and justice in contemporary societies ... But whereas Habermas speaks in the name of emancipation, Lyotard warns us of the dangers of speaking 'in the name of'. He shows how one can, in defending the idea of emancipation, deny this very notion of freedom (Steureman (1992) p 100).

Here Steureman identifies a problem in Habermas's position regarding emancipation through a communicative strategy out of the wreckage of Enlightenment: it is the very process of 'rational' philosophy that has caused us to arrive at the contemporary predicament. This is what Lyotard calls 'The Endless Torment' (Lyotard (1984) p 29). The language of emancipation – freedom, rights, morality, justice – construct the boundaries at which these emancipatory concepts are deliminated in a regulatory strategy of repressive governmentality. Lyotard identifies the danger of nomination, the power to name which creates the relations of domination, subordination and exploitation.

It is possible to take issue with Lyotard's rejection of modernist 'metanarratives' in order to defend the continuing salience of a generalised social theory. We can distinguish between metanarratives of a macro social theory that conceptualises and interprets a complex diversity of phenomena within a global or totalising context. This suggestion misses the point that the difference between narrative and metanarrative is not simply one of degrees of generality: we can tell narrative 'stories' about the entire course of creation. The metanarrative, according to Lyotard, is defined by its second-order function and by 'the modern proclivity to define the conditions of a discourse in a discourse on those conditions' (Lyotard (1984) p 38). This function extends beyond epistemology. Lyotard does not reject the metanarrative as 'victim' of the crisis of metaphysics (progress, enlightenment, emancipation) and he is entirely in favour of narratives, what he rejects is speaking in 'the name of' the narrative. Lyotard returns to Kant's notion of the sublime which is reserved for all those phenomena which exceed logical containment and which elicit simultaneous pleasure and terror. Lyotard uses the notion of the sublime as a metaphor for the absolute nature of those limitations placed on what can be said, seen, shown, presented, demonstrated, put into play and he implies that each encounter provides the single lesson that there is a *beyond our grasp*.

It is possible to conceive of emancipation through the transcendence of the name and in the evolution of alternative patterns of non-hierarchical emancipatory strategies: beyond the limit of the name and that which utilises the space which is beyond-within-between that limit. It is a possibility positioned between the no-place of the two meanings of 'subject' – a no-place (*ou-topia*) which is just that, a place owned by no body, a space between the *enouce* and the *enunciation* where questions of agency, causation, intention, authorship and history are irrelevant. These questions dissolve into a sublime and asocial immediacy. The sublime is installed in each case as the place of epiphany and terror, the place where the ineffable stands over and against all human endeavour.

Finally, whereas narratives of the personal (second-order) may be, according to Lyotard, the site of immediate legitimation, the struggle which is raging between the legitimating-regulatory devices is not one of metanarratives competing for determinacy but between the regulating strategies themselves (in a hegemonic conflict between specialist agencies). The content of the legitimising myths is empty, the form survives and it is the articulation of the empty form through the legitimating strategies wherein lies the struggle of the present. Whether this is a struggle of 'narrative knowledge' as opposed to 'rational norms' assumes significance in the method of transmission of authority through regulatory regimes.

Following Lyotard, I have suggested there occurs a delegation of legitimation from centre to margin and that the source of legitimation eventually becomes the individual. This process of delegation of authority occurs on the level of intermediate fulfilment in which narratives/norms in contemporary urban culture are within the territory of the sub-groups (cultures) awaiting final transmission to the individual. If the narrative is what is told, then the norm is how it is told. The process of legitimation is one of a transition of symbolic authority between first order and second order regulatory cultures, between established centre and outside margin.

2 Culture

The transition in legitimation occurring in the contemporary is on the level of a struggle for symbolic authority over the signs of delineation within the cultural sphere of the urban through the pluralisation of regulatory orders. The urban, following Castells' analysis, provides a specific arena of action in which regulation exists as a particular field in the transmission and circulation of legitimating devices (Castells (1977)). The regulatory environment is constructed through a number of competing cultures of authority in hegemonic conflict. The individual is both a subject of the tensions inherent in this conflict between regulatory cultural regimes and a member of multiple subgroups (both regulatory and non-regulatory) between which this struggle for delineation is being conducted. The individual is therefore in the position to exploit a series of options regarding the construction of identity. This depends upon which arena for action is utilised at any particular moment in a personal history – a series of both ordered or potentially dis-ordered 'lifeworlds', dominating cultures and resistant subcultures.

The individual becomes part of the process of psychic metaphorisation (Rose (1987)) which results in either Jameson's displacement of the alienation of the subject by the fragmentation of the subject or Deleuze and Guattari's triumph of the schizophrenic ethic which deterritorialises the constraints of commodity exchange through the achievement of the opacity of the capitalist regulatory structure. For Jameson the individual is the totalised and consuming subordinate entity. The 'self' is experienced as a fragmented and incomplete being, composed of multiple 'selves' or identities in relation to the different social-cultural worlds which are inhabited, something with a history, which is 'produced' or in process (Jameson (1984) p 63).

In comparison, Deleuze and Guattari suggest that the individual becomes the liberated survivor of shattered capitalism. The intensification of the schizophrenic tendency within capitalism occurs through the creation of group subjects forming transverse connections between deterritorialised flows that are no longer subject to the constraints of the process of reproduction. This process of intensification suggests the eventual cancellation of conflict between competing regulatory cultural regimes and the supremacy of an economy of transgression in a de-regulated environment. The margin of transgression or deviance becomes the centre of authority. This is the space of the transpolitical, the postpolitical sphere of existence understood as opposition without appearance. In the interim – on the journey to marginality – a number of preliminary comments can be ventured regarding the thrust of Deleuze and Guattari's thesis in terms of hegemony.

Culture, following Althusser (1969), is constructed as conflictual. A conflict model of culture assumes the existence of dominant and subordinate groupings. The urban consists of increasingly fragmented cultural subgroupings subject to interdeterminate flows between dominant and subordinate status. This fragmentation is consequent upon the circulation of competing signs (legitimating codes) in a territoristic struggle over the frame of reference (the construction of identity and desire). A series of signs constitutes a particular form of legitimating device. Each series of signs represents an attempt to give their specific interests universal meaning.

If social relations and processes are appropriated by individuals only through the forms in which they are represented to those individuals (Althusser, 1971; Althusser and Balibar (1968)) then the gradual emergence of multiple forms at increasing levels of circulation leads to dilution in the potential of a particular form to frame the boundaries of regulation of conduct: the importance of contesting the reproduction of power relations. In Gramscian terms this hegemony exists as a precarious 'moving equilibrium' achieved through the orchestration of conflicting forces by particular factions. The sign (the delineating mechanism in the articulation of form) is an element in the communicative systems for the transmission of authority and equates a narrative dimension to every signification. The sign no longer determines the universal but only the particular. Signs which initially served as determining narrative systems are eventually transformed into non-signifying signs (Deleuze and Guattari (1977)) or the fourth order of simulacra (Baudrillard (1993a) pp 50-87) in which in its final diachronic stage the sign bears no relation to reality and is its own pure simulacrum.

The dispersal of signifying forms which formerly served to delineate the boundaries between cultural regimes and which can be read as legitimising practices results in the modification of dominant-subordinate oppositions. Hegemony in this context refers to a situation in which provisional alliance of certain social groups can exert 'total social authority' over subordinate groups. This occurs through both coercion (the imposition of prevailing ideas-practices) and through the moulding of consent so that the power of the dominant appears to be legitimate. Urry suggests a classification of a 'concealment of interests' (strategic investment) (Urry (1981) pp 60-62). Hegemony can only be maintained so long as the dominant succeeds in framing all competing definitions within the range.

This process of framing by the dominant requires constant reproduction to be sustained. There is therefore a continuous conflict between dominant and subordinate subgroupings. Within Gramscian analysis hegemony describes the ritual production of an always only apparent consensus or 'moving equilibrium' between classes of people divided between unequal access to political and economic power. Central to Gramsci's analysis is a postmodern conception of the plurality of cultures. Gramsci argued that the reproduction of domination involved the active participation of the dominated (Gramsci (1973); (1985)). Hegemony is a dynamic antimony or interplay of forces and stands in relation to the power of those outside hegemony who, by 'virtue' of their position, push against it and whose force determines the shape and content of hegemony. Rather than being a singular vector of social-cultural action, hegemony appears as a response to the potential threat of domination by those under subordination. The threat is precisely that they represent a potentially more powerful force. There is no single primary vector, culture is a differential of forces and hegemony a structure of containment. 'Power is a power precisely because it is always threatened, always matched by a real counter-force which is a potential counter-power. And the two forces form an oscillating differential devoid of identity' (Ryan (1989) p 191). The dominant or subordinate serve as necessary oppositions in the universalisation of the particular by the dominant (see Jackson (1988) pp 52-54). This conceptualisation of culture emphasises the affirmative value of hegemonic conflict.

This conflict occurs on the contested level of the sign and is expressed as a struggle of signification for possession of the sign which extends to all areas of the existent field. It is a struggle for the 'symbolic' power of signification in terms of nomination. The naming of emergent signs – and hence the determination of legitimating narratives – in this mode becomes the strategy of groupings engaged in struggles with other groups. The power to name destabilises existing symbolic hierarchies and produces classifications in line with particular interests. Nomination involves determining the conditions for the communication of legitimating classification (Bourdieu (1971); (1979)). In terms of representations – what has become named – it follows that there is no single 'true' representation but multiple representations, each bearing its own legitimating burden and each serving particular interests. Bourdieu suggests that such a process is 'an illusion, consistent with interest, but a well-grounded illusion' (Bourdieu (1984) p 74). The multiplication of regulatory groupings can be interpreted as the formation of 'new cultural intermediaries' who rapidly circulate information between formerly sealed-off areas of culture through new communication channels under conditions of intensified competition.

This process is part of Bourdieu's field approach in the economy of symbolic goods involving the processes of competition and monopolisation and struggles between the established and outsiders. A field is a social arena within which struggles or manoeuvres occur over specific resources or stakes and access to them. Every field has a distinct logic and structure of necessity and relevance which is both the product and producer's of the habitus which is specific and appropriate to that field. The field is a structured system of social positions (either of individuals or of institutions) the nature of which defines the situation of their occupants. It is also a system of forces which exist between these positions: the internal organisation of power relations (Bourdieu (1990) p 88). A field, is by definition, a 'field of struggles' in which agents' strategies are concerned with the preservation or improvement of their position with respect to the defining capital of the field.

This field model of social organisation provides a model for an analysis of the structure of material life. But Bourdieu's analysis of power relations within this model is one in which power and authority flow from the top down. Resistance becomes an impossible activity if the reproduction of relationships of domination (the staking of the parameters of value within and between fields) is maintained as the determining structural form. Social change is imposed upon the individual rather than negotiated between individuals.

It is possible to suggest *contra* Bourdieu, but utilising the field basis of analysis, the fragmentation of fields of action consequent upon the success and inevitability of their determination through the transition from hierarchical networks to linear networks. This in part has been the project of Ernesto Laclau and Chantal Mouffe (1985). They proceed from the assumption that social relations can be differentiated in terms of specific discourses which endow them with meaning. Laclau and Mouffe distinguish between the general field of the interdiscursive and intersubjective as a complex series of 'elements' available for integration into specific discourses. The latter fix the meaning of these elements in relation to an overall discursive system and thereby transform them into relatively fixed 'moments' in that discourse. But they also argue that no discourse can totally fix the meaning of these moments (there is always polyvalence and a surplus of meaning) and that no element is totally without some points of articulation with other discourses. It is possible that the inherent instability and interdependence of meaning suggests a linear in addition to a hierarchical structure of power relations. This is a point developed by Lyotard and Deleuze and Guattari.

Within modernity the process of the determination of power relations between fields was conducted hierarchically but in the postmodern the process is conducted on a linear basis. The organisation of nomination through signification occurs on the level of competitive subgroupings (regulatory and non-regulatory). This competition is accentuated between regulatory groupings attempting to delineate particular areas. The determination of the universal is no longer possible; what is left is the determination of the local (the provisional or contingent).

Lyotard proposes that this is the result of the computerisation of society and the development of increasingly elaborate networks of communication. For Deleuze and Guattari it is the result of the development of transverse networks or rhizomes which are non-hierarchical, horizontal multiplicities which cannot be subsumed within a unified (regulated) structure and whose components form abstract, random unregulated networks in which any element can be connected with any other element (Deleuze and Guattari (1977) pp 302–303). These networks develop within the contemporary processes of urban capitalism as a result of the tension between groups involved in symbolic production. These are the networks of the transpolitical.

Deleuze and Guattari utilise the figure of the machine to describe the emergence of the alternative networks of the transpolitical. The schizophrenic condition of contemporary capitalist relations is encompassed in the desiring machine and the nomadic subject. During desiring-production a moment approaches when the desiring-machine congeals and forms an enormous undifferentiated subject. Everything stops dead in that moment, everything freezes in its place (Deleuze and Guattari (1977) pp 7;13). That undifferentiated object is the body-without-organs, the desiring-machine at degree-zero intensity. This is the moment and space of antiproduction, anticommodification and antiregulation signifying a constant feedback into the processes of reproduction. It is a moment of rupture when a gap between the logic of the process is available. It is the moment when the codes are scrambled and deterritorialised and the nomadic subject is produced. The nomadic subject is a point of pure intensity traversing the grid of the body without organs, a mobile locus of becoming commingling identities which traces a process of becoming other (Bogue (1988) p 95). This is the subject not of resistance but of the inevitable consequence of the production of intensity within the process of regulation. It is a moment – for it can only ever be a moment – when the noise stops and there exists an expression of pure desire undetermined by ambient capitalist relations.

This form of analysis is developed in the work of Michel de Certeau who exploits the proliferation of networks through the fragmentation of urban order: 'Beneath the discourses that ideologize the city, the ruses and combinations of powers that have no readable identity proliferate; without points where one can take hold of them ... impossible to administer' (Certeau (1988) p 95).

These theorists of resistance suggest the possibility of a phase of cultural declassification through the dehierarchicisation and demonopolisation of previously established legitimate cultural enclaves. The signs of order find themselves constantly put to flight and worthless in an exercise of increasingly meaningless and abstract nomadic governmentality over deterritorialised space. An empty conflict rages between regulatory cultures in an urban cultural sphere marked by localisation and intimate legitimising forms. The action is no longer at the regulated centre but at the de-regulated margin. The dilution of the authority of the symbolic producers ensures an economy of transgression. Tension and desire exist as distinctions and differences inside the margins of the network. It is an economy of transgression necessarily determined by the violent symbolic laws of capital. Without the stringencies of legitimation capital pursues a frozen moment of accelerated sclerosis. But it is from within this culture of excess – albeit on the edge of the unknowable confines of the urban – that the marginal spaces and the interstices of anger and fear, desire and change emerge. This is the space of the deregulated and decolonised nomadic subject of a transpolitical governmentality.

3 Regulation

The discussion has been concerned with the tensions inherent in the regulatory strategies ordered in the governance of urbanisation. It is possible to identify a process of accelerated sclerosis as an external skeletal layer forms over the machine of regulation. It is necessary to comment upon the nature of regulation so as to articulate the possibility of this frozen moment regarding the possibility of the flight of capital and the emergence of an economy of transgression along the integers of the transverse network. So far the discussion has been concerned with regulation at the level of the struggle for the sign of signification in the process of naming and the tensions between signifying regimes in the colonisation of decolonised space. To clarify this process it is possible to discuss the 'materialisation' of regulation in terms of the form in which regulation as the artificiality of coherence takes on an appearance.

The work of the *Parisien* School of Regulation demonstrated the inherent tensions within capitalism in terms of organisation: 'the unity of unity and struggle'. They posited how capitalism could survive even though capital relations inevitably produce antagonisms, contradictions and crises – all of which make continuing accumulation improbable and generates ruptures and structural shifts as capital develops (Aglietta (1979); Lipietz (1986)). There are echoes of Deleuze and Guattari's schizophrenic ethic here. The analysis of reproduction as regulation was the starting point for much of *Parisien* regulation theory. It represented not only a reaction to the Althusserian account of social reproduction but also to the schemas of economic reproduction. In explaining how both types of reproduction problem were solved the *Parisiens* looked to specific institutional forms, societal norms, and the patterns of strategic control. These expressed and regulated conflicts until the inevitable tensions and divergencies among these various regulatory forms reached crisis point (Jessop (1990) p 171).

Aglietta suggests that accumulation and regulation are the two sides of the capitalist system and that economic analysis has hitherto been too concerned with the former.

Aglietta's work provides a broader framework of analysis encompassing social relations, their cohesion and transformation. It is possible to compare Aglietta's approach to regulation with that of Foucault's work on governmentality. Central to this synthesis is the idea of the tension between regulatory rationales. Whereas the *Parisien* School operated within a dialectical tradition of the inevitability of crisis articulated as conflict within regulatory schemas, Foucault's work analysed the nature of regulation as an attitude of government, the representation of and responsibility for which has been delegated to the expertise of the individual.

Foucault did not approach the issue of governmentality as a necessary relation of repression, as the *Parisien* School did regarding the class struggle. Foucault's analysis suggested a two-way relation between power and identity. Government becomes a notion which encompasses the multiple ways in which identity is related to power and which embraces all those interests which manage and administer social and personal existence in the attempt to introduce economy, order and virtue. Foucault's concern was the question: 'How to govern oneself, how to be governed, how to govern others, how to accept the one who is to govern us, how to become the best possible governor' (Foucault (1979a) p 5). His excavation of these questions led him to conclude that contemporary political power 'now reaches the very grain of the individual, touches his body, intrudes into his gestures, his attitudes, his discourses, his apprenticeship, his daily life' (Foucault (1980) p 39). Foucault is forced to confront the consequences of liberalism and the final question of 'how not to be governed'. This final question – that of the deconstruction of a post-regulatory/disciplinary order – is the subject of Part II of this book.

What Foucault's work establishes is the pervasiveness and insidiousness of government. He addressed political power in terms of 'political rationalities' and 'technologies of government' and drew attention to the diversity of regulatory mechanisms seeking to give effect to government, and the particular importance of indirect mechanisms that link the conduct of individuals and organisations through 'action at a distance'. Government in contemporary urban culture attempts to achieve an alignment of interests balanced between freedom and control, an ordered or disciplined individualisation.

In his development of Foucault's concept of governmentality, Robert Castel (1990) proposes that in contemporary urban culture the purpose of government has not been control, because the organisation of risk and dangerous marginality has become manageable through bureaucratic and managerial technologies so that the individual no longer has the option of deviation, but the constant reorganisation and alignment of interest toward neo-liberal competitive pathways.

Foucault's work suggests a multiplicity of regulatory strategies from the juridic to the administrative and extending from the hierarchical to the linear and the consequential devolution of regulatory techniques to individuals (Miller and Rose (1990) p 1). The earlier ideas of hyper-differentiation and hyper-rationalisation lurk here. The *Parisiens*' identification of crisis can be translated as a stage of hyperinflation of regulatory strategies in the maintenance of legitimation. When the subject, upon whom government operates, becomes the sovereign legislator the nature of government is questioned and the possibility of resistance to government is activated:

> At the very heart of the power relationship, and constantly provoking it, are the recalcitrance of the will and the intransigence of freedom. Rather than speaking of an essential freedom, it would be better to speak of an 'agonism' – of a relationship which is at the same time reciprocal incitation and struggle; less face-to-face confrontation which paralyses both sides than a permanent revolution (Foucault quoted by Gordon (1991) p 5).

Foucault concluded that contemporary governmental rationality is simultaneously involved in the dual processes of individualising and totalising. It is a conclusion which encompasses the tension between the political economy of the market and the governance of the individual. The analysis of the relations between the 'self' and power is a method of investigating the ways in which subjectivity has become an essential object and target for certain strategies, tactics and procedures of regulation. It is possible to utilise this tension as a positive project of self-understanding. An example of this analysis is found in Foucault's concepts of biopower-biopolitics. Foucault (1979b) introduced the term 'biopower' to designate forms of power exercised over persons specifically in so far as they are thought of as living beings: a politics concerned with subjects as members of a population. Foucault suggested that biopolitics generates a new kind of counter-politics, the subversive configurations of the technologies of self. As governmental practices have addressed themselves in an increasingly immediate way to 'life', in the form of the individual detail of individual sexual conduct, individuals have begun to formulate the needs and imperatives of that same life as the basis for political-counter demands. Biopolitics becomes one example of the 'strategic reversibility' of power relations into a focus of resistance, or the way in which government as the 'conduct of conduct' is interwoven with the dissent of 'counter-conducts', the linear and nomadic of the figure of transpolitical. It is possible to place Foucault's concept of *heterotopia* within this schema of analysis, in which the site of order is juxtaposed to the counter-site of disorder. The possibility of 'strategic reversibility' is examined in Part II of this book, utilising the desire not to be governed as a result of the extension of the satiation of governmentality. This is an affirmative conceptualisation of power relations. Power is not a negation of the vitality and capacities of individuals but rather a creative force which shapes and utilises individuals as subjects. This affirmative conceptualisation works in conjunction with the regulatory paradox: the 'truth' of the Law is the justification of an administrative 'rationality' in which truth is applied but as a truth which has operational limits (a source of legitimation crisis). As Judith Butler notes:

> The point is not to stay marginal, but to participate in whatever network of marginal zones is spawned from other disciplinary centres and which, together, constitute a multiple displacement of those authorities (Butler (1990) p13).

CHAPTER THREE

REGULATION AND URBAN ORDER: DETERMINING FORCES

> Along with Marx, we all dreamed of the end of Political Economy, the extinction and transparency of classes and the transparency of the social according to an ineluctable logic of the crisis of Capital. Then we dreamed of the denigration of the very postulates of Political Economy and Marxist critique, in the same movement. We dreamed of a radical alternative denying any primacy to the economic and political in first and second instance. Political economy is simply abolished as an epiphenomenon, vanquished by its own simulacrum and by a superior type of logic (Baudrillard (1992) p 25).

This chapter deals with the socio-economic and psychological forces that determine the construction of identity in contemporary urban culture. These forces enable the delegation of authority through the multiplication of alternative sub-groupings resulting from the conflict between dominant regulatory forms. The forces I refer to are affluence, anomie and alienation. These forces are central in the operation of the simultaneous fragmentation and stabilisation of experience within the contemporary urban sphere. These forces represent the effects of the excess of the processes of commodification, differentiation and rationalisation. These forces were identified in modernity and were confined within the discourses of social and political theory. Here I retrieve them from their moribund state and deploy them as significant terms within postmodernity. These are the forces which result from the reproduction and circulation of the signs which constitute the empty narrative force of the tensions between competing regulatory regimes. These are the forces which constitute the economy of transgression and structure the formation of sub-groupings on the margins in opposition to the authority of the centre. These are the forces which form the transverse connections between the alternative networks of control in the deterritorialised space of the deregulated arena and which mark the end of production, the final outcome of the excess of reproduction.

AFFLUENCE

1 An Urban Culture of Consumption

It would be obscene to describe contemporary urban culture as a site of universal affluence. Inequalities in the distribution of wealth are maintained. What has emerged is the ethic and appearance of affluence which permeates all areas of contemporary existence. This ethic will be discussed in two ways. First, as the sovereignty of consumption. Second, as a determining force in the transition to the economy of transgression through both the excess of affluence and the absence of affluence.

Jameson and Baudrillard both identify postmodernism as part of a 'new cultural logic of capitalism', the purest form of capital yet to have emerged in a prodigious expansion into hitherto uncommodified areas. Baudrillard has been engaged in the task of extending Marx's critique of the commodity form in the context of contemporary capitalism (Baudrillard (1975); (1993a)). In an era of multinational capital, characterised by the controlled programming of commodity production and the pervasive penetration by the mass media, we experience the hegemony of what Baudrillard refers to as 'signifying culture' in which the social world becomes saturated with shifting cultural signs. Society is no longer determined by production but is now constituted post-industrially through processes of reproduction. This analysis is based upon the assumption that the development of commodity production and the advance of information technology has led to the 'triumph of signifying culture'. The significance of this development in terms of the reversal of the direction of determinism is that social relations become saturated with shifting cultural signs to the extent that we can now no longer speak of class or normativity and are faced, as Baudrillard puts it, by *the end of the social*:

> Now we have passed from the commodity law of value to the structured law of value, and this coincides with the obliteration of the social form known as production. Given this, are we still within a capitalist mode? It may be that we are in a hyper-capitalist mode, or in a very different order (Baudrillard (1993a) p 10).

The triumph of the market is crucial in this analysis of the economic dialectic. The global spread of capital means that all centres of authority are either differentiated or have been absorbed by the interlocking cultural and economic systems that constitute 'late capitalism': flexible accumulation. The holding system that was the nation state has been replaced by the market. The market promises and denies affluence through the constant reproduction of images of materiality. The market is the site of the signifiers which form the *locus* of capital's cultural investments and social inscriptions; the sign increasingly replaces the product as the site of fetishism. The 'value' of the product lies in its exchange value as an image – the distinction it has or will acquire in the market. The product becomes the consumer, the production of the demand for consumption. It is possible to reject the simple dichotomies between consumer sovereignty and consumer-as-dupe in advancing a theory of consumption as a signifying practice in people's everyday lives. Advertising offers pleasure and denies satisfaction. In terms of spatial organisation it is possible to distinguish (after Lefebvre) between 'spaces of representation' (such as shopping malls) and 'representations of space' (as in contemporary advertising).

Consumption rather than production becomes the new dialectic. But it is consumption on a symbolic level. The representation of images of materiality and the inexorable process of commodification ensures a transition to an economy based upon simulation. Social space (or what is left of it) becomes saturated with signs (an emptiness filled with signs). The force of affluence turns on the images of consumerism, images which are themselves engaged in conceptions of identity rooted in commodified relations. Images which linked commodities with identity no longer need to be oriented toward non-commodified regions of meaning because commodified meanings become self-referential. For Baudrillard this process marks the fourth and final 'phase of the image'. The absence of the real induces a 'panic' reaction, in which nostalgia blooms, cults of authenticity arise and culture is abandoned to the 'panic-stricken production of the real' (Baudrillard (1988) p 268). It is a process which renders the individual part of a 'silent majority' as opposed to historic subject, becoming inert in the face of the 'territoristic' mode of signification in which signifiers emit meanings to which no response is possible. Consumerism through symbolic consumption becomes the conformism of the ambient malls of reproduction (Baudrillard (1983a)). Baudrillard's forecast is bleak: the subject knows no better and submits to become a spectator. In material terms desire is manifested as compulsive consumption always founded upon a lack, because satiation is a mere fetish, a sign of itself which takes the idea of lived experience as its referent. As an active mode of relations which systematically reduces all individuals to 'the individual' and which institutes mechanisms of social control, consumption is the virtual totality of all objects.

But this process can also render the individual part of an alternative opposition of refusal within an economy of transgression. The insistence that everything – objects, experiences, individuals – has a value, whether through exchange or use, is central to both political economy and its critique; neither can tolerate its transgression. But symbolic values count for nothing; they generate no wealth and indicate no use, and it is precisely in this symbolic realm that the possibilities of a subversive ridicule of political economy emerge. It is an economy which is activated by two paradoxical consequences. First, the consequences of the excess of consumption in which the primary desire becomes to consume no more (refusal through satiation/obesity). Second, the consequence of the absence of consumption in which the primary desire becomes the alignment of absence (the exploitation of the position of the refuse[d]): Those who cannot consume because they cannot afford to, know just how shallow the preoccupation with consumption can be.

2 An Urban Economy of Transgression

An economy of transgression develops in two ways. First, if the processes of commodification and consumption operate on the level of pure signification then the force of affluence is operative only through images and representations. The control network of the market through the regulatory culture of the media and advertising determines that actual material possession becomes secondary to perceived material possession. The activity of accumulation is no longer as important as the form and appearance of possession. The individual as producer and consumer is engaged in a series of symbolic acts in the satisfaction of desire through materiality: the satisfaction of desire through objects is *without* object (Baudrillard (1988) p 46). Although the act of consumption remains a collective act in the sense of being a function of production and a transaction in the exchange of signs, the individual becomes, in one sense, emancipated through the reproduction of signifying values. If material values are purely symbolic then participation in the exchange of these values through actual or perceived acts of accumulation is no longer trapped by the 'reality' of such values. The consumer's 'fixated egoism' is a recognition of being the exploited subject: resistance and 'egoism' drives the system to insoluble contradictions, to which it responds by reinforcing constraints. This confirms that consumption is a gigantic political field. The recognition of this fact becomes the emancipatory strategy of transgressive opposition.

The second strand in the development of an economy of transgression through an ethic of affluence involves an examination of allocation and opportunity of access to resources. An image of affluence is maintained in regulatory terms so that allegiance to the system of reproduction is secured. The perpetuation of the possibility of the achievement of desire is a primary regulatory strategy. This strategy is subject to a tension through the *actual* differential achievement of desire. Amongst particular sub-groupings, goal achievement is realisable and expectation exceeds conformist value. This results in the internal generation of non-conformist values of achievement and satisfaction and trangressionary behaviour. Over-allocation, in terms of potential for consumption and the provision of spatial-temporal opportunity of satisfaction of consuming desires, leads to oppositional (non-conformist) behaviour through excessive consumption. Such behaviour occurs in sub-groupings which were once central in the regulatory structure and which subsequently become marginal through achievement and results in the *internal* undermining of centralising authoritative regulatory strategies.

In other sub-groupings, similar behaviour is realised through *absence*. The fracture in the traditional patterns of the socio-economic structure results in accentuated differentiation between sub-groups along non-aligned networks. The impossibility of realisable accumulation through consumption in a culture dominated by signifying images of consumption generates tendencies of anomie and alienation manifested as oppositional (non-conformist) behaviour. An order of imagined prosperity in which localised sectors are subject to forces of scarcity and unachievable means, results in hostility toward the dominant order and the constraints of its regulatory culture. Differential affluence creates both sub-grouping and individual opposition regarding established orders of regulation. The totalising force of commodification, including the reproduction of 'cultural' capital in a symbolic order of exchange, fragments existing regulatory strategies in a process of hyper-differentiation of urban culture between affluence and absence.

ANOMIE

1 Access To and Absence of Means

The differentiation occurring between both sub-groupings and individuals as a result of affluence, produces anomie. It may be simplistic to retrieve a sociological concept such as anomie and place it as a central explanatory tenet in this analysis. Mestrovic has recently noted: 'It is tragic that anomie, a term that is helpful in understanding the impact of modern economies on social life, has been relegated to an obscure status' (Mestrovic (1991) p 166).

Anomie, as Durkheim realised, is a classical term relating to the human condition as opposed to a variant in descriptive social organisation. It is a condition central to an understanding of the expression of opposition by the individual. It is important to understand Durkheim's conceptualisation of anomie as both an external element in the determination of social structure and also an internal element in mental life.

Anomie is an apposite descriptive device in the analysis of the malaise and fragmentation of the prevailing regulatory regime. Anomie is operative as a sociological and psychological condition against existing legitimating structures. The paradox is that these regulating structures and the advent of hyper-commodification results in the subversion of prevailing legitimating strategies through the excess which they produce. The desire to control, through the provision of images of attainable affluence, has backfired and resulted in the blurring of barriers between ordered and disordered behaviour. Control networks which previously articulated legitimating codes have become overloaded and fractured into multiple regimes of confused regulatory scenarios leaving a new void for the emergence of marginal non-regulatory orders, in opposition to a collapsing central authority.

Anomie as a prevalent condition within postmodernity is operative partially as a result of affluence. Durkheim's original formulation was a state of economic prosperity that could be conceived as being more disordering of and discontinuous with 'the normal state of affairs' than economic depression. Prosperity appeared to encourage dangerous illusions (the tyranny of unbridled passion), while depression (recession) enforced the hard lessons of the Protestant Ethic. Prosperity encouraged the profligate, depression served to validate the prudent: 'This asceticism turned with all its force against one thing: the spontaneous enjoyment of life and all it has to offer' (Weber). Durkheim's use of anomie in *The Division of Labour* characterised the pathological state of the economy, 'this sphere of collective life [which] is, in large part freed from the moderating action of regulation'. Durkheim's formulation operated as a socio-psychological condition within an urbanised economy. Like alienation, it refers first to the relationship of the individual to elements of the social environment and second to a state of mind. Durkheim initially considered the division of labour to provide the necessary regulative force that produced solidarity because it created a system of obligations which linked individuals together. Anomie becomes prevalent because of the rapid growth of the market which fractures this collective and cohesive series of shared obligations through the inability of effective moral regulation ('For precisely because the economic functions today concern the greatest number of citizens ... it follows that as that world is only feebly ruled by morality, the greatest part of their existence takes place outside the moral sphere').

Merton's analysis of anomie assumed a general differential scarcity of socially structured means for the achievement of widely and diversely accepted culturally defined goals to a usual, and perhaps permanent condition in capitalist societies (Merton (1938); (1957)). Merton's writings on anomie are realised around a struggle for access to, utilisation of, or commitment to means. It was the differential availability of means that prompted Merton to suggest that the tendency toward anomie was prevalent amongst those social groups who were the most alienated from modes of access regarding the production of means. Merton's analysis was therefore couched as a process of social transformation which involved an anomie of scarcity.

Merton's conception of an anomie of scarcity operates within a definition of modernisation which includes defined patterns of industrial development and the progressive and administrative rationalisation and differentiation of the social world.

Central to the process of modernisation which a commentator such as Featherstone (1991) attempts to define is the idea of cultural change via a loose base-superstructure model against which modern identity emerges, centred around self-development. The construction of self within a process of developing industrialisation entails conformity to norms which are generated through the process of industrial development, which is only differentially productive. A process of social transformation toward an economy of sustained (apparent or virtual) affluence entails the generation of norms through periods of scarcity (depression and recession) in which universal conformity is only temporarily available, depending upon economic status. The promises which were made in the period of development of the industrial process of modernisation were only ever differentially adhered to; the promises made in the postmodern of urban culture are constantly reproduced and the means of enforcing them increasingly credible.

2 Excessive Abstract Fantasies

At this point Merton's frustration theory of deviant adaptations (differential availability of means) must be revised in the light of the retrieval of Durkheim's original interpretation of anomie as a consequence of affluence. Not all members of society have equal access to the means of externally defined success. The gap between the anomie of affluence and the anomie of scarcity is increasing, complete with an increase in the capacity for leaps across that gap in either direction: dramatic success may be as rare as dramatic failure, with each requiring equally substantial effort. Economic power differences become fluid and negotiated so that any individual may have widely differing levels of economic potency in a lifetime. The co-existence of affluence and scarcity alters both forms as historically identified, with the latter being somewhat more profoundly influenced by the former. The experience of affluence creates a novel set of conditions under which differing groups and cohorts can judge both the opportunities to achieve and the experience of achievement itself (Simon and Gagnon (1976)).

A social order that makes promises and then proceeds to keep them with such apparent ease and abundance can trivialise them to the point where achievement no longer affords what has been called 'consummatory gratification'. It also no longer affords constraining gratification – the condition in which gratification as a process further ties the individual to the prevailing normative order of weakening such ties.[1] The transformation of consumption, because of hyper-commodification, encompasses

1 In these circumstances the goals of the society do not represent some homogeneous set of desires for all sectors, if indeed they ever did. Instead, there is a complex series of adjustments and tensions between commitment to and gratification from a varied set of societal rewards which are themselves under relatively frequent review, in terms of both personal salience and objective valuation. The weakening of attachment does not necessarily free the individual totally to invent the values through which experience is evaluated. Still less does it allow for a genuine expression of some ill-defined original nature or biological mandate. There is a basic reliance on institutional value systems. Though in greater variety and requiring fewer universal assumptions in addition to requiring a reflexive assimilation of the response of others (though with possibly less permanent significance) these systems remain a characteristic of those subject-ed to the anomie of affluence. In the same way they are attributable to those describable in terms of the anomie of scarcity as markers of denial of access to resources through institutional closure. The basic source of both experience and its meanings remain the very matrix of social life; the comparative remains intrinsic to the human evaluation of the human (see Simon and Gagnon (1976)).

all desires except excess. The system ultimately induces a form of subject auto-seduction: the self consumption of the subject (Gane (1991) p 60). But this universalisation establishes new orders within the political field of gratification in which the evolution of desire dictates the value of accumulation. It is at this stage that the prospect of an affirmative anomie of affluence arises. As Durkheim says:

> But the man who has always pinned all his hopes on the future and lived with his eyes fixed upon it has nothing in the past as a comfort against the present afflictions, for the past was nothing to him but a series of hastily experienced stages. What blinded him to himself was his expectation to find further on the happiness he had so far missed. Now he is stopped in his tracks; from now on nothing remains behind of him to fix his gaze upon. Weariness alone, moreover, is enough to bring disillusionment, for he cannot in the end escape the futility of an endless pursuit (Durkheim (1951) p 256).

The transition between scarcity and affluence ensures a break with the past wherein lay the authority of collective metaphors and the establishment of an order of personal metaphors. To adopt the narrative terminology of Lyotard what occurs is a transition from the metanarrative of external legitimation to second-order narratives of internal legitimation. Durkheim's pessimism is based upon his synonymous use of the terms 'individualisation' and 'anomie' reflecting his concern for the ascendancy of the existential over the abstract. For Durkheim the stability of social life and the possibility of retaining social integration depended on long-term value internalisation and the linkage of elements of the individual life-style to the collective meanings of society. In contrast, long-term prosperity appears to be a greater threat to social integration in that it emphasises and enables immediate material gratification and fails to punish individuals for acting out their deepest desires. The transformation and the development of the market mechanism no longer provides either the cohesive pattern of collective solidarity or the imposition of restraint through regulation.

Contemporary urban culture is increasingly an arena marked by the ascendancy of personal metaphors, dominated by the existential, the transient, and the provisional, which increasingly constrain individuals to test concretely their most abstract fantasies. Crucial to the values of an achieving (modern) society was the mechanism of delayed gratification, which involved not only the postponement of gratification but the existence of an ordered set of gratifications so that postponement became an investment which could yield intensified experiences of pleasure. In the contemporary, where the objects that stood for this pleasure are devalued by (apparent) affluence, the other side of the peak of achievements becomes the margin of transgression. Durkheim's image is of the individual suffering the necessity provoked by opportunity to test the limits of their gratification: individuals consuming themselves in 'an orgy of escalating appetites' (Simon and Gagnon (1976) p 367).

Durkheim's model of human nature is essentially consistent with the tradition that runs from Hobbes to Freud: the human, unregulated by the hard 'facts' of life, becomes the instrument (or victim) of overwhelming passions that in the absence of imposed constraints will exhaust the host society-organism before individuals themselves are exhausted. In *Suicide* (Durkheim (1898/1951)) anomie is deployed to characterise the pathological state of individuals who are insufficiently regulated by society and suffer from the 'malady of infinite aspiration'. Paradoxically anomie becomes a peculiar mark of moral distinction in that it is a reaction to the collapse of regulation within a turbulent economic sphere. It is therefore a reassertion of individuality in a desire for limits to desire, a need for control as a part of self-realisation (the re-assertion of a lack). Anomie becomes a signal of individual need for normative moral restraint in the absence of external imposition of authority:

> To limit man, to place obstacles in the path of his free development, is this not to prevent him from fulfilling himself? But ... this limitation is a condition of our happiness and moral health. Man, in fact is made for life in a determinate, limited environment (Durkheim cited by Lukes (1977) p 83).

Within the postmodern, excess as abstract gratification is possible and the abstract fantasy of the modern can become the concretised realisation of the postmodern. The problem is whether the gratification of the fantasy of the abstract is itself determined by the social construction of production and consumption and therefore regulated (as Baudrillard would suggest) or is an indication of breach from the shackles of accumulation toward the imperative of liberated expression through the fulfilment of individualisation in a non-regulatory order. Has the individual progressed beyond the need for externally imposed restraints and social cohesion? The erosion of the metanarrative (the confirmation of status) and the ascendancy of the second-order narrative (the confirmation of experience) becomes a process either of the establishment of new orders of authority (regulation) or an emancipation from all orders of authority (deregulation):

> Indeed, much of what appears to be anomie, for example a rejection or moderation of the achievement motive, might well be reinterpreted as being expressive not of decay but of transition. It is a more flexible approach to human motivation that seems very much in order ... the need to conceive of social structure as active, as producing fresh motivations which cannot be predicated on the basis of knowledge about man's native drive (Simon and Gagnon (1976) p 376).

It is at this juncture that the contribution of Baudrillard must be examined and challenged as one of the few theorists of the postmodern to consider the nature of contemporary consumer society. Baudrillard develops Durkheim's model of the human regarding consumption (Baudrillard (1988); see also Gane (1991) pp 57-61). Baudrillard's formulation is that the practice of consumption is 'the most advanced form of the rational systematisation of the productive process at the individual level' (Baudrillard (1988) p 43). Gane points out that the notion of affluence as the liberation of human desires neglects the paradoxical reassertion at particular moments of puritanical ideologies (the mode of nostalgia) which, in a particular economic-ideological form, becomes the reinvented economic liberalism of the so-called 'enterprise culture' (see Keat and Abercrombie (1990)). The moment in which the individual realises her own pleasure is in fact the site not only of new consciousness but of a new discipline parallel to apparent emancipation. These disciplines embody their own forms of systematisation, concentration, seduction, gratification, and repressive *de-sublimation* ('alienation correctly understood' Baudrillard (1988) p 43). It is Baudrillard's contention that contemporary consumer society invites the individual to attempt a constant extension of the experience of consumption (the gratification of the fixated egoism). The invitation to consume becomes the primary social relation and the code of the subconscious ideological apparatus (*dispotif*). It makes its appearance in the form of involved emancipation and free choice, under the power of individual will, yet the code determines this process, effectively inducing the deepest form of social control.[2]

Baudrillard inverts Durkheim's original conception of anomie. In modernity consumption was unregulated and its processes subject to the particular crisis of anomie experienced in the specific form of productive compensation relative to market demand. In postmodernity the problem of the instability of demand has altered. It is no longer that proposed by Durkheim, where the deregulation or breakdown of former norms gives rise to an explosion of insatiable 'needs', but rather the field becomes increasingly regulated by new ideologically driven obligations which surge toward a new structure of instability that is not anomic.

For Baudrillard there is no escape or resistance, only the totalising force of consumption pervading all levels of experience. Violence as resistance is sanitised into the disequilibrium of fatigue and withdrawal; resistance through hyper-conformity. All conflicts are displaced into the regime of the regulatory code of consumption. Security is sovereign in safeguarding the ambience of consumption. This is merely a different modernity typified by reflexivity, the guarantee to the individual of the minimum risk in return for the submission of individuality. The potential for latent revolt resides with the 'silent majorities' through the expression of fatigue and non-participation, the activity of excessive passivity. Pfohl echoes Baudrillard's position:

> Material access to spaces in excess of dominant order is exactly what is being denied us in the emergence of the ultramodern society. The more we move within the dense and high speed world of image simulations that characterise the ultramodern, the more we find excess modelled to fit prepackaged formats of access and then sold back to us so that we might consume what's different and what's the same all in the same bite/byte (Pfohl (1992) p 16).

---

2 The danger in the contemporary is the erosion of alternatives through the totalising of non-legitimated (hyper-legitimated or legitimation in the finite) strain of capitalism. Baudrillard stresses that this is the condition of the present, that capitalism has achieved the ultimate level of totalisation in the reproduction of signs (simulation) (Baudrillard (1983a); (1983b)) It is, for the individual, the condition of the satiated totalitarianism of capital: 'Everything is in motion, everything is changing, everything is being transformed and yet nothing changes. Such a society, thrown into technological progress, accomplishes all possible revolutions but these are revolutions upon itself' (Baudrillard (1968) p 217). Lyotard makes a similar point regarding legitimating strategies in contemporary urban culture when he writes:

> It would be of great importance to examine the present status of capitalism from the point of view of totalitarianism. Capitalism adapts itself to the republican institution, but it has little tolerance for terror (which destroys its market). It can make a good bedfellow for despotism (as we saw with Nazism). It is scarcely troubled by the decline of the great universalistic narratives, even the liberal one of the enrichment of humanity. It would seem that capital has no need for legitimation, that it prescribes nothing in the strict sense of an obligation, and that consequently it does not manifest an instance which makes its norms prescriptive. It is present everywhere, but as a necessity rather than a purposiveness. I believe that one can understand why it appears as a necessity by analysing the canonical formula of the genre of discourse that is its own. One would see that a purposiveness nevertheless hides beneath this appearance: to gain time. Is this a universally valid end? (Lyotard (1992) p 69).

But it is within this social-psychological condition of non-participation that opposition and resistance is activated. Baudrillard's contention that anomie cannot evolve under conditions of affluence through its erosion by elaborate networks of control is at one level a capitulation to the authority of the market and at a second level a denial of the potential for opposition through the closed expression of non-participation. *Contra* Baudrillard it can be argued that non-participation and closure is a central element in the revolutionary strategy of transition to an original de-regulated order. There is a seductive pessimism to Baudrillard's analysis of 'consumer society' but his notion of resistance through refusal demonstrated as hyper-conformity appears only as a token gesture towards subversion.

Baudrillard's regime of signification suggests a capitulation to external excess in which all that is left is 'anomaly'. Anomie, for Baudrillard, is that which escapes the jurisdiction of the Law; anomaly is that which escapes the jurisdiction of the norm. Anomaly is at play in an aleatory, statistical field, a field of variations and modulations which no longer knows the margin or transgressions characteristic of the Law, since all is reduced to a statistical and operational equation, a field so normalised that abnormality no longer has a place in it even as a kind of madness or subversion: 'Yet there still remains anomaly' (Baudrillard (1990) p 26). Anomaly no longer has the tragic side of abnormality, nor even the dangerous and deviant side of anomie. It is somehow harmless and inexplicable, representing the echo of another. But it is a very faint echo in Baudrillard's schema when there are more direct counter-forces and moments available to be utilised within the system of totalisation that Baudrillard has described.

The issue of closure has been examined by Parkin (1979) in a development of a Gramscian-Weberian model of culture. Parkin identifies two forms in the exercise of power in terms of access to resources. The *exclusionary* process of closure is the denial of access by the dominant grouping. The *usurpationary* process of closure is the exercise by subordinate groupings of a strategic seizure of access. It is possible to extend this analysis into one of a *refusal* to exercise power and withdrawal allowing for the possibility of articulating alternative *desires of power* and resources of fulfilment. The force of the market and its related regulatory regime is, it is granted, capable of fulfilling all desires (no matter how apparent or differential) and as such still exerts a force through which it can determine individual behaviour. But it is through this very process that anomie as an expression of opposition evolves, through the logic of accumulation and the maximisation of the appearance of satiation which ultimately determines the disappearance of accumulation. This proposition can be analysed on four levels.

First, on a sociological level it is unclear whether Baudrillard considers anomie to be a potential determinant of opposition through an expression of non-conformist trangressionary tactics (following Durkheim's model of the human). It is however, feasible to suggest that anomie (without law) either through affluence or scarcity is an expression of either/both subgroup/individual opposition through non-compliance against the prevailing legitimating regulatory order. It is therefore an expression of resistance against established regulatory regimes.

Second, on a psychological level, anomie is the expression of the exhaustion of desire. Desire which is constantly determined by ideologically founded social relations is a perversion of desire. Desire which is an expression of reproduced and simulated images of need is a false desire. Durkheim's fear of overwhelming passion (unregulated desire) is articulated through the requirement of revitalising constraints or the imposition of collective metaphors. But in the contemporary, in which metanarrative fixation is being eroded through multiplicity, the myth of the collective metaphor is shattered and replaced by the contingency of subgroup (second order) narratives upon a pragmatic and less structured plane of regulatory operation. This is the 'logical' transmission from regulated centre to de-regulated margin. Here the movement of desire, the excitement contained in the event-moment of the fulfilment of desire is significant, even in the affirmation of a lack in desire.

Third, regarding 'individual' desire, it can be suggested that there is an ascendancy of a personal metaphor of satiation. If the market achieves its desire through its logic of fulfilling individual gratificatory consumption, then logically the last desire of the individual is to refuse to consume, to participate no longer: the ultimate desire is to be liberated from the shackles of consumption. In the alternative, the outcome of excess becomes difference. In the triumph of Baudrillard's signifying culture and in the articulation of individual gratification determined by that culture, the ever rapid circulation of signs of value and therefore of desire generate levels of excess in which the final stage is the desire for excess itself which can only be satisfied through transgression or deviant modification. In the constant quest to affirm the invitation to consume, the regulated market network is at constant risk from implosion through over-extension and continual fragmentation. Alternatively, within this process of the manufacture and commodification of desire, in which the individual becomes the auto-seductive self-consuming subject, there is the possibility of the implosion of the regulated market network simply through the inversion of the reproductive tendency in which the consumer becomes the consumed and thus exhausts (completes) the logic of the process.

Finally, to follow Deleuze and Guattari ((1977); (1981)) regarding the evolution of subsumed non-regulated networks (rhizomes), the market generates random forces which act upon the very regulatory structures which have been produced to control such activity. The fragmentation of control networks into competing regulatory regimes determines the emergence of alternative transverse networks through the conflictual tensions within the regulatory order. These abstract rhizomic patterns are translated into oppositional sub-groupings and individual transgressionary strategies of withdrawal through the very processes which created them. They act as parasitic mechanisms upon the host system. There has to be something for the forces of reproduction to act upon (in terms of the hegemonic potential of the dominant to determine the universal field). In the contemporary of urban culture in which legitimation is achieved through multiple regulatory strategies the anomic as both a social and psychological condition of both subgroups and individuals within and without those groupings is the resultant condition of the availability of excess and excessive control. It is the consequence of the schizophrenic freneticism and the subsequent comatose state of exhausted (ambient) capitalism. The hierarchical system becomes the root in the creation of alternative networks of opposition.

ALIENATION

1 Market Transformations

The final element in the disruptive forces of contemporary urban culture is the concept of alienation. In modernity alienation means an estrangement or separation between parts or the whole of the personality and significant aspects of the 'lifeworld'. It can therefore be interpreted in three ways. First, as an objective state. Second, as a state of feeling estranged from personality. Third, as the motivational state tending toward estrangement. In Marxist theory the individual is alienated from labour objectively by the relations of economic production and the system of class domination (Marx (1959) pp 67-84). In Freudian theory alienation is a consequence of the requirements of civilisation (Freud (1953)), although as Marcuse suggests, Freud was aware that the demands of social structure hostile to the core of the self could be exaggerated by the existence of class domination (Marcuse (1955) p 45ff). Such a usage views alienation as the state of or result of conformity with institutional expectations in segmented roles resulting in the deprivation of 'total' personality (the ability to exercise rational judgment and thereby to determine the individual conditions of existence). According to Fromm, the individual is alienated when:

> He does not experience himself as the centre of his world, as the creator of his own acts – but his acts and their consequences have become his masters, whom he obeys, or whom he may even worship (Fromm (1955) p 120).

From this conception of alienation as an objective state of separation, alienation becomes the malaise that results from this condition accompanied by a transition in emphasis from structures of domination to the value content of culture as the primary causal factor. There is a loss of emotions which are part of 'normal' experience. A withdrawal of emotional interest from the 'lifeworld' evolves because it is threatening to an exaggerated concern with self. This may express itself either in extreme sensitivity and altered feelings or in depersonalisation and isolation when overcharged feelings are repressed or dissociated from conscious personality. Marx considered alienation from 'species being', from the active function of 'life-activity' and therefore from the body, external nature and mental life. Horney considered alienation as the lack of comprehension of self:

> We cannot suppress or eliminate essential parts of ourselves without becoming estranged from ourselves ... The person simply becomes oblivious to what he really is. Without knowing it he may live the life of his image ... The person loses interest in life because it is not he who lives it; he cannot make decisions because he does not know what he really wants; if difficulties mount he may be pervaded by a sense of unreality – *an accentuated expression of his permanent condition of being unreal to himself* (Horney (1946) p 111; *my emphasis*).

In postmodernity it is possible to construct a source of liberation through the excess of alienation resulting in an economy of transgression. This construction has two aspects. First, regarding a transformation in the market mechanism in the organisation of work and leisure. Second, regarding the psychological interpretation of alienation as a condition of reality or collective experience of absolute alienation.

The rationalisation and commodification of social life through modernisation occurs under the pervasive influence of systems of production. Postmodernisation involves a reversal of determinacy so that fragments of a hyper-differentiating culture impact upon, disrupt and deconstruct arenas of social structure which might previously have been thought impervious to change (Crook, Pakulski, Waters (1992) pp 166-170). The particular vector of the impact of culture on production is the market. Paradoxically, under modern conditions, especially those of organised capitalism, the market is something of a myth. The oligopolisation of the market by international conglomerates develops a command relationship with consumers. Such is the success of these [re]productive units in determining market practice that markets become saturated and consumers begin to exercise choice. Production systems are forced through the vagaries of demand into structural change that enables flexible response. The systems themselves hyperdifferentiate and become choice driven. The market mechanism and the exchange of commodities with which the mechanism is concerned possess mythological qualities. The symbolic nature of exchange determines the totalisation of accumulation.[3] The market becomes the ultimate mechanism in the perpetuation of both repressive regulatory strategies of the everyday and simultaneously the point of erosion of those strategies – when their power becomes visible against the silent opposition of the invisible – and the emergence of possibilities of transgression and affirmation.

For Marx ((1971) p 162-163) this post-capitalist evolutionary stage enables the exercise of the latent potential for human liberation and development. This potential is realisable within a postcapitalist organisation of work as a consequence of the technological implications of the labour process in a post-regulatory order. It is precisely here that Marx and Durkheim differ radically. Marx attributed importance to the wealth of human needs, and consequently also to a new mode of production and a new object of production as well as to a new manifestation of human powers and a new enrichment of the human being. He began from an image of man in society, where a morality of

3 It is important to add that it is not only the market that has been transformed but the commodities in which the market deals. If the market is a myth then so too are the commodities themselves: financial capitalism has become a series of transactions in money as opposed to goods and services. Money has developed the capacity to act as a medium of exchange for itself, and is itself the basis of what it signifies. Therefore the conventional vector of cause and necessity which pointed from trade to finance, from things to money, has been reversed. And the things which are themselves traded are often transacted on a futures basis. This is the arena of symbolic capital. Speculation is no longer surplus value but surplus to value, as Baudrillard makes clear. It is the ecstasy of value without reference to production or its 'real' conditions. The very term 'economy' begins to alter its sense. It is no longer the motor or the productive infrastructure. It is the sphere of the process in the destruction of value. The 'economy' becomes cleared of all 'real' economic effects and becomes a viral economy which has to align itself with all other viral processes (see Gane (1991)). See further on this in Chapter Four.

duty would be unnecessary because irrelevant, an image in which aesthetic criteria were of predominant importance in assessing the quality of man's relationship with the natural and social world (Lukes (1977) p 87). In terms of the organisation of reproduction this appears as the final stage of capitalism, the stage of the automatic system of machinery, set in motion by an automaton, rendering the operative merely a conscious supervisory limb. This vision finds parallels in the transformation of the spatial and temporal organisation of production which is part of the process of postmodernisation. Mechanical and intellectual technologies have transformed the nature of both work and leisure. Technology becomes a liberating factor, a factor which creates several human possibilities. It is possible to argue that the development of organisational possibilities through technological process enables a reintegration of work into culturally ordered lifeworlds, for a form of emancipation in terms of Marx's concept of the relationship between the social-cultural, psychological and the economic.

The emerging postmodern configuration of production is one of flexibility. Flexibility has become the legitimating ideology within the organisation and production of materiality. The practical outcome of its institutionalisation is that the emerging pattern is an absence of pattern, a chaotic mixture of forms of ownership, varieties of task organisation and forms of relationship. Substantive differentiation has the effect of reintegrating the economic and domestic arenas. Material constraints are reduced and what is privileged in the cultural flow of knowledge becomes preferred models of organisation rather than reliance upon the mode of technology itself.

The absence of pattern within the network of the organisation of tasks through the emergence of technological capabilities *within* capitalism results in the freeing of the individual from the determining constraints of the industrial regulatory order. Baudrillard interprets this transition as merely an alternative form of repression. Rather than liberating the individual from the constraints of the material system, the individual becomes subject to ever more pervasive control systems, as a consumer and as an operative. In Baudrillard's early work ((1969a); (1969b) discussed by Gane (1991) pp 28-34) the fragmentation between culturally ordered fields of action (professional, domestic and so forth) into autonomous zones neutralises these zones as sites of potential contradictions and political differences. The order of needs which is constantly reproduced in the contemporary leads to the measuring of pleasure in strictly proportioned repressive rituals of order: an anomie of desire which forges a new repression. For Baudrillard, liberation can only be attained through a perspective which bonds the pleasure principle with transgression ('desire in all its unpredictable and irrational force, in its heretical and insurrectional surge toward totalisation' (Baudrillard (1969a) p 7). We have been seduced into managing our own alienation through ambient capitalism and the anomie of desire. Alienation is no longer possible because the prior space in which disjuncture was felt has been subjected to the forces of hyper-commodification articulated as the passion for control, which by governing both objects and subjects, and subordinating them to itself, delivers them up to abstract manipulation (Baudrillard (1981) p 92).

2 Accelerated Sclerosis

Within the emerging form of consumption reality is composed of signs. These signs are not representations but codes or shared systems of meaning which are without material foundation and have no terms of reference but their own. The simulations established by these codes become lived experience rather than representations of it. There is nothing to become alienated from. This is the regime of the totalitarian code. It can be argued that the processes through which alienation as threat is systematically eradicated is at the same time the moment in which alienation becomes a strategy of liberation. Manipulation of these codes offers the possibility of hyper-differentiation and a genuine decomposition of divisive control categories including the repression of desire. This is the result of the contradictions within capitalism:

> Capital in fact has never been linked by a contract to the society it dominates. It is a sorcery of social relations, it is a *challenge to society* and should be responded to as such. It is not a scandal to be denounced according to moral and economic rationality, but a challenge to take up according to symbolic law (Baudrillard (1983b) pp 29-30).

Alienation as an emancipating strategy emerges in the transpolitical. Politics as control through codes of legitimation has fragmented into multiple regulatory fields. It is a process of overdetermination and of the transfinite. Baudrillard's paradox in identifying this process is that the excess of regulatory codes through hyper-commodification and hyper-differentiation is both repressive and de-sublimating, as fascinating and repulsive, as de-alienating and re-alienating. This is the consequence of ambivalence in which everything has become indiscriminately political and which marks the end of the specifically political allowing for the emergence of transpolitical figures. It is within Baudrillard's transpolitics (1987) and Deleuze and Guattari's rhizomic nomadology (1983) that liberation through the realisation of desire and the economy of transgression is achieved. As Gane comments:

> Now the question concerns the saturation (obesity) of systems of memory, of information, the escalation into excess (*excroissance*) even thinkable as a new metaphysic cancerous equilibrium: an ecstatic state of crisis. The basic nature of transpolitical forms, and their enigma, can be seen in the shift from the secret to the transparent, from the scene to the obscene (the enigma reduced to a puzzle). This is a new era which marks the movement from the violent world of transgression and anomie to that where basic forms escape the norm, and, as error, lead to the event without the consequence (Gane (1991) pp 130-131).

Despite an 'ecstatic state of crisis' through the saturation of regulation it is within the violent world of transgression that liberation is a 'becoming' in the sense of the affirmation of the possible. The culture of excess which has evolved through regulatory strategies is subject to its own strategy in that the regulation of desire has resulted in the desire to become de-regulated and de-alienated through hyper-consumption and hyper-alienation. The commodification of reality has spurned both a plane of hyper-reality and a plane of transgression that is the real of confusion, pain, suffering, isolation and despair. Desire on this plane becomes refusal, withdrawal and the violence of non-participation. Regulation has become total (overdetermined) and it is because of this that the 'basic forms escape the norm', that the instinctual has been forgotten and has slipped away to the margins. This is not the language of centres and voids, and of extremities of position but the language of alternative spaces and a re-interpreted humanism.

In *Anti-Oedipus: Capitalism and Schizophrenia* (1977) Deleuze and Guattari suggest that these liberated spaces emerge from within the schizophrenic condition of capitalism, in the form of desiring production and the nomadic subject. During desiring-production there is a moment when the desiring-machines congeal and form an enormous undifferentiated object. Everything stops dead for a moment, everything freezes in place (Deleuze and Guattari (1977) pp 7; 13). That undifferentiated object is the body without organs, the desiring-machines at degree-zero intensity, a moment of anti-production constantly fed back into the process of production. It is the moment when the codes are scrambled, or deterritorialised and the nomadic subject is produced (Bogue (1989) p 95).

Deleuze and Guattari's 'micro-politics of desire' represents a miniaturised society: discourses, subjectivities, the body as elements in the anarchic series of desiring machines which produces and undermines the identities upon which governmentality was reliant. The fluxes of energy constituting this micropolitical world are channelled and ordered by particular configurations of social codes, and in every form of social organisation the processes by which desires are coded and colonised are continually subverted by their own internal movements of deterritorialisation. Codes are established and scrambled in an endless play of stability and destabilisation produced by the desires which traverse all social relations. Deleuze and Guattari describe an urban culture in which there is continual play between order and disorder and in which any form of organisation is subject to the interruption of its own composition: accelerated sclerosis. While 'new' territories are mapped and desires are colonised by giant webs of reproduction the spiralling proliferation of commodities simultaneously decodifies earlier forms of regulation and allows the radical egalitarianism of their free circulation to flourish:

> [T]he very condition that makes the State ... possible ... constant capital ... continually recreate unexpected possibilities for counterattack, unforeseen initiatives determining revolutionary, popular, minority, mutant machines (Deleuze and Guattari (1989) p 442).

The form of resistance which the elements of affluence-anomie-alienation suggest is a 'molecular' struggle. Configurations of desires rather than solidarities between individuals or groups prevails as the oppositional tendency:

> Today, individuals disinvested as subjects and robbed of their fixed relations, are drifting in relation to one another, into an incessant mode of transferential fluctuations: flows, connections, disconnections, transference/counter-transference (Baudrillard (1993a) p 23).

Impossible to locate according to the coordinates of central control, individuals produce their own axes of reference and establish underground, transversal connections, and randomly undermine relations of reproduction: the family, the body, sexuality. Molecular struggles assert the multiplicity of desires, social groups, strategic interests and forms of representation which cannot be aligned within the regulatory order. Here we have an inversion or postmodernisation of Durkheim and a re-working of *The Rules of Sociological Method*. For Durkheim, the challenge was to pursue an objective that retreats when advanced upon in an attempt to maintain an equilibrium in a disintegrating world and therefore to impose constraints and obligations considered necessary in the establishment of well-being (Lukes (1977) p 87). In the postmodern, the challenge is to exploit the disintegration and the anarchic instability of desire and constitute a challenge to the entire system by all those whose experiences are excluded by it.

MEGALOPOLIS: TEARS IN THE FABRIC

The triumph of regulation through the satiation of consumption in which the value of identity becomes a sign of itself affords the possibility of diversion from the tyranny of the sign of consumption through refusal and movement within the integers of the tensions and frictions established by regulatory strategies as they arrive at a point of implosion and rupture consequent upon their accelerated sclerosis.

In the vacated space of the imploded regulatory regime resides the possibility for the development of strategies of resistance and opposition through the movement of transgression. It is a result of the excesses of regulation that the syndromes of liberation through affluence (absence and excess) anomie and hyper-alienation emerge as potential oppositional strategies. An economy of transgression develops through the contradictions of capitalism and in the emergence of de-determined non-economic and non-repressive cultural forms.

Deleuze notes that Law cannot specify its object without self-contradiction, nor can it define itself with reference to a content without removing the repression on which it rests (Deleuze (1990) p 85). Everything which separates a force is reactive as is the state of force separated from what it can do. Every force which goes to the limit of its power is, on the contrary, active. It is not a law that every force goes to the limit, it is even the opposite of Law (Deleuze (1983) p 58). The articulation of the norms, habits, laws and the other available control strategies of a regulatory culture in operation within the contemporary of the urban landscape has entered a stage of accelerated sclerosis. That upon which regulation acted and repressed is now no longer part of the equation but is part of the refused, the expelled: the disappeared. But as Goodrich ((1990) pp 174-175) notes the refuse[d] may also refuse and form its own network of communication, its own rhizome. It is a transverse network *within and as part of* the network of authority.

The concept of refusal can be related to the idea of enthusiastic resignation. A symbolic field is always structured around a certain deadlock. This deadlock (sclerosis) does not entail resignation but rather enthusiastic resignation applying the Kantian sense of enthusiasm, as indicating an experience of the object through the very failure of its adequate representation. Enthusiasm and resignation are not then two opposed moments: it is in resignation itself that the experience of a certain impossibility incites enthusiasm. This experience of the impossible becomes the realisation of the network of the transpolitical.

★

> I am surrounded by a multitude of signs as I traverse the landscape of urban culture. Taken as a whole they make up the mythology of the world I inhabit, the collective subconscious of society. They are the representations it wishes to give out of itself and the mirror of the troubles that haunt it (Robbe-Grillet quoted Chambers (1990) pp 51-52).

Behind the signs lie the sites and sights of struggle resulting from the fragmentation of order, the deterritorialised space of the legislative guerrilla. This is a hand-to-hand combat zone. Here joyriding 'kids' crash vehicles for the fun of it in the green avenues of market towns. Here 'raves' take place in empty factories in a blur of Ecstasy. Here computer hackers access surveillance systems. Here crack dealers conceal their cubes in the mouth as the only place which can not be searched by the police on the street. Here on the council estate forests of satellite dishes have sprung up and are reprogrammed to receive 'foreign' pornography in the dark hours of the night. Here, along silicone valley, ambient factories appear empty of labour as the computers process microchips. Here on the train you pass through barricaded suburbs in which every dwelling is wired to the police station and it is *behind* the front door that is 'environmentally friendly'. Here you can pass through postnuclear zones of devastation (soon to be subject to urban 'redevelopment') and across the river view the pinnacles erected in praise of mammon. This is a land where the economy is one of 'invisible' earnings generated through the peddling of minimum risk. This is a usurer's economy. This is a land in which it is no longer possible to differentiate between the billboards of political parties touting empty ideology. Here the signs on the side of the road are images of bloody African civil war selling designer clothes whilst the hoardings mask the pools of dead water caused by environmental excess. Walking across the urban wilderness, picking through the cardboard box villages, into an Enterprise Zone, a City Challenge area, a YTS centre, a job 'club' (learning how *not* to work), a private hospital in all its sanitised glory (but which can only undertake cosmetic repairs) next to a public hospital where the kitchens are infested with rats and the geriatrics are tied to their filthy beds as the television transmits endless 'soap'; where Community Care means release into an alien environment without supervision and without recourse to medication. And here, where every high street has exactly the same shops selling exactly the same products against a background of dubbed Gregorian chant, 'bread' riots take place as racism and nationalism become the final outburst of ideology. Here two older boys lead a smaller boy across a crowded precinct to be slaughtered. This is the site of urban survival.[4]

New York is death ... (Sarah Schulman, letter of 19 June 1991).

★

The struggle between the regulated and the deregulated, between the franchised and disenfranchised, between the arena of conflict and the arena of discourse. As both the spatial and temporal planes of existence become colonised through regulatory crisis, so deterritorialised spheres emerge represented by alternative subgroupings and the withdrawal of the individual from the freneticism of the schizophrenic repetition of the desire to control, for the gaze to encompass all. This is resistance activated through refusal consequent upon the loss of control of meaning, value and reality.

It is a resistance that puts an end to the myth of revolutionary praxis. At this point the ultimate violence of capital emerges as it becomes its own myth as an interminable aleatory machine leaving at one moment no possibility of reversal and at the same moment complete possibility of refusal as the machine stops in a frozen state; all intermediary and countervailing structures are eliminated because refusal has no need for opposition. If materialist theory is 'correct' this is reality, the contradiction, a transgression without a norm.

---

4 To all these things have I been witness. Such a self-indulgent describing of my experiences of the contemporary of urban culture serves a purpose beyond the mere creation of an atmosphere or establishment of an ambience. This is a landscape of the banality in affluence and the absence of affluence, of anomie and alienation as both social and psychological conditions of existence; the banality of the violence of the symbolic laws of capital. More importantly I have attempted to set out a little narrative of dissensus, prefiguring similar stories which are the concern of Part II of this work. I do not make direct reference in this text to an incidence of such a magnitude as that of the slaying of James Bulger in Liverpool in 1992. By referring in a footnote to this narrative I do not mean to either avoid the telling or deny the significance of that story. Neither do I wish to marginalise the story. However, to make direct reference to it requires another space to be able to do *justice* to it. It is useful to note the narrative significance of the Bulger case. For three weeks in November 1993, Preston Crown Court was less a site of law than the site of convergence of different narrative styles. The judge drew up rules for how the trial could and could not be reported. Counsel for one of the child defendants argued that the story could not be told because it had already been told by the press (the jury 'had already seen the last page'). The most compelling narratives are always journeys and this one began on 12 February 1992 when two older boys were caught on a surveillance camera leading away a smaller boy (by a perverse irony the iconographic still showing James Bulger being led away was dominated by the single word *MOTHERCARE*). From there the court – we the audience – followed the boys through a landscape that vividly expressed the contemporary urban condition of Britain: shopping mall, canal tow path, reservoir, subway, flyover, alley, and finally, the railway tracks. These spaces exist *in order* for bodies to be discovered within them. When it was over the protagonists-murderers-children went to the video shop, the 'vicarious hearth of all provincial towns'. This malignant habitus of differentiated affluence and poverty ensured that the boys were perfectly at home in the atrocious topography of the poverty of this wild-zone of industrial decline. In part the narrative ends here, at this cliched 'heart of darkness'. But for a narrative which bought us right to the brink of some terrible insight to end or to be closed (for the book to be shut) it must not only be resolved, it must be seen to be resolved. But of course, there is no resolution here, the book cannot and should not be shut because that would be merely a further capitulation to what is known, to what can be answered within the bounds of a norm or a rationality. Other stories can be told and this story and other interpretations can be given no matter how horrific. No matter how unbearable, the other must be spoken, for that is a *justice* which denies the inevitability of closure (see Dyer (1994)).

It is at this stage that the politics of representation becomes the central analytic tool of interrogation. How the world of the contemporary of urban culture is re-represented to us and how its order is precariously maintained on the level of everyday regulation. What follows must be a series of exercises in the interpretation and interruption of representation.[5] The question which determines such a series of exercises becomes the possibility of emancipation through transgression without opposition (witness to the unrepresentable) or the triumph of repression through the order of reproduction (the witness as traitor).

Either:

> The human species has passed the dead point of history: we are now living out the ecstasy of permanent catastrophe, which slows down as it becomes more and more intense (*une catastrophe au relenti*, slow motion catastrophe), until the supereventfulness of the event approaches the uneventfulness of absolute inertia, and we begin to live everyday catastrophe as an endless dead point, or perpetual freeze frame (Morris (1988) p 19).

Or:

> To cut and intersect the flow of simulation, to effect decoupage and to find new vital lines of escape. In other words not to attempt to step outside the flow, but to reterritorialise the self within it, to ambush it as we assimilate it (Wakefield (1990) p 151).

'We can no longer map the modern' writes Chambers 'for that suggests that we know its extremes, confines and limits' (Chambers (1990) p 54). We cannot know the excess of the urban, but in our failure to know resides the possibility of the exploitation of that excess. 'Disciplinary power ... is exercised through its invisibility; at the same time it imposes on those whom it subjects a principle of compulsory visibility' (Foucault (1977b) p 187). The putative chain of economic determination has become a meaningless global capitalism. It is a global capitalism representing circuits of international rentier capitalism in a hypertrophic financial state. Production has turned to consumption and the material hierarchy where markets are a result of production, capitalism a consequence of markets, and finance the enabling mechanism for capitalist

5 Such exercises attempt to analyse specific social phenomena - as diverse as 'serial killing', 'hacking, joyriding and raving' and 'sado-masochism' - and interrogate them not as 'problems of deviance' but as forms of resistance and opposition. As with the attack upon sociology the task is to escape the rigid and jaded positivist paradigms of modernist criminological discourse, where these activities would have been conveniently accommodated devoid of any form of analysis in terms of identity save in the extreme margins of psycho-sociological pathology. The question becomes: does this phenomena exist and if so *how* is it re-represented to us and *what* does it represent? Within a framework of resistance the activity becomes a determinant in the series of activities which allegedly transcend the most basic law (that of cause and effect) since in certain accounts they appear to lack motive. These 'outrages' are constructed as possible spectacles occurring within and between the regulated zones of the urban and represent territoristic activities in the setting of a series of alternative (nomadic) social practices subject to norms and conventions premised upon opposition and resistance. The way these events are represented to us (as ordered spectacles of a *necessary* atrocity) becomes part of the final dynamic in the order of regulation through the politics of naming in the repression of desire: if these activities are named then they cease to be a part of the decolonised but are subsumed within the forces of colonisation. In terms of opposition - which these activities seemingly transcend but must be constructed as being maintained within order - the activity becomes subject to regulation in its presentation. The analysis is a study in the deconstruction of the event and spectacle of these transgressions, without submitting these transgressions to the gaze, which if they succumb, will negate the possibility of emancipation which is temporarily made available.

intermediation no longer holds. This material hierarchy has dissolved. This is the site of urban survival, a zone without-laws. Individual 'emancipation' is a challenge within the paradoxical conflict between the assumption of individual responsibility (legitimation) and the unattainability of continuous gratification (excess) in which all is possible and nothing is achievable.

I have provided one possible image of the urban, which coincides with Sarah Schulman's letter ('New York is death ...'). It is a bleak picture where Harvey's economic logic meets Baudrillard's ecstasy of simulation. Michel de Certeau and others provide an alternative vision. Certeau walks the street and interprets the process as one which defines a 'space of enunciation', the city as a space-place created by myriad actions, all of which bear the stamp of individual intent. This 'pedestrian rhetoric' of trajectories reflects a mythical structure where it is possible to identify clandestine forms taken by the dispersed, tactical and makeshift creativity of groups or individuals already caught in the nets of discipline. Certeau melds Foucault, Deleuze and Virilio into a pragmatic observation of a pedestrian politics of the imaginary (Certeau (1988) pp 91-111; see also Shields discussion of Maffesoli (1991)).

It is relatively easy to line up the opposing factions. Either to succumb to the inevitability that the banality of consumption has triumphed and identity disappears. Or to interrogate what space is available and what unforeseen consequences the processes of capitalism have created as the edge of its implosion is approached and capital takes flight leaving new cultural forms to emerge from the ruins of the site of the spectacle of consumption. These forms express an inversion or appropriation of commodified desire. They may be unpalatable because they are often violent and unpredictable. They nevertheless represent an alternative construct of identity, justice and community premised upon different sources of value and meaning.

To summarise the paradox. The individual becomes a mere fraction of self and loses the sense of being in the process of change. The relevance which was the place of self in time and space has given way to the relevance of mobility and speed in re-inserting the self in ever disappearing social processes. This brings the individual nearer to others, in that the density of relations is increased. But this nearness is counter-balanced by enhanced psychological distance which constrains relationships that demand more of the self. Under material pressure the self activates a psychic defence, distanced from others and isolated with greater indifference. The loss of the ability to give meaning becomes the desire not to risk the self to the stimulus of reality which can no longer be interpreted (powerfully articulated in Wim Wenders' film *Wings of Desire* (1988).[6]

---

6 This film, as David Harvey has noted ((1989) pp 314-321), is a particularly fascinating illustration of urban experience. Even Harvey is perplexed and seduced from his reflexive economic-cultural determinism for a moment. Wenders utilises the figure of the Angel to communicate the innate humanism of alienated strangers within the urban (Berlin). These angels condense past, present and future. Under their gaze we find ourselves caught between the apparent ineluctability of time and continual crisis. They remind us, as Chambers notes, of the spark of eternity that is revealed as we unravel the uniqueness of the present and assume responsibility for the oblivion of the past and the multiplicity of possible futures (Chambers (1994) p 134). Here everything appears as fragmented and ephemeral, each incident is recorded in the same monotone as the other. This extraordinary evocation

Is it still possible to fuse 'self' and 'we'? This 'we' is the imaginary community which remains unspeakable within postmodernity – literally unspeakable in Baudrillard who presents the myth of the masses as a 'black hole' drawing all meaning to its non-existent centre (Baudrillard (1983b)). In Gramsci the 'we' is neither 'fatal' nor pre-existent ('out there') in the post-erus sense. Instead it is itself the site of struggle. The 'we' in Gramsci has to be made and re-made, actively articulated in the double sense, both spoken, uttered and linked with and combined. It is a 'we' which has to be articulated and where the 'social' is neither a beautiful dream nor a dangerous abstraction, neither a contract made and re-made (Habermas) nor an empirically non-existent 'Idea in Reason' which bears no relation to experience (Lyotard). The social here is a post-social series of relations which uses power as a positive force in the satisfaction of desire. It is sociality premised upon community and consequently a form of sociality beyond the name: a sociality of the excess. It is a post-social phenomenon as a continually shifting, mediated relation between groups, a nomadic field of governmentality as a set of lived relations in which complex powers can be actively combined, dismantled, bricolaged so that new political alliances can be secured between different factional groupings and selves: the formation of new communities representing new identities.

★

Identity in the No Place of Megalopolis: decontextualised, s[t]imulated, renewed, restyled. An urban of cultural disorder and stylistic eclecticism. The mobilisation of spectacle and display becomes a positive force in urban existence, pointing to the deconstruction of existing symbolic hierarchies and an opening up of playful and popular democratic impulse. Spectacle might even be successful in the reconnection to territory and used for positive political ends to reconstruct civic identity and transform urban relations.

The city as a physical structure and system embodies or incarnates particular social significations; these significations are realised or 'institutionalised' in and through the urban fabric. This imaginary institution of the city defines the scope – the possibilities and their limits – within which, at any particular time, we can imagine, think and experience city life; it defines the aesthetic field within which transformation will take place. The crisis of urbanisation in an imaginary dimension. Megalopolis assumes 'an alien subjectivity, to have become something with which one has dialogue, as one would with a stranger' (Mazzoleni (1993) p 297).

6... of an urban landscape, of alienated individuals in fragmented spaces caught in an ephemera of unpatterned incidents, has a powerful aesthetic effect. The images are stark, cold, but endowed with all the beauty of the nostalgic. The facts of production, and the necessary class relations that attach thereto are absent: they are abandoned. This is the urban of Simmel not Marx. Death, birth, anxiety, pleasure, loneliness are all aestheticised on the same plane, transcending the determination of ethical or moral commentary but representing a humanism forged through the fabric of the urban. Wenders attempts to re-define the spirit of communication between strangers, a becoming out of the ashes of a 'monochromatic and dead-pan postmodernist landscape of feeling' (Harvey (1989) p321).

Megalopolis is no longer a place, because its dimension exceeds the perceptive apparatus of the inhabitants. The wi[l]dest sensory aperture – sight – is shattered in both the gaze of state and subject. In Megalopolis there is no longer the possibility of panorama (Mazzoleni (1993) p 297). The sensory field of Megalopolis is the field of the total aesthetic, where aesthetics supersedes ethics and the possibility of investiture of the multiple I/Eye is made available. Here even capital attains its own aesthetic of excess, no matter how banal and/or violent:

> The metropolitan condition: the loss of logical linearity, the soldering of deductive reasoning into an obsessive circle-madness. But also the epistemological post-metropolitan breakage; the catastrophe of obsession where an increasingly whirlwind-like motion, obsessive in its excessive speed, finally becomes elusive, and the circle forms a mandala-ecstasy (Mazzoleni (1993) p 300).

In Megalopolis the aesthetic justifies existence: this is the novelty and the revolution. This aesthetic dimension, this playing with one's attitudes with respect to the present can be built into a vast range of possibilities, from depths of feeling to superficiality, skin-deep stimuli of images, and ultimately to kitsch. Ethics is replaced by multiple games and possibilities in aesthetic attitudes. Morality becomes entertainment and imagery and is lived aesthetically. The scenario in which all that is social becomes sociality deadens and pluralises all values. The unit of reality is given to the instant and intuition, the possibility of a game, the image because we believe in the possibility 'of finding in every detail of life the totality of its meaning' (Simmel quoted by Frisby (1985) p 6), the most important of which is the meaning of desire devoid of the totality of self. The ethics of eros must be analysed beyond the mere surface of consumption but without necessitating the narcissism of the psychiatric dupe. For only then will the form of the bonds between slaves in the fractured and repressed urban become understood as part of a transition toward the nomadic governmentality of the community of selves as the site of a justice of alterity.

CHAPTER FOUR

SPECULATIONS ON THE DISORDER OF CAPITAL

> Today, we no longer have to dream of this end. Political Economy now expires before our very own eyes, disappeared by its own self-mutation into a speculative transeconomy which undermines its productivist logic (the law of value, the laws of the marketplace, production, surplus value, the logic of capital itself), and which no longer has anything to do with either the economic or the political – a pure game of floating and arbitrary rules, a fatal game of catastrophe (Baudrillard (1989) p 67).

THE TERRITORY AND TYRANNY OF MONEY

In representing the landscape of the power relations of the urban I have alluded to sharp contours between cultural arenas in terms of the relative distribution of resources (differential access to affluence). If these contours are pronounced in the contemporary then the common 'affliction' of anomie and alienation which bind these dichotomised arenas serves as a basis for resistance and change through transgression in challenging the instability of the norm.

This chapter is concerned with fragmentation within an apparently coherent cultural arena: the financial markets, the central nervous system of capitalism (Harvey (1989) p 96). Erosion through excess regulation combined with a free-market economic imperative shatters the supposed cultural unity within this arena. In the brain of the machine a regulatory conflict is occurring encompassing politics, economics and morality. The market which determines the law eventually accedes to its own 'logic' of law-lessness (becomes with-out law). For a moment, when the machine stops, the laughter can be heard. But it is very faint in the distance. This is a becoming in the moment of the economy of transgression.

If information is central to capitalism then it is within the enclosed world of the trading floor and the exchange that decisions concerning the deployment of capital are made. The processes of postmodernisation involve a transition in terms of use-value from production to information. The economic structure can be visualised as an inter-related system between units of production, units of information and units of regulation (industry-finance-state). What has occurred during the recent development of the global financial markets has been a fragmentation between these units and the advent of regulatory conflict. This conflict proceeds within both the system of formalised rules (for example between regulatory and de-regulatory strategies) and within the structure of market practices and behavioural norms. The principal conflict exists between the achievement of 'free' market initiatives and the maintenance of an ordered market for information. The consumer is encouraged to participate in the attainment of wealth generation through financial speculation and to adjudge the probity of its provision: the final commodity becomes the purchase of the minimalisation of risk. For the consumer, the conflict becomes crystallised into a tension between speculation (greed) and risk (the avoidance of loss).

The de-regulation of the capital markets of London, New York, Paris and elsewhere involved the simultaneous acknowledgment of the supremacy of technological communications networks as the principal mechanisms in the conduct of capital transactions and the imposition of a self-regulatory regime in which responsibility for the conduct of trading practices and ethical standards was placed on the practitioners themselves. The market for financial transactions became an arena of highly charged free-market practice. Capital over-accumulation resulted in capital over-consumption in both the nature of transactions ('panic money' could exist because the ability to 'panic' had been granted) and in the cultural arena in which these transactions were conducted. The credo became 'Greed is Good': the legitimation of excess. It is the effect of the assumption of this ethic of affluence which is of concern here, in terms of the ascendancy of a de-regulated cultural arena and its resultant effects in terms of anomie and alienation.

In this chapter I analyse developments in the City of London between 1984-1989. A number of questions will be asked: What factors and circumstances set this period as being different to the prior regime of the City? What changes were wrought during this period which have perceptibly altered the dominant ethos of market practice in the City? What 'ended' so that in the future the period will be adjudged as having been a transient era of change? There are particular changes which can be stated as markers in the transition of the City of London (for example 'Big Bang' in 1986) but these are artificial points of reference. Although not unimportant, these markers are illustrations of what were perceived as significant structural alterations in the nature of financial practices in the City. They serve to describe particular re-definitions in the relationship between the City and the State and in the patterns of relationships within the City. In part these markers represent change at a deep level of cultural practice. I examine a number of these markers to illustrate the nature of change which has occurred in market practices and place in a cultural context their actual significance as part of the imposition of a re-constituted metanarrative of economic liberalism through which to impart a sense of the nature of change in the activity of the City of London.

★

The analysis is developed in two parts: 1 The Symbolic Laws of Capital and 2 Panic! Coke-Blip Capitalism. Each part is sub-divided into a further two parts.

1 The Symbolic Laws of Capital

   (a) At the start it appears to be important to consider global capitalism as the ascendancy of information as a commodity. This analysis contextualises the subsequent discussion of regulatory conflict in addition to relating to the conceptualisation of consumer society and the nature of value.

   (b) The transition in the nature of capital transactions (in purely technological terms) occurred at the same time as the ascendancy and imposition of so called

'New Right' policies of economic liberalism (involving de-regulatory financial strategies). The effect of these two structural alterations is analysed regarding the arenas of conflict: the London Stock Exchange, markets, banks and finance houses. This conflict is conceived as a development of tension between 'Old' City and 'New' City. The term 'Old' City is used *descriptively* in the sense of defining the scope and context of financial activity. The term 'New' City is used *prescriptively* to imply the imposition of a series of standards premised upon distinct ideological precepts (the precepts of 'enterprise culture'). This analysis emphasises the artificial conditioning by the central political administration whilst indicating the possibility of a conflicting subcultural evolution and the maintenance of an alternative standard of normative behaviour which operates in competition with the transitory survival of the political generation of perceived values. Whilst there has been a significant structural change in the fabric of the City the economic rationale of profit (greed) as a base-point standard of conduct serves to generate a subcultural code of ethics which is manifested as a sanctioning device to prohibit malpractice and deviancy from the accepted code. The enterprise culture as the imposition of a set of values, whether or not conflicting with existing City values and norms, served to legitimate behaviour previously perceived as deviant which has created a conflict between city and state.

2 Panic! Coke-Blip Capitalism:

(a) The effect of the imposition of an ideology upon a 'local' arena is analysed through the concepts of *city crime* and *state crime.*

City crime is that behaviour which deviates from normified conduct and is a transgression of the previously prevalent subcultural code. City crime may be a deviation from the self-generated set of principles evolved within the City. Changes in the nature of financial activity have served to generate transgressive activities which have been uneconomic beyond the limited range of immediate self-gratification because performed within a regulatory framework founded upon a rationale operating to validate transgressive activity. Previous examples of transgression would have been contained through the prohibition of temptation or through a ritual penalisation and stigmatisation resulting in ostracisation in terms of opportunity and advancement. The regulatory strategy of the state through the ideological vehicle of the enterprise culture has legitimated market malpractice.

State crime is the condonement and reaction of the central political administration to resultant deviant market practice. Externally imposed legitimation premised upon an ill-founded economic rationale challenges the internally evolved economic system of regulation. Therefore an analysis of the politics of regulation (the legitimation of greed and speculation) is presented which demonstrates that an externally imposed value-position has resulted in the generation of an uneconomic system of regulation. This development has served as a symbolic gesture spurring a collapse in the validation of authority. What was coercively generated in a brief period was a confused scenario of cultural fragmentation. This development concealed the imperative of the legitimation of market malpractice resulting in the erosion of previously internally evolved regulatory mechanisms. It put into play doubt over the continuity of confidence which had been previously developed and maintained.

(b) In conclusion to this chapter we move to a different part of the city, a landscape of urban deprivation and the absence of affluence. It is a simple comparison to make but serves to distil the central determinants of contemporary material life (affluence-anomie-alienation) and accords to the general paradox within the regulatory system regarding the maintenance of order through the encouragement of consumption and the satiation of desire. The example is the arena of petty entrepreneurship and criminal activity in the East End of London (which in spatial terms resides literally in the shadow of the City of London). The terrain may be different but the tensions and processes of fragmentation consequent upon economic and ideological change are very similar. A previously stable (mythological) subculture generated a series of codes of conduct. The fragmentation of this cultural stability has accentuated the contours between previously generated normative behaviour and new forms of arbitrary violent behaviour. The old forms of customary practice (traditional 'wheeling and dealing, ducking and diving') have been eroded, given the invasion of more violent forms of entrepreneurial-criminal behaviour in the form of drug related transactions. The violence in the streets of the East End may be more 'real' in the sense of a growing physical fear but is only a shadow of the 'symbolic' violence being waged in the dealing rooms of the finance houses of the City. As Baudrillard writes:

> The violence appearing today is an altogether different kind, one we no longer know how to analyse because it eludes the traditional model of explosive violence. It is an implosive violence no longer resulting from the extension of a system but from its saturation and contraction - as in the physical system of stars. Violence as a consequence of unlimited increase in social density, resulting from an overregulated system, from overloaded networks (of knowledge, information, power) and from hypertrophied controls that invade all the interstitial paths of facilitation (Baudrillard (1982) p 3).

1 The Symbolic Laws of Capital

From Finance Capital to Panic Money

> The City's not mine any more so let it fall (Churchill (1987) p 30).

The transition in the nature of capital relations can be examined in terms of hierarchies: how finance relates to capitalism, capitalism to markets, and markets to basic routines of material life. The formulation of this hierarchy is taken from Ferdinand Braudel ((1977) pp 47-63). There is nothing especially novel about the place of finance at the apex of this hierarchy, which has existed wherever merchants have been able to pursue long-distance trade.[1] While international financiers and property developers might effect an effortless displacement of one micro hierarchy (the domestic financial City/the domestic unit of production), this feat should not be misunderstood simply as the ascendancy of sophisticated finance over less developed forms of economy. It is a process in the ascendancy of a vastly more powerful and complex hierarchy over a no less differentiated hierarchy. The visibility (obscenity) of the financial markets, which form the apex of the hierarchy, has to be related to the rhythms of material life at the base of the economy. The point is either the implosion of the apex of the hierarchy and the retrieval of local arenas of production or the continuing domination of this structure upon the local arenas of production in which the pinnacle of the structure is 'finance' (reproduction) devoid of a relation to the actual (production) hierarchy of material life. Either consequence involves violent internal revolution.

Caryl Churchill's play *Serious Money* opened to critical and popular acclaim at the Royal Court Theatre, London, in March 1987. The period Churchill depicted was one in which the massive flows of global finance enabled the swift personal accumulation of wealth.: 'Never had so many unskilled 24 year olds made so much money in so little time' (Lewis (1989): Preface). Just to dip a finger into the stream generated super-profitable commissions. The popularity of Churchill's play mirrored the fascination with money which had gripped popular imagination. In the 1980s money became a valid possession *in its own right*:

> The creation of wealth is not some unpleasant habit to which we have set our hand when we have nothing morally superior to engage our interests. It is the foundation of our civilisation (Brian Walden quoted by Rushbridger (1990)).

Serious Money was just one of a number of representations which set up a mirror to a world which had been closed from view, a mysterious game, only vaguely understood by the populace.[2] But the public had been encouraged to take note of the game through the economic imperatives of prevailing Conservative administration in terms of the

1 Whimster and Budd ((1992) pp 3-4) use the example of the Bengali community around the locality of Brick Lane in London, one block away from the Bishopsgate financial centre. At the top of the hierarchy are the financiers and international merchants. These are rich Gujarati and Pakistani families who act as intermediaries in an international flow of goods, predominantly clothing. On the basis of this, merchant capital accumulates and the most successful families have moved on to property development on the City fringes, thus joining the peculiarly English road to financier status. Beneath the level of international trade in clothing, which is organised by the merchant, lies production for the market. In the Braudelian schema these markets need not be capitalist. So in villages on the Indian subcontinent, or in the backstreets of Spitalfields, a predominantly domestically based economy can produce for village or street markets. At the bottom of the hierarchy are the enduring routines of material life as it encompasses domestic life and the rhythms of family existence.

2 The City professional was both villain and hero, someone who became rich by fair means or foul, a figure of attraction and hatred and, as such, was glorified and vilified in television, film, drama and newspapers. The 'yuppie' was the cultural hero of the 1980s, the embodiment of the 'go for it' enterprise culture. Throughout the period representations of financial speculation became a staple of popular consumption. In addition to Caryl Churchill's play *Serious Money* there was also Tony Marchant's play *Speculators* and revivals by the two national theatre companies of plays such as Bulwer-Lytton's *Money* (RSC) and Granville-Barker's *The Voysey Inheritance* (RNT). These two productions by the subsidised theatre were particularly interesting in their timing given their nature as both were concerned with the presentation and examination of the virtues and sins of wealth and

privatisation of public utilities and in initial steps toward the creation of a 'shareholder democracy'.

The action of *Serious Money* is the enclosed world of the trading floor of LIFFE (London International Financial Futures Exchange), a site of international financial transactions encompassing figures beyond mere mortal imagining, conducted in seconds as global capital circulates in a furious shouted rage of trading. The characters of the play are a meritocratic selection representing the material desires and aspirations of international community: a LIFFE dealer, a commercial paper dealer, a gilts dealer, a stockbroker, a jobber, an arbitrageur, a corporate raider. They all subscribe to the idea that 'These are the best years of our lives, with information from inside' (p 111). Churchill's portrait is far removed from the staid picture of the City of London as the bastion of financial prudence, a righteous spirit of trust and commercial municipality cast in Portland stone and served by restrained bowler-hatted, umbrella carrying Lloyd's brokers. The transition is captured by Churchill in her inversion of the City maxim 'My word is my bond' when it becomes 'My word is my junk bond' (p 105). The City of London simply became 'the City', the anonymous international financial metropolis in which a trade can be made between LA, London, Paris and Frankfurt within a matter of minutes and one can fly to JFK and be back the next morning all for the sake of a signature to 'close the deal' and where the same signature can annihilate a small oil town in Kansas whilst simultaneously opening up a tin can processing plant in Kiev.

There were two cities representing two conflicting cultures. As a subculture the City possesses its own style and ethos - its own system of legitimation for action, which is closed from other forms.[3] The conflict played out between 1984–1989 was for control in terms of the legitimation of determination of action between the Old City and the New City, between the City of London and the City of the Enterprise Culture, between old money and new money.

2... enterprise in the Victorian age which were now being reinvented as the nostalgic values of an 'enterprise culture' by the prevailing Conservative administration. There was also a spate of productions of Shakespeare's *Timon of Athens*, again an allegory on greed. Churchill's *Serious Money* is prefaced by a scene from Thomas Shadwell's eighteenth century drama *The Volunteers, or The Stockjobbers*. Even in 1993 the RSC staged a production of *The Merchant of Venice* drawing heavily on the design ethos of the City of London (the designer Shelagh Keegan visited the stockbrokers Smith New Court; David Calder who played Shylock visited Lloyds). Television dramas also pursued the theme with series such as *Chancer* (Central) and *Capital City* (Thames). In the cinema, films such as *Dealers*, *Wall Street*, *The Bonfire of the Vanities* and *Other People's Money* in addition to variations upon the theme (*Something Wild*, *Nine and a Half Weeks*, *Pretty Woman*, *Working Girl*, *White Palace*) all sought to capture the popular imagination with varying degrees of success. The relationship between financial power and sexuality became a dominant one within cinematic representations and is discussed in an analysis of the nemesis of the genre captured in Bret Easton Ellis's novel *American Psycho* (1991).

3 The homogeneous subcultural enclave ('the City') is in a relationship with and exercises hegemonic power between the industrial sector and the state. The City is in conflict with both these sources and also involved in the maintenance of equilibrium and stability in conjunction with these two sources. However, this homogeneity becomes fractured. The Old City exerted exclusionary closure in opposition to the New City. The New City successfully exerted usurpationary closure in opposition to the Old City. There was a realignment of interests within the nexus State-City-Industry and a consequent 'culture for regulation' crisis as value positions were challenged in the response to a new economic imperative.

The structural changes which took place in the London financial markets have been well-documented elsewhere (see for example the essays by Stafford (1992) and by Coakley (1992)). What has been given insufficient attention were the changes which occurred in the nature of global finance as a landscape of power from a cultural-aesthetic perspective. If Churchill's play is adopted as a starting point an intimation can be given regarding the nature and development of the financial transactions that occurred consequent upon the introduction of information technology into the securities markets within a broader cultural as opposed to a narrow economic analysis.

Churchill's play uses verse to convey the atmosphere of the trading floor. The discourse of the City is internalised. Only those operatives who can appreciate the discourse will be able to participate. The language of the City is like verse complete with rhythm. It is a language spoken through a machine (telephone or computer screen), a technological language which is mystical to the extent that its subject is money (the constant referent being numerology and alchemy). It is self-referential, it is almost always shouted. The use of metaphor is numerous, often alluding to sexual, animal or death imagery: Big Bang, Big Swinging Dick, bulls, bears, stags, poison pills, golden parachutes. It is a language constructed through acronyms: LBO, SIB, ADR, MBO, DTI, LIFFE. It is a construct of *real* language but reconstituted so it has to be learnt (the authenticity of jargon):

> Scilla (on phone 1) Going out later – hang on.
> (on phone 2) 4 for 10 nothing doing. Will he go 5?
> (To the floor) 5 for 10! 5 for 10!
> Grimes (on phone) Bid 28 at the figure.
> Mate (to Grimes) I'm only making a tick.
> Grimes (to Mate) Leg of it.
> Scilla (on the phone) Grimes?
> Grimes (to Mate) Futures are up.
> (On the phone) Champagne bar at six?
> Mate (on the phone) Selling one at the figure.
> (To Grimes) I'm lifting a leg
> (Churchill (1987) p 3).

If the language of global finance is akin to verse then so too is the architecture of global finance: it has to be translated from the real of dwelling to the imaginary of the institutions of finance which look real in the sense of being visible but which are in fact constructed of opaque glass. The Manhattan style skyscraper, like the logo-form NatWest Building or the Meccano style Lloyd's, clash with the classicism of the commercial municipality of the Bank of England and the Mansion House. These new buildings represent the inside-outside paradox where the 'pure' inside must be protected from the 'impure' outside (Cooke (1988) p 488). The mirror glass skins of the buildings repel the City outside in the same way as the language. The glass buildings appear to allow openness and penetration but merely provide an artifice masking closure behind which there is an opening only for those who can hack into the maze. Global capitalism represents the circuits of international rentier capitalism in a hypertrophic financial state and postmodernism architecture becomes its representation as a 'Warholesque' transformation of the City where the 'postmodern tower is merely a package of standardised space to be gift-wrapped to the client's taste' (Davis (1985) pp 108-109).

Zukin (1988; 1992) portrays the urban landscape as one of the dominance of the vertical – the polished architecture of the centre – over the horizontal segmentation of vernacular city life that lies around the centre. Modern office blocks rise above the vernacular topography of the city to impose a powerful visual imprint. The vernacular landscape belongs to the old working class, the immigrant ghettos and the artists colonies. These are areas of 'resistance, autonomy and the originality of the powerless' (Zukin (1992) p 198). Economic and financial power confers the ability to buy up property and devise plans for wholesale reconstruction such as the doomed Canary Wharf. But it also controls symbolic representation: a new visual syntax of consumption styles attends to the tastes of the global finance sector and takes precedence over the old vernacular. The elimination of immigrant enclaves through gentrification, and the replacement of local retail outlets by high-volume chain stores, the redevelopment of wholesale markets and manufacturing sectors into prestige housing, historical artefacts, bistros and 'craft' workshops are the victories of the centre over the vernacular (Zukin (1992) p 201). The apex of the financial hierarchy leaves deep marks on the landscape and determines a transitory culture of consumption and style, where the vagaries of taste move almost as rapidly as the transactions which facilitated such change in the first place.

Baudrillard's 1976 essay *The End of Production* is relevant at this juncture. The essay bridges his development from Marxist theorist of consumer culture into the critic of the culture of reproduction and simulation. Baudrillard considered affluence and consumption to have profound consequences for social structure and cultural integration. It is an analysis stemming from Bataille and Mauss. Central in Baudrillard's analysis is the importance of the relationship between the semiotic order and the symbolic order. Following Mauss, the semiotic order represents the cash nexus whilst the symbolic order represents the obligation of the gift. Baudrillard (1970) suggests the superiority of symbolic over semiotic while witnessing the apparent destruction of the former by the latter. In *The End of Production* he develops his analysis and considers the ironic evolution of the semiotic order itself. In this work he suggests that contemporary capitalism is not one of the mode of production but of a code dominated by the 'structural law of value'. A mode of production suggests an order of causation between the spheres of production and consumption; a 'structural law of value' suggests the end of this moment of causation and that reproduction alters the nature of the rationality of production. The moment of implosion occurs when the gift can no longer be exchanged, at which point the sign (semiotic) loses all value. In Baudrillard's analysis the mode of production inverts itself and begins to destroy the separations it was built upon. Capital proceeds to destroy the hierarchy of base and superstructure, of production and reproduction.

Baudrillard specifically considered the role of finance. 'Purged of finalities and the *affects* of production, money becomes speculative ... hot money and generalised flotation, money is transformed from a referential sign into its structural form' (Baudrillard (1993a) p 21). Money becomes a free floating signifier in the sense that it abandons every signified in semiotic terms (every 'real' equivalent) as a brake to its proliferation and unlimited play. Global financial transactions involve the incessant splitting and increasing of their own abstract substance. Money ceases to be the medium or means to circulate commodities and becomes the process of circulation itself:

> Money is the first 'commodity' to assume the status of a sign and to *escape use-value.* Henceforth, it intensifies the system of exchange-value, turning it into a visible sign, and in this way makes the transparency of the market visible. Today, however, money sanctions a further step: it *also escapes exchange-value.* Freed from the market itself, it becomes an autonomous simulacrum relieved of every message and every signification of exchange, becoming a message itself and exchanging amongst itself. Money is then no longer a commodity since it no longer contains any use-value or exchange-value, nor is it a general equivalent, it is no longer a mediating abstraction of the market. Money circulates at a greater rate than everything else, and has no common measure with anything else (Baudrillard (1993a) p 22).

Money in this stage signifies the separation between the fictional and the real economy: it is a separation which makes the possibilities of the real economy impossible as it enters the transeconomic stage of implosion and deterrence (the simultaneous balance between the possibility of collapse and the continuous simulation of the impossibility of collapse): the hyper-realisation of global capital which escapes the necessary connection with reality itself. 'Money' in the fictional economy is simply not convertible into the real one. Hence Baudrillard is able to write: 'Today we no longer have to dream of the end. Political Economy expires before our very own eyes' (Baudrillard (1989) p 67). The term 'economy' begins to alter its sense. It is no longer the productive infrastructure but rather the sphere of the process of the destruction of value. The era is one of pure speculation, the emergence of an 'economy' cleared of all 'real' economic effects, a viral economy which has to align itself with all the other viral processes (Gane (1991) p 142). Global finance has the literal power to conjure profits from its own transactions devoid of the messiness of the real economy (see further Strange (1986)).

This analysis has been developed by Kroker and Cook. It adds an interesting element to the material hierarchy thesis of Braudel. Kroker and Cooke suggest that 'Money is caught in the grand cancellation of the sign of political economy. It finds itself homeless and constantly put to flight. It is abandoning the 'worthless' world of contemporary capitalism' (Kroker and Cooke (1988) p iv). Rothman, in his work on the semiotics of zero, notes that within the London financial markets less than five per cent of the billions traded everyday mirrors an equivalent transaction in goods and services. Finance capitalism is now distinguished not by the selling of goods, labour and services, but money. Money has attained the capacity to act as exchange for itself, the basis for what it signifies. Transactions are dominated by the purchase of interest rate options, fluctuations in currency rates, purchase of futures, financial derivatives and in highly complex swaps. As Rothman notes 'The significance of this is that the conventional vector of cause and necessity which points from trade to finance, from things to money, has been reversed' (Rothman (1987) p 95). And the 'things' themselves (actual units of production) are traded as commodities on a futures basis so that in fact they do not exist. With the cancellation of the referent, money circulates faster and more violently to maintain itself as the universal clinamen and its 'value' only appears 'at the vanishing-point of its afterimage' (Kroker and Cooke (1988) p iv). It is no longer one's filthy lucre, only that of the sanitised electronic display of the computer monitor:

> Numbers flashing across screens, numbers which can be erased with the touch of a finger, or a loud voice. Numbers which point to imaginary properties of imaginary things. Companies with made-up names, whose productivity is measured in imaginary numbers concerning losses and gains. Money going in and out of hidden accounts. Money attached to nothing but imaginary numbers attached to made-up accounts, built on the transactions and imagined doings of imaginary companies. Careers built on who can best manipulate this imaginary political economy of signs (Denzin (1991) p 91).

> *On the floor of LIFFE the commodity is money.*
> *You can buy and sell money, you can buy and sell the absence of money, debt, which used to strike me as funny* (Churchill (1987) p 31).

Particularly important is the role of credit. This is distinct not only from control over production but also from the role of money as a means of circulation. What has developed is a system of credit, separate and de-synchronised from the global system of production. The global credit system is unregulated to a greater degree than money. The market for credit, and especially for new financial innovations, and the private hierarchies of the credit-creating enterprises dominate the public hierarchies of national and international regulation. These new global forms of credit are beyond the control of nation-states, but nevertheless exert structural power over each of them (see Thrift and Leyshon (1992)).

Two comments can be ventured regarding this analysis of the contemporary disorder of capital. The first concerns violence. The second concerns dissolution of the material hierarchy. Capital as a free-floating sign is able to circulate at increasingly rapid levels suggesting a violence of randomness. The laws of economics are disrupted in a movement toward a transeconomy of excess: hyper-circulation. It is an economy of violence even though its appearance is one of satiation and ambience. It is a banality of violence as certainties and the predictable degrees of causation between production and consumption are flung into a void and liquidated in the storm. The possibility of controlled external planning through a regulatory conduit is annihilated: there are no laws here, only the symbolic law of capital. This is either the end of the dialectic or the implosion of the order of exchange. With the disappearance of the signifier in terms of economic value there is a corresponding transition in the nature of value attaching to the commodity in terms of morality and ethics; the commodity has become an element to which substantive or normative values can no longer be attached.

The material hierarchy thesis must be altered. The commentator is faced with the problem of either revelling in the prospect of implosion or the anxiety that the reversal of the material hierarchy (already tenuously poised in terms of access to material resources) has become so dislodged as to scupper any possibility of a revival of a community based system of production based upon 'actual' exchange in terms of 'positive value'.

This problem can be approached in terms of the differentiation of the 'lifeworld' (those spheres of production beneath the apex of the material hierarchy: Habermas (1987)). Baudrillard's analysis can be interpreted as a progressive decoupling of the 'lifeworld from system' – steering mechanisms become more remote and uncontrollable by individual actors, so that the lifeworld becomes encapsulated and powerless. However, as this differentiation is accentuated the lifeworld can no longer be protected adequately against invasions from the system: there appears a 'coloni(ali)sation of the life-world' as 'subsystems of the economy and the state intervene with monetary and bureaucratic means in the symbolic reproduction of the lifeworld' (Habermas (1987) p 356).

This accords with Baudrillard's prediction regarding the ambience of consumption. It is possible to invert Habermas's 'lifeworld' analysis and suggest (ironically following Baudrillard) that the 'lifeworld' becomes de-determined from the strategic process of alignment within the material hierarchy. Baudrillard's totalitarian code of consumption (the order of simulation) suggests a new code of lived experience ('lifeworld') consequent upon de-coloni(ali)sation as capital relations premised upon the mode of production disappear. The severing of the forces of economic determination suggest a 'lifeworld' where opportunities for new forms of production relations are possible.

Cultural forms are liberated from structural determinants and develop the capacity for independent development in an extreme form of code manipulation which offers the possibility of hyper-differentiation and decomposition. The availability of technology enables the material hierarchy to be altered consequent upon the virtual implosion of capital at the apex. The economic-lifeworld (where goods and services are produced within a utility framework) becomes possible.

Bourdieu's analysis of patterns of inequality demonstrated an order of cultural differentiation which intersects and challenges the order of economic differentiation. Former political-economic communities become hyper-differentiated and hyper-reified through the mass media. Multiple communities characterised by common ascriptive tastes, habits and concerns emerge (Bourdieu (1984)). The order of simulation can encourage a sense of fellowship, common interest and shared identity as a result of the failure of simulation to organise allegiance when the last possibility of identity becomes refusal and withdrawal of allegiance through usurpationary closure (when consumption no longer determines identity in terms of possession but in terms of use). These communities do not depend on an actuality of shared situation, much less on dense interpersonal networks: their common assumptions and concerns become the re-investiture of value beyond simulation. It is the value and order of excess generated at the apex of the material hierarchy through the processes of deregulation and fragmentation.

Old City and New City

> I'm not talking greed.
> I'm talking how I mean to succeed (Churchill (1987) p 25).

There are two cities. There is the city of global finance and the city of petty entrepreneurship. There is the city of domestic financial transactions and there is the city of international financial transactions. There is the white city and there is the black city. There is the city of affluence and the city of the absence of affluence (from Holland Park to Hackney Downs, from Mill Hill to Herne Hill). There is the city of modernisation and the city of postmodernisation. Everywhere there is division and fragmentation. Everywhere there is regeneration and degeneration. Everywhere the force of gentrification is measured by the force of degentrification as *habitus*[4] becomes increasingly awkward to identify save in terms of the festival of *heterotopia*. Here I am concerned with the internal conflict between subcultures in terms of the regulatory (value) tensions between the Old City (domestic finance) and the New City (global finance). It is an illustrative conflict of the way in which deregulation results in a crisis of legitimation.

The conflict between the City of prudence and the City of enterprise is illustrative of the transition from modernisation (production) to postmodernisation (reproduction). The point of analysis at this juncture is the consequence of this transition in terms of the crisis in business ethics within the financial markets.

The Old City of domestic finance is best described through the analogy of the English Gentleman's Club. In the period prior to the election of the Conservative administration of 1979 the City of London relied upon self-regulation with occasional intervention from the external legitimating organisation of the State to enhance effective prohibition. If external intervention was needed it took place at the request of the City. The 'club atmosphere' was reinforced through traditions, institutions, self-interest and the essentially homogeneous character of its members. This culture provided a fertile ground for self-regulation to develop and attain respect. It enabled the City of London to become a leading financial centre with a reputation for probity and trustworthiness. It was a microcosm of the prevailing corporatist industrial climate which prevailed in the post-war years in British society. The club developed a code of conduct based upon the threat of exclusion should its authority be challenged. It was a practitioner based system of regulation which deployed essentially informal methods to exercise discipline and to gain compliance with (perceived) normified trading and dealing practice. The senior

4 The concept of *habitus* is illustrative of some of the perplexities involved in analysing the ways in which ideas of time and space have been reconstituted. Following Bourdieu (1984) a district has a particular set of material and cultural characteristics. An identifiable social class lives in a district, the housing and collective services such as transport, education and culture are all of a particular type. In short, a social class, or part of one, could secure a section of the city, benefit from its collective services, and impose aspirations upon it. This social fixing of an area becomes part of the process whereby social classes reproduce their position in the class hierarchy over time. *Habitus* assumes a degree of empirical discernibility of material and cultural practices. The question becomes whether the concept can be adapted to the ephemeral events and fragmentary contacts, the collage of spaces and people, within the contemporary of urban disorder.

levels of the financial institutions of the City exerted exclusionary pressure to ensure that homogeneity was maintained and 'common' values and 'informal' codes of financial practice were enforced:

> The effectiveness of this club-type arrangement rested on the membership of the financial world being fairly exclusive. One cannot control people if they do not share the values of the club and are free to decide whether to join or not (Veljanovski (1988) p 3)

> The class system, with its institutions of social control, invariably subtle and exclusionary in their orientation, functioned with a predictability and efficiency which probably surpassed any practical system of legal regulation (Rider, Chaikin, Abrams (1987) p 11).

> *The stock exchange was a village street.*
> *You strolled about and met your friends.*
> (Churchill (1987) p 12).

Paradoxically the development of global financial processes presupposed particular local configurations: spatial proximity ('the village street') helped to sustain trust, everyone was within walking distance and this not only ensured control but it also allowed the development of a particular conception of time with enormously powerful conceptions of 'invented traditions'. The Old City was a localised social and cultural system which served to maximise trust. The empirical analysis provided by Scott (1982); (1985), Ingham (1984) and Thrift and Leyshon (1992) illustrates this homogeneity. In his work *Markets and Ideology in the City of London* David Lazar (1990) usefully brings these studies together in an analysis considering the differences between the Old City and the New City in terms of attitudes to the market. He concludes that the Old City operated a system of social closure which in fact was uneconomic in terms of the laws of the market:

> ... the City has constantly striven to erect non-economic barriers to entry since the mid-nineteenth century, through the establishment of exclusive associations based upon the discount houses, the accepting houses, the Stock Exchange and Lloyds (Lazar (1990) p 16).

This empirical analysis of the Old City can be placed within the broader conception developed by Bourdieu in terms of 'distinction' accruing 'social' and 'cultural' capital. Social capital refers to each person's insertion into, and accumulation of, a network of 'relationships of acquaintance and mutual recognition'. In terms of the City this is a network of family, friends and business contacts. Cultural or symbolic capital refers to each person's accumulation of a stock of socially accepted competencies all the way from a family name through ownership of 'appropriate' goods to formal educational qualifications. The sentiments expressed by commentators such as Veljanovski and the empirical studies conducted by Scott and Thrift and Leyshon substantiate Bourdieu's analysis with specific regard to the social structure of the financial system of the City of London. The social cohesion of the Old City meant that control systems were informal although no less effective: 'moral suasion, raised eyebrows, the stern rebuff over drinks.' These devices enabled the City to maintain its protectionist and autonomous position within the polity. But from the late 1970s both the spatial and cultural form of the City began to change. Pryke summarises this transition:

> The City was to become the hub not of a culturally familiar, empire-orientated regime of finance but of a new fast-moving capitalism ... The growth in numbers and size of foreign capital began to threaten the supremacy of the Bank's style of spatial policing, which in many ways required incoming capital to subordinate itself to British rule (Pryke (1991) p 210).

It was a subordination which both foreign institutions and new indigenous layers were not to accept (Stanley (1992a); (1992b)). Global and political pressure in conjunction with developments in telecommunications ensured that the closed structure of the system was blown apart. The void left by the rapidity of change meant that there was a regulatory vacuum. Significantly what occurred during the period under review was the external imposition of an alternative symbolic and formalised regulatory regime which disrupted the established control strategies of the old regime. The code of conduct became the arena of conflict between two loci of power: politics and economics. The former determined to impose ideology and the latter struggling to maintain position as an equalised member in a constellation of interests.

The impact of globalisation and technological innovation upon the London financial markets has been documented elsewhere (Coakley (1992)). The particular point of analysis here is the effect of the imposition of an enterprise ethic. Throughout the 1980s the concept of enterprise emerged as the central motif in the ideological agenda of the governing political administration. Stuart Hall suggests that the Conservative agenda was determined in part as a response to a perceived deep and long-running 'organic crisis' within society:

> [I]n their conception and project: the aim is to struggle on several fronts at once, not on the economic-corporate one alone; and this is based on the knowledge that, in order really to dominate and restructure a social formation, political, moral, and intellectual leadership must be coupled to economic dominance (Hall (1988b) p 154).

> They actually do believe that you have to struggle to implant the notion of the market; and that if you talk about it well enough, effectively and persuasively enough, you can touch people's understanding of how they live and work, and make a new kind of sense about what's wrong with society and what to do about it (Hall (1988b) p 188).

Policies which coerced individuals to confront market forces were a crucial means to facilitate the desired ideological-moral change in values. The enterprise culture can be interpreted as an economic vehicle for social change. The distinctive nature of the enterprise culture can be analysed in terms of the processes of transition from modernisation to postmodernisation. Following Cooke ((1988) pp 483-484) and Gamble (1989) the socio-spatial determinants of modernisation included:

- the geographical spread to the periphery of modernisation processes
- the partial convergence in income and unemployment indices between classes and the regions
- an inclination towards producing standardised products for volume markets and towards economies of scale
- economic development in close proximity to new 'collective consumption' environments

- a demand for skilled and semi-skilled labour to fill secure, 'lifetime' occupations
- the determination of specific regulatory goals in relation to socio-economic welfare.

The principles underlying postmodernisation include: the appeal to unadorned market relations as the source of economic success, the rolling back of the 'nanny state' with its all too comforting disposition towards 'lame-ducks' of society and economy, the weakening of established solidarities in the workplace and the elevation of the private over the public sphere in the matter of cultural and social provision (Cooke (1988) p 483).

- the uneven spread of postmodernisation characteristics
- an inclination toward divergence of income and unemployment indices between classes and regions
- an inclination towards customised output for niche markets and towards economies of scope
- economic development occurring in areas of privatised consumption (the 'sunbelt')
- labour market opportunities limited and insecure.
- the determination of specific regulatory goals through de-regulatory strategies in terms of socio-economic opportunity.

The process of postmodernisation entails the decoupling of political divisions and processes from the socio-economic structure and the market-shaped relations of production and exchange. This decoupling of political conflict, including dominant values, orientations and repertories of political action change under the impact of new social movements. Political constituencies are effected by changing political allegiances. The new conflicts are contingent and conjunctural and erupt around values and lifestyles involving status, situs and generational categories rather than socio-economic groups. Under these conditions traditional 'milieu' parties lose ground and are displaced by 'third parties' and less permanent social movements representing ephemeral concerns. The political imperative of postmodernisation (following Crook, Pakulski and Waters):

- a shift from centralised to decentralised apparatus
- a shift from authoritarian to manipulative forms in the organisation of control
- the severing of the idea of the state as an autonomous entity enjoying privileged links with politics and the public sphere
- the removal of determinist regulatory organisation of the socio-economic sphere and the emplacement of de-regulatory organisation of individual opportunity
- the simultaneous enfranchisement of individual enterprise and disenfranchisement of traditional strategic-group interests (Crook, Pakulski and Waters (1992) pp 221-222).

In terms of the relationship between enterprise (economic-moral values) and politics (political-ideological precepts) the triumph of the entrepreneur marks a change in governmental rationality: 'Here a certain idea of the enterprise government promotes and capitalises on a widely disseminated conception of individuality as an enterprise, of the person as an entrepreneur of the self' (Gordon (1987) p 300). The central features of contemporary political rationalities and technologies of government has been the attempt to establish connections between the self-fulfilling desires of individuals and the achievement of social and economic objectives. Rose notes that the 'success' of neo-liberalism 'operates within a much more general transformation in "mentalities of government", in which the autonomous, responsible, free, choosing self ... has become central to the moral bases of political arguments from all parts of the political spectrum' (Rose (1990)).

Postmodernisation weakens historicity when defined in terms of private temporality. The determinant of the future is technology which constructs a new economic order of reproduction as opposed to production and the sovereignty of consumption. This is achieved through the rise of new international rentier circuits in the current crisis phase of capitalist relations. In this sense the dominant ethos of postmodernisation is the legitimation of the temporal and the contingent. The tendency toward hyper and panic money which took over the international financial markets became perceived as an inevitable if not natural process in the immanent attainment of an uncertain capitalist equilibrium. The erosion of history, save in the form of nostalgia, eradicates the need for an historical base in terms of the forging of legitimating narratives of the contingent. The responsibility for legitimation no longer lies with the state (save in terms of safeguarding the possibility of individual economic achievement through economic imperative) but with the enterprising individual as the sole source of the legitimation of economic and ethical practices. The process is one of the 'naturalisation' of normative values of individualism:

> It is through this process – a kind of inevitable reflex of all social life – that particular sets of social relations, particular ways of organising the world appear to us as if they were universal and timeless. This is what Althusser means when he says that 'ideology has no history' and that in this general sense will always be an essential element of every social formation (Hebdige (1979) p 11).

This sentiment receives greater potency when considered in the light of Baudrillard's totalitarian code of the sign of consumption, the order of simulation and the banal violence of cultural ambience. The emplacement of the enterprise culture as a reaction to the failures of industrialisation was marketed through the images of a reinvented and mythical Victorian virtue of 'enterprise' and 'self-help'[5] – that the regulation of personal existence is not a question of authorities seeking to impose norms of conduct through intrusive regulatory bureaucracy. This nostalgic return to economic liberalism was mythical in the sense of responding to the virtues of certain elements of the modernisation process within the frame of the postmodernisation process. But it was a myth which has become entrenched in both individual and institutional activities.

5 The myth of the English industrial spirit has been documented by Weiner (1985). He notes an early speech by Margaret Thatcher when she announced 'I am a reformer and I am offering change' she sought 'to turn the clock back' and to restore economic dynamism by re-introducing the disciplines and incentives of the market. In another speech in 1979 she announced 'Our aim has always been more than just economic progress; it is to renew the spirit and solidarity of the nation' (Weiner (1985) pp 162-163; on the historical lineage of 'enterprise' see Perkin (1992) pp 36-61).

The City of London, Old and New, offered certain elements of commonality in terms of inhabiting specific parameters of ideological space (a belief in the sanctity of the market). The point of divergence was the primacy that the enterprise culture endorsed in the paradigmatic status afforded to both the achievement of the goals of financial acumen in the rewards of 'enterprise' and the role of the consumer; meeting the demands of the sovereign consumer became the imperative. Both these elements were an anathema to the Old City which spurned the qualities of the 'enterprising self' because these qualities represented a removal of the paternalism of financial welfare which had prevailed and the obliteration of the myth of greed which the Old City had privately endorsed but had publicly sought to deny. Greed in its most vicious form represented the hard material edge of the enterprising self:

> Here one finds a rather loosely related set of characteristics such as initiative, energy, independence, boldness, self-responsibility for one's own actions, and so on. Correspondingly, then, an enterprise 'culture' in this second sense is one in which the acquisition and exercise of these qualities is both highly valued and extensively practised (Keat (1990) p 3).

To institute and endorse these qualities determines that the sphere of consumption becomes a vital training ground in the nurturing of the spirit of the 'enterprising self'. The commodification of previously state supplied services (pensions, health insurance) ensured that the citizen becomes an individual and 'responsible' for the purchase of these items. The problem for the Old City was that during the period of the post-war settlement it had been the State which had relied upon the City to organise the provision of these services to the dependent sectors of society. These sectors were reliant upon distinctions within public life as differentiation between provider roles was perceived to be equated with efficient supply. The consumer was now encouraged to participate in the attainment of these services and to question and challenge the standard of their provision.

To compound this situation of external pressure for expansion upon the Old City there were demands for new procedures and new players. The procedures consequent upon the implementation of new technology (for example the doomed TAURUS programme) included the capacity for 24-hour 'Follow-the-Sun-Trading'. An example of internationalism and technology operating together to generate change is to be found in the development of the Eurodollar market in London. The new players included foreign finance houses for the first time allowed onto the London market (consequent upon the forced removal of restrictive trading barriers) and the expansion of recruitment in London based houses. These new procedures and new players ensured that the previously existing stability of norms and codes were irrevocably disrupted. New organisations introduced powerful competing regimes of conduct. The new ethos of enterprise encapsulated the importance of the development of non-external referent points in the determination of behaviour:

> Enterprising individuals are self-reliant and non-dependent. They make their own decisions, rather than wanting or expecting others to make these for them; and they take responsibility for their own lives, so that when things go wrong they do not assume there is always someone else to blame, or whose job it is to put things right (Keat (1990) p 5).

These individuals are goal orientated and their activities are directed toward the advancement of these goals and they are motivated to acquire whatever skills and resources are necessary to fulfil their aims effectively. They are dependent upon their own resources. These attitudes limit the effect of community-corporate generated norms (collective metaphors) in that individual conduct is assessed upon self-generated criteria of success. A subcultural construction of codified action will therefore be obeyed only to the extent that it contributes to the facilitation of individual goals and will be transgressed if it poses an obstacle to individual advancement.

These characteristics accord with the classifications 'yuppie' and 'the Disestablished'. Regarding yuppies, Whimster (1992) argues that certain continuities rooted in the expansion of the resources open to personality marked the character formation of this second generation of babyboomers. Yuppie-egoism is a feature of a differential personality that embraces both a much harder and more competitive world of work and career as well as a well developed sense of the needs of self and personality in comparison to the countercultural first generation of babyboomers. Equally interesting is the rise of the Disestablished. Commentators such as Hodgson (1990) and Perkin (1989) have noted that what occurred in the 1980s was the fall of the Establishment and the rise of the Disestablishment. The Establishment were those possessors of power and influence who shared values and used informal personal links to promote and defend those values. Not a distinct class in socio-economic terms but a distinct cultural enclave in terms of wielding power as identified by Parkin (1979): an interlocking power network operating between the key institutional structures of the state, industry, the city, the church, the universities and the arts. The Disestablishment represented the demise of this nexus of exclusionary power relations of social and cultural capital. The Disestablishment was characterised as 'meritocratic rather than egalitarian, efficient rather than generous, individualistic rather than corporate' (Lloyd (1988) p 155). In the New City the 'disestablishment' became a highly visible coalition of private business interest that sought to challenge the old regulatory mechanisms of the established order. In this the activities of the disestablished in the financial markets were legitimated through State endorsement of conflicting regulatory rationales and structures. The effect of these changes will be examined specifically in relation to deviant activity in the financial markets, city crime and state crime.

2 Panic! Coke-Blip Capitalism

> Fuck the DTI, Zac. I refuse to be defeated.
> I don't care if I go to jail, I'll win whatever the cost (Churchill (1987) p 98).

Money Crime and State Crime

The imposition of an enterprise ethic complete with variably articulated norms in addition to a series of external pressures served to collapse the consensus between state and city and engendered a hegemonic conflict within the City resulting in changes in attitudes toward transgressive activity. The question of structure is significant: 'Structure is both medium and outcome of the reproduction of practices. Structure enters simultaneously into the constitution of the agent and social practices, and 'exists' in the generating moments of this constitution' (Giddens (1980) p 5). This structured approach to deviancy can be considered in terms of 'location of agents' structurally within the confines of specific historical situations, so that particular courses of action come to be viewed as 'desirable' and 'able or unable' to be achieved. The delimination of norms is never strictly determined through the social structuring of power relations but it is never entirely free of the systematic influence of power as structured at particular moments in history. The same goes for individuals as actors or agents in a world which is only partly of our making. In the ritualised activity of our everyday lives we are at once structuring and structured by our relations of power. In our expressions of social, political, and economic power we are at once creative or self-structuring subjects and created or structurally subjected selves. We are 'decentred subjects'; subjects who actively assess our situations and make historical choices, while experiencing our choices as limited by the objective possibilities available within the structural confines of our position in history.

In the context of this chapter, city crime is identified as fraudulent activity. The fraud consists in the appropriation of property through fraudulent means. In the financial markets this implies an intentional abuse of position, trust and confidence. The abuse could be the utilisation of unpublished price sensitive information for personal gain or the disclosure of information which is known to be incorrect to a potential investor. The gain will be of economic benefit (in terms of personal-corporate accumulation or strategic advantage). The 'victim' will often be difficult to identify. There can be no doubt that fraudulent activity has always existed in the securities market and this is the reason for the development of regulatory mechanisms, be they self-generated or externally imposed. A capitalist system engenders fraudulent behaviour because the criterion for the operation of the system is premised upon economic principles concerning profit maximisation and therefore the moral-legal boundaries regarding ethical and moral conduct are determined through economic premises. Therefore, the organisations in which profit maximisation is pursued are crimogenic in the sense of subsuming moral-legal values to a speculative end. But for the system to work effectively (in the sense of encouraging investment) the profit maximisation rationale is tempered by the conflicting requirement of trust and confidence which can only be guaranteed through the operation of a degree of apparent or ostensible control. During the period 1984–1989 competing regulatory mechanisms and neo-liberal economic principles facilitated in undermining any effective governing strategy.[6] Rapid change in market practices and products gave rise to an atmosphere of uncertainty and the belief in instantaneous profit: greed. The veneer of control was tarnished as a jungle mentality took hold of many of the players and became the natural inclination of the new entrants. The homogeneity of beliefs which had been the principal control mechanism in the City's regulatory operating collapsed.[7] The game became one not merely of survival, because there was sufficient work to go around, but how much one could consume – and how many opponents one could annihilate. It was an atmosphere of the anomie of affluence consequent upon a regulatory void and the accessible realisation of the achievement of goals.

The use of Durkheim's analysis of anomie is significant because of his concern with the culture for action. A determining factor in the construction of 'deviant' behaviour is the culture in which the individual operates. Durkheim used the term anomie to describe a state of normlessness consequent upon a rapidly changing economic structure outstripping particular regulatory forms which engenders the fragmentation of solidarity (community) which the division of labour had imposed. A culture beset by anomie was said to lack the regulatory constraints necessary for the adequate social control of its members (and therefore resembles social disorganisation and normative chaos). There is a moral void where the norms over individual conduct break down. Durkheim's original formulation concentrated upon the higher echelons of the social stratum for it was '[P]ower and not poverty that facilitated the personal achievement of socially inculcated cultural ambitions' (Box (1983) p 40). Economic success fuels the desire of the 'inextinguishable thirst' for further satiation of desire; 'greed is aroused without knowing where to find ultimate foothold. Nothing can calm it, since its goal is far beyond all it can attain' ('Naturally there's a whole lot of greed and that's no problem because money buys freedom' (Churchill (1987) p 109)). Durkheim's analysis foreshadowed the success-at-any-cost 'ethic' as well as the lack of a formal code of ethics in business practice. The disruption of an order weakens the normative structure of that order. Within an economic frame sudden success or recession causes a declassification of norms and the moment of the de-subjected individual. The successful experience the sensation that anything and everything is possible: the less limited one feels, the more intolerable all limitation appears. As Durkheim noted:

6 A survey conducted by the accountants Ernst and Young revealed that sums totalling £4 billion were risked over the period, one hundred times more than sums risked between 1964–1969. This figure does not represent the full degree of fraudulent activity only of detected cases. There is the dark figure of unrecorded fraud. There has been no decrease in the number of cases involving investigation, prosecution and conviction of fraud despite the transition to the corporate-governance conscious 1990s.

7 This 'jungle mentality' was reflected in the growing popularity of a number of classic texts on the strategy of warfare. Machiavelli's *The Prince*, Clausewitz's *On War* and Sun Tzu's *The Art of War* became 'standard texts':

> A couple of hitherto quiet types with Prussian names were now keeping copies of Clausewitz's *On War* on their desks. Investment bankers usually read *On War* secretly, not because they are embarrassed to be caught with it, but because they don't want to let anyone in on their technique. I recommended Sun Tzu (Lewis (1989) p 173).

> Such is the source of the excitement predominating in this business part of society, and which has thence extended to the other parts. There, the state of crisis and anomie is constant and, so to speak, normal. From top to bottom of the ladder, greed is aroused without knowing where to find ultimate foothold. Nothing can calm it, since its goal is far beyond all it can attain. Reality seems valueless by comparison with dreams of fevered imaginations; reality is therefore abandoned (quoted by Mestrovic (1991) p 175).

Applying anomie as a cause of deviance in the City of London between 1984-1989 suggests a breakdown in regulatory strategy consequent upon subcultural conflict. The Enterprise Culture as a neo-liberal economic-political imperative can be identified as promulgating a commitment to the achievement of individual economic goals as the criteria for success, but the individual still operated within a culture in which the means of legitimating the achievement of this goal was only differentially available.[8] A commitment to goals is assumed; the means of achievement were problematic. What occurred in the period under review was a transition from the legitimation of goals beyond mere conformity (modernisation) toward the demonstration of individual goals as the measure of individuality (postmodernisation). These goals were determined by speculation because the culture in which they were formulated was one of consumption. They were goals achieved through the articulation of individual metaphors as opposed to collective metaphors. The City has traditionally been successful in generating collective metaphors of control, restraint, confidence and trust. The Enterprise Culture attributed primacy to the personal metaphor of success. This was enterprise as the 'state of nature' in which benefits accrued to the will and the wits of the individual.

According to Simon and Gagnon (1976) environments which encourage the ascendancy of personal metaphors are those dominated by the existential, the accidental and serve to challenge the individual to test out their most abstract fantasies and desires: overconsumption and immediate gratification. The player in the whirlpool of global finance was encouraged to indulge desires. The crimogenic atmosphere of the finance house, the ethos of enterprise and regulatory void provided individuals with the opportunity and justification for realising desires. Following Simon and Gagnon, the individual becomes a 'conforming deviant' when, having achieved the means of gratification, there is a necessity to explore the dimensions of pleasure which brings them to the 'margins of deviance' (Simon and Gagnon (1976) p 362). The individual will receive gratification from the performance of deviant activity as a new experience in the exploration of desire-power and will not feel constrained by the norms which would be activated to punish the less successful. The legitimating ethos of enterprise and greed served to de-stabilise such punitive regulatory controls. What Durkheim called the 'habit' of feeble morality is transferred into the core of public life:

8 As such anomie points to a central contradiction in the organisation of capitalist society: the promise of a free market for opportunity in which those who work hard can rise as far as their abilities permit *and* a systematic limitation of access to decisions affecting the allocation and distribution of economic resources to those who control the processes of reproduction.

Naturally, we are not inclined to thwart and restrain ourselves; if, then, we are not invited, at each moment, to exercise this restraint without which there is no ethic, how can we learn the habit of morality? (Durkheim cited by Mestrovic ((1991) p 171).

The Report on County NatWest Ltd and County NatWest Securities Ltd by Inspectors appointed by the Department of Trade and Industry (DTI) under investigatory powers pursuant under the Companies Act 1986 s 432(2) ('The Blue Arrow Affair') is the story of a group of individuals within a finance house who were prepared to be enterprising and exploit the regulatory void in search of corporate advantage:

The story of The Blue Arrow Affair began in July 1987, the high point of a bear market on the London Stock Exchange (LSE). Blue Arrow, a recruitment company, had been launched on the Unlisted Securities Market (USM) at a capitalisation of £3 million. In discussion with its financial advisers in the UK, County NatWest Limited (the merchant banking subsidiary of the National Westminster Bank plc), and in the US with Dillon Reed, it was decided that a bid should be launched for the largest temporary employment agency in the world, Manpower Services, based in the US and capitalised at £600 million.

The bid was launched in the US with Dillon Reed successfully securing 131,200 shares in Manpower at a cost of $7,913,195. This purchase considerably exceeded Blue Arrow's disclosure limits under The Companies Act 1985 ss 198-200 representing 11 per cent of Blue Arrow's asset base. In the UK Blue Arrow did not wish to officially launch its bid until the financing for the bid had been put into place through a rights share issue of £837 million. Taking account of the fact that its US holdings in Manpower were already substantial, Blue Arrow would have had to persuade the Stock Exchange Quotations Department to waive the stake that had already been acquired. The issue of disclosure was raised so as to reduce the financial impact on Blue Arrow of the costs that it would incur in the event of a rival, higher offer, causing Blue Arrow's offers to fail. Under the Stock Exchange Class II requirements a listed company is required to make an immediate announcement to the market of transactions for a consideration representing between 5 per cent and 15 per cent of the listed company's assets.

The stockbrokers for Blue Arrow-County NatWest were UBS Phillips and Drew (a subsidiary of the Union Bank of Switzerland). Phillips and Drew were left taking up the remainder, significantly exceeding their own disclosure requirements and with the consequent probability as mentioned in the Report of the offences of insider dealing, market fixing, the making of negligent misstatements and the avoidance of Chinese Walls at various strategy meetings held over the period.

Three executive directors of National Westminster Bank plc were informed that their subsidiary, its market makers and Phillips and Drew had taken significant stakes in Blue Arrow with County NatWest's stake amounting to 13.5 per cent. The share price of Blue Arrow continued to fall due to the effect of the crash in equities in October 1987 (Black Monday). This resulted in a loss to National Westminster Bank plc of £40 million. The Bank announced in December 1987 that it was injecting £80 million into its merchant banking division and admitted a 9.5 per cent state in Blue Arrow (67.9 million shares) on which it has lost £49 million. The Inspectors noted that there was nothing illegal about this announcement but that it may have been clearer if reference had been made to the actual holding of 76 million shares. At the end of 1988 County

NatWest resigned as adviser to Blue Arrow after the appointment of the DTI Inspectors. By the year end the total losses of the Bank were £65 million and the Chairman, Lord Boardman, had resigned. Blue Arrow's £837 million rights issue to finance a bid for Manpower was intended to be the high point for County NatWest and Phillips and Drew in their respective attempts to become major players in the City's booming equity market.

The Report of DTI Inspectors concluded that:

- County NatWest should have disclosed its interests in more than 13 per cent of Blue Arrow shares (para 4.26)
- The market was 'deliberately misled' several times over the progress of the Company's rights issue (para 8.30)
- The conduct of senior corporate financiers at County NatWest was 'well-below that to be expected from responsible executives' (para 12.11)
- Three NatWest main board directors were criticised for failing to ensure 'the lawful conduct of business' by the Bank (para 11.20).

The Report was sent to the Serious Fraud Office and charges were brought against 11 people relating to theft under the Prevention of Fraud (Investments) Act 1958 s 11 and relating to conspiracy under the Criminal Law Act 1977 s 1(1). The indictment alleged conspiracy to induce investors through the use of fraudulent statements, conspiracy to deliberately withhold information from the LSE and the creation of false market for shares.

A number of the statements given in evidence and the Inspector's own comments pointed to an attitude of contempt for the rules of the market prevailing at County NatWest and at Phillips and Drew:

- We regard Mr Wells' attitude toward compliance with Class II requirements of the Stock Exchange as irresponsible. Mr Stainforth took no steps to discourage Mr Wells. The willingness of Messrs Fraser and Alcock to be parties to a misleading of the Stock Market enabled Mr Wells to succeed in his objective (para 4.26)
- We can find no justification for the way the market was misled ... Those involved in making those decisions must have appreciated that the market was going to be mislead (para 8.29)
- We regard Mr Wells as responsible for the failure of County NatWest to fulfil its relevant statutory duties. His conduct fell well below the level expected (para 4.24).

The Report by the DTI was received as a serious indictment of the National Westminster Bank and its investment banking subsidiary. It served to undermine the view that commercial banks could successfully merge with securities houses to create immediately successful multi-service financial institutions which could compete on a global scale. It also served to suggest that market makers were primarily concerned with the letter of the law rather than the spirit. The Report pointed to misleading the market as a matter of routine and the fact that had the market not crashed the extent of these fraudulent practices may never have been revealed. The Inspectors were told that it was common practice to ignore Stock Exchange rules and that at all times the principals were concerned only with the form rather than the substance of the rules with regard to the disclosure of share holdings. The people to whom they were ultimately accountable – the main board of National Westminster Bank plc (let alone the shareholders) – did not have sufficient grasp of the investment business to supervise the activities of the subsidiary effectively. At a vital moment … 'none of the three executive directors had sufficient experience to examine critically what they were being told … having raised one or two obvious points and having received some comfort in relation thereto, they accepted the position.'.

This last point illustrates the divide created over the period between trading floor and boardroom and the cultural conflict in terms of organisational power structures which emerged. Spiralling activity within the financial markets created an unstable corporate atmosphere in which the traditional (Old City) blue-chip players no longer dictated the pace or the process of change. Those in County NatWest were prepared to blatantly disregard the rules (of statute, of regulatory institutions, of the corporate culture) as if these rules did not apply to them. The goal was the success of the deal at all costs and to enhance the market share of the operation. At boardroom level the senior executives of the National Westminster Bank simply did not comprehend the nature of the transactions that their subordinates were conducting in their name. County NatWest was simply playing by the rules of an unstable and temporarily buoyant market. The Old Guard were out of touch with the game and with the Young Turks who played it. The flare and greed that characterised the contemporary investment bank was far removed from the qualities of prudence which characterised the traditional clearing bank. In the event the prosecution resulting from the case failed on appeal. The eleven individuals on the indictment were either appointed to similar positions in other institutions or maintained their positions. The reward for financial malpractice appeared to be consolidation of position.[9]

---

9 As one financial journalist commented:

To give clearing bank executives responsibility for an investment bank dealing in securities and corporate finance is like putting the paycorp officers in charge of an SAS unit. Financial controls at head office are not much help when your hardened troops are fighting it out in the streets for rewards that it would take half a lifetime for a bank manager to earn in a high street branch (*The Guardian* 26 July 1989).

Scilla's been named by Business Week as Wall Street's rising star.
Greville walked out of prison but didn't get very far.
Grimes does insider dealing for Scilla and Marylou (and he bought Greville's house) (Churchill (1987) p 69).

Recent empirical work demonstrates the prevalence of pro-market legal-ethical indeterminacy amongst financial service practitioners:

- Lazar's 1990 empirical analysis studied how participants in the financial markets of the City of London viewed the markets in which they work and the market mechanism in general. Lazar also provides an empirical investigation into how ideologies function. Since financial markets are flex-price markets where prices change continuously participants stand in direct relation to market forces. The consciousness of participants and their hour-by-hour activity is determined by this immediacy. In particular, the volatility of financial markets means that constant examination of price movement is central to the work of the participants. The positive view of the values of the market mechanism displayed by practitioners flows from their experience of the 'efficiency' of the market. These views are shaped by the brutality of market forces which serve to coerce participants to compete and markets attract individuals who already assume a belief in market forces in terms of insecurity and risk. Lazar's analysis demonstrates an adherence to views and values close to or coincident with pro-market neo-liberal economic precepts and political ideology, views which are held prior to entry and enforced through participation and socialisation.

The final aspect of 'The Blue Arrow Affair' was the role of the regulatory organisations empowered by the Financial Services Act 1986 to detect fraud and monitor the conduct of licensed financial institutions. In the case of the Blue Arrow take-over The Securities Association (TSA), The Securities and Investment Board (SIB), The General Council of the Stock Exchange and The Bank of England could all claim providence in the conduct of the bid. For example, the design weakness of the SIB structure was such that ownership of responsibility was undefined. County NatWest was both a bank and a finance house, the extent of its economic resources and the division of its functions were vulnerable to abuse and it was its aggressive mergers and acquisitions team which instigated the abuse. Under self-regulation the Bank's compliance officer should have prevented illegal share-buying and ensured disclosure. In the event the compliance officer at County NatWest was charged with conspiracy. The Securities Association might have been expected to proscribe certain activities of its members. One of the reasons for this failure was that TSA assumed that County NatWest was monitored by the SIB. The behaviour of the DTI, the ultimate regulatory authority, was at best erratic and at worst a refusal to assume responsibility. This gives rise to the suspicion of collusion: not so much a design weakness as weakness by design.

It is possible to relate the erosion of the boundaries between legality and illegality in terms of financial transactions (and therefore the issue of the source of legitimation) to the economic aspirations of neo-liberalism and the imperative of de-regulation within a strong state:

> The New Right seeks to create a free economy and a strong state; only if the state is strong can the economy be free. For the new right the remorseless growth of the modern state, measured by its spending programmes and the range of its interventions, has been a disaster and must be reversed if a free and prosperous society is to survive (Gamble (1989) p 5).

9... – Weait's work studies the role of compliance officers in financial institutions. These are the officials who operate within both the empirical reality of the organisational structure and its legal characterisation as an organic system. Consequently they have a very complex perception of role. They are involved in the development of new financial products, assessing their regulatory implications and, as such, are concerned with the firm's commercial success. They are also responsible for monitoring compliance by directors and staff within the complex of rules and regulations of the FSA. They are in a situation of potential conflict. They have an incentive to ensure the firm's profitability and owe a primary obligation to the firm as their employer. They are also engaged in a role which may demand criticising the firm, requesting dismissal of errant employees, or even alerting regulatory authorities to misconduct. Weait's fascinating analysis pursues the use of imagery and metaphor in the language employed by compliance officers in describing the complexity of their function. Significantly compliance officers, who in reality are the front-line troops in the enforcement of regulatory strategy, did not wish to profile themselves as policeman ('You're not a policeman you're an interpreter of rules and a persuader of people'). As Weait notes:

> They know what it involves, what it is constituted by, and what it is like and what it is unlike, but they appear unable to present a broad, holistic image, which captures succinctly what their role in fact is. This is unsurprising. The typical compliance officer has moved into compliance from accountancy, the law or other areas of financial services work. For those in the former categories, they have come from structured professions with a high-degree of institutionalised procedure and standards of ethical conduct, into a non-man's land where determining what you do, how you achieve it, and so on is much more open to debate and interpretation ((1992) p 63).

The sanctity of the market engaged four issues: the limitations of effective state intervention; alternatives to markets having only limited effect; the continuity of market dominance over that of central government; the sanctity of individual rights and freedom of action without state intervention. This policy was implemented through initiatives such as the encouragement of competition, privatisation, re-commodification of the residual public sector, tax deductions, internationalisation. With regard to the City (which benefited from many of these initiatives) the most significant in terms of structural change was the policy of de-regulation. In terms of legitimation the authority of City to govern its own practices was eroded through two devices: the ostensible imposition of external authority through a re-defined regulatory framework and through a process of symbolism and duplicity in the enforcement of this framework.

The imposition of ostensible authority: The imposition of a new regulatory structure was the cornerstone of the State's effort in limiting the influence of the City in terms of the governance of the implementation of economic policy. The Financial Services Act 1986 (FSA) was a symbolic gesture in both its effect of offering to protect the 'innocent investor' who was encouraged to participate in the operation of the City through privatisation issues and in its introduction of an impressive array of regulatory machinery, which did not achieve this aim.

9... – Bosworth-Davies usefully complements the findings of Weait, again using the example of compliance officers. As opposed to interrogating the problem of the definition of role in relation to compliance officers, Bosworth-Davies investigated attitudes held regarding financial malpractice and criminal opportunity with particular reference to insider dealing. Weait's work suggested endemic ambivalence regarding regulatory strategy and enforcement consequent upon indeterminacy in the nature of function. Weait provided useful evidence regarding regulatory confusion given the specific example of the enforcement within the financial institution. Bosworth-Davies interrogates attitudes which are held by compliance officers toward financial malpractice and perceptions of criminality and opportunity afforded to them by benefit of their position. He demonstrated that compliance officers possess a high degree of congruence of business, cultural and social norms with the practitioners within their industry. The likelihood of conflict (which Weait identifies in the perception of role) is minimised because there is a low degree of correspondence between what individuals are prepared to admit ought to happen in theory and what they would do in practice, for both practitioners and compliance officers. Bosworth-Davies' research identifies a distinction between perception of 'real crime' in the views and values of compliance officers:

> It is clear that they do not accord a high status to insider dealing which indicates that its offensiveness as a prohibited attribute is small ... If this feeling is indicative of the minimalist level of proactive regulation which the industry is prepared to donate and Government is prepared to accept then such a finding provides an uncanny degree of confirmation ... of the existence of certain statutes adopted for essentially political reasons and not meant to be enforced ((1993) p 355; see further Stanley (1994a) (1994b)).

Bosworth-Davies identifies the nub of the problem regarding a regulatory framework which depends upon self-regulatory enforcement. In relying upon a self-regulatory framework in the maintenance of an ethos of fair market practice in an environment of regulatory conflict (between demands for enhanced autonomy of regulatory agencies on the one hand and demands for re-regulation and greater intervention on the other) Bosworth-Davies' research demonstrates the fact that those individuals who will play the most influential part in the formation of policy for the future are those most likely to resist adopting pro-active methods to implement those policies ((1993) p 355).

The history of the introduction of the new regulatory regime is illuminating because it illustrates the division between the State and the City in the formulation of policy.[10] The government's enforced removal of restrictive trade practices in relation to share trading commissions was the first move. Its appointment of an independent expert to consider wide-scale reform consequent to the collapse of the Norton Warburg and Johnson Matthey investment banks was the second move. The Gower Report (1982) gave the government the opportunity to use a respected external authority to legitimate its own neo-liberal *real politik* aims. The Gower Report suggested a detailed set of investor protection laws:

> Logic and tidiness ... are of importance only in so far as they contribute to a legal regime which can be understood, which will be regarded as fair by those it affects and which, as a result, will generally be observed and can be effectively enforced (Gower (1982).

As an 'outsider' Gower had great difficulty conducting his research in the City; as a lawyer his Report was attacked for not being premised upon rational economic grounds, particularly in its neglect of any form of cost-benefit analysis (see further Veljanovski (1988) pp 7–12). Gower suggested a basic principle of a comprehensive system of regulation within a statutory framework based on self-regulation subject to government surveillance:

> If self-regulation is to survive, the surveillance to which it is subject must be sufficient to provide a genuine curb on undesirable restrictive practices and a sufficient spur to ensure that rules are kept under review and their observance efficiently monitored (Gower (1982)).

The Government departed from Gower's proposals in its introduction of the FSA. The Government's White Paper accepted the need to improve the laws relating to investor protection but it warned of the dangers of 'excessive' regulation: regulation should be no more than necessary to protect the investor, and therefore should reflect the needs of the market to operate with minimum restrictions. The prevailing regulatory philosophy was to be *caveat emptor*, the sovereign consumer was to be charged with the task of simultaneously being encouraged to participate in the orgy of speculation whilst being prudent enough to know what the dangers were. The FSA became a symbolic gesture assuaging investor protection. The rhetoric of its provisions can be detected in its ostensible objectives:

- the promotion of efficiency and competition
- the inspiration of confidence in issuers and investors that the financial services industry would be 'a clean place to do business'
- ensuring that the regulatory framework was flexible so as to facilitate future structural changes.

10 See further on the political background to the de-regulation of the City, Jessop and Stones ((1992) pp 171-192).

The mechanisms for the achievement of these objectives were the principles of supervision, compliance, disclosure and accountability. The instigator and principal regulator in the formulation and enforcement of the rules which would encapsulate these principles was to be the hybrid SIB. The SIB was given unprecedented authority to implement statutory powers whilst being a private body but accountable to the DTI. In addition the SIB was to reign over a series of Self-Regulatory Organisations (SROs) each empowered by the SIB to regulate its own sector of the financial services industry. An impressive array of regulatory machinery.

But an examination of the economic principles underlying the implementation of the FSA suggest deliberate paucity in the response of the State toward investor protection beyond mere symbolism. A simple economic analysis of the operation of financial markets points to the fact that efficient markets afford investors adequate protection given the cost of that protection. An efficient market is one in which all information is reflected in the share price. Therefore, the principal regulatory mechanism is an enforceable definition of 'fraud on the market'. This simple rule (given either by the judiciary or a regulatory authority) is all that is required. Further regulations do not improve the quality of the provision of information and serve only to place additional costs of regulation on the securities industry (and therefore on the investor) and there is no account for regulatory institutional failure or regulatory capture. Another interpretation is the simple enforcement of a series of rules relating to the conduct of investment business. Given adequate sanctions compliance will follow.

The government arranged for a complex combination of legal and quasi-legal regulations and institutions to come into operation, without a governing principle of 'fraud on the market'. The costs of this regulatory regime are borne by the market and the investors. The regime is one of ostensible self-regulation but with ultimate authority residing with the government. In the absence of a general definition there is scope for liberal interpretation of what will and what will not constitute fraudulent behaviour. In the absence of external funding there is pressure to negotiate and by-pass the rules so as to minimise costs. The amorphous nature of the regulatory regimes means there are inevitable problems of capture between organisations and mutual assumptions that one organisation bears responsibility. This centralisation of ultimate authority enables the government to take regulatory decisions on ideological grounds. A system of 'codes of conduct' even if backed up by statutory powers means that not all participants will choose to abide by the code. It is a regime which has served to irrevocably limit the internal authority of the City. The 'innocent investor' has been left to take the consequences of Barlow Clowes, Eagle Trust, Ferranti, Maxwell, Lloyds, Guinness, Roger Levitt, Barings and so on.

The appearance of action by government illustrates the partially successful articulation of duplicity and symbolism. An obvious example is the introduction of a self-regulatory regime where ultimate power resides with government. Guidelines for the interpretation of the enforcement of the FSA has not been forthcoming. Two further examples substantiate this accusation.

The statement made by Cecil Parkinson (then Secretary of State at the DTI) in the House of Commons introducing the Companies Securities (Insider Dealing) Act 1985 in 1984, claiming that this legislation would protect innocent investors from the abuse of unpublished price-sensitive share information. These investors would otherwise be 'at the mercy of the unscrupulous'. At the time of his speech it was alleged that the first major investigation by the DTI into insider dealing activities probed into the affairs of Parkinson's own broker, Walter Walker, who was involved in asset stripping and illegal share dealing involving Parkinson's personal share portfolio.

The evidence given by Nicholas Ridley (then Secretary of State at the DTI) to the House of Commons Select Committee on Trade and Industry in 1990 is illuminating. Ridley declared that he did not consider insider dealing to be endemic in the City and that 10 convictions out of 19 cases was a good record in the five years since the legislation had been introduced. On the same date the SIB published figures that it was investigating 15 cases of insider dealing a day.

These examples of duplicity serve as illustrations of an underlying symbolic imposition and of ostensible action. There is the appearance of a legitimating code but one which is denied its function. On one level of analysis this is representative of a conspiracy between interest groups with shared motives (Box (1983)). But with specific regard to the relationship between the City and the State this level of symbolism and duplicity legitimates the re-definition of competing norms. The emplacement of an enterprise culture could only be achieved if enterprising agents were able to achieve their personally defined goals which meant the de-classification of the limits of deviance. The government enabled individual goals to be established and executed through the disruption of competing norms and the creation of new and mutable referents. But the limits of individually legitimated action had to appear to be determined through a compromise between agents and state. There was a requirement for a symbolic legitimating framework and the apparent enforcement of sanctions.[11]

*

As a footnote to this analysis it is possible to consolidate the argument with reference to recent regulatory failures. Blue Arrow in addition to Barlow Clowes, Maxwell, Levitt, Dunsdale, Barings, home income plans, Garston Trust and most recently the mis-selling of millions of pensions all suggest regulatory collapse in the financial services sector. Indeed, one of the most significant markets in the area, that of financial futures (LIFFE) remains unregulated. The rising stakes in the financial markets include the uncertainty of economic performance given the boom-bust cycle of recession. Individual practitioners have become trapped in the regulation-deregulation conundrum, between heaven and hell. In times of boom (following the anomie of affluence thesis) the fulfilment of personal goals is unconstrained by particular external limitations. In time of recession (following the anomie of scarcity thesis) the fulfilment of personal goals becomes increasingly difficult but the culture of excellence and individualism remains in addition

11 It is impossible not to be seduced by Matza's opinion that 'By pursuing evil and producing the appearance of good, the state reveals its abiding method – the perpetuation of its good name in the face of its own propensity for violence, conquest and destruction' ((1969) p 196).

to the institutional pressures of target fulfilment. Individuals are coerced into taking risks so as to maintain their position in relation to differentially available cultural goals. In terms of the financial institutions (who pay for regulation), a self-regulatory system (even within a statutory framework) can only operate effectively if the system engenders the compliance of the regulated. Recent evidence suggests the increasing fragility of existing regulatory structures. Three examples can be provided:

- The continuation of overseas competition squeezing the possibility for business and importing yet further new financial products in addition to alien corporate cultures and attitudes to compliance. London has operated as open-door policy and the balance has continued in favour of the free market.
- The Personal Investment Authority (PIA) introduced as a consequence of the Maxwell fiasco (another layer of regulatory artifice) was launched in a state of confusion and embitterment with a senior practitioner resigning on the issue that a public interest constituted membership did not reflect the 'spirit' of self-regulation under the FSA. Two further regulatory initiatives have been undertaken which constitute another layer to the complex system of regulation:
  - The first regulatory initiative has been the creation of a Market Conduct Regulators Group established under the auspices of the SIB and charged with establishing 'coherence' to the varied regulations regarding equity trading. The SIB has called for 'explicit standard of market integrity and investor protection'. In part this regulatory initiative is a response to the proliferation of marketplaces and the development of financial derivatives such as futures and options which have inevitably outpaced the regulations of the FSA. The new Group will consider strategies for enhanced disclosure of financial information in relation to trading in equities. However, regulation through disclosure which has remained the principal rationale underlying the control of corporate and financial organisations operates to deter both practitioners and investors and thus reduces liquidity.
  - The second regulatory initiative has been undertaken by the House of Commons Treasury Select Committee. The Committee launched a review in 1994 of the regulation of the financial services industry. The Committee identified five questions. First, to what extent is self-regulation working? Second, what is the cost of regulation? Third, is it still appropriate for the Lloyd's insurance market to be regulated by the DTI as opposed to the Treasury (which, indicatively, is avowedly against assuming a regulatory role). Fourth, how will regulation in the EEC affect British consumers? This question raises the issue of 'regulatory arbitrage' through which financial institutions elect for registration in the most conducive regulatory jurisdiction and then operate their business in the correspondingly conducive financial market. Finally, is the government co-ordinating regulation efficiently? Again, this question raises the issue of the failure to develop the concept of a lead regulator given the inadequacy of the SIB to fulfil this role.

- The final regulatory problem is one of capture. It is clear that the current FSA regime is a complex and burdensome regulatory structure which in addition to its pyramidal organisation has to co-operate with policing institutions (the SFO and the City of London Police) and economic institutions (the Treasury and the Bank of England). All possess a stake in either enforcing or hindering regulation. The ideological-economic imperative of a particular strategic interest in this regulatory miasma is determined by the scope of the jurisdiction of a particular organisation. An efficient regulatory regime requires clearly delineated networks of communication and exchange of information. The imposition of a regulatory system upon an established series of informal mechanisms engenders confusion. This confusion is exacerbated because regulatory organisations must justify their existence; if indetermination exists in terms of jurisdiction this pressure is compounded again. A particular financial institution might be subject to regulation by a number of authorities with the consequence that it escapes regulation by a particular authority granted the inevitability of regulatory capture and regulatory lapse (see further Stanley (1994a); (1994b)).

Tame Zones and Wild Zones

> My school reports used to say I was too aggressive
> (but it's come in quite useful).
> My old headmaster wouldn't call me a fool again.
> I got a transfer fee like a footballer. He thought I was a hooligan (Churchill (1987) p 7).

There are two cities: the City of London and the Inner City. The City of London over shadows the Inner City, literally and metaphorically. To the east of the Bishopsgate development, within two minutes' walk, there is Whitechapel and Shoreditch. From the opulence of the facades of the City of London (Old and New), the city of international finance we discover very different streets reflecting an urban wasteland:

> No more than a few hundred yards to the west of Brick Lane, Middlesex Street forms the boundary between Tower Hamlets and the City of London. On the City side of the street a huge glass and concrete behemoth has just been completed and is waiting the arrival of a firm offering financial or commercial services. It dwarfs the tiny shops on the other side of the street which are retailing clothes, watches and electrical household goods. In some streets off Brick Lane, the hulks of substantial Georgian houses are being restored to their original condition and offer the convenience of a trouble-free walk to work in the City. They sell for prices which exceed the annual turnover of many of their neighbouring Asian businesses (Rhodes and Nabi (1992) p 333).

In terms of human geography it is ever the same: the wind blows to the east and carries pollution with it, the radius of affluence never flows outwards but causes the absence of affluence to situate as near to the centre of affluence as possible, railway stations serve to bring the service workers to the office but also attract the transient population, other centres of affluence lie on the green-belt margins of the City. The rest becomes the Inner City. As Soja has written, the development of urbanisation has been marked by a selective dispersal and decentralisation, emptying the centre of many of the activities and populations which once aggregated around it: a submergence of the power of central places (Soja (1989) p 234). But there are similarities between the City of London and the Inner City of the East End which remain unexplored.

Both cities have been subject to de-regulation. The City of Finance was de-regulated so as to encourage trade. The Inner City was de-regulated because it served no purpose. Local authorities, denied financial power because of government centralisation and the delegation of power to agencies, are left to negotiate the detritus. The occasional re-development programme served as a sop to the inhabitants but more often serves to further marginalise them as dwellings are converted into maximum security condominiums for the affluent. Conscious enclaves have developed which had previously only been loosely determined. Now Dalston belongs to West Indians, Brick Lane to Asians, Stoke Newington to Turks and so forth. Cultural, ethnic and religious enclaves have always existed within urban culture but have now become far more obvious in terms of the delimination of territory. And it is territory which is subject to forces of violent invasion and protection. The tension between enclaves is manifested not as an external resentment against the forces which have determined the erection of these barriers but as an internal friction between enclaves as dispossessed fights with dispossessed.

There is a tangible atmosphere of violence here. The violent symbolic laws of capital which now mark the trading floors of the City of Finance is mirrored in the hard edge of the actual violence which stalks the Inner City. The night is interrupted by the wail of the police siren. Drug and drink violence, the violence of breaking and entering, the violence of joyriding and ramraiding, gang violence, domestic violence and sexual abuse, racial violence: all this violence makes life in the Inner City a perpetual series of anxious backward glances and Chubb locks. It gives the Inner City an uncomfortable edge and the curious feeling of the solidarity of the fractured community, the community which has been forgotten and which has become the community of out-laws. Unlike the crimes of the City (including the tangential destruction of vast tracts of the immediate urban environment and the violent disruption of formerly stable communities) these are 'real' crimes, the domain of the criminologist and the sociologist of deviance, where the old assumptions about criminal behaviour still run and where only the solution has changed as the state withdraws and places barriers which declare 'NO GO': the ungovernable space of the wild zone.[12]

12 According to Hobbs the three East End boroughs of Hackney, Tower Hamlets and Newham had unemployment rates of over 50,000 with an aggregate registered unemployment rate of 25%. The highest unemployment rate of the outer London boroughs was in the outer East End in Barking and Dagenham where the figure was 11%. The knock-on effect in terms of health means that the East End has a figure for deaths from tuberculosis which is six times the national average. Over 16% of dwellings in Hackney and 12% in Tower Hamlets and Newham were classified as unfit for human habitation, and over 10% of East London's denizens were living in overcrowded conditions (Hobbs (1989) p 217).

More immediately (1994) on the Kingsmead Estate on Hackney Marshes, one in three people are unemployed; 60% claim benefit and 90% are in rent arrears. Hackney has 180 children on the 'at risk' register. The estate is where in 1985 a paedophile ring, led by tenants Leslie Bailey and Lennie Smith, murdered two children in a squalid flat in Ashmead House. Jason Swift, 14, and Barry Lewis, six,

The contradictions of the Inner City were symbolised in Rachel Whiteread's art-installation *House*. This 'monument' was created in 1992–93 and was simultaneously awarded the Turner Prize and the K Foundation Prize, the former a mark of excellence the latter a mark of derision. *House* was originally part of a terrace of houses on Grove Road, Tower Hamlets. As the terrace was systematically demolished to create a park, No 119 was left standing and the occupier forced out. In between the eviction and the final demolition, Rachel Whiteread was granted permission to create *House*. This took the form of a mould of the inside of the original structure. The resulting work was uncanny, an inversion of private space (Home) into public space (House) and a representation of a presence of an absence. In one sense *House* was a violent reminder of the shattering of memory, that *House* was Home, but simultaneously its presence as a ghost of a House disrupted that certainty of origin and belonging and imposed the impossibility of recovering memory, in that *House* represented the destruction of Home and therefore of memory. In terms of the politics of identity-community *House* became an important metaphor for the complexity of social relations in the contemporary. Simultaneously *House* became an important transitory element-event in the politics of locality in that its position within the shadow of Canary Wharf Tower and the NatWest Tower (symbols of panic money) represented the relationship between the local and the global. In addition the political dispute which *House* prompted in Tower Hamlets was framed in terms of appropriation by local political factions. *House* became a representation of what the East End of London had been in a mythological interpretation whilst simultaneously drawing attention to immediate problems of homelessness and urban degeneration, of justice in the community.

The dis-organisation of capital forces the replacement of socially structured space by unstructured space, the displacement of the 'live zone' by the 'dead zone', the 'wild zone' by the 'tame zone'. When socially structured space is not replaced by information and communication networks, the result is not individualisation but anomie and social disorganisation and retrenchment into neo-tribes. Areas where subsiding social structures are not yet adequately displaced by information and communication structures suffer a deficit of regulation and become deregulated and disordered.

The processes of reflexive accumulation which served to generate the individual as consuming subject (and therefore disrupted class patterns of social organisation) have also generated a 'two-thirds' society. This section of society represents a structural downward mobility into a restructured stratification ladder in which the hierarchy of capital is replaced by a three-tiered ordering of professional-managerial, an under-resourced working class and a new class of dispossessed and disenfranchised. This is a bleak dystopia of increasingly wild zones deserted by the mobile informational and communicational structures and by the mobile tourists who hurry past to progressively well-defended tame zones. In the terms used by Deleuze and Guattari this is the zone of nomadic governmentality, beyond the banal coercive rationality of hierarchical and external

12... were killed to mask appalling sexual abuse. It was also in one of the Kingsmead blocks, Malmsmead House, that 'devil-worshipper' Gerald Dowden, who regularly conducted black magic masses, battered his stepson, Daniel Vergauwen to death with a pool cue. In 1992 a gang of nine teenagers burgled their neighbour's homes 189 times and carried out 48 major crimes.

government and forming a linear and internal network of an alternative (forgotten) organisation of individual action. It is a potentially dangerous subterranean network, a margin where the power of images no longer runs (save as relayed impressions of chaos and examples of the success of surveillance strategies in containing the problem).

But the wild zone as ungovernable space is subject to its own material hierarchy which perversely reflects that of the formal system of contemporary capitalist relations, informed as it is by the sovereignty of enterprise and the supremacy of the violent laws of capital. This may be a twilight economy but it is nevertheless potent in its uneasy maintenance-subversion of the division between the legal and illegal; an economy of transgression. There are many layers to this economic framework. There are struggling families attempting to maintain the vestiges of 'civilisation' (satellite television and other electrical household goods) purchasing through a network of catalogues with extended periods of credit. There is extensive use of loan sharks and the purchase of stolen goods. Street markets still thrive and have extended their scope to include general domestic hardware in addition to the more traditional food items. Car boot sales boom every Sunday on disused factory land and the allotment is back in vogue.

A major feature in this fragile economic framework is the effect of enterprise ethos upon the material relations of East End culture. Certain enclaves (for example the Asian community) have always subscribed to a variation of the enterprise ethic. Other enclaves, particularly the 'wheeling and dealing, ducking and diving' community have also traditionally subscribed to a variation of 1980s enterprise. Petty entrepreneurship and negotiation of the division between the legal and the illegal have been investigated in the work of Dick Hobbs:

> Physically, culturally, and metaphorically the East End of London stands on the very periphery of British capitalism. Informed by historical precedent, East Enders exist on the brink of the City of London's legitimate commercial enterprise and legality. Bourgeoisie cultural hegemony may define, via the coercive force of the market-place, the parameters of the area but it rarely impinges upon the day-to-day dynamics of East End culture (Hobbs (1989) p 140).

In Hobbs' empirical study we encounter a gallery of grafters, jump-up merchants, skilled escapees who subscribe to a version of the enterprise ethic: 'whether this manifests itself in a commercial transaction or as an attitude or pose, a central dynamic of the culture is provided by the imagery of the entrepreneur' (Hobbs (1989) p 142). The City of Finance has the trading floor as its principal site of interaction, the Inner City has the bar. This may be a separate reality but it bears striking resemblance to the reality of the world beyond Middlesex Street.

There is a material hierarchy here despite (or because of) the absence of affluence. It is a fragile system but one in which there is 'no' excess. Whereas the financial system of contemporary capitalism deals exclusively in excess, the forgotten Inner City deals in hard edge commodities where even if the exchange is not for money there is at least some remaining value attached. What has occurred is a strengthening of this hard material edge. Partly due to the pressures forced upon it by the encroaching City of Finance and the destruction of communities, partly due to its neglect by central government this arena has had to resort to neo-tribalism for survival. Criminal activity has increased and negotiated policing strategies have been abandoned in favour of either coercive policing or the abandonment of policing. The disappearance of the community as defining the social structure (where, as a subculture, there was the generation of patterns of informal legitimating techniques which meshed with the formal system of state legitimation), has left a violent void of fear. The stable structures and codes of the cosmopolitan East End have broken down into more vicious forms determined by a marginalised economic existence: a transition from a culture of stability to a culture of instability consequent upon political imperative. The 'controlled' gang violence of the 1960s and the 1970s has declined in favour of new and more arbitrary forms of violence. Where gang rule provided a veneer of respectability in the distribution of the criminal activities of protection, gambling and vice (for example in the reign of gangs such as the Krays and the Richardsons) the dominant commodities are now drugs and guns implicating embryonic Jamaican Yardie and Asian Rajamuffin influence. The effect of an entrenched neo-liberal political regime has ensured that policing has been centralised and a policy of restricted response in certain designated areas prevails.[13]

In the course of this excursion I have drawn attention to the forces of capital within postmodernisation in terms of legitimation and the relationship of these forces to the complex fabric of power relations which characterises contemporary urban culture. The established assumptions of sociological and criminological science are no longer able to adequately provide coherent accounts of this complex of forces and fields, spaces and times. The point is that people do not live materially and then add culture; they live and have culture simultaneously. There is no material existence that is not accompanied by culture, by forms of interaction and structures of meaning. At the very moment of material survival representations are at work which are cultural representations, which constitute the field of the community involved in the production of materiality and the forces which are generated by it and therefore determine discipline and order. At the end of his study of penology, *Discipline and Punish* (1977b) Michel Foucault comments that what ultimately presides over all these disciplinary mechanisms is not the unitary functioning of an apparatus or an institution, but the necessity of combat and rules of strategy:

> That, consequently, the notions of institutions of repression, rejection, exclusion, marginalisation, are not adequate to describe, at the very centre of the carcereal city, the formation of the insidious leniencies, unavowable petty cruelties, small acts of cunning, calculated methods, techniques, 'sciences' that permit the fabrication of the disciplinary

13 There is an understated insidious relationship between 'alternative' and 'official' regimes of governmentality. To the extent that an area such as London's East End has been neglected and cordoned off there has been an implicit derogation of responsibility to alternative mechanisms of order and control through drug-trafficking syndicates. However, it is possible to identify 'official' discipline and surveillance mechanisms in operation in co-operation with drug-bound communities. Under the guise of health policy, the drug substitute methodone is now commonly prescribed as an element of a drug reducement policy. Methodone ('Nazi Juice' as it is colloquially known) replaces the need for street drugs and is intended to act as a method of reducing addiction. However, the politics of methodone programmes suggests an alternative form of social control in that its controlled distribution through state agencies (clinics and health centres) which serves to reduce the possibility of 'anti-social' behaviour through the removal of the need for reliance upon the recourse to criminal activity regarding drug culture.

> individual. In this central and centralised humanity, the effect and instrument of complex power relations, bodies and forces subjected by multiple mechanisms of 'incarceration', objects for discourses that are themselves elements for this strategy, we must hear the distant roar of battle (Foucault (1977b) p 308).

To hear the distant roar of battle. The task is to glimpse sight of the heterotopia between the detritus of the carcereal archipelago of the punitive city where we are subject(ed) to the force of the symbolic laws of capital as either the possessed or the dispossessed. In Part II I signal the potential of a hyper-regulated society to be transformed into a post-regulatory society. In one sense proactive 'regulation' is no longer required (following Baudrillard) because computerisation and administrative rationalisation begins to make possible for the first time a 'real' governmentality of population; we are simply no longer able to realise the nature of discipline and surveillance, the choice to deviate having been removed in the supremacy of the violent banality of satiation of desire through external validating regimes without reference to value. Government in this mode is able to appropriate forms of expertise and assessment and become a purely pragmatic bureaucratic and managerial source of post-legality and legitimation. It becomes capable to identify all those who manifest some combination of specified factors which demonstrate that they are a risk to themselves. Marginality in this mode instead of remaining a dangerous 'wild zone' can become a colonised zone within the social, toward which those individuals will be directed who are deemed incapable of following hyper-relational and competitive pathways. The priority for this neo-liberal/postmodern governmentality becomes not to annul, but rather to dissipate and disperse into organised (legitimated) 'wild zones' (see further Castel (1991)).

But like all important transformations there is a process of rupture and discontinuity. Excessive regulation and order may result in implosion and unexpected deregulation and disorder, dangerousness and risk. Dominating hierarchical networks may spawn subordinate linear networks and alternative rhizomic patterns of governmentality in both culture and materiality. The contemporary neo-liberal ideologies of postmodernisation are overarched by a grandiose technocratic rationalising dream of symbolic and absolute control. It is a desire to control the accidental and the unpredictable: that upon which the desire of the norm attains self-realisation. The randomness of individual desire, that which for a moment escapes the banality of external excess, which is irrational, 'dangerous' and 'affirmative' becomes the source of undetermined resistance and refusal precisely because these desires are refused. The individual as subject no longer finds reflection in the post-regulatory order of external power relations in the construction of an asocial sociality conforming to a managerial rationality which enables the deterritorialisation and utilisation of spaces of refusal, the actuality of the wild-zone of the without-law. As Ryan has noted this is the possibility of an 'alternative group life, one in which work is no longer the paradigmatic narrative of social life, in which the capacity to script alternative life stories becomes a privileged goal rather than a marginal, merely, cultural event' (Ryan (1989) pp 23). Part II of this book interrogates this possibility in terms of excess and absence of affluence; it draws out of the patterns of repression which have been described the potential of patterns of resistance in the space of the without-law.

CHAPTER FIVE

DEREGULATION AND URBAN EXCESS: THE LAWS OF DESIRE

> In defiance of etymology, one needs to understand 'exceed' here in terms of the following three Latin verbs taken together: *ex-cedere*, to pass beyond, to go out; *ex-cidere* (from *cedere*), to fall outside of, to be dispossessed from; *ex-cidere* (from *caedere*), to detach by cutting, to excise (Lyotard (1990) p 17).
>
> The task of extremist writing is to put through the call for a justice of the future. Henceforth, Justice can no longer permit itself to be merely backward looking or bound in servility to sclerotic models and their modifications (their 'future'). A justice of the future would have to show the 'will to rupture' (Ronnell (1992) p 21).

Excess, Critique and the Limit: Introduction

The desire to evade and contest regimes of power has led to the invocation of other spaces and places both real and imagined. Within the city a significant counter-site is the wild zone as heterotopia. The wild zone is the other side of the external ordering of spaces and places. The wild zone is a field of disorder and ungovernability and signifies the arena of the without-law(s). This arena consists of a dangerous topography that does not offer itself conveniently to the disciplinary maps and surveillance nodes of the city as an extension of the *polis* and *civitas*. The spaces and places constituting the wild zone are not beyond but within and between the sources and sites of legitimating power relations and colonising forces of the city. These are spaces and places existent within the disciplinary networks of the urban and can be provisionally identified as subordinate networks. Subordination here should be understood as linear and heterogeneous as opposed to hierarchical and homogeneous. An important aspect of the wild zone is that it is arena separate from the hegemonic contest which orders the activity of the city. The wild zone as an interstitial space or place is not identified through reference to other ordered spaces and places but rather avoids direct identification in preference to its existence as a partial sighting. It is a contingent site of occupation and colonisation which evades the objective processes of ordered territorialisation. Territorialisation as a strategy in the expression of power relations can be analysed in terms of excess and nomination. This preliminary discussion enables further clarification regarding the political and ethical significance of the wild zone and introduces the central theme of this intervention: the possibility of a collective expression of desire without Law:

- The operation of power relations as an expression of legitimation, regulation and governmentality produces the effects of both order and disorder. The dominant arena in which these power relations are organised is the city. The city has become an arena of total discipline achieved through surveillance and results in the colonisation of all that constitutes risk and danger. But this process of colonisation simultaneously produces effects of disorder. An order of governmentality which has been achieved through legitimatory and regulatory strategies premised upon the political imperative of deregulation serves to determine the expression of individual desire and simultaneously locates responsibility for legitimation upon individuals. This process of delegation involves inadvertent effects as a result of the production of counter-forces in the organisation and distribution of power relations. The hyper-inflationary condition of repressive regulatory strategies in the city ensures both internal conflicts between dominant cultural-economic producers and the possibility that through the continual process of rupture unpredictable and random flows of cultural-economic power are produced. Alternative networks evolve along the margins and in the interstitial spaces between dominant orderings. These networks are disordered and are sites in an alternative production of legitimation.

- To nominate these alternative spaces and places is dangerous. A strategy utilising an expression of political or ethical opposition must not offer itself to colonisation. These spaces and places must remain unrepresentable if they are sites in the expression of counter-forces. The representation of power determines its force. Consequently that which cannot be represented, which is unrepresentable or denies representation is effective similarly as a force. The strategic interest of dominant groupings in the city is the colonisation of danger and risk through spatial organisation. A mechanism for attaining this aim is the organisation of unpredictable forces through nomination and representation. That which is constituted as decolonised attains political and ethical significance granted its spatial indeterminacy and transitory situation. These are spaces and places which do not coalesce into fixed spatial zones or fields.
- Finally there is a question of what is occurring within these spaces and places. In one sense the siting-sighting of them is not as important when compared to their construction as arenas of possibility. They are spaces and places in the expression of becoming and belonging in the sense of representing the movement of phantasy and desire in being other to law. They are spaces and places of those narratives which represent other histories and arenas which represent other geographies. They are sites and sources of counter-power in terms of a collectivity premised upon the de-determination and the politicisation of individual desire. They serve as arenas of discourse in the articulation of a resistance to the external and the dominant. These are the spaces and places where aesthetics and ethics merge and where there are no defined boundaries and constant ruptures in terms of value. They are spaces and places where individual bodies and groups of bodies, actions and inactions, become manifestations of alternative knowledge and experiences and where critique in the sense of becoming ungoverned is articulated as a challenge to the negative constraints of freedom in a reading of liberalism. They are the spaces where the paradox between Nietzsche's 'will to power' and Kant's 'freedom' are melded in alternative patterns of obligation.

Is it possible to achieve a sympathetic account of the wild zone which does not immediately invest in a process of repressive territorialisation and colonisation? It may be possible to invoke the discursive vocabularies of the wild zone through an interrogation of the excesses which constitute it. Excess can be equated with a condition of satiation and a situation which is beyond and outside of. These other spaces and places are the arenas of the dispossessed as opposed to the possessed and of the refuse and the refused. This interpretation does not construct these spaces and places negatively as arenas of emptiness or vacuity. Refuse in this interpretation is an affirmative condition. To state that a limit has been reached implies that there is arrival at a final point and that there is no where else to go. The limit can be the end-point and also the point which deliminates fixed space-place and determines the terrain behind it. But the limit can also operate as the boundary or border between spaces and places: following Heidegger a border is not where something stops but from where something commences its presencing; it is an affirmative topographical or metaphorical condition (quoted by Hebdige (1988) p 228). From the border as the mark of the limit of the territory there is the possibility of seeing or entering that which is other to the territory. However, here there is partial investment in determination: that there is an other which can become subsumed by that which is not other. At which point the relationship between the limit and excess assumes significance. For in the city of excess there is No Limit. With the shattering of Limits the organised production of reality collapses:

> Metropolises are no longer real 'places', because their dimensions exceed by far the dimensions of the perceptive apparatus of their inhabitants. The widest sensory aperture, that of sight, is shattered. It was the visual field, in some respect, which defined the city dimensionally: in the metropolis there is no longer pan-orama (the vision of all) because its body overflows beyond the horizon. In the metropolitan aesthetic the eye fails in its role as an instrument of total control at a distance (Mazzoleni (1993) p 297).

The expression of a geo-political struggle is no longer the struggle over rights in emerging territory. Processes of sectorisation and colonisation reflecting the division of the city between competing and coalescing dominating groups, technologies and rationalities in the determination of spatial and temporal relations enables interstitial spaces-places between and within the ordered zones of the city to emerge. The continuity of order through colonisation assumes a rupture of colonisation through disorder. The limit in this process of ruptured colonisation is the point of the crack, the point of fragmentation, fracture and discontinuity. There is no longer the utopian desire for uncolonised space-place (space-place that is other to the limit and *ou-topic*); rather there is the heterotopian desire for decolonised space-place (space that is of the otherness to the existence of the limit). This process involves the investigation of the potential of the tame zone to be transformed from its status as that of governed, regulated and ordered to the wild zone of the ungoverned, deregulated and disordered.

In establishing a non-territorialistic siting-sighting of the space-place of the ungoverned within the wild zone as an interstitial network, the points (spatial) and moments (temporal) of identification enable the possibility of signifying a presence within the disciplinary order. It is a presence of identity enabled through intersubjectivity. Fragmentary philosophical and psychoanalytic commentary suggests a project of opposition to the political and philosophical certainties which have determined both cultural and individual identity as that conforming to a symbolic and external order. (Encompassed in the question: Who comes after the Subject?)[1]

I suggest four related strategies which represent possible points of intervention in a statement of an ethical and political discourse which enables the collective expression of desire without law. The four strategies consist of a politic-poetics of the unrepresentable, the production of the body-without-organs, transgression as affirmation, and the flight of the Phantasm. It is in the Phantasm that we find the three earlier strategies coalescing into a figure of political and ethical possibility. The four strategies are related in that they endorse a general strategy of ungovernability within a political economy of abundance and therefore suggest a possible utilisation of certain excessive tendencies within the city consequent upon the inadvertent effects of the political imperative of deregulation and the triumph of technology. As opposed to identifying the affirming opportunities of the wild zone or heterotopia the statement of four potential strategies of interruption enables a process of grappling with a political and ethical discourse of difference premised upon an economy of desire.

1 The Politic-Poetics of the Unrepresentable

The politics of the contemporary is a politics of representation. The cold pessimism of Baudrillard (1993a) has to be confronted in this inevitability. The 'endless replication of signs, images and simulations' and the attendant accession of a cybernetic visual culture (Featherstone (1991) p 15) apparently eradicates desire and difference. This closed structure directs an order of appearance in which simulation becomes the dominant organising principle of contemporary existence (ontology replaced by hyper-ontology). The simulatory explosion within contemporary culture has fashioned an existence seemingly dependent on the infinite production (inflation) and proliferation of signs. This regime of signification implies a transition in value from use value to sign value. The use and exchange value of a commodity becomes nothing more than an alibi of its sign's value. The hyper-reality of a commodity-sign culture presents a vast synthesis of fictions and realities into which modernist reference points collapse and we are confronted with the ultimate exhaustion of meaning. Baudrillard (1990) suggests that rather than increased understanding, this implosion of meaning within the

1 In adopting the elements of representation, the body, the affirmation of transgression and the relationship between law and desire I follow Foucault's idea of technologies, each a matrix of practical reason. Foucault expressly sets out the relations between macro and micro power, which I have utilised as those relations between order and disorder, regulation and deregulation, in law and without law:

(1) Technologies of production, which permit us to produce, transform or manipulate things; (2) technologies of sign systems, which permit us to use signs, meanings, symbols or signification; (3) technologies of power, which determine the conduct of individuals and submit them to certain ends of domination, an objectivising of the subject; (4) technologies of self, which permit individuals to effect by their own means or with the help of others a certain number of operations on their own bodies and souls, thoughts and conduct, and ways of being, so as to transform themselves in order to attain a certain state of happiness, purity, perfection of immortality (Foucault (1988) p 18).

contemporary mediascape has resulted in the cold seduction of the masses in which information is entertainment as opposed to political or cultural education.

The proliferation of systems of hyper-real commodity-signs within the contemporary mediascape 'seduces' the masses through an inversion of the relative importance of discursive codes and affective investments. In terms of the regime of signification the non-discursive articulation of a commodity-sign has triumphed over its discursive identity. This implosion has been characterised by Chen (1991) as the de-rationalisation of ideology and an accompanying de-irrationalisation of emotion. It results in a commodity-sign culture which historicises inner mechanisms and articulates conjectural inflections in an affective economy. The affective realm constitutes an economy of different forms of emotional responses and involvement. Affect is the energy invested in particular cultural practices and emotions are the specific forms that this affective investment assumes. The implosion of ideology and affect within the multiple circuitry of the mass media creates a network of hyper-real cultural practices and identities which mobilise affect, and results in the increased encroachment of the mediascape into the experiences of the everyday. Affect has a power over difference, a power to invest in difference and make specific differences of value in particular ways. The structure of ideology is unrealisable without its inflection through an affective economy, for it is affect which enables particular differences to matter.

It is the sign which determines the structure of particular realities. It is the sign which has become the source of culture rather than an effect of culture. The issue in terms of politics becomes the exploitation of this explosion and invasion of signs. The explosion is simultaneously an implosion for no particular sign can maintain its effect as a determining sign. This explosion-implosion of signs enables a reinvestiture of value into the spaces and places which have been vacated or de-signified. The nature of representation within this schema of politics becomes part of the agenda of an emancipatory semiotics or cultural de-doxification. It is a politics which exposes the structure of how we represent ourselves to ourselves. It attests to the possibility of the recognition of a polyphony of voices in the assertion of the value of identity in the reality of the particular as opposed to the universal. It is a question finally of value invested through the inversion of the assumptions of the regime of signification.[2]

This project is achieved through a poetic investiture in the political act of representation, a deployment which neutralises the ideological element of the sign and reveals the diverse expressions of contemporary sociality. Maffesoli has called this an aesthetic paradigm operating in opposition to the political paradigm. Maffesoli associates

---

2 As Goodrich makes clear in his 'Introduction' to *The Languages of Law: From Logics of Memory to Nomadic Masks*:

> The law of the image, where the sign plays the law, where the sign organises the very content of daily life – that I suspect is the future of law. Government in such a context, in such a culture, is a matter of moving the signs, of controlling the avenues of circulation of images, of intercepting the hallucinated messages of the microchip age. Its law is the law of the image, the law of the sign. It is a moveable law, a collapsible structure, its hermeneutic that of simple survival. In the place of the logics of memory we now find, we now glimpse, the intimations of another law, a pragmatically nomadic law that fixes itself to the momentary apparitions of the various screens, the televisual apparatuses of post-contractarian communication (Goodrich (1990) p 11).

the aesthetic paradigm with an 'ethical immoralism', which is 'the carrier of a morality that is created collectively and not imposed in an overwhelming manner' (Maffesoli (1986). *Aisthesis* operates on 'shared experience' and 'favours interaction'. The micro-processes of association and dissociation generate their own ethics apart from the imperatives of the rationalising and totalising sign-state: 'One enters the aesthetic order which pre-empts the logic of morals or the politics of the "must-be"' (Maffesoli (1992) p 251). 'On the one side the accent is placed on the monad and its counterpart the rational association, and on the other it is placed more on the group and its "affective cement"' (Weinstein and Weinstein (1993) p 18). Maffesoli's sociology of the social imaginary is an attack through the 'immorality' of aesthetics upon the 'rationality' of external sign-systems. The central tactic of this affective project is the intervention-interruption of the process of the transmission of the hierarchical network of signs of legitimation. To recognise the nature of the representation, if only for a moment, is to interpret the form of its reproduction. This is a utilisation of the alternative break-flows of power in the circuitry of signification, in this instance the crisis of nomination. The vacancy created through this crisis can then be occupied with that which has escaped nomination and which is therefore unrepresentable.

Maffesoli's attack upon the regime of signification through the assertion of an investiture in the social imaginary has a possible spatial dimension analogous to Foucault's concept of heterotopia (1986). Maffesoli's conceptualisation of contemporary culture is characterised by a continuous series of transitions occurring along fluctuating and short-lived networks of affinity, interests and neighbourhoods between which subjects are continuously shifting. Maffesoli's image of the city privileges the local of multiplicity as opposed to the global of universalism. It is a city which denies totalisation from a central point and privileges the investment made by those elements which are excluded from or deny signification:

> Within it, the individual is no longer seen as isolated monad according to a dichotomy of subjects and objects, but as part and parcel of an emotional geography of sites and places, all of which participate in the investment of effect which characterises sacred sites. These are no longer strictly religious, however, but 'high-places' of local and splintered devotions and interests (Shields (1991) p 4).

Lyotard's clarion call at the end of *The Postmodern Condition* included an ethical demand that we become witnesses to the unrepresentable:

> The postmodern would be that which, in the modern, puts forward the unrepresentable in presentation itself; that which denies itself the solace of good forms, the consensus of a taste which would make it possible to share collectively the nostalgia for the unattainable; that which searches for new presentations, not in order to enjoy them but in order to impart a stronger sense of the unrepresentable (Lyotard (1984) pp 81-82).

Becoming a witness to the unrepresentable is an expression of critique and therefore an element in the paradoxical identification of the ungovernable which in turn is an element in the establishment of a space (both of the spatial and of discourse) of and for a justice of or as resistance. In *The Differend* (1988) Lyotard's justice of the unrepresentable is established at the points in a framework at which 'political' representation performs a victimisation. The task of witnessing requires a series of parological experiments which displace the governing frame of representation and seeks to 'perform' justice as opposed to merely representing an appearance of justice which is an injustice (Lyotard (1988) p 5).

Maffesoli's identification of an alternative network of value situated within a social imaginary premised upon a series of interruptions or interventions in the fabric of the regime of signification can be related to Lyotard's institutionalisation of the context of language. Lyotard identifies the force of a statement as its institutional context not its psychological correlate. It is the institutional position in which a statement is uttered which is important. The institutional position of the statement regulates its circulation. The unutterable or the unintelligible is that which cannot be represented or exceeds the institutional constraints of representation and becomes the unrepresentable and corresponds with Maffesoli's ethic of immorality. Lyotard's aversion to the violence of the metanarrative and his affirmation of the paganism of the multiplicity of discourses or incommensurability of language games accords with a multiplicity within the statement of justice. Immorality and injustice identified as processes of violence become important markers in the affirmation of resistance to the morality and justice of the banal. The *aporia* of justice would be the act of being a witness to the unrepresentable. It would be an act of affirmation in a political strategy of resistance and an act of activating differences through the incommensurability of language games:

> To regulate the political by reference to a justice of multiplicity would be to open up the closed categories of thought that govern social and political life to the 'violence' of endless experimentation, and in this way to make possible the expression of injustices which are otherwise borne in silence (Barron (1992) p 34).

Maffesoli and Lyotard would dispute Baudrillard's assertion that subjectivity corresponds with subjection and that resistance can only be activated through hyper-conformity. Baudrillard suggests that the effects of anomie and alienation have evaporated because of the erosion of the political and the ascendancy of the transpolitical in a culture of consumption. The eradication of difference destroys justice. All that remains is the trace of the other in the form of an 'anomaly' which is an unconvincing substitute for a justice of multiplicity because it signifies only a memory of something other and not the possibility of something other. Lyotard refuses both the idea of a system and the possibility of a 'winning strategy'. For Lyotard, power relations are multiple and unstable, order and discipline contingent and fragile (Lyotard follows Foucault's analytic of power relations (Foucault (1983) pp 224-226)). Lyotard utilises that which is available but, unlike Baudrillard, does not rely on the excess generated by the system but on an 'alternative' configuration of a counter-excess. The point has been made by Barron:

> However, the nature of the counter-move is always indeterminate. Situated as we are at the 'nodal points' of many communications circuits we are bombarded and displaced by many conflicting messages, and it is precisely this positioning within a fragmented universe that enables a whole field of possible responses, inventions and new combinations of phrases to open up (Barron (1992) p 39).

That which is unrepresentable becomes a point of disturbance in the sense of enabling discourses which transgress established boundaries. The space-place of these discourses of the unrepresentable is the heterotopia. The heterotopia is a space-place where otherness disturbs speech and dissolves myths. In this space-place limits are shattered and language is brought to the threshold of impossibility. In terms of the present analysis (the relationship between the unrepresentable, the body, transgression and the Phantasm) the issue is the relationship between a dominant legitimating narrative form and particular or potential categories of the unrepresentable. This relationship is developed in terms of an analysis of the tension between the colonising function of the law of the sign and the process of decolonisation achieved through the emergence of an absent sign which signifies excess and the possibility of multiplicity. It is a tension operative in the following way.

At the moment a particular event of excess becomes subject to nomination there appears a fracture or division in the legitimating mechanism of the regime of signification. At the moment of nomination a process of closure occurs. The event of excess escapes nomination because there is no possibility of translating its discourse into a common tertium, there is no category available because the event is unrepresentable and in excess of nomination. The event assumes significance as a moment of intersubjectivity or unrepresentability within a schema of representation not as a subject of representation but rather as a category within a schema of representation which is beyond representation. It is therefore a moment of justice in a violent politic-poetic of resistance.

2 Disciplined Body to Body-Without-Organs

A central location in a politics of representation is the body. Within the context of the present analysis the concern is with the relationship between the notion of the represented and unrepresented body, the body as a site of transgression and affirmation and as a locus of power in the manifestation of the Phantasm. The question of the body in this analysis is addressed in different modes, allowing for a broad semantic range for 'body' – biological entity, psycho-sexual construction, cultural product.

The significance of the body in terms of representation can be stated with reference to Barthes. Toward the end of his study of narrative, *S/Z*, Barthes enigmatically claims that the 'symbolic field' is occupied by a sole object, from which it derives its unity 'This object is the human body' (Barthes (1974) p 220). This is a claim that the body is the referent of reference itself, the object for which reference, as a notion or an activity, exists. The body is the ultimate field from which all symbolism derives and to which it returns. This is the body as the primary source of symbolism-representation. Brooks states the point thus:

> Our bodies are with us, though we have trouble saying exactly how. We are, in various conceptions or metaphors, in our body, or at one with our body, or alienated from it. The body is both ourselves and other, and as such the object of emotions from love to disgust. Most of the time, the body maintains an unstable position between such extremes, at once the subject and object of pleasure, the uncontrollable agent of pain and the revolt against reason. As such, it is always the subject of curiosity, of an ever renewed project of knowing (Brooks (1993) p 1).

- The first body is the physical body. It is the body of flesh, blood, sweat, tears, faeces, decay from birth to the dust of death: the mortal body. It is a body which exists only for a moment in time and space. It is a cage and a vessel for the expression and articulation of the physical manifestations of thought and emotion. It is the body of joy and laughter, grief and despair. Its humours give up their juices into elemental fragments which once determined character. Its palm can be read, its scalp interpreted. It is a body entwined with another body in love and hatred and production. It is both a parchment and a script upon which can be written pain and pleasure. It is the root-route of an idea of self/selves/slaves. It is simultaneously a point of origin and a point in the erasure of origin. It is a reference point and a marker of orientation, an inhabited space in the world of other bodies and therefore a body which conveys obligations and responsibilities (togetherness). It is a mutable body both as a subject and a sphere of subjection to the power of others. But it is also an autonomous sphere, mutable only to the will of the self, enabled so as to modify its form, to adapt its appearance and to be a vehicle of excess and a reference point of a limit. It is alienable and detached from the world and as a world of itself and for itself (apartness). But it is also the socio-cultural body, a construct and ideological product which represents precultural and prelinguistic phenomena: sensations of pain and pleasure constituted outside language (of the presemiotic chora). The body which ends in death is not simply a discursive construct. This is the body presented as a fall from language and therefore the assertion of a presymbolic space in which a 'primal' desire reasserts its force. There is a political-ethical tension and ambivalence between docile-governable bodies (within-law) and ecstatic-ungovernable bodies (without-law). The ghost of Rousseau appears as the first to recognise the body as a problem in the determination of the life story, and sets himself the task of giving a narrative account of that problem: how the private realm of the body becomes the object of the public realm of the body politic.[3]
- The second body is the 'body politic'. This body is a strange fiction crystallised in modernity complete with personality, the presence of an absence figure which bonds society through guilt. A mystical body echoing the sovereignty of a divine right and encompassing a social memory of obligation and responsibility. The authority of the body politic resides in its nature as an absence. There is no presence (no face) and no origin. The memory it recalls and reproduces in its iconography

3 Rousseau's body remains a problem as Goodrich playfully recognises in his *Conclusion* (Goodrich (1990) p 323) which I discussed in the Introduction. Rousseau's body is represented in the installation created by David Walliker and depicts the significance of the body as absence and presence (in addition to representing the symbolism of the failure of delivery – the breach of *the* contract):

> Rousseau, the author of the contract, has died. An admirer, a private citizen, builds a park outside Paris to house Rousseau's tomb on an island in an artificial lake. The tomb will memorise the author of the social contract as a hero of the People, as the author of the first modernist contract, a consensual and democratic agreement between equals or, in legal terms, a considered and wholly fictive bilateral deed. Later the state comes to recognise Rousseau, both as hero and as threat, and his body is removed from the tomb and taken to the Pantheon in Paris: the state appropriates the contract and symbolically removes the body, the text, from the periphery to the centre, from the private domain to that of law (Goodrich (1990) p 319).

represents the desire to be bonded and is achieved through the image of an orginating violent sacrifice of authority which creates a collective guilt of a sociality premised upon tutelage. Community is forged via a collective memory of an apparent origin and original body. Goodrich notes:

> Such is the power of sacrificial memory that we can further and briefly redefine the presence that such memory invokes as being more than simple presence; it is, indeed, the presence of the immemorial, of the beginning, an orginary presence which is of crucial importance because what it signifies is the continuity of the origin ... Presence is not what is before our eyes, it is not what is directly experienced; presence is indexical, it is *prae-sens*, in advance of the senses, in excess of the immediate, imminent, the bearer of a history, a predefined alchemical being' (Goodrich (1990) p 61).

The body politic re-presents the immemorial and the continuous through the repetition of its image as apparition. The process of repetition is demonstrated through the continuous violent judgment forced upon the subject. The force of Law is a mystical foundation of authority replicated in a constant failure to expunge the guilt of the founding sin of the community ('The body as a surface of writing demands the cruelty of a corporeal wounding without which there would be no codes, no culture, and no memory' (Wyschogrod (1990) p 204)). At the site of the absent body there is the presence of the body politic, a presence recorded through the inscription of its being upon the body of the individual in the form of laws. The body becomes a parchment upon which juridical authority as the incarnation of the body politic inscribes its authority. The material support for the relations of power and knowledge in society is the body politic. The political anatomy of society is the political economy of the body. Both images involve a set of correspondences and transferences that define strategies by which power works. The body politic is:

> [A] set of material elements and techniques that serve as weapons, relays, communications routes, and supports for the power and knowledge relations that invest human bodies and subjugate them by turning them into objects of knowledge (Foucault (1977b) p 28).

> All the stupidity and the arbitrariness of the laws, all the pain of the institutions, the whole perverse apparatus of repression and education, the red hot irons, and the atrocious procedures have only this meaning: to breed man, to mark him in his flesh, to render him capable of alliance (Deleuze and Guattari (1977) p 190).

The power of the mark inscribed by the body politic is now only a trace of a violence that was performed through physical torture. This violence is now performed in two ways. First, through a suspended inevitability in the form of a threat. Second, through the technologies of the microphysics of power and the insidious government of surveillance and movement. The voice of the Law says 'Give me your body and I will give you meaning; I will make you a name and a word in my discourse'. The contract is in the form of an exchange of private desire for public desire. As Deleuze and Guattari note *socius* need not inscribe its Law literally upon the body since the person has become private in reality, subject to the violent banality of cynicism and piety.

But when the metanarrative coherence of the body politic is subject to re-interpretation, interrogation and interruption, the discourse of order assumes a fragility previously lacking in its construction. The fragmentation of the universal decisively marks the body. By accepting historical and cultural differentiation it is no longer possible to think of the body as a passive ground or constant of subsequent social activity. The assumed referent of the body has become a flexible zone, interleaved, crossed and composed of multiple discourses, constructed in different languages, tempos and places, received and lived with disparate meanings that are diversely em-bodied. But the body politic does not disappear or vacate its absent presence swiftly. It maintains its authority through transmuting itself into more insidious and indirect forms in a hidden series of obligations and violences. A tension exists which is ever on the threshold of an awakened contingency of the body.[4] The body politic becomes a dangerous and sclerotic body; a fragmented body where the synapses no longer connect as swiftly as they once did and where its cancerous decay seeps outwards and infects the parts of the whole in ever more diverse hierarchical networks or semblances of order.

- The third body is the contingent body-without-organs: the space of a body sited in the interstice, the transverse and the linear. In Foucauldian terms this body is that which cannot (will not) be allotted a space within the grid. This body presents itself as the gravest challenge to the body politic. The body-without-organs is the paradoxical absent embodiment of the materiality and physicality of the Phantasm of desire. The body-without-organs is the nomad body, the existence of which signifies an alternative governmentality. As a site of the Phantasm the body-without-organs becomes an assemblage of experiences, emotions and bodies on the edge of transformation.

The space of the body-without-organs is the contingent and multiple space of a rupture which becomes the space of the with-out law. Following Deleuze and Guattari, the body-without-organs is a manifestation of desire operating as a locus of connection for all the machines of desire:

> Non-hierarchical, horizontal multiplicities which cannot be subsumed within a unified structure (and) whose components form random, unregulated networks in which any element may be connected with any other element (Bogue 1989) p n 13, 107).

The body-without-organs is an entity of desiring machines and involves heterogeneous independent parts which work 'only when they break down, and by continually breaking down' (Deleuze and Guattari (1977) p 8). The body-without-organs is 'the field of immanence and desire, the plane of consistency proper to desire' on which flow 'pure intensities, free, prephysical and prevital singularities' (Deleuze and Guattari (1984) pp 191, 58). It is the source of the nomadic subject and that point of pure intensity traversing the grid of the body-without-organs

4 Foucault notes that in the contemporary order the human body enters a spatial machinery of power that explores it, breaks it down, and rearranges it allocating to each person a place, and to each place a person. In this 'grid' each position is coded as a value so that distribution of functions is transposed into relations fixed in this structured grid. The success of this arrangement depends on the coding of this space (Foucault (1979b) pp 137-138, 143).

which is a mobile *locus* of becoming which commingles identities as it migrates from desiring-machine to desiring-machine (Bogue (1989) pp n.13, 95): the nomadic subject that traces an alternative ontology of becoming-being. The figures of the body-without-organs and the desiring machine as described in the work of Deleuze and Guattari provide alternative configurations in the relations of power and in the articulation of the laws of desire:

> Deleuze reminds us that the Greek *nomos*, law may be traced to 'division' or 'sharing', and he describes this kind of distribution – the establishment of a realm of strict boundaries and limits – as 'the sedentary structures of representation'. It is overshadowed by Being in the transcendental or ontological meaning which divides in an hierarchical and nomadic way, a wandering with no fixed boundaries, a power which surpasses limits. The equalities of the first hierarchy are suspended unequally within the second which is univocal only in this ontological boundlessness or 'unmeasure' – everything is equally subjected to this inequality: 'Univocal being' is at the same time nomadic distribution, and crowned anarchy (Rose (1984) pp 104-105).

The importance of division and border can be explained in terms of the deconstruction of the normative order through the relationship between the monad and the nomad. This necessary violent relation corresponds to the relationship between law and transgression. Granted the immediacy of this relation (in the spatial terms of inside and outside) there is a tension between stability and instability which can be expressed in two oppositions: absence and presence, force and counter-force. Deleuze and Guattari recognise power as strategy not privilege and that the body as capital is the primary site in the exercise of this strategy in the subversion of the existent order.

In configuring the body in this technological frame, Deleuze and Guattari utilise desire as a force or power in a political-economic discourse as opposed to a psychological-philosophical discourse. This process activates possibilities beyond metaphysical confines in terms of a political radicalisation of psychology and philosophy. The relationship between the desiring-machines and the body-without-organs becomes a relationship of interruption and possibility in the alternative configuration of the body (of self and the politic) and the machine (of the mode of production). The body-without-organs can be defined as an entity manufactured through desiring practices. It is not a fundament that can be reached but a limit that is always ultimately in the process of being attained and a material version of Kant's regulative ideal (Deleuze and Guattari (1977) pp 149-150). The inversion or destratification of the machinic order becomes the strategy of affirmative schizo-revolutionary events, affording potential movements of deterritorialisation and lines of flight toward the manifestation of the desiring-machines/body-without-organs. These events occur within and through the regulatory-repressive structures and orders of the city as constant random movements which might be translated as affirmative transgressive tactics in the emancipation of a non-repressive social desire (see Wyschogrod (1990) p 204).

3 Transgression as Affirmation

'The Law is our symptom. The symptom is our Law' This sad correlation appears to negate the possibility of emancipation from repression, for law is what we desire. 'That the feeling of guilt precedes the Law, and that the latter is presented appears phenomalized only in its own transgression: without ever presenting itself' (Borsch-Jacobsen (1985) p 36). In this sense guilt is the announcement of the gift of the Law. This would appear to be the psychoanalytic impasse which blocks – through lack – the possibility of transgression as a positive psycho-political or schizo-revolutionary strategy. It is an impasse which is violent in three senses. First, in premising social obligation upon a negation. Second, because it is a command which cannot command respect because law subjects ethics and logics by escaping them and it escapes them by compelling them. Third, in the banal violence of being the subject of absence.

It is important to consider strategies of transgression as a series of affirmations. Otherwise the moment of transgression merely becomes a further moment in the extension of the gaze of the Law. Each transgression determines that which it is not and serves to create further boundaries and borders of discipline. The moment of transgression defines a territory to be colonised or negatively marginalised. A strategy which utilises transgression must be conceived as a relation of affirmation. This is meant both in the sense of acts and moments of transgression and in the transgression of knowledge and meaning. The act or moment can exist without conscious understanding of its transgressive force and enable itself to be an element in a structure of knowledge which is transgressive. The act or the moment of transgression must be random and destratified otherwise it affords itself only as a negative moment in the construction of repression. A knowledge which is transgressed must be de-ontological in the sense of ignoring the boundaries and limits of established paradigms of thinking and become a continual interrogation and interruption of established values.

The problematic relationship between law and transgression has been discussed by Mark C Taylor in his essay *Desire of Law Law of Desire* (1990). Taylor posits a series of rhetorical questions in response to Fish's essay *The Law Wishes To Have A Formal Existence* (1991) to illustrate the nature of the relationship between law and transgression:

> 'The law wishes ...' What is the law that wishes? How can the law wish? What does (the) law want? What is the want of (the) law? What does (the) law desire? What is the law of desire? ...
>
> In wishing to have a formal existence, Fish has argued, the law wishes its own autonomy ... it wishes to be only itself. This wish, however, is impossible. By wishing to be itself, the law is found wanting. To desire is to want and to want is to lack. The desire for autonomy, therefore, testifies to its lack. Never able to be only itself, the law is forever wanting. The lack of the law is the opening of transgression. Transgression, which in one sense is what the law does not want, is also precisely what the law desires.
>
> To interpret transgression as the desire of law is to refigure the relationship between law and desire. Law and desire appear to stand in an antithetical and dialectical relationship to each other. Law struggles to control, direct, or repress desire, and desire attempts to express itself by eluding the strategies of lawful control. This antagonistic relationship between law and desire is, in effect, a play of forces (Taylor (1990) p 1269).

In spatial terms there are insides and outsides: within-law and without-law. Fish has argued that the determination of what is 'inside' will always be a function of whatever 'outside' has been assumed. If what is 'inside' is a function of what is 'outside', then the 'outside' is 'inside' and the 'inside' is 'outside' (Fish quoted by Taylor (1990) p 1271). This inversion of interiority and exteriority illuminates the interplay between the desire of law and the law of desire. The internal which appears 'outside' the law becomes an 'inside' as an 'outside' which cannot be properly inwardised: if law is force then force is law. It is wrong to consider that desire is repressed because it is law that constitutes both desire and the lack on which it is based. Deleuze is able to state: 'The discourse of transgression is the basis of legalism'. The inside-outside paradox opens the interstitial space in the affirmative manifestation of transgression as deed and thought.

There are only spaces in-between because beyond order there are only moments and spaces of disorder constituted through that which can never be represented and is the refused or the waste. The moment of transgression becomes a moment at the limit in the delimitation of ordered space. 'Transgression is an act which involves the limit' (Foucault (1977a) p 33). When law and transgression are interpreted as force and counter-force then transgression becomes not the violation of law but an alternative law in the sense of determining the boundary of that which is with-out law through its reference to that which is within-law. Foucault discusses this relationship in terms of the movement of a line. Transgression refers to the incessant crossing and recrossing of a line which immediately redraws itself only to be crossed again. It is a political activity without apparent reference or determination, a perpetual revolution made and unmade by the excess which transgresses it:

> Limit and transgression depend on each other for whatever density of being they possess: a limit could not exist if it were absolutely uncrossable and, reciprocally, transgression would be pointless if it merely crossed a limit composed of illusion and shadows (Foucault (1977a) p 34).

In order to utilise transgression as an affirmative act-thought in a psycho-political schizo-revolutionary strategy what must be interrogated is not the crossing of the boundary which causes the limit to arise but the movement of the line at the boundary. As Taylor notes 'By establishing a limit, the boundary stone marks a frontier that forms a point of passage. At this threshold, inside and outside join and separate to form an undecidable play of perpetual displacement' (Taylor (1987) p 102). It is this displacement which is central in an affirmative conceptualisation and expression of transgression.

For Bataille, law is the imperative to the preservation of discrete being. The law summarises the condition of existence. Being servile to the law is unconditional and involves the submission of consumption to its reproduction and eventually to its complete normative suppression within an obsessional productivism. The word Bataille employs to mark the preserve of law is 'discontinuity'. It is the condition of transcendent illusion or ideality and for this reason it cannot be grasped by a transcendent apparatus or by the inter-connected series of conceptions involving negation, logical distinction, simple disjunction and essential difference. Transgression as the perpetual challenge to the limit of law can be observed as a displacement in the sense of marking the point of discontinuity in the limit of the law. This point of discontinuity-displacement operates in a paradoxical simultaneity in that it both determines the logic of the frame of reference of law and also, in the moment of that framing, challenges the frame of reference. In one sense law is always transgressed and in the exact moment of its transgression it affirms repression. In spatial terms this moment of violence occurs at the limit, the point of the interstitial section. It is this space which must be interrogated for it is within this space that the movement of the line betrays the interior space or psychological condition that is not yet fixed, a space-condition which is undetermined, unmotivated, random, chaotic and affirmative ('Nothing is negative in transgression' Foucault (1977a) p 35). For Bataille transgression surpasses and completes the prohibition. Transgression is a source of social harmony and solidarity and simultaneously a movement which confirms the law in the act of its violation.

The affirmation of transgression can be utilised at the fragile moment of the interstitial space because here is the simultaneous play of the negative and positive forces of lack and desire. Where there is desire the power relation is already present, a power relation that is multiple, immanent and affirmative. Desire as an element of transgression denies the fundamental and violent law of reason which is external, irrational and illogical:

> [Law and Desire] both rely on common representations of power which, depending on the use made of it and the position it is accorded with respect to desire leads to two contrary results: either, the promise of a 'liberation' if power is seen as having only an external hold on desire, or, if it is constitutive of desire itself, to the affirmation: you are always-already trapped (Foucault (1979a) p 83).

The Foucault-Bataille conceptualisation of the relationship between law and transgression is echoed in the debate between Baudrillard and Deleuze. It is possible to utilise the inversion of the 'psychic metaphorisation' of the political economy of desire in the relationship between law and transgression. Baudrillard would suggest that desire has become hyper-real because it is always charted along the trajectory of, and disseminated with, or as, capital itself. Baudrillard radically extends Lacan's insight that the subject is an effect of the signifier by theorising that the signifier itself is no more than an effect of the commodity form. Deleuze and Guattari utilise the capitalisation of the other in suggesting an alternative political economy of desire. Here desire is social before it is individual and desire is capital. Desire in this Deleuzian frame of political economy assumes startling possibilities in comparison to Baudrillard's cold binarisation assuming the satiation of desire. As a commodity, desire has exchange-value and is therefore a moveable economic force. This proposition enables Deleuze and Guattari to dispense with an essential nature of being and to utilise the metaphor of the machine and circulation. It becomes possible to construct desire as force and as counter-force and the circulation of desire as both a free-flow and an interrupted flow.

Deleuze and Guattari do not reject the mode of production of desire in a proto-revolutionary schema, rather they utilise the mechanisms of the system. The system deterritorialises desire by subverting codes that limit and control the social relations of production and then reterritorialises desire by channelling all production into the narrow confines of equivalence-form. Desire as a commodity is valueless until invested with external value. Desire is an unbounded free-floating energy-power. The repressive regime of capitalism subjects desire to a hierarchical order of external values premised upon lack. It is an order of political economy which conceives of that which is scarce being subject to planned and organised distribution. But desiring-production operates along a linear as opposed to a hierarchical structure and is production as an internal series which represents the manifestation of excess as that which is always left after exchange.[5] Their analysis of a general economy of abundance operative through desiring-machines enables Deleuze and Guattari to subvert systematised desiring-production through attacking the very operation of the machine and disrupting the production of desire which releases the nomadic subject, the body-without-organs.

The strategy of interruption discussed in relation to the process of representation can be utilised in the activation of affirmative transgression in the light of the production of the nomadic subject. Taylor's notion of displacement and Bataille's notion of discontinuity suggest that the limit is not a fixed point of arrival but rather a fluid point of departure and subject to rupture. In operating within limits and in presupposing the existence of positive and negative configurations of power and force it is possible to envisage an interruption in the creation of limits through an affirmative transgression in the form of the nomadic subject and the economy of transgression. These incursive moments along the line of the limit occur within the relation of law-desire-transgression and can be interpreted as affirmations through the inversion and appropriation of the production of desire along those lines. The limit here is not breached and there is no transcendence into a beyond of law but merely the recognition that through random redistributions of ordered desire law can be neutralised and transformed from the negative of the external to the positive of the internal. We sight-site a(n) (a)societal structure of bonds between selves as opposed to the bonds of guilt and violence between

5 It is possible to detect the figure of Bataille in Deleuze and Guattari's notion of production and antiproduction in terms of Bataille's discussion of the conceptualisation of an economy of abundance as opposed to a restricted economy of scarcity. In terms of value, the *potlach* is that element of the exchange which always remains to be fulfilled and which is therefore the determining mechanism in the organisation of need. But *potlach* is decisively a negation of production and in Bataille production is subordinate and posterior to destruction: people create in order to expend, and if they retain things they have produced, it is only to allow themselves to continue living and thus destroying. The *potlach* as excess to/of production becomes an affirmative notion in the disorder of production. Deleuze and Guattari argue that debt is not an accidental by-product of a stable system of reciprocal exchange but a primary disequilibrium which sets in motion the circulation of gifts and counter-gifts. Every gift-exchange presupposes an already established debt or obligation on the part of the giver and a certain prestige (a 'surplus value code') on the part of the recipient. Deleuze and Guattari use this idea as an attack upon Saussurian linguistic analysis in the order of signs and suggest that in capitalist representation signs are not part of a stable code of clearly delineated and hierarchically organised signifiers and signified, but 'non-signifying signs, point-signs having several break-flows or schizzes that form images through their coming together in a whole. The capitalist sign means nothing but functions within the economic process as a medium for transcoding and co-ordinating various components of the circuit of production, exchange, distribution, and consumption. Occasionally deterritorialised flows escape the rigid circuits of capitalist production, at which point redundant, regulated commodity signs become schizophrenic flux-signs of desire (Bogue (1989) pp 95-103).

slaves. Power does not contest power, transgression does not transgress law, but carries the law away with it by losing it, forgetting it. The point has been made by Shapiro in his commentary on Blanchot:

> Transgression is not, finally, a negation; it is an affirmative movement that by its mobility and excess both generates and disintegrates social and individual 'arrangements' of power. It is therefore in a still profoundly Bataillean inspiration that Foucault is able to describe a 'power' that is multiple, immanent and affirmative, and attack the restrictive logic that would represent power in 'juridico-discursive' terms. When Bataille affirms transgression, he is recalling that the logic of utility and negativity is not exhaustive, even though the movement of transgression itself is most frequently, and with horrible effectivity, captured for the purpose of utility, negativity, and power (Shapiro (1990) p 80).

To carry away the law through transgression implies movement, a line of flight. In terms of narrative we search for the 'molecular' plot between the anarchic play within language and between the paranoiac 'molar' narrative of relentless repetition. In terms of space we forego the space of the other and move toward the fluid space of otherness, that of the interstice, the dangerous deterritorialised space-place of the intermediate and the hybrid. It is no longer the hierarchical of ordered signification of desire but the linear of the presemiotic which constantly moves within the limit. How is it possible to arrive at such an investment, such a dangerous assumption which marks the affirmative moment of a socialisation of limitless desire without-in law? One possible route-root is through the figure of the Phantasm.

4 Law, Desire and the Phantasm

A politic-poetics of representation, the production of the body-without-organs and the process of affirmative transgression coalesce within the figure of the Phantasm. There is a dilemma involved in a conceptualisation of desire expressed in terms of knowledge and practice. The movement of desire as commodity involves both the 'social production' of desire on an external plane (as ordered and controlled) and on an internal plane (as disordered and random). Regarding the latter, it is tempting to be seduced by the possibility of overcoming the paranoiac (structured) impulse through intensifying the schizophrenic tendency in the contemporary 'mode of production' of desire to the point that the system shatters through implosion. A schizo-revolutionary manifestation of desire within an economy of abundance is achieved in the creation of group-subjects that form transverse connections between deterritorialised flows that are no longer subject to the constraints of the commodity-exchange system of desire. An ethics formulated in terms of the art of the ungoverned and the possibility of becoming without-law promotes an anxiety which is an inversion of the strategy of resistance proposed by Baudrillard in his formula of resistance demonstrated through hyper-conformity.

A socialisation of desire manifested as phantasy is never individual but group phantasy.[6] This affirmative response can be examined in terms of repression and resistance. Repression is both a psychological-philosophical and political-sociological condition. For example, repression 'occurs' when to satisfy an instinct or drive – though likely to be pleasurable in itself – it would incur the risk of provoking unpleasure because of impinging requirements (socio-political contingents, disavowal and defence). Resistance constitutes that which obstructs the analysed from gaining access to the unconscious. Resistance is constituted within Freudian psychoanalysis as a resistance to recovery. Within a radical political economy of transgression, resistance is an element in a perpetual movement toward transcendence (otherness) when recovery is revealed as merely the manifestation of the mythical-ideological foundations of a repressive external-symbolic order. It is important to maintain an investment in a conceptualisation of desire which is not an idealisation of desire (fascistic) but a consequence of a group production of desire (schizo-revolutionary).

The figure of the Phantasm at this point is the manifestation of desire as a line of flight representing the scene or event of desire: phantasy as the presentation of an original desire and the event of reverie. Desire which exists prior to the individual and as a power relation suggests a Phantasm (the figure of phantasy in flight along the line between law and transgression) as a political element which marks the event of the deterritorialisation of a collective phantasy of resistance (psychoanalytic) and resistance to the external regulation of desire (political-economy). In *A Thousand Plateaus* (1987) Deleuze and Guattari develop a linguistic analysis in the politicisation of the Phantasm. This analysis simultaneously serves as a critique of the organisation of language in structuring desire and as a subversion of this organisation of language in a manifestation of desire within a humanistically-orientated replacement discourse.

The territorialisation of desire through language (the linguistic structuring of desire) is fixed by the Oedipus complex and serves to produce subjects of utility and docility situated within the external order. The juridic subject is the consequence of juridico-semiotic production and of the insertion of the subject into a discursive subject-position within the order of juridico-semiotic production. This process of positioning occurs as a result of *the regime of signs* which determines that context is a critical determinant in the stabilisation of meaning. The signifying regime produces signs which spiral outward from the centre of the production and which intrude first into the speaking subject (the producer of the utterance) and ends in the subject of the statement (the grammatical *I*). In the *post-signifying regime* (the authoritarian social formation) signs travel along this path

6 A distinction must be made between the German *phantasie* and the French *fantasie*. In the former, *phantasie* means imagination in the sense of the faculty of imagination, its contents and the creative activity which animates it. In the latter, *fantasie* is interpreted in a philosophical sense: *fantasme* refers to a specific imaginary production, not to the world of phantasy and imaginative activity in general. Here I follow a Freudian interpretation in linking phantasy with desire, specifically phantasy as the *mis-en-scène* of desire – a *mis-en-scène* in which what is prohibited is always present in the actual formation of the wish. This interpretation accords with my later development of the Phantasm following Deleuze in that phantasy as a scene of desire is thus the *locus* of defensive (resistant) operations and an affirmation in the sense of representing a domain of reverie which is heterogeneous and resistant and which is alone in being 'real' compared with the marginality of physical phenomena (see Laplanche and Pontalis (1980) pp 314-319; also Cowie (1990) pp 149-162).

and culminate in statements by subjects in conformity with the dominant reality, irrespective of a coherently materialised omnipotent centre. It is no longer necessary for the process to be policed. The domination of the subject's internal mental structure is congruent with the externalised statement so that every subsequent discourse formation serves only further to limit thought-imagination. Imagination is subjected as soon as the individual enters the symbolic order of determination and becomes a juridic subject. The juridic field determines the discursive subject-position within which the *I* can exist. The grammatical *I* is the subject which takes up residence in a discursive subject-position, is but the presence of an absence. It is no longer the *I* as desiring-subject but as determined legal subject:

> What is crucial in the post-signifying regime is the doubling of the subject, in the speaking subject and the subject of speech, and the reduction of the one to the other. The speaking subject reveals a mental reality, the subject of speech a dominant reality, and the post-signifying regime ensures the conformity of mental and dominant reality via an internal process of subjection. There is no longer any need for a transcendent centre of power, but instead for an immanent power which merges with the 'real', and which proceeds via normalization (Bogue (1989) p 142).

A conceptualisation of desire expressed in terms of the formulation of an emancipatory critique of linguistic violence suggests that the field of desire is the realm of the imaginary: the realm of the Phantasm. The Phantasm as imagination topologises the materiality of the body in mapping out otherwise mute animal instincts and drives. In the city bodies appear to be docile and disciplined. But inwardly bodies and souls seethe, their 'secret dreams of mastery without mercy isolated, intensified and incorporated', driven inward and cut off from the old links of the public spectacle of atrocity and cruelty (the inscription of the memory of guilt-law upon the body) the soul turns from 'jousts to Phantasms' (Foucault (1977b) p 193). As Deleuze notes, 'What appears in the Phantasm is the movement in which the ego opens itself to the surface and liberates the acosmic, impersonal, and preindividual singularities which have been imprisoned. It literally releases them like spores and explodes as it gets unburdened' ((1990) p 213). No matter what the external order (the regulatory semiotic process) may dictate, the dreamworld of imagination remains beyond good and evil, beyond reason and rationality and outside of territorialised and disciplined desire. It is a state akin to madness, a secret frenzy with all the 'ambiguity' of 'chaos and apocalypse'. Given any 'healthy, normal and law-abiding adult' it is possible, according to Foucault, to bring out the chaos within – the 'nakedness of desire as the lawless law of the world' – by asking 'how much of the child he has within him, what fundamental crime has he wished to commit?' (Foucault (1977b) p 193). Foucault urges that 'Phantasms should be freed from the restrictions we impose upon them, freed from the dilemmas of truth and falsehood and of being and non-being ...; they must be allowed to conduct their dance even though the results are cruel' (Foucault (1977a) p 170). After Sade, 'violence, life, death, desire and sexuality will extend below the level of the representation, an immense shade, which we are now attempting to recover, as far as we can, in our discourse, in our freedom, in our thought' (Foucault (1970) p 211; (1984) pp 31-78; Miller (1993) pp 223-224; Miller (1990) pp 470-491).

The Phantasm is the element which, in signifying the line of flight, constitutes the possibilities provided in the deregulated arena of desire. The Phantasm is simultaneously the manifestation of desire as movement and the figure which illuminates the space-place of desire (the *mis-en-scène* of desire). Deleuze presents the characteristics of the Phantasm:

- The Phantasm represents neither an action nor a passion, but a result of action and passion, that is, a pure event.
- The Phantasm is inseparable from chaos and randomness.
- The Phantasm represents the event according to its essence, that is, as a noematic attribute distinct from the actions, passions, and qualities of the state of affairs (following Deleuze (1990) pp 210-216).

There is a Phantasm of thought (language) and a Phantasm of act (the event of desire). The two are related through discourse, the movement of discourse as a line of flight, from within to without, from structure to destruction, from monad to nomad, from the word to the mark, from the representable to the unrepresentable and from the semiotic to the presemiotic. In *The Revolution in Poetic Language* (1984) Julia Kristeva discusses the presemiotic *chora*[7] in terms of the production of affects, drives and flows of energy representing the condition of the pre-vital organisation of power. The semiotic here is composed of 'discrete quantities of energy' moving through the body, 'a nonexpressive totality formed by the drives and their states ... articulated by flows and marks' which subsequently becomes ordered through the entry to the symbolic (Kristeva (1984) pp 25; 40). Once expression and representation are situated through the violence of language then the nomadic subject becomes the juridic subject, caught by the imposition of the structure of determination and particular subjectivity (repression) but always, however, undermined by the bodily scream (Milovanovic (1992) p 114). The instinctual drive (deregulated desire) is trapped within the syntax and rules of language so that even though the subject is established above the semiotic chora there is a sublimation-repression of the physical origin and remembrance of a mythical guilt. It is only in dreams that the event-arena of disordered desire becomes possible (the presemiotic *chora*), the moment of that which has been otherwise disavowed. This is the mark of the return of the repressed (in the margins of the law) in the excess of language. The instinctual drive of desire is charged with both psychic and somatic energy, the semiotic being the frontier between the two but its determining characteristic is excess (the pre-verbal) in the sense of the inevitable addition of meaning into any particular discourse. It is this excess which is the trace of the presemiotic disorder of the instinctual drive and the mask of the mythical origin and the original memory of the absence of an all mastering subject: traces of otherness imposed through the structure of language itself.

7 The process of the organisation of language has been theorised in the occidental philosophical tradition in the concept of the unitary subject, that which is repressed and denies its origins in the semiotic chora (pre-verbal organisation of drives). *Chora* in this sense can be interpreted as a receptacle where elements are mixed in chaos before there is an ordering into a cosmos. In this state instincts acquire an unstable and contradictory organisation out of which the subject is formed.

The body is marked literally and metaphorically, territorialised and traversed by lines of flight. Deleuze and Lecercle rely upon the assimilation of phantasy with the Stoic's concept of *lekton*, that which is the significate and of the incorporeal, the attribute which dwells upon the body. The body-without-organs is composed of fragmented marks of a prior inscription, letters which are disordered and in random lines, without beginning or end, and which oppose the singular unity of a body determined by the words of juridic inscription. Deleuze and Guattari politicise the original (psychic and somatic) manifestation of the presemiotic-instinctual drive. The figure of the Phantasm becomes the mark of the event in a movement of a counter-force of desire without lack. It marks the emancipation of the presemiotic chora and the arrival of the nomadic subject. Deleuze and Guattari develop the line of flight as that process in the movement of desire which connects multiplicities of desire in excess. The line of flight is surplus and of the unrepresentable and interruptive. These are the lines along which desire flows and along which the subject takes flight (Deleuze and Guattari (1987) p 21). The hierarchical structure which orders desire through the processes of the internalisation of language and the territorialisation of the body can be contrasted to the linear structure of a desire operative through the displacement of language and the deterritorialisation of the body (the moment of desiring production which produces the body-without-organs).[8] The former is a process in the displacement of the real from originating expression. The latter – the line of flight of the Phantasm – is that excess of language which has been called *delir* (the scream, the language of madness and non-sense) (Lecercle (1985) pp 147-177). *Delir* as the articulation of the inarticulable nature of the movement of the Phantasm along the line of flight is that subversive and destabilising force which is only 'potentially steps removed from a fully articulated oppositional discourse' (Milovanovic (1992) p 114). But every moment in the recognition of the line of flight is but a fleeting moment crystallised in practice and temporarily captured as the discourse of the legislative guerrilla on the margins of a disordered political economy of a psychoanalytic and philosophical order.

There are a number of connected possibilities: the pursuit of the line of flight, the manifestation of the Phantasm, the connection with the pre-semiotic chora, of becoming part of the excess (refuse(d)), the ability to scream and to enter the event of the *mis-en-scène* of phantasy, the possibility of becoming nomadic. But within each possibility there is the violent external imposition of language and lack. The subject exists to be captured by the order of language and on this level *delir* is a false experience of freedom, not an attempt at liberation but the symptom of a failure to conform to the law. There appears to be no possibility of breaking away from law of lack and out of the

8 It should be noted at this point that Lacan utilises the figure of the body-without-organs in his discussion of the mirror-stage of identity formation:

> The fragmented body .... usually manifests itself in dreams when the movement of the analysis encounters a certain level of aggressive disintegration in the individual. It then appears in the form of disjointed limbs, or of those organs represented in exoscopy, growing wings and taking up arms for interstitial persecutions ... But this form is even tangibly revealed at the organic level, in the lines of 'fragilisation' that define the anatomy of phantasy, as exhibited in the schizoid and spasmodic symptoms of hysteria (Lacan (1977) pp 4-5).

violent circle of metaphor (the production of meaning) and interpretation (the consumption of meaning).

But the figure of the Phantasm which determines the *mis-en-scène* of desire (the space-event of desire) and which is articulated as *delir* is one characterised by a movement. A linguistic structure which is not static and externally determined but which is fluid and chaotic represents a configuration of desire which is not structured but rather of pure event, neither imaginary nor real, internal nor external, neither active nor passive. As opposed to a singular subject (language, body) which makes its itself available to capture and territorialisation, the Phantasm can also be a simultaneous manifestation of the event of a social (group) desire and an expression of a presemiotic chora as a political moment independent of a political subject.

The Phantasm becomes an event in and of the Limit. The space-place of the Phantasm is simultaneously the *mis-en-scène* (individual and social) and the space-place not of the Other (which determines the existence of the law) but of otherness (the space of movement in the margin and the line of flight along the interstice). The time of the Phantasm is a Nietzschean temporal instability which accords not with a manufactured-mythical history of origins but rather with a period without origin and of a beginning in a void and as a moment. The Phantasm as representation represents not an originary presemiotic or prelinguistic *chora* but rather the trace of that condition expressed as *delir* or schizophrenia in a molecular narrative. It is not a code in the sense of representing a value accorded by nomination but a scrambling of codes and therefore unrepresentable (incapable of nomination) save as a liberating narrative of dissensus, a provisional and contingent short-story. The Phantasm as the figure of affirmative transgression exists not as an act beyond the limit of the law serving to determine the existence of the law. The movement of the Phantasm carries away and displaces the law and serves as a mark in the discontinuity of law. It is an encapsulation of the violent liberating movement of the line which constantly draws the border. The Phantasm encapsulates a non-repressed socialisation of desire of the bodies-without-organs as opposed to singularly trapped bodies of selves. There is no separation between the personal and the social because desire and politics interpenetrate. There is no division between the 'rational' and the 'delirious'. The Phantasm becomes the representation of a nomadic or linear governmentality as opposed to a monadic or hierarchical governmentality. The nomad is the without-law, the figure of a non-repressed desire (desire without lack), whose main value is not authority (stability and order) but flight (instability and disorder). The nomad is a by-product of the manufacture of desire as a consequence of the excess of the system of order and repression. The nomad is still a political subject but can be constructed as a counter-political subject not of the external-symbolic of negative paranoia (psychological-philosophical repression) but of the internal-real of affirmative schizoanalysis (political-sociological resistance) and therefore an independent political subject of a possible alternative and humanistically disorientated social grouping. The arrival of the without-law marks a possibility in the articulation of collectivity of desire in an abundance of difference.

CHAPTER SIX

THREE STORIES IN URBAN EXCESS: *AMERICAN PSYCHO*

He addresses the world from the crack; he has also spent a lifetime listening at it. Everything that can be said about him, and more particularly against him, he already knows; he has, as he says in a typical paradox, overheard it all, invented it all. 'I am a sick man … I am a wicked man.' In the space of that pause Dostoevsky introduces the unifying idea of his tale: the instability, the perpetual 'dialectic of isolated consciousness' (Pevear and Volokhonsky (1993) p 4).

American Psycho can be seen as a classic text at the end of the high postmodern period and simultaneously playing its part in the slow emergence of an American renaissance that attempts to transcend these fictional games, and re-establish, from deep within consumer culture, other ways of writing fiction and apprehending American society as it approaches the millenium (Young (1992) p 122).

AMERICAN PSYCHO, VISUAL CULTURE AND GENRE

'New York is death' writes Sarah Schulman in a bleak plea from the front-line of urban chaos; her aim is not to fall apart 'It is virtually impossible to set a goal higher than this right now'. Schulman writes a postcard as a victim of a nightmare world of urban-fall out from a city that is a imploding and where the boundaries have been irredeemably confused. From the packed trading floors of Manhattan to the packed sewers beneath there is a stench of excess and refuse. This is the stalking ground of an American Psycho.

We cannot get beyond the modern until the lure of ethics and aesthetics as totalising narratives or legitimations that mask contradictions and fissures is recognised: only the most extreme and disruptive images or experiences can penetrate the bland vacuity of the contemporary. This representation of a transgression – how transgression *might* appear – is a fiction. It is not real, it only mirrors the real as a recognition of discontinuity (But remember Baudrillard's claim 'There is no more fiction' (Baudrillard (1983a) p 148)). In interrogating the moment of Bret Easton Ellis's novel *American Psycho* (1991) it is only possible to convey the effect of this cultural artefact through the medium of the visual.

The contemporary cultural terrain is defined almost exclusively in visual terms including the display, the icon, the representations of the real through the camera's eye, captured on videotape and given in the moving picture.[1] Cultural and social theory is dominated by examinations of the law of the representation, because it is through such

1 As noted by Denzin ((1992) p 8). See also on the dominance of the visual Ulmer ((1989) pp i-ix) and Hebdige ((1988) pp 13-14). As Young comments: 'We are in another country where the author is dead and 'character' comes to us in wraiths, projections, pastiche, mutating entities, archetypes, comic cut-outs and intertextual refugees from history, film, fiction and myth' (Young, (1992) p 20).

laws that the individual is constructed as a re-represented subject, the subject within the gaze. *American Psycho* exists only as text, as an exercise in the imagination passing itself off as literature, as respectable 'art', subject to supplementary magazine 'copy'. In part this interrogation is concerned with the ways in which the i-eye becomes seduced by this storyteller and his story and how it is translated into a visual imagination through the minds i-eye, and whether it can be so translated. Or is it so grotesque as to be untranslatable?

An initial attempt to translate this text into visual image can be suggested through the medium of film. This translation or transformation will be 'realised' when the film 'rights' are sold and what might naively be considered to be unrepresentable becomes clearly represented on video tape. It would be a film marketed as an epitaph to an age of excess or as the demise of a particularly temporal social group labelled the 'yuppies'. It would possess the gloss of social documentary, a metaphor by Scorsese out of de Palma having lunch with Lynch, screenplay by Schrader: *realised* by Cronenberg, music by The Talking Heads and Eno (in addition to the soundtrack provided by the protagonist's musical sensibilities: Genesis, Whitney Houston, Huey Lewis and the News). The garish excess of lifestyle contrasting with the black and white ordinariness of carnage in *Silence of the Lambs* meets *Miami Vice* via Soderbergh's bleakness of videotape as *Henry: Portrait of a Serial Killer* moves to Manhattan. *Serial Killing as Designer Death*. Here the details of dissection and cannibalism become displaced moments of sound and only intermittent flashes of blood. We cannot witness this attempt at transgression, become conspirators to it, it is not translatable into the visual image, caged by our censorious liberal qualms of being party to a slasher or snuff experience in witnessing the 'real' reel.[2]

American Psycho exists as an example of three related genres of fiction: the fiction of the 'post-punk' generation, the representations of greed, and finally the 'genre' of serial killing thriller. First, it exists as part of the genre of fiction which has become known as the 'post-punk generation' (a sub-division of the 'blank generation')[3] concerned with excess defined in terms of 'drugs, clubs and MTV'. These novels describe the eternal verities of urban life: fashion, music and style. They are the novels which represent and reflect the aesthetic considerations of consumption in terms of the condition of anomie-affluence-alienation: the repressive fun-house of desire ruled by spectacle, simulation and media. In the novels of Douglas Coupland, Bret Easton Ellis, Tama Janovitch, Jay McInerney in the US and in the novels of Martin Amis, Michael Bracewell, Geoff Dyer, Kate Pullinger in the UK the arena of action is the satiated play-ground of the urban

2 Bret Easton Ellis is the author of two previously filmed novels *Less Than Zero* (1985) and *The Rules of Attraction* (1988). A week before *American Psycho* was to be published in the United States its publisher, Simon and Schuster, decided to breach its contract with the author and refused to publish the novel. At 28 his third novel met with inevitable hostile critical attention including an initial ban by one of Britain's largest retail book store chains, Dillons (as discussed by Kmetyk (1991)). In America the publication of the novel threatened to end in obscenity charges similar to those which had been bought against the artist Robert Mapplethorpe and the rap-band Two-Live Crew. The novel has now faded into obscurity. Together with the age it represents. It remains a *noir Bonfire of the Vanities* (Wolfe (1987).

3 On the 'Blank Generation' and 'Post-Punk' see Young and Caveney (1992) and Redhead ((1995) pp 87-95)

where identity is mutable. The most extreme attempts at expressing individuality are doomed because personality itself has become a commodity. At the outset *American Psycho* is a study in the failure of identity through violent excess in which the 'real' violence of serial killing cannot transcend the 'apparent' violence of banal commodity fetishism. For Easton Ellis's characters the shadow always falls between the person and the personality. 'Even to be natural is to decode and assume the elements of a consumer crux' (Young (1992) p 20). Against this background of consumer frenzy and fragmented fictional landscape, Easton Ellis and his literary peers take to the streets hoping to tell the truth as they see it but with the realisation that it is difficult to see anything, let alone render it through the:

> [B]lizzard fall out from an uncertain, nervously apocalyptic world which seems constantly poised, like a psychotic at bay with no hostages, on the brink of shooting itself in the head (Young (1992) p 20).

The genre of the 'blank generation' confronts the constraints of consumption. But *American Psycho* is also part of another genre where the narrative pulse is greed. It will be recalled that the credo of the 1980s was 'Greed is Good'.[4] Money developed the capacity to act as a medium of exchange for itself. Money became the basis of what it signifies and eliminated the need for any underlying material value. This is the ecstasy of value without reference to production and the reversal of the conventional vector of cause and necessity. I will investigate the effect of this transition in a wider cultural context using the narrative events of *American Psycho*.

The cultural logic of contemporary capitalism is the excessive consumption of the self-referential signs of consumer society. Existence occurs in a political economy of consumption. The commodity system establishes itself without an autonomous cultural impetus into the order of the abstract object. Capital attains its own 'angular momentum', perpetuating a whirlwind of dissolution, whose hub is the virtual zero of impersonal metropolitan accumulation. At the peak of its productive powers the human animal is hurled into a new nakedness, as everything stable is progressively liquidated in the storm and infected by the viral economy. This is the stalking ground of the *American Psycho*, the violent aesthetic of greed. To convey a sense of the aesthetic dimensions of money requires an understanding of money as particular form of 'psychological commodity':

> Money demands constant vigilance. To become poor, one has only to let oneself go. But to enrich oneself requires greed. Our relationship to money demands a tension which is

---

4 As proclaimed by Wall Street *arbitrageur* Ivan Boesky to the graduating class of the Berkeley Business School in 1985. Boesky was later jailed for insider dealing. In Oliver Stone's film *Wall Street* (1988) the protagonist, the corporate raider Gordon Gekko (gekko means lizard), makes this statement to a stock holder meeting: 'The new law of evolution in corporate America seems to be the survival of the fittest. Well in my book you either do it right or you get eliminated ... The point ... is that greed, for lack of a better word, is good. Greed is right' (for an analysis of this film see Denzin (1991) pp 82–95). This speech echoes Boesky's original declaration and also that of Sir James Goldsmith before the US House Committee on the proposed bid by his consortium, Hoylake, against the conglomerate, BAT Industries (see also Stanley (1992a) (1992b) (1994a) (1994b)).

> not reducible to any other. It is through money that the Other confronts us. The monetary act is always aggressive (Amar (1976) p 283).

> The cult of money has its asceticism, its self-denial, its self-sacrifice – economy and frugality, contempt for mundane, temporal and fleeting pleasures; the chase after the eternal treasure (Marx (1973) p 232).

We are constrained at every turn by the divisions of western philosophy – logics, ethics, aesthetics – all knowledge belonging in one or other of these categories. In this structure there can only be consideration of the true, the beautiful, the good. Each realm is autonomous with its own set of concerns, its own rules. Along the edges, those who scavenge for the cast off scraps resulting from attempts to fit recalcitrant bits of information into these realms will find some rich pickings in the border skirmishes, the incursions into foreign territories which take place in these regions.

Aesthetics proper has nothing to do with logics and ethics, notwithstanding the assumption of high-minded truth and goodness expressed by art, which is manifest amongst the high cultural followers of the aesthetic experience. As Grace notes, it has certainly nothing to do with money, '[A] distasteful substance, which does not fit into any of philosophy's categories' (Grace (1991) p 115). Money appears only as an abstraction which does not oblige philosophy actually to handle it. It is left to a function of language to produce the desired effect and to carry the power of arguments which are presented initially in forms which belong to the realm of logic rather than aesthetics. But in considering the world of economic reality – contemporary urban culture – in that reality we are dealing with fictional entities: futures, yields, junk, something called credit that is in fact debt. This is a world of high fiction, a daily soap opera full of the most extreme occurrences, an everyday life which becomes a fiction of terrifying realism, a horror scenario with such convincing special effects that at times it is easy to become part of it (see Grace (1991) pp 115-119).

American Psycho is an urban folktale taking place in the darkest part of the forest, the horror scenario of the world of money translated back as a serial killing narrative. And in this mode the novel falls into the genre of fiction where the dominant narrative is violence. *American Psycho* is The Master of the Universe transformed into a Devil Incarnate, a tale of absolute corruption by materiality played out through the satanic rituals of the contemporary. This Devil is searching for the extreme of experience ('the limit experience'), playing out every phantasy in the exercise of power (a power articulated as transgression (resistance) to the formality of the dominant). As Homi Bhaba notes, when the demonic dimensions of fiction are acted out in the psycho-mythology of everyday life, then it is time to turn to the novel to learn what forms of language are appropriate for this 'neurasthenic hour', that description of the anxiety-producing reality of the contemporary American city, chaotic, random and discontinuous ((1991) p 62). Easton Ellis places the warning Preface that Dostoevsky employed in his story *Notes from Underground*:

> Both the author of these *Notes* and the *Notes* themselves are, of course, fictional. Nevertheless, such persons as the composer of these *Notes* not only exist in our society, but indeed must exist, considering the circumstances under which our society has generally been formed. I have wished to bring before the public, somewhat more

> distinctly than usual, one of the characteristics of the recent past. He represents a generation that is still living out its days amongst us. In the fragment entitled Underground this personage describes himself and his views and attempts, as it were, to clarify the reasons why he appeared and was bound to appear in our midst. The subsequent fragment will consist of the actual 'notes', concerning certain events in his life (Dostoevsky (1864/1993) p 1).

To plunge into the novel itself, rather than the stories that surround the production of its telling, what Easton Ellis intends in the dissection of the alienated world that is contemporary America, cutting into the underbelly of American affluence. He consolidates his literary journey in following the tenor created in his two previous excursions. He ends up in the Gothic, a world of dazed consumers, urban deviants, middle-class bohemians, sexual outcasts and other disconsolate riff-raff who drift through the metropolitan jungle. To raise the level of our awareness ('this is the *real* real') Easton Ellis avoids a psychological or motivational discourse of violence. Rather he develops an alternative 'tactful' or aesthetic description of violence and murder that is closer to the writings of 'actual' killers, whilst maintaining a high degree of ironic black humour that the 'real' action lies elsewhere.[5]

American Psycho is a narrative which inverts, in the most violent way, the ideals of the American Dream, and invokes them as a series of apocalyptic nightmares. The critic of the American Dream can never be wholly successful since the overwhelming nature of the ideology that is 'America' is simply too large to grasp in any rational or aesthetic way. The power of the idea encompasses the whole of the geographic space that the continent swallows. Easton Ellis, similar to other artists, retreats to Manhattan and Long Island, which as 'islands' off the Eastern seaboard assume manageable proportions: from there to look toward the *terra firma* of real America and to dissect it from afar.

As the dust jacket commentators remark 'The horror is not in the novel but in the society it reflects' (Rawlinson) and 'It is a serious novel that comments on a society that has become inured to suffering' (Mailer). Consider this statement: 'American culture contains a strong core of norms, values and beliefs that tend to approve violence and also facilitate it.' Some would instantly – perhaps indignantly – reject this as an unwarranted criticism of the 'American Way Of Life.' But as Holmes and de Burger note:

> Violence has accompanied virtually every stage and aspect of our national existence … apart from its role in the formation and preservation of the nation, violence has been a determinant of both the form and substance of American life (Holmes and de Burger (1988) p 27).

Easton Ellis's protagonist serves the role of an Everyman – every-yuppie – taking the reader by the hand on a journey toward the rotten heart of contemporary American civilisation. As the novel progresses the increasing anonymity of the character heightens this capacity as Easton Ellis attempts to ascribe the characteristics of his principal as a metaphor for the sickness through consumption that is perceived as spreading through America, a sickness through excess and the quest for something other as a result of the

5 See for example the account of Pierre Rivière edited by Foucault (1982).

restraining banality of the ordinariness of the everyday. As Denzin makes clear the contemporary (post-industrial urban America in this example) is marked by a *ressentiment* based upon the repeated inability to experience the pleasant emotions promoted by popular culture. Self-hatred, anger, envy, false-pride and a desire for revenge against the Other takes hold as the Other assumes the position as the mechanism for release. Sexism, racism and homophobia are the undersides of this condition and from these spring the violence and the prejudice (Denzin (1991): Preface). Easton Ellis describes the effect of these dominant characteristics of the contemporary in graphic and unrelenting detail. At the rotten heart is the constant theme of corruption through consumption and of the exercise of power in a quest for transgression (to become other) through the fulfilment of the desire for excitement. But the blackness/blankness which lies hidden constantly affirms that this is not transgression, only a playing at the margins of an ever-increasing regulatory sphere of repression. Herein lies the ironic paradox between repression and transgression, order and disorder.

'THIS IS NOT AN EXIT'

The novel opens with a statement, scrawled in blood red lettering on the side of the Chemical Bank near the corner of Eleventh and First, Manhattan: ABANDON ALL HOPE YE WHO ENTER HERE. It concludes with another sign: THIS IS NOT AN EXIT. The reader is *signed* and enters the first circle of hell. The first sign points to the principal themes of the book: blood, despair and banking. In between these two apocalyptic signs a 400 page history unfolds concerning moments in the life of Patrick Bateman. In a first person narrative a 'yuppie' meditation is written in which the banal Manhattan lifestyle of a young investment banker is counterpointed by his violent nocturnal activities. His day-time existence is marked by intermittent periods of work (which are never fully described in terms of function) between a highly developed series of social tableaux (He works for Pierce and Pierce, the fictional investment bank which Tom Wolfe created for his protagonist, Sherman McCoy). It is the social setting that is of primary importance to Bateman and his acquaintances. His 'alternative' persona, which becomes increasingly dominant as the narrative unfolds, is a nocturnal beast whose bouts of depravity are revealed in a series of escalating atrocities, a continuation of a depravity already alluded to through the laundering of blood stained sheets early in the story. The narrative progresses through a series of grotesque masques of violence. The indictment reads as follows:

- The physical persecution of a beggar (Jesus, will you get a fucking shave, *please*).
- The murder of a black beggar (Do you know what a fucking loser you are?).
- The disembowelling of a homosexual and his dog (An arc of red blood splatters the white BMW 320i).
- Acts of sado-masochism with two prostitutes (We're not through yet ...).
- The murder of a colleague with an axe (It takes Paul five minutes to finally die. Another thirty to stop bleeding).

- The murder of female partner with a nail gun (No one cares. No one will help you).
- Incident with homosexual acquaintance (Listen, you want to *die*? I'll do it, Luis).
- Murder of a child at the zoo (Though I am satisfied at first by my actions, I'm suddenly jolted with mournful despair at how useless, how extraordinarily painless, it is to take a child's life).
- Murder of prostitute using a power drill and a rat (I can imagine that my virtual absence of humanity fills her with mind-bending terror).
- The cannibalism of the above (I can imagine my own vacant face, the disembodied voice coming from its mouth: *These are terrible times*).

The style is stark in manner reflecting the nature of its content. It is literally pared to the bone wherein lies the drama of intensity through clinical attention to detail, bordering on the fanatic. Each grotesque act of violence spans pages in a graphic catalogue of description. This is the violence of repetition, in which one vile act is followed by an even more horrendous one. Reading, we recoil, these scenes provoke nausea, disgust, revulsion – but also engage our perverse fascination with detail. Slow, meticulous, ceremonial, it is a kind of pornography – a pornography of murderous pleasures, and, on the printed page, mute pain: 'It is probably this that can be called the horror: to an unsuspecting glance, the encounter with dead things which are laid open, a certain tortuousness of being, where open mouths do not cry out' (Foucault (1986b) p 84). As Deleuze notes '[T]he gathering momentum of repetition tends to force us onto the side of the torturer and make us identify with the sadistic hero' (Deleuze (1989) p 34).

In the psychological thriller, the reader is made to participate in the murderer's own vertiginous experience of suspension from worldly reality and moral law. This suspension is heightened in *American Psycho* through the use, post the 'crime', of a meditation on a particular popular music artist written in the 'serious' and in-depth critical style of a 'Rolling Stone' magazine format which contemplates the relative merits of Genesis, Whitney Houston, Huey Lewis and the News. The moment of transgression is, after all, followed by the banal and becomes of itself banal. What Easton Ellis achieves through these apparent inconsequential postmassacre musings is an exploitation of the gap, of rupture and suture.[6] To pursue an extended description of violence and to counter-point it with an equally extended description of an element of the cultural debris of the contemporary serves to accentuate the banality of both activities. At once the reader is gripped through the repulsion of the immediate and then hurled into the monotony of excessive consumption. Their presence is deliberately at odds with Bateman's narrative performance and exaggerates the anonymity ('not-there-ness') of Bateman in Easton Ellis's continued concern with 'the absent presence'. Of course, Bateman is not there – we, the reader, create him as a necessary palliative to our mundane, regulated and repressed, contemporary existence. But Easton Ellis' subtlety denies us this pleasure through his careful construction of Bateman as a serial killer who *cannot* exist beyond the realms of the narrative structure that Easton Ellis determines:

6 I am grateful to Glenn Bowman for this point.

Bateman is annihilated in language. The gap is the reader's desire for this reality and the author's continuous seduction and denial of this desire through the monotony of the banal. 'Thus we are forced by the author to confront the definition and function of fictionality itself' (Young (1992) p 116) or as Baudrillard suggests 'There is no more fiction that life could possibly confront, even victoriously – it is reality itself that disappears utterly in the game of reality' (Baudrillard (1983a) p 148).

In part the banality of the excessive act becomes the most disturbing aspect of the work. The reader is seduced by the protagonist's quest for knowledge and excitement and is then confronted with the most mundane aspects and *conclusions* of contemporary existence (in a video store Bateman lets out a terrifying silent scream: 'There are too many fucking movies to choose from'). This is the mimetic function, the forcing of the reader into an examination of the surface of fiction and reality and desire beyond the artificial border of the ethical and the moral. There are few judgmental comments allowed by the narrator regarding the nature of his acts. The reader becomes involved with the narrator's increasing attempts to satiate his desire through further destruction and carnage. Simultaneously Bateman becomes possessed by a need to reveal himself through the primary device of the narrative structure in which the identity of the protagonist is constantly erased. Throughout the book Bateman is constantly mistaken for someone else. As he desperately attempts to 'confess' or rather to reveal himself (at one stage to a private detective investigating the death of one of Bateman's colleagues, and at another making a full confession into a telephone answering machine) this displacement of identity becomes ever more apparent. No matter how hard he tries no one will listen. Everyone therefore appears to be engaged in the affirmation of their own identity through the negation of another. Bateman, the homicidal artist, desperately seeking to reveal himself for what he 'is' or rather believes himself to be, cannot escape himself through becoming other, the constraints of his existence denying him that final pleasure:

> 'Wait. Stop,' I shout, looking up into Carnes' face, making sure he's really listening. 'You don't seem to understand. You're not really comprehending any of this. *I* killed him. *I* did it, Carnes. *I* chopped Owen's fucking head off. *I* tortured dozens of girls. That whole message I left on your machine was *true*.' I'm drained, not appearing calm, wondering why this doesn't feel like a blessing to me. 'Excuse me,' he says, trying to to ignore my outburst. 'I really *must* be going' (Easton Ellis (1991) p 388).

'ABANDON ALL HOPE YE WHO ENTER HERE'

The ephemerality of Easton Ellis's characters is more than just postmodern self-consciousness about the fictional device of 'creating' character. It is one of the bleakest and most ominous aspects of his vision: the synaptic overload integral to contemporary urban culture. There are too many people, there are too many things and they have both become interchangeable. There is no space for humanitarian behaviour or emotional connections: 'If you're not busy being born you're busy buying.' Thomas Pynchon and Don DeLillo have tried to deal with the labyrinthine ways of information overload in contemporary society but only Easton Ellis manages to evoke the awful emptiness of human disposability and meaningless, 'the misanthropia that licks daily at our consciousness' (Young (1992) p 30). Easton Ellis's characters do not exist as archetypes, since the qualities he gives them are so spurious, negligible and second-hand as to be not worth mentioning. Easton Ellis plays with the ironic connotation that contemporary America continually promises personality and personal liberation to individuals as part of the cornucopia of consumer choice but constantly fails to provide actual emancipation. This is the dupe to keep the consumer continually on the edge either through satiation or tantalising promise. It is a theme central in the Durkheimian inspired musings of Jean Baudrillard (see for example (1970) (1983a) (1993b)). Easton Ellis is not inclined to invest character and therefore reflects a society overloaded with the endless circulating signs and signifiers of consumerism which are themselves devoid of meaning and doomed to revolve forever with-out substance or hope of signification in an 'orgy of indifference, disconnection exhibition and circulation' (Baudrillard (1988) p 96). The only roles available are those of spectator, consumer or star: identity without signification save for panic. The predicament has been captured by Whitebrook thus:

> As one New York analyst wrote recently *a propos* this new frenzied consumer consciousness, there is now a 'new type of patient' who is presenting himself. The classical neurotic for whom psychoanalysis was invented suffered from symptoms which were lodged in a self that was otherwise intact. By contrast the 'new patient' of the post-modern period has not even progressed to the point where a stable identity structure has coalesced. 'Typically he or she suffers from feelings of emptiness, isolation and futility, pre-Oedipal rage and primitive separation ... which are masked by grandiose narcissistic fantasies', fuelled by 'the marked intensification of the pursuit of material success, power and status; an increased preoccupation with youth, health and glamour, accompanied by difficulty in forming relationships with emotional depth'. Excessive alienated narcissism frequently masked by social adaptability has come to dominate our era, according to this perception, just as hysteria and (later) neurosis did Freud's (Taylor with reference to Whitebrook (1985) p 150).

For the reader, this serves only to heighten the awareness that this is not real and that means of escape are not available. The device serves to accentuate the gruelling monotony of everyday existence in which intense emotional experience is shaped by anxiety, alienation, ressentiment and a detachment from others. In addition, this displacement of identity serves to confirm the reader's suspicion that Bateman is in fact an outsider within this social network, a white anglo-saxon protestant of the second order, desperately attempting to belong. The metaphor – the corruption of the American Dream – becomes one in which the *real* wasps are engaged in actual events (city crime) and practices of corruption (state crime) through their power and influence in the control of the American (and therefore the global) corporate economy and are servants only to the symbolic laws of capital and *Serious Money*. To provide an Hegelian twist, Bateman's 'power' is one of internalised nocturnal (dark) hatred, whilst those of the *real* wasps is one of clear (light) demonstration of power beyond any formalised constraints at the behest of the laws of capital involving sacrifices beyond the imagining of Bateman.

To counter-point these acts which serve to challenge this routine of the everyday, acts which attempt to confirm his power and identity, Bateman's life is determined by a collective preoccupation with consumption and the assumption of lifestyle. To *be* in this vision of eighties Manhattan is to exist through an intensely determined ritualisation of everyday behaviour (social mores/norms). On the publication of the book Easton Ellis wrote:

> [I]t's really about the 1980s greed generation and how no one looked beyond what kind of suit someone wore, how much money they earned and where they ate their meals. That's how a man like this can keep doing what he does without getting caught (quoted by Kmytek (1991)).

In this society you are what you wear. Bateman's obsessional behaviour therefore appears to become 'normalised' as all the characters are similarly obsessed. The text assumes the tone of a litany in its ritual incantation of designer labels and products, which juxtaposes with the almost religious nature in which the atrocities occur (it takes six pages to describe the process of shaving). There are no restraints regarding 'correct' consumption. But, as Easton Ellis ironically notes, 'In civilisation there have to be some restraints. If we followed every impulse we'd be killing one another' (from the frontispiece). What emerges is a study of a group of 'civilised' and affluent people involved in a quest for an acceptable level of excitement/excess (how far *can* you go?) through a combination of drugs, sex and shopping. Through his actions Bateman merely expresses a desire for something other than this collective impulse:

> '*I'm* pathological? *You're* telling me that *I'm* pathological?' I ask. 'We look at the world differently, Patrick.' She sniffs. 'Thank god,' I say viciously. 'You're inhuman,' she says, trying, I think, not to cry. 'I'm' – I stall, attempting to defend myself – 'in touch with ... humanity' (Easton Ellis (1991) p 341).

There is much in both *American Psycho* and in Easton Ellis's other works which suggests that this partial, glimpsed achievement of the other is the only possible and genuine one in the complex world of the contemporary of urban culture. Throughout the book we are continually reminded of the unknowable nature of this culture. In the Babel of New York things stream across the eye in a series of disconnected atoms, and subject and object blur each other's image. In Poe's tale of the journey of Arthur Gordon Pym the hieroglyphs that the hero discovers, that might form the first tongue of Adam, though undecipherable are inscribed on solid rock. The hieroglyphs that Bateman's wanderings inscribe on New York are inscribed in air or are simply a figment of Bateman's imagination. To seek for absolute knowledge (identity) here is madness.

THE AESTHETICS OF VIOLENCE

There are two specific issues which this interpretation regarding excess raises. The first concerns the aesthetic function of violence in terms of knowledge and desire. The second is concerned with formulating a politics of transgression (the liberation of the other) through the order of sacrifice and catharsis.

The novel operates on the level of the psychological thriller from the perspective of the perpetrator. It thus forms part of a genre of fiction which departs from the orthodox detective story. The popularity of the serial killing/psychological thriller has little concern with the orthodox detective narrative of systematic scientific examination leading toward the successful revelation of the criminal in a process of retribution on behalf of the victim. Rather its concern is with the motives of the perpetrator and the nature of the act of violence. Violence and murder have consistently been denied a rigorous aesthetic consideration as Shklar notes 'Perhaps cruelty is too deep a threat to reason for most philosophers to contemplate' (Shklar (1984) p 8).[7] But it can be argued that an act of violence in representational terms reveals the nature of excessive tendencies lurking within the contemporary predicament. The only method through which individuality can be exerted is through the potentially transgressive act, if only in reaction to the violence of the contemporary regulatory order. Thus violence deserves to be read as having an aesthetic function as a representation of a search for liberation and as a reaction to jaded logic and ethics.

Violence within modernity was confined to the categories of sociology, criminology and pathology. But our customary experience of violence is primarily aesthetic rather than moral, physical, natural or whatever term we choose as a synonym for the word 'real'. Only the victim knows the brutal 'reality' of murder, the rest of us view it at a distance, often as rapt on-lookers with regard to its 'reality' as a peak aesthetic experience. But because our aesthetic sensibility often conflicts with our moral sense, we are tempted to subordinate the former as deceit and illusion to the 'truth' of the latter. This disavowal of our aesthetic experiences serves to create a moral 'reality' that is a supreme fiction. This grand artifice of moral reason can only maintain itself as truth at the continued expense of the individual's own subjective feelings, the aesthetic and erotic responses to the world. In societies governed by moral-rational values these responses, and their objective embodiments as artifacts (or art-facts), are periodically stigmatised and art becomes suspected of promoting violence, and of subverting the established moral order. Often however, the violence depicted in works of art ultimately seems directed against the idea of art itself, and should be seen as art's suicidal attempt to pass beyond its cultural conditioned self-image of falsity, and to achieve some transcendent or nihilist – but in any case, pre-aesthetic – 'reality'.

In Bataille's general economy of excess, art is excessive (beyond use-value in the restricted political economy of scarcity), and therefore central to the postmodern economy. Art is both the highest stage of capitalism in its fully aestheticised phase whilst simultaneously reinforcing capital by transforming the commodity-form into a purely self-referential and excessive state of power. The continued media representation of violence exposes us, liminally and subliminally, to the transformation of the violent act into the aesthetic experience.

It is possible to envisage the violent act within an aesthetic series of representations. The problems encountered concern ethical questions that are raised when considering

7 However recent attempts have been made to theorise violence: See for example Scarry (1985) and Girard (1977).

violence in this mode. Particularly with reference to a novel such as *American Psycho* the objection can be raised that the acts of violence within this narrative (which *are* the narrative) are motiveless on some form of spurious rational level. This is not a violence of politics or an obvious political act, it is entirely self-interested and inhabits a personal void, an intimacy: an individual demonstration of ungovernability. This is even more pointed given *American Psycho* is a representation or recitation of events by a voice that may be present or absent, embodied or disembodied, inhabiting a purely mimetic function (It should be noted that Plato was suspicious of these arts precisely because they blurred the fundamental distinction between fiction and reality). But it is the mimetic function that a novel such as *American Psycho* serves in pointing out the themes in contemporary urban existence, themes which transcend rationality, logic and ethics and which can only be recognised on the level of the aesthetic.

Dostoevsky intended to illustrate that violence may not only be a moral transgression or even an artistic performance, but could be considered a cognitive and even a creative act. He performed the post-Nietzschean feat of upsetting Kant's philosophy of art by a literature of action. Violence becomes a creative act when analysed on the level of pre-aesthetic action. This is what Nietzsche seemed to say when he urged his readers to undertake 'The creation of our new tables of what is good' and to 'stop brooding about the moral values of our actions'. Nietzsche was prompted to call for the re-creation of morality through his realisation that the causes, essence, and meaning of human action are fundamentally unknowable and that action therefore eludes both moral and aesthetic judgment: '[A]s one contemplates or looks back upon any action at all, it is and remains impenetrable' (Nietszche (1974) p 265) (impenetrable to all those but the perpetrator who acquires knowledge through the act). Pure violence therefore is a thoroughly unmotivated, disinterested act, a supreme fiction that is only possible in the realm of art, which sets off by contrast all the impurities and contradictions associated with human existence (Black (1991) pp 4-5). As Holmes and de Burger remark in their study of serial murder:

> Serial murder is the ultimate violence because its perpetuation reflects a polarization of the worst of our values and because it exemplifies the greatest negation of benevolent values, norms, and beliefs in the ... socio-cultural context (Holmes and de Burger (1988) p 45)

The reader of *American Psycho* is forced to abandon the search for a motive or a 'truth' in the text and becomes complicit with the protagonist in the quest for knowledge through excess.

SACRIFICE AND CATHARSIS

This leads us to the second element in this dissection – the acquisition of knowledge through sacrifice and catharsis and the attempt at a transgressive (political) gesture. Bateman's quest for knowledge/power/excitement and the possibility of 'revelation' in terms of truth and meaning as opposed to the confines of satiated existence provide a degree of motive, if such a concept is desired. Nietzsche writes that '[T]o practice cruelty is to enjoy the highest gratification of the feeling of power' (Nietszche (1974) p 265). Foucault notes 'It might be said that all knowledge is linked to the essential forms of cruelty' (Foucault (1962) p 606). Within the novel there are references to motives which Bateman makes in the course of his acts (for example that beggars should get work and that prostitutes are paid to suffer) and in one respect he is satisfying a sexual desire. If a criminological-psychological typology were applied to Bateman as serial killer then it could be suggested that he exhibits a typically 'nonrational' *intrinsic* motive system originating from an internal manifestation. This governs and structures the serial killer's homicidal behaviour. These motive systems ordinarily reflect neither passion nor personal gain nor profit tendencies. As the text progresses Bateman's general abandonment of motivational proclamations points to a quest for self-knowledge and fulfilment. In terms of excess there need be no motive in Nietzschean terms, only action. However, Bateman's existence becomes one in which he attempts to exert his identity and his anomistic power through affluence.

There are two possible psychoanalytical interpretations of identity given this analysis. A Freudian interpretation utilises the collapse of the public-private lifeworld referents. Bateman's 'agony' consists of the way his interior life keeps leaking into the public arena only to be inauthenticated, so that he has to reinforce his 'self', his 'identity', in ever more extreme and violent ways. A Freudian examination of the postmodern implosion of the public-private distinction would place Bateman at this juncture of collapse and in the consequence destroying his autonomous 'ego'. Bateman does not understand the boundaries of the appropriate and the inappropriate, the acceptable and the unacceptable; his 'personality' debouches haphazardly along a spectrum from the most secret and interior desires to the mannered conventions of a highly-sophisticated society. An individual 'personality' cannot sustain these contradictions; an individual 'personality' in which Id, Ego and Super-Ego go into melt-down is doomed. It is doomed to psychosis, schizophrenia and gibberish. Bateman exists only to implode and to become void: he becomes feminised.

The quest for identity in excess of affluence can also be explained within a Lacanian psycho-analytic interpretation following the analysis provided by Salecl (1993). Here the key element of the perverse intensity of the serial killer is the prevalence of the maternal Super Ego and the unresolved Oedipus complex. *American Psycho* can be interpreted as Bateman's bonding to the power of the pre-Oedipal maternal desire which is not subject to Law. Bateman's quest becomes one that in the absence of the Name-of-the-Father his slaughtering is a demand for Law, an attempt to establish the agency of the Name-of-the-Father, which in turn leads the subject to symbolic castration. Bateman understands Law only as a force that impels him to kill each time in a different way. So he does not relate to social norms with a feeling or an awareness of his acts being wrong, within the bounds of those norms. He does not mount a spectacle but only a ritual which means that he has no desire to unmask authority because he does not resist authority or question the Law. Bateman relates to external symbolic authority as a mere fact, he is Law's equal and becomes a Law unto himself, creating Law in his own image and is therefore an outlaw within-Law. It is this fact which becomes political in the negation of Law through the quest for identity through the absent Father. As opposed to the implosion of personality Bateman becomes Law because his identity is beyond bounded rationality (dreadful desire, uncontrolled libido, the unconscious).

Motiveless crime violates the fundamental law of cause and effect. It is therefore a crime against reason itself and becomes a subversion of ethics by aesthetics and a perverse political act through negation. This political act is operative upon two levels: the sacrificial and the cathartic.

Sacrifice can be interpreted as an act that organises and neutralises the violent forces of disorder in primitive societies and thereby lays the foundation for a new social order. The public spectacle of cruelty was an ideological device in that it was through such festivals that the social memory, and with it, the spheres of legal obligation and morality were first brought into existence:

> Blood, torture and sacrifices were the way in which man created a memory for himself ... only that which never ceases to *hurt* stays in the memory – joining a group a man pledged himself to obey shared rules on pain of cruel punishment if he did not, punishments which produced an increase of fear, a heightening of prudence, mastery of the desires: thus punishment *tames* men, but it does not make them better (Nietzsche (1953) p 192).

But sacrifice also served a fundamentally cognitive, heuristic purpose: sacrifice as an instrument for exploring the world. Bateman's pathological interest in the mechanisms of his act certainly conform to such an idea, for example in his 'experiments' in the production of sausages out of human intestines and his general demeanour of being fascinated by the technical aspect of his dissecting activities. Bataille noted this fascination in his analysis of the fifteenth century child murderer Gilles de Rais: 'He loved to look'. In this sense violence becomes an act of knowing and of creation because it is a foundational or originating act. But its originating potential is inseparable from its violent, destructive and excessive character which goes beyond Kant's moral universe. In modernity, the problem is how to control this desire (and becomes translated into psychological and therapeutic practice). Cruelty, abolished as public spectacle, reappears as shadowy sexual obsession fuelled by phantasies of butchery, death, and violent domination. But in the contemporary experience of the world we have found ourselves confronting the open space of irrational, pre-aesthetic action in which humanity's Dionysian lunges at self-knowledge are repeatedly performed: 'The infinite void that opens beneath the feet of the person it attracts' (Foucault (1977b) p 46).

The American Psycho merely accedes to the 'rational' of the pre-modern, assisted by the power granted to him through his affluence (that which grants him identity in terms of anomie and alienation). At the same time he is trapped by this affluence in an anomistic state of false-delivered satiation and awaited gratification. To inhabit a social order that makes promises and then proceeds to keep them with such apparent ease and abundance can trivialise them to the point where achievement in terms of self-knowledge no longer affords consummatory gratification and an individual's ties to a normative order are weakened. Here the other side of the peak of achievements becomes the margin of deviance and the possibility of transgression in an orgy of escalating appetites.[8] The American Psycho 'achieves' this state both literally and metaphorically. The shackles of consumption in which perceived (regulated) desire is ever satisfied ensure that the final desire becomes the desire for excess itself. Only through passing through the border, or entering the alternative of the other, of the contemporary regulatory order, can the individual become aware of the potential of the interstice inhabited by the unregulated and unrepresentable. Therefore the individual partakes in a political act from within the carnival of consumption in a movement toward the possession of self-expression and knowledge beyond the barriers created by the multiple regulatory forms. Or within those barriers.

In terms of radical psychoanalysis an affirmation of a quest for knowledge and creation can also be interpreted as a negation, in that acts of transgression against the limits of the normative order merely validates these limits. It is against the world, attempted because of the constraints of the world. It is therefore not simply a search for knowledge but also an expression of opposition against the repressive authority of the contemporary order. In this mode the violent act becomes a cathartic statement of a psychological or spiritual need. Crimes against the person can be read as demonstrations of individual power and as a cathartic release of rage. The challenge is to escape a situation that has come to be viewed as inexorably humiliating in which 'the killer leaps at the possibility of embodying through the practice of "righteous" slaughter some eternal, universal form of Good' (see Katz (1989) p 9).

In his work on the aesthetics of murder, Katz uses the word transcendence as opposed to catharsis, in that the former implies a desire to go beyond the established moral definitions as opposed to the crude articulation of instantaneous rage. Much the same can be said of transcendence regarding transgression, in that to transcend does away with a struggle involving opposition. Nevertheless, catharsis also denotes (together with sacrifice) the possibility of purity and purgation. As Aristotle notes in *The Poetics*, catharsis includes the aesthetic experience of the spectator, those persons partaking of a ritual of purification of the 'morbid substances'. We return to the nature of representation and the gaze which reflects ourselves as the audience of these events of the everyday. On this level the fatal attraction of *American Psycho* in Blanchot's terms is that we are seduced as sympathetic witnesses by an unfolding of events which engage our primal instincts for destruction in terms of racism, sexism and homophobia.

8 As Durkheim noted: 'Thereupon the appetites thus excited have become freed from any limiting authority. By sanctifying them, so to speak, this apotheosis of well-being has placed them above all human law. This restraint seems like a sort of sacrilege'. Later, Durkheim discusses this 'private passion' in terms of social injustice, remarking on the fact that hegemonic supremacy is only ever contingent and unsatisfactory: 'To be sure, the strongest succeed in completely demolishing the weakest, or in subordinating them. But if conquered, for a time, must suffer subordination under compulsion, they do not consent to it, and consequently this cannot constitute a stable equilibrium. Truces, arrived at after violence, are never anything but provisional, and satisfy no one. Human passions stop only before a moral power they respect. If all authority of this kind is wanting, the law of the strongest prevails, and latent or active, the state of war is necessarily chronic' (Durkheim quoted by Mestrovic (1991) p 172). In terms of Bateman this predicament is demonstrated in his destruction of others, which is always unsatisfactory.

Our protagonist, Bateman, carries us with him through both the literal and metaphorical system of 'ritual' purification which, although unsatisfactory, perhaps provides a temporary moment in the process toward transgression. (Such activities can only ever be unsatisfactory: there has to be a crime for the rage to work and a crime means a transgression of a norm and an act which will lead to the desire to be discovered and granted redemption). We, the audience, the spectator, become baited, we become Bate-Man. Or is it perhaps merely the black joke of contemporary 'civilisation' that the Bate-Man merely fulfils the desires of the repressing and violent regulatory order of which he is an essential part, as he becomes the final incarnation of the regulator, the policing operative of regulation? An embodiment of the authority of the violent symbolic laws of capital.

Sade in the revolutionary spirit of the 1790s insisted that his cruelties were liberating (cathartic) and that it was right to set free sensual appetites, no matter how gruesome the consequences. The chilling idea that murder might be a philosophical advance is exploited in Easton Ellis's drawing of Bateman. The fictional killer, burning with resentment and frustration accuses us: 'You created me. All that talk about breaking away from the timid compromises of bourgeois morality, all those liberal gestures, all that sex where ever you looked – I am the monstrous result. I am what you are' (Winder (1991)). But as with Dostoevsky's Underground Man there is a quality about him that sets him apart. Dostoevsky states this on the last page of his book: 'Excuse me, gentlemen, but I am not justifying myself with this *allishness*. As far as I myself am concerned, I have merely carried to an extreme in my life what you have not dared to carry even halfway' (Dostoesvsky, (1864/1993) pp 129-130). Submitting to the testing of full acceptance, the testing of this irreducible human existence, the 'heightened consciousness' of the rationalist, like the sentimental impulses of the romantic, runs into disastrous and comic reversals: the paradoxically defiant double-mindedness of the Underground Man/American Psycho.

Within such a reading of aesthetics, violence as embodied in Bateman cannot be considered a transgression at all, but only a misplaced attempt at transgression, an articulation in the failure of the possibility of transcendence which produces only a further site of authority – this is the blackest of black comedy. But as Black notes:

> They are ritual enactments of a higher sacred law that combines and transcends the antithesis of the law and transgression. Ritual provides the basis for both an aesthetic and an aristocratic existence; the very acts that a bourgeois ethic, founded on individual self-interest and a closed economy, stigmatizes as scandals are precisely acts of ritual self-sacrifice and prodigality whereby the individual transcends his mundane social identity ... No longer appear merely as transgressive ... rather they stand revealed as ecstatic acts of transcendence, or what Bataille called acts of excess that rupture ... the discontinuous individualities that constitute the confined, fragmented condition of human existence (Black (1991) pp 208-209).

The paradox is that the individual attempting a perceived act of transgression engages in the act the Law desires. Transgression cannot do away with morality-value altogether since it depends upon the Law to retain its seduction as transgression. This echoes Baudrillard's concerns with the all-consuming seduction of the order of simulacra that has become contemporary consumer society. The site of a new transgression is simultaneously the site of a new discipline and a new regime of order. As Arendt noted in her commentary on the Eichmann trial, the consistency of evil results in banality: evil articulated as violence as a technique of escape merely becomes another in a series of repressive discourses, an 'administrative massacre' (Arendt (1977) pp 282-284). In the contemporary evil is everywhere and therefore nowhere:

> Terrorism in all its forms is the transpolitical mirror of evil. For the real problem, is: where did Evil go? And the answer is: everywhere – because the anamorphosis of modern forms of Evil knows no bounds. In a society which seeks – by prophylactic measures, by annihilating its own natural referents, by whitewashing violence, by exterminating all germs and all of the accursed share, by performing cosmetic surgery on the negative – to concern itself solely with quantified management and with the discourse of the Good in a society where it is no longer to speak Evil, Evil has metamorphosed into all viral and territoristic forms that obsess us (Baudrillard (1993b) p 81).

It is Baudrillard's contention that 'We can no longer speak Evil' (Baudrillard (1993b) p 85). It is a contention which clearly signifies the failure of the American Psycho: it is now impossible to articulate the horror because the horror is everywhere, inside each one of us as hyper-alienated operatives of the system, articulated so clearly as communication and information that it has ceased to exist. The sublime of the moral-ethical void has in Baudrillard's analysis been traversed and the *real* of Evil has been replaced by the constant re-play of the simulation of Evil: on the video camera two boys will always be leading a smaller boy towards slaughter. Is it possible to turn the television off?

However, playing with the difference and the displacement available within the contemporary fractured state of the regulatory order it is possible to discern (or perhaps it is only a desire to discern) the emplacement of acts of transgression which do violate the norm, liberated from the shackles of opposition and taking place in the interstice that is the space of otherness. The possibility of de-regulated desire. As Deleuze and Guattari write when they become our guides: 'The sign of desire is never signifying, it exists in the thousands of productive break-flows that never allow themselves to be signified within the unitary stroke of castration' (Deleuze and Guattari (1977) pp 111-112). The point is to attain access to de-centred excess. Violence may be one avenue through which such a state becomes possible. But to *know* the possibility of transgression becomes, within the contemporary of urban order, the ever-almost impossible gesture. The American Psycho, as his precursor the Underground Man, refutes his opponents with the results of having carried their ideas to an extreme in his life. These results are *himself*. This self, however, as the reader discovers at once, is not a monolithic personality, but an inner plurality in constant motion. The plurality of the person, without any ideological addition, is already a refutation of *l'homme de la nature et de la verité*, the healthy, undivided man of action who was both the instrument and the object of radical social theory. Unity is not singularity but wholeness, a holding together, a harmony, all of which imply plurality. What the principle of harmony is, the American Psycho cannot say; he has never found it. But he *knows* he has not found it because his inner disharmony and his dividedness are the sources of his suffering and consciousness: the inner fixity of death-in-life. At once a source of good and at the same time a source of the tragic horror of the violence of banality and the banality of violence.

But inner movement is always a condition of good: what moves may also rise, this is the affirmation of transgression, even in failure. To escape determination requires not merely the exercise of physical opposition but the imagination to perceive the impossible, the American Psycho realises this but he is ultimately trapped by the ambience of consumption to become an agent of the order he desires to refuse, but the possibility, no matter how untenable, remains. It is the possibility of affirmation and articulation of the s(ub)lime of desire. And that is the hardest thing of all. Hard because it fuels the barbarism of the individual and serves to discredit the social. But it is a risk which might result in a recognition of a new limit and an alternative post-social community of nomadic governmentality based on a positive negation of the limit of excess. It is a possibility which I explore in relation to two further stories in excess: hacking, joyriding and raving (excess through absence) and sado-masochism (excess through inversion and appropriation) in the following two chapters.

CHAPTER SEVEN

THREE STORIES IN URBAN EXCESS: YOUTH CULTURES

By exploring the relation between cultural practice, social identity and the social and spatial organisation of the city, we can pay attention to the ways in which these discourses play, and who participates, in the multiple, power-laden discursive arenas of actually existing democracies (Willens-Braun (1994) p 102).

We are in fact always multiple and contradictory subjects, inhabitants of a diversity of communities (as many, really, as the social relations in which we participate and the subject-positions they define), constructed by a variety of discourses and precariously and temporarily sutured at the intersection of these subject-positions (Mouffe (1988) p 44).

NARRATIVES OF DISSENT IN THE WILD ZONE

This second narrative of dissensus occurs in a place in a different sector of Megalopolis. If the American Psycho is a displaced and dysfunctional operative of the contemporary urban order and a violent consequence of satiated consumer culture then he is a desiring-machine which has broken down but into the dangerous negative mode of excess: paranoia and repression, the external and the symbolic. Certainly the figure of the American Psycho is a discontinuous and displaced one and therefore represents an affirmation of something other, but his quest is blocked through the methods he employs to satisfy his desire, which are merely the methods which the urban order grants him. He is therefore only an occupant of another (tame) zone with-in law and represents the extreme detritus of the contemporary, the worst of all possibilities.

American Psycho is not real, only an attempt at representing the unrepresentable. However, it serves as a useful examination of the excesses of urban culture and the problems inherent in the maintenance of legitimating systems which have become subjected to hyper-inflation, simultaneously more insidious because of the technologies of surveillance and also less effective because of the delegation of the responsibility for legitimation to increasing numbers of experts and operatives (and the parallel construction of a new disenfranchised sector 'the urban under-class'). *American Psycho* is a *coda* to *Panic Money* and a demonstration of the need for a realignment of a fractured sense of being in an increasingly disorganised and dysfunctional arena of urban existence. The failure of the American Psycho is the failure to effectively renegotiate the repression of desire and to rely upon the pathologically and externally structured psyche to establish independence. Far from being a figure within the margins, the American Psycho ends up representing the centre. We have to look elsewhere, within the absence of affluence, for other possibilities in the deregulation of desire and the disruption of order.

In my final short story of excess I excavate strategies of inversion of law and order in the private realm of the bedroom as dungeon. At this juncture I am concerned with a story of excess within the public realm and the public space of Megalopolis. But rather than the spaces of affluent post-industrial civilised urbanisation which the American Psycho inhabits, the spaces here are the forgotten spaces of industrial decline (joyriding and raving) and the alternative spaces of technology (hacking). These are the fenced-off spaces, spaces where we are not supposed to go. They exist as de-regulated spaces, nominated as 'wild zones'. They may not necessarily be spaces of the without of law but they are spaces of without-laws.[1] They are spaces which have always been with us and which are therefore of the everyday and the continuous. Indeed, if consumption is a form of production, as Certeau (1984) suggests, but only within prescribed syntactical forms (temporal modes of schedules, paradigmatic orders of space), then a change in the prescribed syntax provides new possibilities in consumption. These disordered and deregulated areas open up alternative spaces within the urban for the creative (even though, or necessarily, through destruction) use of individuals and bondings, providing new possibilities for tracing the indeterminate trajectories which Certeau celebrates. The wild zone is both a tactical subversion of rationalised space and also a space of a becoming of alternative systems and representations that can be utilised in particular manifestations of desire. They may be constructed as 'negative' narratives in the establishment of legitimation but they may also be constructed as affirming narratives of dissensus.

These activities occur in the cracks and within the margins of the contemporary urban order and in one interpretation they represent the spaces which define the centre. They are the spaces of a continuum of disorder serving as reference points in the delimitation of order; but they are also affirmative spaces in the economy of transgression which transform public-repressed space into private-resistance space.

These are activities in the expression of deregulated desire and urban disorder and their space-place are representations in the possibility of Foucault's heterotopia. In their nomination and investment as 'deviant' activities or 'social problems' they are territorialised and subject to urban surveillance (even if fenced off and 'forgotten'). However, it is also possible to invest them as activities which confront the technologies of contemporary surveillance mechanisms and which do not offer themselves to nomination within particular political-ideological categories of the existent order. Their space-place is not a particular aspect of the contemporary punitive archipelago but rather a moment of alternative colonisation (deterritorialisation) either as a resistant challenge to the contemporary urban order or as a strategy of escape-emancipation from within that order and a movement toward alternative subjectivities of community.

---

1 I am aware that in the ensuing analysis the outlaws (hackers, joyriders and ravers) are adolescents. Predominantly, in the examples of hacking and joyriding, they are adolescent males. The narrative confronts the importance of youth culture but I do not specifically deal with the gender element in this analysis. This is not to neglect the importance of the construction of masculinity which is an element in computer hacking and joyriding, but rather my concern here is to emphasise the theoretical dynamics of these acts of excess within an alternative remit of analysis. This may be a somewhat artificial response to feminist criticism. I do not deny the importance of gender but rather pursue lines of inquiry regarding the activation of strategies of resistance which may become available to all and which represent moments of de-regulated desire and political resistance deliberately not universal strategies such as feminism.

The relationship between action and space is important in that the culture which the action comes to represent is both a determination of the space available to it and a constitutive element of that space. There is correlation between the environment and the activities which determine or are determined by that environment. This relationship has been discussed by Foucault in his commentary on Bachelard:

> [We] do not live in a homogeneous and empty space, but on the contrary in a space thoroughly imbued with quantities and perhaps thoroughly fantasmic as well. The space of our primary perception, the space of our dreams and that of our passions hold within themselves qualities that seem intrinsic: there is a light, ethereal, transparent space, or again a dark, rough encumbered space; a space from above, of summits, or on the contrary a space from below, of mud; or again a space that can be flowing like sparkling water, or a space that is fixed, congealed, like stone or crystal' (Foucault (1986a) p 23).

This element of space is referred to by Foucault as internal space. But he also discusses external space as heterogeneous space. This space is that which is lived and produced as 'a set of delineated sites which are irreducible to one another and absolutely not superimposible on one another' (Foucault (1986a) p 27). These heterogeneous spaces of sites and relations – heterotopias – are counter-spaces, simultaneously concrete and abstract. There is a correlation between Foucault's reading of space and counter-space and his reading of power and counter-power, both as socio-political relations of production (according with the Deleuzian concept of the social production of individual desire). For every site of regulation there exists a site of deregulation. This point can be related to the issue of governmentality and the construction of the order of discipline and surveillance. There is again a tension between centre and margin. As Soja notes, in contemporary orders the authoritative and allocative power of the urban centre is purposefully obscured and granted the stretched-out appearance of democratic ubiquity. The process of urbanisation has been marked by selective dispersal and decentralisation, emptying the centre of activities and populations which once aggregated around it. This signals a negation of nodality and a submergence of the power of the centre. Yet, as Soja concludes, the centre holds. 'Even as some things fall apart, dissipate, new nodalities form and old ones are reinforced' (Soja (1989) p 234). To be urbanised still means to be trapped in the collective ideology rooted in the *polis* (politics, policy, polity, police) and *civitas* (civil, civic, citizen, civilian). That which is not of the urban is comprised of *idiotes* ('one's own private person'), unlearned in the ways of the *polis*. To be urbane can be contrasted with the rustic. The tensions and possibilities in terms of regulation and deregulation exist in an urban cartography of power that is often hidden in ideographic histories and geographies.

The difficulties of controlling the sprawl of the urban from a disappearing centre, as a result of both policy (deregulation) and inevitability (the 'logic' of the post-industrial), is one of the demographic control of the organisation of movements between regulated (ordered) and deregulated (disordered) spaces-places. Regulation is the application of a governmentality which represents a Law which has become dangerously (negatively) nomadic. It is a law of movement which seeks to control paths across space (Goodrich (1990) p 298). It is a technological and bureaucratic law of dispersal, transmitted through computer networks and other sophisticated surveillance mechanisms. It attempts to maintain the structural regularities of ordered space-place through an increasingly affirmative nomadic and transgressive deterritorialised urban sphere which has arisen because of the inherent chaos which this inflated system of regulation has manifested.[2] It is a law not merely of physical movement but also the psychic movement of desire, the order of individual thoughts monitored and achieved through both the coercive and seductive manipulation of the mediascape, an attempt to maintain docile minds in docile bodies of utility. The recourse of Law in terms of a determinate space-place is that which is within a static site: the gaze (found in the figure of the panopticon) is now represented by the punitive archipelago of the urban which attempts the maintenance of stability (order) but is limited through its very nature as one of stasis which therefore exists only as partial failure regarding instability (disorder). The eye of the gaze may have assumed negatively nomadic proportions of movement but it cannot encompass all. Megalopolis defies the completion of site, the gaze cannot penetrate everywhere (no longer panorama) through its inextinguishable extension (Mazzeloni (1993) p 300). Regulation becomes the process of suture over rupture when the body politic is a state of accelerated sclerosis.

There is both a tension and a possibility here in the recognition of a regulatory scenario premised upon movement. A nomadic law which has evolved because law is essentially antinomadic attests to the inevitability of the failure of surveillance as a control mechanism. In order to map a disciplinary grid of social order the subject of discipline must be fixed. The remaining strategy in the achievement of this stability is either to attempt regulation through movement or through the nomination of deregulated areas. The first strategy entails a double recognition: of the failure of stability in the establishment of a fixed centre, and also the weakening of coercive and seductive tactics through a dilution throughout the system. The second strategy operates through the nomination of areas as deregulated within the regulated urban sphere. Areas become fenced-off as wild zones as opposed to tame zones (following Urry and Lash (1994)). These zones exist within the scope of Megalopolis but attest to the failure of the regulatory-organisational principle of surveillance. Through nomination the wild zone is bought within a regulatory initiative but not so as to be able to regulate it directly but rather that through representing it as such it is therefore confined in terms of territorialisation. The wild zone becomes a space possessing a mythical or demonic quality, constructed as a 'problem area' containing specific 'social problems'. It is within the domain of *polis-civitas* but as a definable other space to that domain. The wild zone is a recognition of a margin by the centre and a strategic admission of failure; but it is a failure which again serves as a reference point in the construction of the order-disorder/regulation and deregulation/law-transgression series of dualities. The wild zone as a potential site of affirmative transition within the urban must be approached with care otherwise one will be seduced by its ideological construction. This is not to deny

2 The affirmatively nomadic, a transient migrating population is a threat to control and order and the maintenance of effective regulation. As Minson has noted 'A vagrant population cannot be easily mapped onto a disciplinary grid of social order' (Minson (1985) p 24). As Foucault noted, 'Discipline fixes and arrests movement, it is static and enables calculated distributions' (Foucault (1977b) p 219).

the significance of the fragmentation of this element of order-regulation but rather to signal the fact that such zones have always been a necessary element in the process of urbanisation and related strategies of repression.

Nevertheless an investigation of the wild zone which recognises its nature as a particular form of spatial production may perhaps lead to surprisingly resistant elements in affirmative transgression, at which point this zone of the out-law becomes a possible site in the socialisation of non-repressed desire and alternative orders of community without-law. A law of movement which is nomadic but premised upon an antinomadic assumption, even though deploying a strategic admission of impossibility, points to both the process of regulatory implosion and the production of unexpected and random configurations of counter-powers and counter-spaces. The metaphor of refusal comes into play: that which is refused may also refuse. The processes of colonisation-territorialisation achieved in part through decolonisation-deterritorialisation as an element of a deregulatory salvage operation engenders dangerous tendencies towards instability in the maintenance of stability.

It is possible to develop the theme of imploding spatial control via the notion of the construction of social problems.[3] The nomination of a particular activity as a 'problem' is an ideological investment conveyed through particular discursive practices. I deal first with the idea of social problems as ideological constructions and then the related idea of discursive practices as a medium in the structuration of activities as being either within or without law. This analysis supplements the earlier discussion of the relationship between law and transgression but which is here presented as a critique of criminology and the construction of deviancy. At this moment the 'problems' of hacking, joyriding and raving have been constructed as deviant activities (and therefore available to social control mechanisms). In the latter part of this chapter I examine these activities as affirmative examples of critique (the art of the ungoverned) and the ways in which they subvert ready categorisation and become elements in non-repressive discursive practices.

Edelman ((1992) pp 263-279) suggests that persistent troubling conditions are a paramount theme of political discourse. Problems come into discourses as ideological constructions since they affirm and signify those who are virtuous and useful and who are dangerous or inadequate, which actions will be rewarded and which penalised. They

---

3 Here I am aware of the importance of telling stories. I do not seek to represent the activities of hacking, wrecking and raving since, as I have made clear, the nature of representation as a political tactic of repression serves to delineate the activity within a determined discursive frame. A narrative of dissensus becomes a story amongst other stories and not merely another subplot of a metanarrative. The story dissents and places itself beyond the metanarrative frame and becomes part of an alternative logic of legitimation. The story of hacking, joyriding and raving has already been told as an element of the metanarrative of the rhetoric of law and order and thus in its particular telling becomes a series of problems to be solved (a story to which there is an end). Such a reading is available in the response of Government in its legislation which seeks to out-law these activities because they have been perceived as dangerous and problems (in the Computer Misuse Act 1990 and the Criminal Justice and Public Order Act 1994). A narrative of dissensus is not a value-free narrative, since every story conveys particular assumptions through suggestive intonations. However, its power as a dissenting narrative is that it is counter-hegemonic and anti-rhetorical; molecular as opposed to molar. It is an alternative political narrative in that its force rests in its affirmative inability to offer itself up to convenient external or ordered interpretation (see Stanley (1995)).

constitute people as subjects with particular kinds of aspirations, self-concepts, and fears, and they create beliefs about the relative importance of events and objects. They are critical in determining who exercises authority and who accepts it (they also serve to divert attention from other problems). The construction of a 'social' problem possesses two elements. The first is the rhetorical frame of requiring a solution to a problem. The second is the insidious politicisation of a problem which serves to reinforce existent political (hegemonic) practices. Both elements invest in an idea that a problem has an origin. Because there are always conflicting explanations, any affirmation of an origin for a problem is also an implicit rejection of alternative origins; such an affirmation is bound to bring to consciousness whatever it denies. As Derrida has noted, the trace of what is negated remains present and so continues to play a part in action and in attitudes, its difference from the affirmation actually constructing the meaning of affirmation. The evocation and reconstruction of origins are pervasive, constant and central to political manoeuvre (which relates to the postmodern political arena as one of representation and nomination). The nomination of the 'problem' serves as a strategic element in the ideological construction of the universalisation of values transmitted as those of a common sense representing an everyday life: the problem becomes an element in the construction of the political spectacle of symbols and fetishes:

> It denigrates the concerns of the construction of everyday existence and personal well-being so as to highlight the constructions that originate in reports about the political spectacle. These change often. They call attention to the long odds against success in changing social conditions and to the irrelevance of personal sensibility. Though the spectacle takes place in a remote universe, it discourages resistance to immanent conditions and rationalises acceptance of the world as it is (Edelman (1992) p 278).

This diversion into the ideological construction of social problems as constitutive of the external enforcement of universal values in the realm of the everyday is an element in the armoury of legitimation and regulatory rationality in the maintenance of a hegemonically determined urban order. Its effectiveness is achieved through media manipulation. It is a device which is related to the general nature of discursive practices as organisational practices.[4]

Social structures are the categories used to classify the events that they actually represent. As such they are strengthened by routine construction in everyday life and by activities organised in relation to them, as though they were concrete realities. The principal means through which social structures are constituted is language and the

4 A theory of ideology is a theory of semiotic value, because within the symbolic order the position and intensity of values are the index of a mediated tactical assertion, the site of a struggle for symbolic power and charged with the traces of that struggle. The ideological structure is coextensive with the semiotic field. It is the process of the articulation-representation of the sign which produces meaning. Baudrillard's idea of a vanishing of reality because of the dialectic of simulation becomes an important element not simply in the transition of ideological production but also in the manifestation of that reality. It is the interruption of the process of transmission which is of importance in the critique of repressive discursive regimes aligned to the status of that which escapes representations and becomes the eventual depository of a reality.

discursive practices that make conceptual distinctions through the play of difference. At the level of the maintenance of order and stability through regulation, the complexity of the everyday is given a static and decontextualised meaning. This 'flattening-out' of complexity through the creation of 'smooth space' enables effective external regulation and the perpetuation of structural regularities. Discursive practices become disciplinary practices in the sense of producing legitimating narratives which anchor signifiers to particular signifieds, producing a particular image claiming to be the reality. These narratives become the semiotic co-ordinates of action which agents recursively use and provide a reconstruction of the original form:

> Once social structures are constituted as summary representations, their ongoing existence depends on their continued and unwitting reconstruction in everyday discourse, a discourse replete with tacit understandings whose basis lies outside the realm of intrinsic intersubjective communication and established meaning (Henry and Milovanovic (1991) p 300).

It is not enough, however, simply to repeat distinctions in order that such representations be sustained as apparent realities. Part of the reality-constituting process involves a routine investment of faith and interest in them; fighting over them, manipulating them and defending them. The 'social problem' is constituted as a symbolic boundary-policing structure. The oppositional discourse which the 'problem' encapsulates, is similarly constitutive of existing reality, since it addresses and thereby reproduces the prevailing distinctions while disputing their content rather than deconstructing them or discrediting them through the construction of new replacement discourses. The 'problem' becomes a necessary constitution of an externally ordered reality through its construction as a negative reference point, whilst the oppositional discourse which the 'problem' represents is a discourse similarly operating only through the negation of an official discourse.

The themes of hegemony, discourse, legitimation and regulation, coalesce at this point around the issue of the construction of reality and meaning. It is an issue complicated by the processes of postmodernisation and the logic of simulation, which have placed meaning-reality into political play. This issue in relation to the construction of 'social problems' and 'categories of deviance' can be approached through the concept of transpraxis developed within the poststructuralist criminology of Henry and Milovanovic (1991). Praxis is taken to be purposive social activity born of a consciousness of the world and mediated through membership of social groups. Within an identification of the ways in which interrelationships among human agents constitute spaces and actions as particular realities and simultaneously how these emergent realities constitute human agents, the concept of transpraxis assumes significance. Transpraxis assumes that critical opposition must be aware of the reconstitutive effects (the reproductions of relations of production) in the very attempts to neutralise or challenge them:

> The dialectic of control is such that praxis assumes dualistic forms – negation/ affirmation, denial expression. In the process of negation, relations of production are often reconstituted along with human subjects that are their supports. But often

> neglected is that with affirmation, relations of production are also deconstructed, along with those same human agents (Henry and Milovanovic (1991) p 295).

Transpraxis, as an oppositional-resistant agenda, actively negates and produces, affirmatively, new values. It suggests that individuals have power to undermine structures that confront them and asserts that individuals use and are used in the generation of knowledge and truth. The individual has the ability to undermine and subvert structures of control, to episodically render them edifices of subordination. In the postmodern city there is a tension between exploding insidious governmentality (all-encompassing disciplinary surveillance through technological methods) and imploding obscene governmentality (fragmented disciplinary surveillance through delegation to intermediaries). The extension of discipline-regulation-organisation through strategies of spatial determination and deregulation means that individuals experience the different reality relations subject to control and the more contempt accrues to disciplinary institutions. As a result, individuals begin to question other distinctions, for example between the legitimate and the illegitimate in the promulgation of normative values. This questioning undermines that which the controls were designed to protect.

The regulatory transition in the London financial markets between 1984–89 put into play fixed values and assumptions which had previously attached to ethical market practices. The tension between the development of capitalism and the maintenance of order was solved through deregulation, one of the effects of which was the destabilisation of previously fixed conceptions of meaning and reality. The delegation of responsibility regarding the maintenance and generation of legitimating practices which this deregulatory strategy engendered meant a dispersal of power to intermediary agencies, experts and operatives. As a consequence, applying the notion of transpraxis (following Henry and Milovanovic) within a narrative framework of legitimation (following Lyotard), the period of indetermination in the delimitation of stable legal-ethical-moral boundaries and the alteration in the constitution of juridic subject enabled a space to become available in which the assumptions of the processes of legitimation and regulation were challenged, exploited and manipulated by the agencies and individuals charged with the responsibility of maintaining order and stability through a strategy of secondary legitimation.

There is an elision between secondary narratives of legitimation and narratives of dissensus. It is an elision consequent upon the inevitability of regulatory implosion and dramatic alterations in the production and organisation of meaning and reality. It is an elision which illustrates the role of the individual in the co-determination of categories of reality. Specifically in relation to the construction of 'social problems' and 'labels of deviance' it is possible to identify an 'alternative logics' through transpraxis which affirms those aspects of intersubjective experience capable of displacing the excess of regulation-order that comes from giving into those energising its continuity on the basis of sustaining hegemonic practices that constitute repression-subordination.

Affirmatively, such an approach, becomes credible granted the disorganisation of economic life in the contemporary, the banal violence of consumption and the reliance upon symbolism-representation as a primary control mechanism given the dispersal of power through the fragmentation of the mediascape communication networks of governmentality. The narrative of dissensus as the narrative of opposition and the spatial form which contains or enables these narratives to become significant texts of the everyday attaching to alternative configurations of meaning and reality becomes a key realisation in the formulation of non-repressive, anti-rhetorical, non-hegemonic formulations of power and identity in the form of an ethics of viral communication. As Foucault noted:

> It is not a matter of emancipating truth from every system of power (which would be a chimera, for truth is already power) but of detaching the power of truth from the forms of hegemony, social, economic and cultural, within which it operates (Foucault (1980) p 132).

The power of truth, in this sense, is a power representing the universal as opposed to the local, the external as opposed to the internal, and is exposed in the realisation that the truth of things is embedded in a ceaseless repetition of an indeterminant act of differentiation between colliding practices. From within this collision or collusion of structuring practices arises a 'true' story – the 'real facts' of the matter, the self-evidency of 'things'. There are no truths aside from this (intertextual) formation. But so also is truth effected as an act of deference. To make something 'truly' present is to make something other. 'Things' become 'real' only in a socially differentiated act of silencing. It is the activation of this silence which becomes the strategic possibility for a constructivist intervention.

Telling different stories. The discourse of space and the space of discourse attains significance in terms of the production of identity in opposition to a constitutive intersubjectivity and is enabled as an interpretative device. If we assume that desire is social before it is individual and that the relationship between desire and lack is a central determinant in the formulation of space and event (of the regulator and the regulated) then it is possible to establish the construction of identity through the significance of spatial relations. Here identity becomes an element in the activation of alternative strategies of (replacement) discourse. The external construction of a narrative as a 'problem' in the propagation of a particular variation of a 'reality' can also exist as a story of 'opposition' in the internal construction of an alternative variation of 'reality'. An identity invested with meaning exists in a discursive arena and is therefore a contestable identity. The 'informal' discursive arena (as the 'wild zone' or heterotopia – the space of intersubjectivity) in the sense of being an arena of contest which is indeterminate in terms of its ultimate delimitation or nomination is both a product of the event or the act and also a space constituted through the event or the act. The recognition of intermediate discursive arenas (between the public and the private and between the regulated and the deregulated) such as computer highways (hacking), back streets (joyriding) and disused warehouses (raving), as sites of intersubjective negotiation of social identities, allows a valuable and critical perspective on cultural practices and politics. By attending to their construction – making them visible without offering them to territorialisation and recognising them as rhizomic or nomadic spaces – it becomes possible to excavate the alternative logics presented by them.[5] It is the instability of these events-spaces which can be affirmatively utilised in a process of reconfiguration in the determination of desire and identity. The indeterminacy and instability of these spaces-events do not betray a fixed space of the other but rather a moveable space of otherness in multiplicity and plurality in the formation of identity and desire. Thus these spaces-events are nomadic, disruptive, disordered, deregulated in the sense that they are ambivalent. These moments of intersubjectivity do not equate necessarily with inversion or subversion. Similarly, the dualisms liminal-everyday, reproduction-subversion, fail adequately to capture the intertwining of multiple (often contradictory) discourses in the activity of subjects, who although unique users and producers of the materials of everyday life, are always already they who are within and because of certain socio-spatial relations. An emphasis upon intersubjectivity – as a relation with otherness which is at once constitutive of self – dictates that attention be directed to the topography of these discursive arenas.[6]

The concepts of intersubjectivity and ambivalence can be seen as elements in the identification of anti-rhetorical and anti-hegemonic replacement discourses of a nomadic governmentality. They deny access to formal structures, hierarchical organisations, stable fields and fixed centres. They are elements in a nomadic governmentality which is informal, linear, unstable and marginal. In terms of transgression the moment of intersubjectivity and ambivalence is one of an affirmative

5 Asking these questions means rethinking not only the literature of criminology and social policy, but also that literature which celebrates the transgressive and liminal. This literature has stressed the discontinuity and transgression of social codes and the de-familiarisation of the familiar in the identification of other spaces, spaces which are other to law and beyond the border (Stallybrass and White (1986)). This interpretation of a space of transgression establishes the space of Law since transgression is what Law desires. To move beyond this relationship incurs the activation and affirmation of discontinuity and displacement not simply an affirmation of the centrality of Law. What discontinuity and displacement suggest in the sense of 'carrying away law' is a movement or a shifting between boundaries which disrupts stable discursive and spatial paradigms.

6 In assuming a spatial-topographical analysis in relation to the 'events' and 'spaces' of hacking, joyriding and raving they can be related to the condition-forces of affluence, anomie and alienation. *American Psycho* is a failed attempt in the demonstration of excess in the de-determination of identity-desire in a satiated culture of consumption and reproduction. Even though *American Psycho* offers partial solutions, the banal violence which overcomes the protagonist ensures that rather than challenging the external configuration of the arena of identity-desire, he is re-constructed as an operative, compliant victim or accomplice. The events and spaces of hacking, joyriding and raving utilise the effects of the absence of affluence in an affluent urban culture, anomie and alienation affirmatively. Taking account of my earlier analysis in which affluence, anomie and alienation were considered in relation to culture and economy it is possible to enable these activities in relation to the organisation of social and spatial relations in the urban. These are events-spaces which are produced and consumed through difference (following Bourdieu) in the sense that whereas a particular (political) analysis of the effects of affluence, anomie and alienation would be couched in purely negative terms regarding the inequality of social and spatial relations, the determination of a culture-economy through these forces can produce inadvertently affirmative reactions in the articulation of difference (if only through refusal). This occurs through appeals to 'alternativeness' and through the differentiation of 'place' which finds its conditions of possibility in a particular configuration of discourses organised through dynamics other than the economic. The manner in which these events re-work and re-assert this configuration results in the production of 'public' spaces in a manner whereby access is unequal, and, not insignificantly, contributes to dynamics which recognise the social and spatial relations of a nomadic governmentality.

recognition of a lack. If Law determines desire through the enabling of a lack (or the maintenance of a fulfilment of a lack) which can never be ultimately fulfilled, then transgression demonstrates the fulfilment of a lack in desire through a limit-act. Transgression becomes a positive identification of the impossibility of the fulfilment of a lack in desire ('enjoy your symptom'). The constant movement of a transgressive force along the line of the limit is not one which removes the line of the limit but rather determines the inadequacy of a limit which can never be approached since the lack can never be fulfilled. It is an ambivalent movement of otherness rather than a determined other, of intersubjectivity rather than a pure subjectivity.

At this juncture, having established a theoretical plane which does not invest in the modernist parameters of criminological science, it is possible to approach hacking, joyriding and raving and draw out other stories about these activities which do not constitute them as negative reference points in the perpetuation of an external construction of an ideologically determined meaning-reality. It is not possible to tell the 'truth' or convey a 'reality' of these events, but merely provide a competing version, an emancipatory representation. I have attempted to activate a theoretical frame in which an affirmative narrative analysis of these events can be given. It is overtly a political activation in the sense of utilising these events as oppositional. But this is opposition through refusal and ambivalence not a structured version of a competing rhetoric.

The politics of these events is related to a notion of critique which demonstrates the possibility of freedom through the art of ungovernability. This politics is a skill or tactic which is a positive consequence of the negative effects of the determining condition of affluent urban culture: anomie and alienation. 'The will to know' as the art of ungovernability is related to the tendencies of excess, inversion and implosion which the contemporary order of hyper-regulation has given rise to. It is a will to know which confronts and contests the external determination of desire and identity, community and obligation and in the process of the constant interruption of colonisation through the banal violence of consumption and the symbolic order of representational politics seeks to establish alternative (non-repressive) systems of value and replacement discourses representing the complex reality of the everyday as a culture of difference. The spatialisation of social difference provides a key to understanding the social construction of meaning. The moments and arenas of hacking, joyriding and raving dissolve the 'ordered' social into a fluid *gestalt* of 'disordered' sociability of strangers.[7] If we are all 'strangers to ourselves' in the city then the spaces of possibility become the places of strangers as transgressors who notify through their actions the spaces of otherness outwith the law.

---

7 The stranger, foreigner or refugee are important characters in contemporary urban culture. Following Shields (1991b), in contrast to Habermas's perception of the public sphere as a world of rational communication, such a purified realm has never been achievable. Rather, the urban public sphere has always included contradictory elements of liminality (heterotopias). Modernity is founded on generalising the rationalised, economic space of the market to other urban spaces as the public sphere. One aspect of this dissemination of the economic to other spaces of economic life is that social exchange with strangers is no less set aside from the everyday but becomes a constituent element of the everyday, we are all strangers and nomads. As Simmel pointed out, the stranger is a banal feature of the contemporary metropolis. In the metropolis nobody is an outsider, but nobody is an insider either.

The analysis is organised into the following structure. First, a working definition of the events of hacking, joyriding and raving is given. The definition is then considered in terms of the construction of a narrative of dissensus 'told' by youth culture (and by implication the irrelevance of received conceptions of youth culture as interpreted by sociologists and criminologists). Second, an exploration of the relationship between the individual and the group ('the subculture') in the formation of these events and the significance of this relationship in the expression of desire. Third, an analysis of the mechanisms of inversion and appropriation of economic forces in operation in these events. Finally, a discussion of these events in terms of excess, movement and spatial disorganisation.

DEFINITION AND DECONSTRUCTION OF EVENTS

Hacking, joyriding and raving are activities which became prominent during the 1980s in the UK. At this time that they were identified as potentially dangerous and subversive activities of a dispossessed youth culture. Subsequently they have become subject to criminalisation and, as I have discussed, entered popular mythology as 'social problems'. The process of classification-criminalisation assumes that the regulatory agencies of the state comprehend the nature of the activities they are attempting to legislate against. In fact, such simple classifications belie the complexity of the activities.

Computer hacking, which has become subject to prosecution under the Computer Misuse Act 1990, involves the appropriation of communications technology through illegal means. Through the use of relatively simple computer technology involving a modem link, the hacker is able to access confidential or privileged information. Through the use of code words and the manipulation of networks and highways the hacker can 'hack' into files containing both commercial and government information, often of a highly sensitive nature. The hacker can either use this information directly (the most well publicised example being the transfer of funds from bank accounts), destroy the information or simply leave a message to be either located immediately or activated inadvertently at some later date, so as to inform the managers of the system that their networks have been accessed. The hacker can also plant disruptive viruses which can be timed to cause confusion within the system at a later date. Hackers, by definition, work alone or in small groups in the actual performance of hacking, but communicate with each other via computer noticeboards and exchange information and alert each other as to triumphs and problems. The hacker can potentially communicate with any similar individual anywhere in the world with ease. In a recent prosecution of two hackers the presiding judge called computer hacking intellectual joyriding.

7... Each is a stranger to the others, a participant in societation yet detached from and about that societation (Simmel (1971)). Following my analysis of the relationship between postmodernisation (economic production) and postmodernism (cultural production) the 'triumph' of a culture of consumption ensures that not only do specific regulatory rationales become deregulatory in both the economic and the social sphere, but that any form of depth in the organisation of the everyday gives way to a surface tension that heightens the effects of alienation and anomie, ensuring that pre-existing obligations, bonds and formulations of legitimation are ruptured and cast into uncertainty.

Joyriding involves stealing motor vehicles with the intent to drive them at high speed and in as dangerous a manner as possible but not necessarily with the intent to permanently deprive the owner of them, although more often than not joyriding either concludes with dumping the car so as to conceal the offence of theft or in smashing the car up. Joyriding is related (somewhat problematically) to the activity of ram-raiding which involves the theft of a car which is then driven at high speed either at other motor vehicles or, more probably, at a shop-front either to cause destruction or to create an access to pillaging (theft is too precise a word when the obviousness of the ram-raiding in the destruction of shop-fronts becomes synonymous with pillaging). Joyriding usually takes place in built up urban areas (although not exclusively so) at night and is only organised to the extent that it is often undertaken by adolescent males either to impress adolescent females or as a mark of a 'dare' which expresses courage in the presence of other adolescents. There is often a drug related element involved in undertaking the activity, either so as to enhance courage or to provide a heightening of the experience. Often there is no intention to deliberately deprive the owner of their vehicle but merely to utilise the vehicle for pleasure and excitement. It is an excitement which becomes crystallised should the joyrider become part of a car chase, preferably involving the police.

Inevitably the police become an element in the event again when we turn to raving. A rave in its most simple sense is a party. Hence another label for raving was/is the 'acid house party' which conveys the involvement of particular forms of music ('Acid House') and also of particular drugs (E/Ecstasy). The nature of the party is that it is paradoxically a disorganised organised event in the sense of occurring 'underground' (without overt publicity and communicated through alternative information networks such as flyers and intermittent radio announcements) and in non-traditional venues such as disused warehouses, derelict buildings and fields. There are also 'official' raves organised in clubs which often manage to conform to the 'underground' ambience through transgressing laws relating to both drink and dancing. The party literally goes on all night and until the early morning or, indeed, for a number of days. The principal components of the rave are music (multiple variations of dance and ambient) often involving sampling and an insistent bottom line beat; additional elements are 'smiley logo's', fluorescent paraphernalia, pastel colours and Lucozade. The drugs component, even though prevalent, is optional. The rave attracts a multicultural group of participants, the majority of whom are adolescents. Rave can be related to the phenomena of other contemporary 'festivals' such as those of the New Age Travellers, and Rave has become increasingly reliant upon a nostalgic reinvention of 1970s cultural icons, artefacts and values although infused with a *fin-de-millenium* spirit of hedonism in hard times.

These are deliberately open definitions of these events-activities. One of the problems of external labelling and classification is that its closes the scope of the activity, it becomes fixed and therefore open to regulation. Sociologists and criminologists require fixed definitions so as to pursue the narrow informing parameters of their respective disciplines. In so doing they provide useful but artificial empirical evidence which can then be appropriated by a strategically dominant regulating group which identifies these activities as subverting particular assumptions of meaning, reality and value. It is in fact impossible to define precisely these events. There is no obvious origin to determine the reason as to why they arose. There are no fixed criteria which concretely define the remit of computer hacking (precisely because it is a product of an ever evolving technology), joyriding (which has certainly existed in one form or another since the advent of cars and exists in a number of forms) or raving (which is ever evolving, subject to entrepreneurship, changes in musical taste and the merger with festival culture and other artistic forms). Therefore, in the absence of dangerous empirical study, only the ambience of these events can be given. I later identify two determining characteristics pertaining to these events which are presented as significant in terms of the structure of a political discourse which I discussed earlier. However, these characteristics are neither explanations of motive nor considerations of value, save in the affirmation that these events coalesce or serve to reconfigure conceptions desire and identity through the appropriation of space and technology.

In one sense these three activities display the inadequacy of previous attempts at explaining youth subcultures and deviancy. Hacking, joyriding and raving have never constituted a new subculture and attempts to utilise subcultural theory to explain them, and to formulate a new youth politics around it are bound to end up in confusion. As Redhead notes:

> Previous theorists of postwar popular music, youth culture and deviance (whether from Cultural Studies or Radical, or New Deviancy, Deviancy Theory traditions) have tended to look beneath or behind the surfaces of the shimmering mediascape in order to discover the 'real', authentic subculture, apparently always distorted by the manufactured press and television image, which in turn becomes 'real' as more and more participants act out the media stereotypes. This 'depth model' is no longer appropriate – if it ever was – for analysing the surfaces of the (post)modern world, a culture characterised by shallowness, flatness and 'hyper-reality' (Redhead (1991) p 94).

Analysis in this area is limited to either standard deviancy explanations (that hacking is a result of criminal intent, that joyriding is a result of social disadvantage, that raving is merely another turn in the subcultural chain) or dangerous criminal justice policy initiatives which construct these events as 'moral panics' or the activities of 'folk devils' (subcultural theorists producing 'authentic' subcultures). In Britain only Dick Hebdige (Hebdige (1979); Hebdige (1988)), Iain Chambers (1986), Angela McRobbie (1989) Mike Presdee (1992) and Steve Redhead and the members of the Manchester Unit for Law and Popular Culture (Redhead (1990); Redhead (1993)) have attempted to develop a cultural politics from within as opposed to from without. These commentators have sought to develop the importance of the examination of cultural practices, discourses and sites often around the theme of transgression (doing wrong rather than simply doing crime) and within a coherent political-philosophical frame which takes account of the complexity of contemporary power relations and cultural production in terms of desire and identity and the formation of the subject. The task of cultural studies, criminology and sociology is to activate alternative conceptions in the description of social activity, such as intersubjectivity, transpraxis and ambivalence, which simultaneously might appear dangerously ephemeral and lacking in a rigorous theoretical grounding but which are the only strategies through which an understanding of the unrepresentable (in the sense of not conforming to established modes of representation) can be glimpsed and humanistically utilised in the articulation of a non-repressive response to the outlaws.

This approach does not deny the relevance of structural determinants such as poverty (the representation of affluence and absence of affluence is a significant determining factor in this analysis) but in making the object of study the realm of cultural practices, which is no more than the personal resolution of structure and agency; the savage and the civilised; then we can discard the positivist notion of 'doing crime' for the indeterminate 'notion of doing wrong' without in any way devaluing the effects of poverty and placing into political play values such as justice and morality (being governable) which are now subject to indetermination as a result of the force of transition in the contemporary. If the structure of legitimation is in doubt as an inherent result of contemporary developments in the organisation of economic life and regulatory policies have acquiesced to deregulatory policies then we must look elsewhere for a rejuvenation of values since there is a void at the centre. In *American Psycho* the attempt to reassert identity and desire in the absence of external stability results in an orgy of existentialist bloodshed. In this narrative of dissensus we can perhaps discern an affirmative assertion of oppositional values created through the void.

This form of analysis, which does not invest in stable-artificial sociological paradigms, centres on the production of meaning and reality. With specific reference to post-punk subcultures there is only confusion and ambivalence for in a sense they are characterised by a speeding up of the time between points of 'authenticity' and 'manufacture' putting into play many of the assumptions of subcultural analysis. As Wakefield has discussed in relation to rave culture (especially 'The Summer of Love' in 1988):

> What we witnessed over the course of the year was an accelerating closure of the gap between the original and its resurrection ... The emergence of acid house as a discernible musical genre in the spring of 1988 completed the ever-decreasing circle of revivalism ... and imploded the past into a permanent (danceable) present (Wakefield (1990) p 11).

INDIVIDUALS, GROUPS AND SUBCULTURES

It was Dick Hebdige (1979) who excavated possibilities between cultural practice and cultural politics in his analysis of British youth culture from the 1950s to the 1970s utilising semiotic and ideological accounts. Even though many of his assumptions concerning the formation of subcultures are now outmoded or have been supplanted by 'ideas from France' his original Gramscian analysis of hegemony and subculture is still relevant. Hebdige could not anticipate the complexities of power relations in the contemporary, the disorganisation of capitalism or the range of psychoanalytic theory. He certainly could not envisage the potential ravages of Thatcherism and the sweeping away of the post-1945 settlement and the Keynsian consensus. In 1979 the millennium still seemed a long way off (and the Gulf War had not taken place). Punk did not seem to be The End of the Century Party but rather the fevered death cry of the anarchic tendency of '68 (no worse for that, even though manufactured). Hebdige fused culture, ideology and semiotic analysis into a coherent explanation of the nature of subculture in terms of style. Hebdige pre-figured later work in his analysis of the political significance of subculture as a moment of refusal (a movement away from the externally imposed consensus between competing dominant groups) and as a disruptive and incoherent 'noise' describing a challenge to symbolic order that such styles were seen to constitute. Hebdige posed the 'political problem of subculture':

> I have tried to avoid the temptation to portray subculture (as some writers influenced by Marcuse were prone to do) as the repository of 'Truth', to locate in its forms some obscure revolutionary potential. Rather I have sought, in Sartre's words, to acknowledge the right of the subordinate class ... to 'make something of what is made of (them)' – to embellish, decorate, parody and whenever possible to recognise and rise above a subordinate position which was never of their choosing (Hebdige (1979) p 139).

Hebdige's insistence on the utility of symbols of resistance such as the 'revolting style' of punk rock have been criticised as reifying particular stylisations beyond their actual significance. However, these commentators miss the point of Hebidge's critique which operates to deny both an essential political truth which can be applied to subcultural formation and, more significantly, points to the fluidity or *bricolage* inherent in subcultural forms which creates them as sites of difference. Obviously there are structural determinants in operation in the manifestation of particular aspects of subcultural activity (for example the element of social deprivation in joyriding) but Hebdige places them alongside other less obvious elements, for example Bourdieu's idea of a 'cognitive acquirement'. In Hebidge and his contemporary cultural theorists the analysis of subculture becomes a complex activity.

It is the indetermination of contemporary subcultural forms which makes them dangerously destabilising in relation to remaindered hegemonic institutions. If Gramsci's 'moving equilibrium' is fluctuating wildly between competing strategic groups within an economic culture which has determined the enactment of deregulatory policies with uncertain effects, then subcultural forms become strategic sites in the possibility of resistance to a greater extent than before. The complexity of power relations at the 'centre' is mirrored by the complexity of power relations at the 'margin' which often utilise and invert not only the detritus of consumption but appropriate the very symbols of consumption which have been offered to satiate desire but to different ends. Gramsci's original model of hegemony requires fine tuning but its essential elements remain pertinent in an analysis of the distribution of power relations in the contemporary. Particularly important is the process of fracturing and consolidation of relationships of consensus between particular dominant agencies and the multiplication of agencies charged with the devolution of symbolic-legitimating norms in the maintenance of order. In terms of a discourse-narrative of regulation-deregulation the edge is blurred between a reliance upon secondary legitimating narratives and narratives of dissensus. The processes through which metanarratives have fragmented into multiple secondary narratives enables the emergence of incoherent and competing rhetorics (the contested spaces of intersubjectivity). At this edge the relationship between the group and the individual is significant.

The contemporary urban sphere enables a re-configuration of identity and desire, community and obligation consequent upon a hardening of the effects (both psychological and sociological) of affluence, anomie and alienation. The 'subcultures' defined through the events-spaces of hacking, joyriding and raving relate to conceptions of identity and desire within broader (political) conceptions of social-group identity and desire. Subcultures have been identified as either agencies or structures which determine individual identity and desire through collective negation in terms of resistance in the failure of the dominant to provide either coherent possibilities of participation or through their closure in the maintenance of their referentiality. The 'subculture' becomes an arena through which perceived isolation from the dominant can be shared and through which alternative societal patterns of obligation can be constructed in the satisfaction of a collective desire (either an *internal desire* such as the challenge of hacking into a system, driving dangerously or raving or an *external desire* such as disrupting a computer network, appropriating a glamorous car or accessing a private building for a party). Whereas previous youth subcultures in Britain conformed to a group solidarity model of resistance, the relationship between the group and the individual, in the contemporary manifestation of youth subcultures this is a less consistent characteristic and demonstrates the increasing instability of the prevailing hegemonic dynamic to maintain stability. For example, both computer hacking and raving are significant individual moments in the movement toward the satisfaction of desire (beyond the norm of universal representations of consumption). The solitary existence of the hacker is permeated only by communication through the computer noticeboard where the hacker can share experiences such as the presentation of a trophy. The raver surrenders to the void in a Dionysian hedonism of an entirely internal satisfaction of desire through the sacrifice of self to the dance. The joyrider, when engaged in driving as fast and as dangerously as possible, is similarly displaced from a group. However, the three forms rely upon the existence of a group for the affirmation and construction of individual desire, without which the experience of desire is altered and the satisfaction of desire is diminished. The hacker must display the trophy, the joyrider demonstrate a lack of fear and the raver experience the intensity of the dance through participation in the event.

The individual assumes importance in a far more significant manner than in previous incarnations of youth subcultures. The individual is both a figure in the articulation of a narrative of dissensus and also a visible subject of and in a multiplicity of subject positions, constructed through a variety of discourses and precariously sutured at the intersection of subject-positions (following Laclau and Mouffe (1985)). The individual as a member of the subcultural group is both a subject of subordination/resistance but is also able to move between cultural forms in the process of centring by an external figure, either that of the affirmation of collectivity in action or that of negation in the banal violence of consumption. Whereas the subculture becomes a determining arena in the expression of identity-desire the fluidity between cultural forms consequent upon the triumph of an (objective) representational culture which only signifies the appearance of cultural fixity, as opposed to a particular version of a cultural reality, serves to accentuate the idea that although identities and desires are constituted within systems of difference, such systems are always subverted by an excess of meaning, which is inherently schizophrenic.

The activities of computer hacking, joyriding and raving exist within the interstices in the sense that as manifestations of an economy of transgression regarding the delimitation of the limit they utilise this excess of meaning through their anti-determination in the sense of relying upon excitement in both an individual and collective manifestation. It is the element of excitement either through appropriation or inversion rather than any eventual outcome of desire that is important in these activities. The quest for excitement as opposed to fulfilment of desire becomes a demonstration in the will to know and also in the art of becoming ungovernable. There is no desire to demonstrate deviancy merely to attain a knowledge at the limit of experience. In one sense this movement in the satiation of desire and instability in the formulation of identity is the most 'dangerous' aspect of these events-spaces in that they deny fixity of placement by an objective (dominant) cultural presence through their nature as indeterminate cultural activities of absence: absence of affluence, absence of normified motivation, absence of ultimate fulfilment of desire. It is this movement, this shifting in the conception of self from an objective to a subjective self, that enables the 'self' to slip away and become imaginary (hyper-individualised), a stranger in a group of strangers, without the risk which the desire to satiate desire entails, and which therefore denies the autonomy of (an objective) culture.

Hebdige's interpretation of hegemony-culture following Gramsci is still relevant but rather than effecting closure downwards through subordination (objective) the contemporary dynamic of transition in terms of economy (postmodernisation) and culture (postmodernity) entails an increasing intensity between dominant regulatory cultures (strategic interests-agencies) in terms of secondary legitimating narratives and the becoming of cultural forms which are not subordinate in a Gramscian sense but rather ambivalent (subjective) in which the 'deviant' subject is only imaginary. The subject is therefore able to slip between formations of meaning and reality, beyond and within the gaze, as part of a group and as individual. It is at this intersection that deregulation and disorder manifest as excess-excitement coalesces into alternative formations of non-repressive discourses of (intersubjective) community.

TECHNIQUES OF APPROPRIATION AND INVERSION

A characteristic of postmodernism is nostalgia. The images and artefacts constituting postmodern culture are reproductions which appropriate and invert the forms of modernity. For adolescents the seductive world of commodities is often the world of their first transgressions. They perceive a common desire to possess, to have and to consume. What they become aware of is the Verblian nature of conspicuous consumption. What Baudrillard describes as 'style through acquisition' which was formerly only available to the 'leisured classes' can now to be experienced by everyone. We are what we consume. Consumption becomes the cultural activity, which by its nature has a short shelf-life and needs to be constantly reproduced. We cannot consume only one day in twenty, we must consume, we must desire commodities all the time. New excitements and desires become an essential part of everyday life. Excitement under these conditions becomes a commodity to be bought, sold and consumed.

But a consumerism which neither satisfies the desire it constructs nor satisfies the social situation of its participants, is futile. *American Psycho* demonstrated this. Personal change as a result of consumerism is only perceived in terms of what importance that ownership carries. What it pretends to offer the consumer is an escape from the realities of the everyday whilst simultaneously becoming the reality of the everyday. But this escape – this everyday – the comfort of the home, the car, the video, the television is only ever momentary and differentially available to participants in images and dreams.

This is a culture that literally 'plays at life' (Presdee (1992)) and where transgression (in the sense of 'doing wrong') can become a leisure activity in itself. Not that leisure becomes a crime, but that crime assumes the characteristics of leisure. For young people, especially the unemployed (taken from all social backgrounds: the Generation-Xers), there has been a continuing congregation within the contemporary shopping mall, the cathedral of consumption in Megalopolis. Here, where desires are created and fulfilled and the production of commodities, the very activity that the unemployed are barred from, is celebrated on the altar of reproductive consumerism, young people push back the limits imposed upon them. In the hyper-stores of postmodernity we are faced with all the hype: of space, consumption, reality, alienation, individualisation. Lost in a space with no outside meaning, a multiplicity of competing discourses between strangers. Young people, cut off from the power to consume but still subject to the representation of the banal violence of consumption, have the power to invade this space of consumption. They become 'space invaders', lost in an ambient everyday of dysfunctionality, dislocation and excitement, suffocated by the glut of artefacts: an 'excremental culture'. Consumerism demands that they touch, take and appropriate. This is a culture that plays at life and where the market becomes, like the pleasure pier, the site of pleasure, leisure and the pushing back of the limits. Power, desire, and disorder, where all, irrespective of affluence or morality, combine in an exhausted world turned upside down (out-with the law of capital). But most of all it is a world of transgression, since objective culture no longer provides the resources for self-development and expression:

> It would seem that what we experience, or the need to experience, in a world based on 'mind' and 'rationality' is coming closer to the realms of desire and excitement, which we must deny ourselves in a civilised rather than savage society. What Katz described as the 'delight of being deviant'. A transient, ephemeral yet sublime experience that like all seductions needs to be played with and experienced again and again (Presdee (1992).

In this culture marked by searing differentiality, the event-space of the experience of excitement (the quest for the fulfilment of desire as opposed to the actuality of the fulfilment of desire – the recognition of a lack) the space invader utilises whatever detritus or remnants are available, not as theft but as appropriation and inversion ('crime' as leisure) consequent upon the disorganisation of materiality, regulation and order.

For the computer hacker the technological apparatus which has now become ubiquitous can be utilised not simply for playing games which are sold by the multinational computing companies but for playing games which engage with the production of objectivised meaning and reality. The hacker (as expert and therefore as legislator) can experience the thrill of deep penetration and disruption of the 'reality' of unauthorised and classified computing networks. The hacker appropriates these networks and inverts them in a statement that 'I was here, it was easy, wise up'. In planting a virus or bug which can be pre-timed the hacker not only exerts his or her (assumed) identity but can also demonstrate a symbolic violence in the ordered world of the 'safe' network. There is the excitement of the risk and the chase but it is only through the distanced corridors of cyberspace.

Similarly, the joyrider experiences the excitement of the sport of the activity. It is viewed as an extension of the playground. The dominant 'leisure class' (for example, the yuppies who do coke and drive Porsches) pursue adventure within the concept of *machismo* and joyriding can fall into the same category. The car becomes the vehicle for excitement, again a ubiquitous but differentially available commodity, which is only 'stolen' to the extent that is borrowed for the event. The car is appropriated to the extent that it becomes a vehicle of transgressive desire in that it is forced to go beyond speed limits and driven in an 'unusual' or dangerous manner.

Finally, the rave party, in which music is the determining element, similarly appropriates and inverts that which is offered 'officially'. Specifically rave music, as with computer technology, can be adapted from copyright sources. The use of sampling and editing demonstrates the possibilities afforded by contemporary recording technology when the original source is 'stolen' from the multinational recording companies. The technology itself, especially computer-synthesiser programming and mixing, can be used to create music which is not mass produced and may only be heard on one occasion (the irony here is that tapes of this music become re-appropriated by the record industry and subject to commodification). By continually reproducing its own means of reproduction – sequencing and sampling – it becomes like a reflexive utterance that is capable only of mediating upon itself: there is no ultimate founding narrative presence (see Wakefield (1990) pp 10-11).

Each example demonstrates alternative forms in the disorganisation of the signs of consumption. The sign – the computer, the car, the music – is taken to its limit and altered in terms of signification, causing a disruption in the patterns of control in the everyday. These activities place a mirror to the received conceptions of meaning and reality and exist because they cannot be reflected back at themselves.

EXCESS, MOVEMENT, SPATIAL DISORGANISATION

The regulatory void of the contemporary displaces the source of legitimation and ensures intersubjectivity as a compensation for the inadequacy of objective culture to the individual's demand for an integral personality. Either the impact of representations upon sensibility drives the individual into a posture of self-protection which is maintained by a multiplicity of defence mechanism, or the individual shares in a response to the excess of stimuli and the dysfunctionality of reproduction, revelling in the excitement and becoming an element in the implosion-explosion. Excitement and movement in the manufacture of counter-space becomes the imperative in the individualisation of desire. This is not the fulfilment of desire but rather the understanding of the limit and contingency of desire and that the lack of desire is a significant element in emancipation from the external determination of desire. We return to the desire of law-the law of desire as essentially nomadic (the movement of the phantasm) generating moments of the transpolitical subject.

In terms of intersubjectivity and transpraxis the imperative in terms of resistance and emancipation becomes movement and excitement between and within the shifting borders of the hegemonic maintenance of order through deregulation. To combine the deregulation of boundaries with the desire and excitement to interrupt the instability in the process of their production and policing, leaves an examination of the creation of boundaries (spatial organisation) coupled with desire. Under the imperative of liberalism which loosely determines the contemporary ideological-ethical sphere of the public realm all emotions are repressed except for excitement.

Excitement is important in the activities of hacking, joyriding and raving. These activities involve the active participation of the individual in the shaping of desires, fantasies, pleasures and identities within established boundaries of meaning but inverting and appropriating these boundaries. The struggle to construct an identity which does not involve hyper-conformity or sublimation engages in the idea of excitement in transgression. For the hacker, the excitement involves the demonstration of power in breaking into a system, technology replacing magic as the social manifestation of power. There is the excitement of trespassing, entering systems which are apparently impregnable and the risk of discovery. For the joyrider there is not only the excitement of risk-taking through driving but also the thrill of the chase. The police chase is an interesting process in an interpretation of joyriding. The joyrider does not intend to become involved a police chase and at this stage the activity is entirely private save regarding the external validation of identity by the attendant compliant spectators. The police chase shifts the register (the discursive organisation of the activity) from the internal to the external, when the excitement comes from the manifestation of disobedience and resistance. Again, can the driver out drive the system? Finally, the rave exists so that individuals can partake in the collective process of excitement generated by a particular atmosphere (music, location, lights, drugs, shared symbols). There is no possibility of discussion-relationships, only the movement in and out between an internal realm (in a process of displacement of self) and an external realm (the collective atmosphere of the rave). There is an element of excitement in the sense of partaking in a celebration which is marginal but equally important is the excitement of the movement which the music dictates. The music is 'impossible' to dance to given the rapid tempo generated by synthesisers and computers. The music does not ask you to engage with it but rather to chase it, to lose it or to establish a transcendental relationship with it. The freneticism of the beat serves to cybernetically suture the various sound textures and different recordings onto a single plane – an unrelenting but mesmeric surface. This syndrome occurs equally 'after' the rave when the individual 'chills out', collapsing through exhaustion consequent upon the event and listening to ambient music which is specifically created to enhance a calm atmosphere through sampling and very slow beats and tempos. The rave encompasses a range of possible responses to excitement, from a signification of lack to a pre-signifying moment of satiation consequent upon lack.

The significance of excitement inherent in these activities can be related to the importance of movement and spatial organisation. All three activities utilise speed and movement in the fulfilment of excitement. They are not sedentary activities reliant upon passive engagement, they actively demand that you become part of the intensity of the movement. The importance of speed and movement – of being nomadic – has already been identified in the sense that to move is to be unstable and therefore to deny fixity from which reference in a strategy of control can be exercised (Sun Tzu: speed is the essence of war). But speed and movement also deny order and fixity in the sense of constantly renegotiating particular spaces. Ordered spaces can be disrupted and plunged into disorder through the event of a rave or joyriders terrorising the avenues of suburbia. These are not events which seek to territorialise in the sense of colonising particular spaces but rather they are events which temporarily re-constitute and re-configure fixed spatial forms and then move on: transitory spaces of nomadic governmentality.

The joyrider ensures, following Goodrich ((1990) p 298) and Virilio (1986), that asphalt becomes the political territory *par excellence.* Quiet streets are invaded, deprived housing estates become reinvented as exciting circuits, again utilising what is available but transforming it through extension and exaggeration. As Virilio notes 'The violence of speed has become both the location and the law'. The joyrider challenges both the physical laws of movement and the Law of Movement in a terrifying demonstration of defying death and then defying the external order.

Similarly, the rave relies upon speed and movement. First, in terms of its organisation and the network of communication through which information regarding time and place of the event is transmitted: a different warehouse, another field. It is possible to recall here Baudrillard's insistence that viral contamination is the only truly postmodern pathology. Second, in the sense of the convoys of vehicles which often form on major roads as people drive out to the venue and become subject to the confusion between the maintenance of social order and the control of traffic. And finally, as I have previously identified, the event itself and the ritual of the undanceable dance – the Dionysian abandonment to the beat that is both unselfconscious and oblivious (each dancer existing as a monad within the technological cocoon of an all pervasive beat). Speed and movement ensure that the self is no longer (nor can be) subject to an external gaze, there is only the giddy neutralisation of self-space a dissolution of boundaries between public and private, order and disorder.

The computer hacker similarly engages with speed and movement but in a somewhat different configuration. Here the movement takes place in an entirely different dimension, another space between the real and the imagined: cyberspace. It is a movement triggered and invaded by codes and systems in a subterranean world of alternative networks of surveillance. The hacker can enter a secret world of an alternative governmentality, the external order of regulation through surveillance by information. This is a totalitarian space created by the corporation and sold to the State as the ultimate vehicle in the maintenance of stability through the dupe that it does not exist. In one sense it does not exist since the system has become so dense that it is no longer feasible to access particular aspects of information required in the surveillance project. The network of surveillance through information technology implodes because it is an impossible project in pan-orama. The hacker can intervene and move between the real and the unreal, where information ceases to convey meaning. Movement through digital interpretation becomes play and fenced-off spaces become targets to be confronted and negotiated. The space of information is neither public nor private but simply a point of entry into the viral economy where the processes in the production of space can be witnessed (indeed you can witness your own 'official' identity being created, or create your own identity through the manipulation of records and data). The hacker has the literal capacity to enter the eye of the gaze.

> Things have found a way to elude the dialectic of meaning, a dialectic which bored them: they did this by infinite proliferation, by potentialising themselves, by outmatching their essence, by going to extremes, and by obscenity which henceforth has become their immanent purpose and insane justification (Baudrillard (1988: 185).

This narrative of dissensus – a story in excess – has illustrated the limitation of the 'official' methods of delimitation and describing 'social problems' and the importance of a particular series of 'social problems' in terms of resistance. The events of hacking, joyriding and raving demonstrate a transition in the nature of the boundary between fixed conceptions of right and wrong, good and bad, order and disorder. They are subsumed conveniently into such categories and become potentially important events marking the impossibility of establishing fixed narratives of reference in terms of value and space. They are contingent activities in recognition of the lack of desire and utilise the processes of the attainment of desire as movement and excitement. As such they are transgressive since they 'carry the law away' in the sense of appropriating either directly or indirectly, elements of the dominant regulatory forms of the contemporary – the satiation of desire through consumption – and inverting technologies of power into technologies of counter-power. In this process they do not claim 'other space' but rather move within established space, reinventing the tame zone as the wild zone in the establishment of particular manifestations of desire.

These activities are the consequences of excess within the contemporary, consequences of the surplus of meaning and the complexities of social and economic relations. They are deregulated and disordered activities but which offer themselves as a potential elements in a resistant cultural politics by putting into play both the relationship between subordinate interests and dominant interests and also the relationship between the individual and the group in terms of the construction of identity and the socialisation of non-repressive desire. These relationships become contestable and unstable enabling both alternative moments of discourse and significant interruptions in the processes of the communication of authority to be made.

CHAPTER EIGHT

THREE STORIES IN URBAN EXCESS: *R v BROWN*

> There are the hoods, the leather gloves, the face is hidden, and quite often many of the acts have nothing to do with sex … There are very few hard cocks in the orgy room (Crouch (1990) p 124).

> BE CRUEL in your erotic play: snap on handcuffs, neck-collars and chains, lock pins and clips on nipples, administer meticulous floggings; or be a slave for a night and, with your master's help, mimic the ancient 'art of maintaining life in pain', tremble with 'the most exquisite agonies' savour the disintegration and humiliation of the self in the *jouissance* of exploded limits (Miller (1990) pp 484-485).

SADO-MASOCHISM AND THE LAW

This story of excess was prompted by two statements. The first was made by Nietzsche in *The Genealogy of Morals*: 'Only that which goes on hurting will stay in the memory' (Nietzsche (1953) p 192). The second was made by Foucault in *Mental Illness and Psychology*: 'It might be said that all knowledge is linked to the essential forms of cruelty' (Foucault (1976) p 73). The relentless story of violence and desire proceeds from the affluent urban terrain of the American Psycho and the cyber-punk space of the hacker, through the forgotten terrain of urban deprivation of the joyriders and the ravers and into the bedroom as dungeon. This space of desire is inhabited by the writhing body.

There are two bodies here. The Body of the Law and the Body of the Individual. Both operate within a matrix of order and desire, disorder and repression. They are both sites of power and therefore sites of interpretation and value. They are sites of violence (literal, allegorical, metaphorical). The relationship between order and desire can be understood as a relationship between the realms of pain and pleasure. Unifying these realms is the play of violence in the organisation of the laws of desire and the desire of law. It is a violence which crystallises the allegorical and the metaphorical into the physical and reflects the actuality and the tension of the force of positive Law.[1]

In a semiotic interpretation the relationship between the two bodies is one of subjection to codification: the human body enters a spatial machinery of power that explores it, breaks it down, and re-arranges it allocating to each person a place, and to each place a person. In this grid, each position is coded as a value so that the distribution of functions is transposed into fixed relations in this structured grid. The success of this

1 Cornell notes that the violent foundation of Law is allegorical rather than metaphorical in that the Law of Law is only 'present' in its absolute absence. The 'never has been' of an unrecoverable past is understood as the lack of origin 'presentable' only as an allegory. The Law of Law, in other words, is the figure of an initial fragmentation, the loss of Good. It is an allegory which is inescapable because the lack of origin is the fundamental truth (Cornell, (1990) p 1689).

arrangement depends on the coding of this space (Foucault (1979b) pp 137-138, 143). The Law as a structure in this codification of material life, is a system of signs and images. It is through the processes of symbolisation (iconic unity) that the Law dwells within the subject: 'The law is in that sense, no more and no less, a sign; it is the spectacle of the scaffold, the aura of judgment, the sense of the normal' (Goodrich (1990) p 210). Hachamovitch comments that regarding the image of Law and the institution of Law *in* the Body:

> Images are instituted: they honour an imperative to produce and reproduce the text of material life, so as to transmit, again and again, the heritable sense of an origin. The history of the image is the history of the conversion of the origin of law: one law on the other: *utrumque ius*, Roman law, canon law. It is the history of fealties such conversions imply. A history of law would be in other words nothing other than a history of faith, a history of faith in the body itself, but also and at once of an absence of faith in the body, a history of (Christian) repression of sensation in the name of law (Hachamovitch (1990) p 190).

This idea of the image of Law as Law can be understood through the nature of its mythology as a construction or reflection of that which it is not. The power of the sign of the Law subsists through its determination of the space that is not Law, that which is other to Law. Through the determination of that which it is not it becomes that which is. This is the desire of Law. It is the desire of the negative, the absent and the dead. Goodrich notes that a semiotics of Law can show us some of the forms of its dying (Goodrich (1990) p 254). The ideational-iconic unity of the Law is maintained through the processes of the transmission of its images, the constant re-representation of an appearance of order. To interrupt this process – a political and critical interruption – is to grasp the power of the representation of a previous experience as opposed to that of lived experience. The revolution of the form of L-law is a circular masque of death and we are the dying. That which inherits the past and determines the future, the dead (non)space, is that which ignored and escaped death, a pointless immortality without foundation, an engulfing and choking web of repression of life as lived experience.

Simultaneously as the sado-masochistic experience is recognised by the Common Law in the case of *Brown* it is placed in a category of social behaviour that is 'beyond good reason' in the legal construction of the public interest. The Common Law classifies the activity within a schema of prohibition but in doing so cannot recognise the activity as conforming to whatever 'fundamental social values' are operative at that time. The sado-masochistic experience is within and without of the Law. It is excluded through the processes of identification by Law. Similarly, the discourse on sado-masochism in other spheres, for example psychiatry, has generally been a discourse on sexual deviation and psycho-pathology. It is the purpose of this narrative of dissensus to activate the sado-masochistic experience as the foundation of a potential-partial psychoanalytic account of dead Law.

Within an analysis of sado-masochistic practices there can be identified a series of inversions of the symbolic legal order (the psychoanalytic dynamic of positive Law). Processes of inversion as ironic reversal of the principal psychoanalytic devices of the symbolic legal order (pain and pleasure/violence and desire) subject the order of Law to de-mystification and de-authorisation. The possibility is created for the establishment of alternative patterns in a de-regulated distribution of power and construction of identity. As Minson notes in his commentary on Foucault's analytic of power '(power) produces too … productive of a range of intended and unintended effects' (Minson (1985) p 44). The critique has the dual function of providing an interrogation of the process of exclusion (closure and denial) in the operation of the legal order of positive law and identifies moments of knowledge and transition in the operation of the body in society. A moment of knowledge through the expression of desire is a political moment of transgression articulated as a refusal – or the mark of the refused – in which the disordered body becomes a site of opposition in the activity of the without-law.

The sado-masochistic experience is presented as a lunatic gesture in the reversal of the symbolic violence of the law in the distribution of pain and the repression of pleasure in desire. The pleasure in the distribution of pain is received in the ecstasy of pain as the liberated pleasure of desire. As an ironic inversion of the social contract, the sado-masochistic experience becomes a political moment in which the order of Law (through the contract and the ritual), where the violence of its pain is disavowed, becomes an order of desire in which the violence of its pain becomes the guarantor of pleasure. In this non-relationship between (alienated) bodies there is no role for the external Law of the symbolic order and the space of the activity is by the internal laws of individual desire. Rather than succumbing to the violence of the external symbolic order of law in which the individual portion of reality is sacrificed or repressed in the formation of the contract which binds the body politic, what occurs is the abandonment of the external referent through the extension of the contract and its ritual enforcement to an absurd logical conclusion. At this conclusion desire is fulfilled (liberated) through the satisfaction of imagination. Participants in this contract-ritual are without-laws.

FROM OPERATION SPANNER TO *R v BROWN*

The story of the decision of the case of *R v Brown* ((1992) 94 Cr App R 302; affirmed in the House of Lords (1993) 2 All ER 75; hereafter cited in the text by reference to the page number in the report of the decision of the Court of Appeal) might be interpreted as having importance only regarding issues of civil liberties or as a particular addition to the doctrine of consent in criminal law. No doubt these issues are not insubstantial and the debate which the case of *Brown* generated was conducted around these themes. Similarly, as I have intimated, discussions of sado-masochism have been undertaken as discourses on sexual deviation or psycho-pathology. The function of this interpretation of *Brown* within the frame of excess is to use the decision of Lord Lane in the Court of Appeal as a preliminary foundation for a critique of the Common Law in its refusal to see the desire of the alienated individual body and which can only see the repressed desire of the body politic. The case of *Brown* is an example of the most obvious technology of regulation and surveillance – the Law – in its relationship to the desire of the individual. It is a story of the excess of action and reaction and the way in which the internal action of the individual (in this case in terms of the sexuality of desire) can be used to undermine the reaction of the external authority of control (in this case the Common Law).

The story of the investigation and prosecution of a series of sado-masochist activities is immediately subject to interpretation in the process of naming for it is a story which has more than one name. As a report of the Law it travels under the name of *Brown*. As a police surveillance operation its travels under the name of 'Operation Spanner'. As part of the political discourse of the gay and lesbian community it travels under the name of 'Spanner'. As part of the doctrine of the criminal law as laid down in the textbook it will travel under the section on 'Consent'. As the story has entered the public domain the people and their lives have faded from memory and have become depersonalised characters or figures in a legal narrative. The story has entered the public domain and has become subject to various interpretations, multiple investments in terms of meaning and significance. How did *Brown* as legal narrative arrive in the public domain? This is a story of reaction in decision making and how the private (the foundation story) became the public. The story moves chronologically as 'process' becomes the imperative in decision making.

In 1987, by chance (and by mistake) four video tapes entered the public domain and were subject to the scrutiny of the Greater Manchester Police. They were tapes that were never meant to have been seen beyond the members of a small group of consenting men. As is the popular mode of recording memory at the end of the millenium the activities of these men ('their happy times') had been 'captured' via the means of the camcorder (the contemporary is defined exclusively in visual terms; the capture of the real through the reel). Based upon the contents of one particular video tape the police set up an expensive surveillance programme known as 'Operation Spanner', a policing exercise targeted at what the police perceived to be a potentially dangerous homosexual sado-masochistic 'torture vice-ring'.

The contents of this particular video tape were subject to an interpretation (an interpretation made with the volume of the tape turned down) and a decision was made for the story to progress. The eye of the camera moves from passive private observer and becomes inverted back upon itself as it becomes the eye of the state, the public eye. Because the video tape depicted scenes of extreme violence between men it was subject to the initial interpretation that it was a 'snuff' or 'slasher' video which relayed scenes of *real* violence and possibly murder. What in the event were scenes in the extremes of pleasure obtained through the giving and receiving of pain and punishment, an orgy of delight in which the suspended orgasm is *un petit mort*, were interpreted as scenes of horror and death. In addition, the interpretation of the scenes on the video tape was determined by the fact that the actors and actions were necessarily by and between homosexuals.

This series of decisions having been taken the operation leading to arrest was undertaken. Some while later, after peering behind the curtains of suburban houses in middle class districts, a 'torture vice-ring' was uncovered/constructed consisting of forty or so men, the majority of professional status. During the investigation – the gathering of the evidence – sniffer dogs were used to search for corpses in the garden.

At this stage the body is only on tape: it is a representation upon which judgment is being made. The accusation emerged out of the interpretation of the contents of a video tape. It is an image, not of the real, merely the subject of interpretation and speculation. It is the subject of what an authority (the police) intended and the reason for their intention to determine in terms of realising their investment (and more than just the £3 million which the operation cost). Based on their interpretation the police had to consider what charges should be brought.

There is a charge sheet and an indictment. There are forms to be completed in which a version of the narrative is given. The indictment appears in the form of *The Queen v AB*. It is the Crown that prosecutes, the accuser becomes the symbol of the immemorium of the Common Law of England and Wales; the monarchical constitution which you have transgressed. You have erred before the icon and the symbol of unitary authority and have broken the contract. There then follows the Counts (in this 'case' there were 29) each divided into the statement of the offence followed by the particulars of the offence. A decision to be crystallised through the process of completing the relevant document. In this story the decision becomes one of what would be the most 'successful' charge to bring (in terms of securing conviction)? And against whom?

Twenty-six were cautioned for the offence of aiding and abetting assault. Fifteen were sent for trial at the Central Criminal Court. Six appeared in the Court of Appeal. Five appealed to the House of Lords. You are named. Your name will be recorded. You have been nominated as important enough – or notorious enough – to merit a role in the story of the Common Law. One name will enter the library of legal knowledge, ceasing to be what he was but becoming part of that sub-division of the Common Law, part of the memory of what went before in which his life becomes his 'offence'.

For technical and administrative 'legal' reasons the prosecutor (the Crown Prosecution Service) decided against charges of gross indecency under the Sexual Offences Act 1967. Those of keeping a disorderly house were considered too trivial. Those of conspiracy to corrupt public morals were thought too difficult to bring successfully. The final recourse became charges under the Offences Against the Persons Act 1861 ss 20 and 47. These can be abbreviated as follows:

> Section 20: Whosoever shall unlawfully and maliciously wound or inflict any grievous bodily harm upon any other person, either with or without any weapon or instrument ... shall be liable ... to imprisonment for not more than five years.
>
> Section 47: Whosoever shall be convicted on indictment of an assault occasioning actual bodily harm shall be liable ... [to imprisonment] ... for not more than five years (*Known within the criminal fraternity as GBH and ABH*).

For the prosecution – the Crown – the issue becomes one of the inevitability in the esoteric and peculiar logics of legal argument. For the 'defendants' the issue becomes one of remand, dismissal, the position of the social outcast and misfit in a society which allows 'the tickle but not the slap'. Could the 'defendants' (once again a renomination, a transfer in status) use a defence of consent against the charges brought against them? For the prosecution the issue is one of academic interest and public policy, the setting of a precedent and the addition of another layer to the memory of the Common Law. Had consent been admitted by the Crown then the charges would have been dismissed. At the Old Bailey trial in 1990 the aptly named Judge Rant QC (Stowe School, Selwyn College, Cambridge) ruled that consent was not a defence, that it was unnecessary for the prosecution to prove that the victim did not consent to the infliction of bodily harm or wounding on him and that the freedom of the individual did not extend to acts of cruelty and 'perverted gratification'. In passing sentence on the men, Judge Rant accepted that all those involved in the activities had consented, that no money had changed hands, that no minors were involved and that the video tapes had not been intended for public circulation. Custodial sentences were given of up to five years.

INTERPRETATIONS AND DIVERSIONS

Six of the defendants appealed against conviction and sentence: Brown, Laskey, Lucas, Jaggard, Carter and Cadman. The appeal was heard in 1992 by the Lord Chief Justice, Lord Lane (the way, the path, the law via Shrewsbury School and Trinity College, Cambridge). In attendance, but silent, were Mr Justice Rose and Mr Justice Potts. The introduction to the judgment (the resume of how we got to where we are) states the following:

> The appellants belonged to a group of sado-masochistic homosexuals who willingly and enthusiastically participated in the commission of acts of violence against each other for sexual pleasure engendered in the giving and receiving of pain … All the activities were done with the consent of the passive partner or victim and were carried out in private. There was no permanent injury; no infection of wounds; no evidence of any medical attention being sought; and no complaint to the police, who discovered the activities by chance (302)

The judgment delivered by Lord Lane is contained in five pages. One of these pages describes the sentences handed down in respect of the convictions by Judge Rant against the six appellants. There then appears the following statement: '*It is, unhappily, necessary to go into a little detail about the activities which resulted in the various counts being laid against these men*' (305). Lord Lane's unhappy little detail runs for one and a half pages. He delivers a detailed and salacious account of the counts on the indictment (In the same way Lord Templeman in the House of Lords describing the facts said: 'The victim was usually marked so that the sadist *could enjoy the thrill of power and the victim could enjoy the thrill of helplessness*'). Since Lord Lane thought this necessary – even if unhappily so – (although, of course, it is entirely *unnecessary* in terms of the delivery of his judgment) – then I shall re-iterate the activities and we can decide for ourselves:

- Branding a man with Laskey's initials using a wire heated by a blow lamp. Scarring from those injuries remains. Matches were taped to the victim's nipples and the navel and having been set alight were then doused.
- Hitting the victim's penis with a ruler and holding his testicles with a spiked glove. Map pins were inserted into the buttocks.
- Stinging nettles were applied around the genital area and buttocks. He was hit with a cat o'nine tails and the insides of his thighs were caned.

- Branding a victim whilst in bondage with a metal shaped into the letter 'S' and heated with a blow lamp. This was applied once above the penis and a second time on the inner thigh.
- Caning on the buttocks and whipping on the back. A cat o'nine tails was used.
- The victim's buttocks were bitten. He was caned on the buttocks and the nipples were bitten.
- Shaving of the body hair and being hit with stinging nettles.
- Beating with the hands, the strap and the cane. Caning with a riding crop.
- Hot wax was dripped into the urethra of the penis. The penis was burned with a candle flame and then a syringe needle was inserted.
- The pushing of a safety-pin through the head of 'L's' penis.
- The nailing of the penis to a bench. He was then caned, hit and rubbed with a spiked strap, then cut with a scalpel to the penis and the scrotum.
- Sand papering of the penis. Clamping of the testicles causing blood to flow.
- The penis was hit and rubbed with sand-paper. The scrotum was clamped and pinned to a board with three pins. The foreskin was nailed to a board.
- The pushing of a piece of wire and the fingers down the urethra. The insertion of safety pins and hooks through the penis. The testicles were pushed out of the scrotum into the groin and there manipulated.

A litany of movements: Pushing, Inserting, Hitting, Rubbing, Clamping, Pinning, Nailing, Caning, Rubbing, Dripping, Beating, Shaving, Biting, Whipping, Branding, Taping, Scarring.

> (1) You may tie me down on the table, ropes drawn tight, for ten to fifteen minutes, time enough to prepare the instruments; (2) One hundred lashes at least, a pause of several minutes; (3) You begin sewing, you sew up the hole in the glans; you sew the skin around the glans to the glans itself, preventing the top from tearing; you sew the scrotum to the skin of the thighs. You sew the breasts, securely attaching a button with four holes to each nipple. You may connect them with an elastic band with the buttonholes – Now you go the second phase; (4) You can choose either to turn me over on the table so I am tied lying on my stomach, but with my legs together, or bind me to the post with my wrists together, and my legs also, my whole body tightly bound; (5) You whip my back buttocks and thighs, a hundred lashes at least; (6) You sew my buttocks together, all the way up and down the crack of my ass. Tightly, with a double thread, each stitch knotted. If I am on a table, now tie me to the post; (7) You give me fifty lashes on the buttocks; (8) If you wish to intensify the torture and carry out your threat from the last time, stick the pins all the way into my buttocks as far as they go; (9) Then you may tie me to the chair; you give me thirty lashes on the breasts and stick in the smaller pins; if you wish, you may heat them red-hot beforehand, all or some. I should be tightly bound to the chair, hands behind my back so my chest sticks out. I haven't mentioned the burns, only because I have a medical exam coming up in a while, and they take a long time to heal … *This is not a fantasy, it is a programme* (Deleuze and Guattari (1987) pp 151-152).

This is the violence of repetition – fascinating and transfixing in its detail. One 'vile' act followed by an even more horrendous one. Reading we recoil. The scenes provoke nausea, disgust, revulsion (for us, the 'normal' ones, the repressed, whose manacled imaginations cannot go this far). But these acts – as with the acts of the American Psycho – engage our perverse fascination, our lurid gaze. We become fixated with the intricacy of the detail. It is a detail which is slow, meticulous and ceremonial: a mockery of the procedures of the Law. The gathering momentum of repetition simultaneously seduces us and neutralises the effect of the 'irrational'. It is a detail where the banality of the violence is accentuated because conducted in the chintz furnished houses of the bourgeoisie of Birmingham and beyond. A most unlikely setting which serves only to exaggerate the absurdity of the processes to which these events became a part.

The judgment of Lord Lane is one in which the values of the Marquis de Sade as distinct from the Marquis de Queensbury are found wanting. After his unnecessary deviation into the sexual activities of the accused Lord Lane spent a short time reviewing the legal argument where the value has become the construction of the meaning of consent in an action for assault. He arrives at his conclusion through the not unfamiliar routes of orthodox English judicial decision making: a reliance upon what has gone before, a reliance upon that much-loved judicial phrase 'the public interest' and finally a refusal to examine in any way the context of what has previously been revealed (the private becoming the public), the sado-masochistic libido. In terms of what has gone before Lord Lane relied upon three previous judicial statements for guidance on the question of consent in assault. He framed the issue thus:

> There are, however, certain circumstances in which the law does not permit a defendant to rely, so to speak, on the victim's consent … Where the consent to assault is given involves permanent injury or maiming – there is no dispute that the victim's consent is immaterial (308)

The first statement Lord Lane relied upon came from the case of *Coney*, a prize-fight decision which established that consent to assault was immaterial. This case, however, also contained broad qualifications. The second statement Lord Lane relied upon came from the case of *Donovan* in which the defendant was indicted for assault for having beaten the prosecutrix with a cane. Lord Lane commented that 'Although some of the reasoning of that Court appears to be tautologous ... the decision is clear' (308). In reaching their decision in *Donovan* Mr Justice Swift in the Court of the Appeal stated that 'If an act is unlawful in the sense of being in itself a criminal act, it is plain that it cannot be rendered lawful because the person to whose detriment it is done consents to it. No person can licence another to commit a crime.' This remark might be rightly denounced as confusing and obscurantist since it might lead the interpreter to question whether an act is unlawful or not. The third statement that Lord Lane relied upon and which was central to his decision was regarding his consideration of the propriety of the circumstances under which 'the beatings' took place. At this point the issue became – at least for Lord Lane – the test for evaluating whether consent is constitutive of legality within the realm of the 'public interest'. Lord Lane relied upon the decision of *The Attorney General's Reference No 6 1980* (1981) 73 Cr App R 63, (1981) 1 QB 715. The judgment in this case was delivered by Lord Lane (betraying the circularity and self-referentiality of the seamless web of the Common Law). In this case leading to a reference by the Attorney-General two youths who had started a quarrel decided to settle their dispute in the street. In his decision Lord Lane posed the following question: 'Starting with the proposition that ordinarily an act consented to will not constitute an assault, the question is: At what point does the public interest require the court to hold otherwise?' Lord Lane answered his own question: 'It is not in the public interest that people should try to cause, or should cause, each other bodily harm for no good reason.'

In neither the 1980 decision nor in *Brown* were criteria established as to what constituted good reason save that 'The satisfying of the sado-masochistic libido does not come into the category of good reason'. Therefore the sado-masochistic libido was situated in a category beyond the public interest; the activity is simultaneously recognised and in the moment of recognition it becomes a category both inside and outside the institution. It is brought within the bounds of formal legal classification as a subject which is external to that system of classification. It is recognised, silenced and neutralised as an activity that cannot come within orthodox reason and rationality. In terms of the legal construction of consent what can be ventured in terms of legal and moral reasoning is that consent renders an activity lawful if there is no perceived public interest against it. Therefore the public interest served to act as the entitlement of the judicial division of the state to trump arguments based upon appeals to rights or moral autonomy by recourse to wider conceptions of public good. The basis for such intervention became the deliberate infliction of corporal hurt which, if not of direct harm to the victim, may yet indirectly harm the network of social relations through which the victim's society is constituted; underpinned, as it will be, by a prudential concern to minimise the occasions upon which harm may be inflicted. It is a formalistic interpretation of Lord Lane's decision. It is also paternalistic in the sense of upholding the position of judges as guardians of a moral order charged with the responsibility of sending out messages about 'fundamental' social values (Stanley (1993) p 220).

There are a number of diversions in operation here. The first diversion is the disappearance of the subject. Lord Lane's decision negates the existence of sado-masochistic activity at the very moment of its arrival in the legal arena. It is a negation which operates through the classification of sado-masochistic activity as outside the category of good reason. The decision establishes moral-ethical norms in terms of the parameters of lawful conduct.

The second diversion is the paradoxical reception of sado-masochistic activity through the process of its judicial categorisation. The diversion operates through the peculiar truth, that at the moment of classification, in which the activity is sanctioned, sado-masochistic practices are becoming part of a series of increasingly acceptable forms of 'safe-sex' in an era of high risk through epidemic. As Brown is reported to have said 'Perhaps there's a tendency for S&M activity to have increased, particularly among homosexual men, as a result of the threat of AIDS. To a degree it's a displacement activity' (quoted by Kershaw (1992).

There is a temptation to regard the decision of Lord Lane as a further example of judicial hetero-centricism. In the popular imagination (for example as related by the tabloid press) the decision involved the prohibition of certain – necessarily – homosexual activities. It was assumed that the 'torture vice-ring' was composed solely of homosexual members. The effect of the decision was to be applied only to members of the homosexual community. The decision neglects the fact that sado-masochism can be conducted between heterosexuals and lesbians. It is an activity which is not gender specific. Would the Law have been activated if this had been a 'torture vice-ring' between the consenting heterosexual couples of Edgbaston?

The 'notorious' video tape must be re-examined. Acts which might be described as resembling murder can be interpreted as having little to do with the 'orthodox' or 'natural' conceptions of sexuality in which penetration is the norm. Regarding the video tape, there is no mention of penetration (there are plenty of other adjectives available). There are 'few hard cocks in the orgy room' in the sense that in the conduct of the fulfilment of desire in the sado-masochistic relationship the central determinant is the suspension involved in the achievement of orgasm: the orgasm is of secondary importance. The tools and props applied in particular sado-masochistic scenarios operate so as to cause pain to the phallus in its attempt to become erect. Penetration is redundant and the 'form' that it may take is that of 'fist-fucking' (the insertion of the arm into the rectum). The act is the achievement of sexual gratification through the displacement of the phallus.

Herein lies the perversion and the danger. The submissive male in the sado-masochistic relationship assumes what, in the judicial consciousness, is the female position. In terms of judicial pronouncements on cases of rape this assumption operates to sanction the mythical operation of consent when one is obviously not present in the male-male relationship ('yes means no'), when consent so often appears to negate a charge of rape in the male-female relationship ('no means yes').

This decision was a refusal to contemplate sado-masochistic activity through its categorisation as an aspect of the heterosexual abhorrence of the absent phallus. The phallus is the weapon, the tool that provides the pleasure in the exercise of its authority. Here the phallus assumes significance as the instrument to which something 'unnatural' is done or through its non-participation and its replacement by different tools and props. The manipulation of the phallus is important but it is as a dormant and repressed sexual entity: not of the symbolic law but of the absent other. At this level of interpretation the proscription against sodomy assumes a spurious logic in terms of the operation of binary oppositions, where, as in the example of sado-masochistic activities, there is a complete displacement and inversion of the role of the phallus, the activity operates beyond the bonds of such logic.

THE COMMON LAW AND A REMEMBRANCE OF TIMES PAST

Goodrich suggests that a semiotics of law can depict the implicit rationalism of legal method. It instances the relationship between the legal gaze – the visual measure of conduct seen and circumscribed from the outside. It is a Cartesian or modernist reason, a heliotropic rationality that silences the imaginary and freezes its images in the name of logical schemata. Enlightenment reason constructed the world from the outside, as an external order and lost the tradition and the temporality that it claimed as the frame of the source of its logic, replacing temporal movement with spatial categories and with a forensic gaze that was essentially a panoptic surveillance of a space inhabited by others (Goodrich (1990) p 251). The forensic speculum – the technology of surveillance – became diagnostic and distanced: the Law opened up the body to the public eye but in so doing it forgot itself.

At the level of the literal reading, the judgment of Lord Lane is simply banal. His later exhortations 'It is hoped that he might now be rid of his sado-masochistic inclinations' (p 311) and that 'It is some comfort to be told, as we were, that 'K' is now it seems settled into a normal heterosexual relationship' (p 310) in addition to his statement prior to dismissing the appeal that the defendants 'Should be prepared for prison' exhibited the displacement of his individual fascination in drawing out – and simultaneously pushing back in – these private acts of sado-masochistic desire. Lord Lane summons his own 'time out of mind', that of the all-male English public school. Small wonder that Lord Lane in the expression of apparent revulsion at the activities presented to him ('*It is, unhappily, necessary to go into a little detail*') is trapped for a moment in the reversal of the forensic gaze. Perhaps Lord Lane yearned for a retrieval of his time at that very English institution remembering a profane body subject to constant reference and exposure to regimes of corporal punishment administered either through the external authority of the Master or through the internal self-infliction of the Game. That:

> (V)ery particular hothouse regime in which our judges are usually trained and in which they are birched or caned, smacked, seated, sometimes caressed: and there is nothing more frightening (or exciting) to the rustic Englishman than the intimacy of that particular caress (Goodrich (1990) pp 252-253).

Lord Lane evades the issue and evokes the memory of the Common Law and the order of reference it institutes. He signals what the Law has always known: that there are those who are like us and there are those who are not. The body of desire is forced to succumb to the body of Law that is the body politic.

It is unsurprising that Lord Lane's judgment in *Brown* treats the question of consent as part of a general public policy issue. It is impossible not to discern that behind the technical arguments regarding consent lie fundamental issues of the unitary foundation of the hierarchy and authority of the Common Law, the processes of closure and its power struggles within the framework of a *corpus mysticum* that never dies (see further on this Kantorowicz (1957) p 4 and Goodrich (1990) pp 169-170). In the House of Lords, Lord Mustill made explicit reference to the case of *Cole v Turner* ((1704) Holt KB 108, 90 ER 120) and to the 17th edition of *Blackstone's Commentaries*:

> The Law cannot draw the line between different degrees of violence, and therefore prohibits the first and lowest stage of it: everyman's person being sacred, and no other having right to meddle with it, in any slightest manner (Blackstone (1830) p 120).

The Body that is the Realm is ultimately Law's subject (and subject to Law) and also its reflection. Every individual within the Realm is therefore a limb, an organ and a microcosm of the whole. The remnants of natural law theory are (among the rest) the solid foundations of a judiciary independent from political force inside the state, stating the Law of the monarch in parliament, the very mouth of the body politic (See Berman (1983) p 83). As Deleuze notes:

> Every force of law is related to others and it either obeys or commands. What defines the body is this relation between dominant and dominated forces. Every relationship of forces constitutes a body – whether it is chemical, biological, social or political (Deleuze (1983) p 39).

Bodies being unequal relationships of forces are the products of chance, the very essence, and ultimate character of force itself. 'Being composed of a plurality of irreducible forces the body is a multiple phenomena, its unity is that of a multiple phenomena, a 'unity of domination'' (Deleuze (1983) p 40). The relation between the dominant and the dominated in the body creates a reality of active and reactive forces, qualified by quantity in relation to the different sources, described as hierarchy.

The Body of the Law, the soul of the Body Politic, died a while ago and only emits putrid gases of repression. In formal terms the logic of Lord Lane's decision in *Brown* exhibits a dead circularity; it is dead in the sense that it institutes a life that masks the life that is lived, that denies that lives are actually led. It has nothing to say and is scar(r)ed: scared of its own desire, scarred by the memory of sin. As Goodrich suggests:

> An institution which has lost its desire to speak, that has abandoned the surface of the text, that tyrannises with the emptiness of reason, is a dead institution, an entombed law, no more than detritus, relic and remains (Goodrich (1990) p 254).

Because *Brown* is the story of writhing, ecstatic and orgiastic bodies, any legal rule that emerges or the articulation of an abstract standard of behaviour ('fundamental social value') cannot escape the brute particularity, the libidinal surface, upon which an idea (of transgression, of affirmation, of violence, of desire) is inscribed, across which or through an idea makes itself felt, makes itself life. The dead language of the Law, the frozen speculum or forgotten body is forced to confront its own desire when confronted with the desire of a body of passion, of imagination beyond Law and subject to its own nomadic laws, laws which are determined by pleasure and not pain, by joy and not guilt. There is no role here for the external and symbolic order of Law. The twitching corpse of the Law in which the life-force has been expelled contains only the decomposition of life as lived experience. For the fading memory of the Law this is the foundation of sin and now forms a deep scar of repression. The dead eyes of the Law cannot see sado-masochism even though it is brought within its gaze.

TECHNIQUES OF APPROPRIATION AND INVERSION

Brown is an example of an activity that poses a deep structural threat because it disrupts the psychoanalytic mechanisms of the symbolic legal order exhibited as the internal logic of positive Law. These activities, contained through exclusion, can be interpreted as significant sites of disorder and opposition because they invert the formal order and are independent from external order.

> The sulphur was lit, but the flame was so poor that only the top of the skin was burnt, and that only slightly. Then the executioner, his sleeves rolled up, took the steel pincers, which had been especially made for the occasion, and which were about a foot and a half long, and pulled first at the calf of the right leg, then at the thigh, and from there at the two fleshy parts of the right arm then at the breasts. Though a strong fellow, this executioner found it so difficult to tear away the pieces of flesh that he set about the same spot two or three times, twisting the pincers as he did so, and what he took formed at each part a wound about the size of a six-pound piece (Foucault (1977b) p 3)

A determination of jurisdiction through absence is part of the cruelty of Law. This cruel Law. Cruel because impossible to respect because it subjects ethics and logic by escaping them and it escapes them by compelling them. There is the violence of the Law in which 'legal interpretation takes place in a field of pain and death' (Cover (1986) p 1601). As a narrative practice the judgment is incomplete without violence. The word and the deed, the proposition and the sentence, the constative and the performative are intimately linked. Legal interpretations and judgments cannot be understood independently of this inescapable imbrication with violent action: 'Modern law is built on representations of aggression, force and disruption' (Sarat and Kearns (1991) p 211). It is a violence which is visible and vivid.[2] It is a violence which speaks clearly and arouses indignation. As a result, its representations threaten to overwhelm reason. One of the problems of representing this violence would appear to be one of being able to discipline these representations. The analysis of this system of violence allows us to determine the variants and the different speeds and parts of the machine that makes bodies the inscription of a text, and to ask ourselves for what I/Eye, this writing, which cannot be read by its supports, is intended.

In this sense, legal interpretation – the operation of the machine – as we have witnessed, is a practical activity, other-orientated and designed to lead to effective threats and violent deeds (Douzinas and Warrington (1991) p 116). The main, if not exclusive function of many judgments, is to legitimate and trigger off past or future acts of violence. In the juridical sphere it is the violence of the word: the force of law. The sentence is both literal and metaphorical, the entrance of desire ('How does it work?')

2 The association between Law and violence is linguistically present in the ease and comfort with which we speak about enforcing the Law. Derrida notes: 'The word 'enforceability' reminds us that there is no such thing as law that doesn't imply itself, *a priori* ... the possibility of being 'enforced', applied by force. There are, to be sure, laws that are not enforced, but there is no law without enforceability, and no applicability or enforceability of the law without force, whether this force be direct of indirect, physical or symbolic' (Derrida (1990) p 925).

(transgression) automatically submitting to the sentence of the juridical ('What does it mean?') (Law). The legal text – the judgment – sees nothing, it hears nothing, its says nothing. It is a written violence, it is a violence which is inscribed by words not marks upon the body. The most graphic illustration of this is obviously Kafka's short story *The Penal Colony* (1919). The prisoner transforms himself into a machine for writing the law, and inscribes it on his own body: the prisoner is utterly out-lawed. The body of the condemned writes the decree:

> But how quiet he grows at just about the sixth hour! Enlightenment comes to the most dull-witted. It begins around the eyes. From there it radiates. A moment that might tempt one to get under the Harrow oneself. Nothing more happens than that the man begins to understand the inscription, he purses his mouth as if he were listening. You see how difficult it is to decipher the script with one's eyes; but our man deciphers his wounds. To be sure that is a hard task; he needs six hours to accomplish it (Kafka (1919/1961) p 204).

In a previously literal and now in an allegorical sense the Body Politic founded itself through the operation of the inscription of its memory upon the individual body. It was through participation at public displays of cruelty, Nietzsche speculates, that memory and with it the spheres of legal obligations and morality were first brought into existence. 'Blood, torture and sacrifices' were the means through which the state created itself through the imposition of a structure on the community (Nietzsche (1953) p 192; Girard (1977) p 317). The authority of Law resides in its memory, the memory to which we all subscribe through the sacrifice inherent in the formation of the social contract. It is a memory founded upon the originating violent act: 'Only that which goes on hurting will stay in the memory' (Nietzsche (1953) p 192). No one is supposed to forget the law on which social life is based. Repression is the inevitable price of being social: we must forget instinct and remember only the Law. The Body Politic must be inscribed in the soul of the individual. In *The Social Contract* Rousseau expressed the fear that, not only would authority grow tyrannical, but also that punishment would be needed to sustain repression, the subject 'forced to conform to wills that are not his own' (Rousseau (1968) IV-II). It is only through the creation of this repressive regime of inscription that the body politic (in this instance determined through the authority of the juridical sphere) can maintain its autonomy and authority over the individual body. The law assumes the monopoly of punishment through writing its authority upon the body. The point is made by Certeau: 'There is no law that is not inscribed on bodies ... This machinery transforms individual bodies into body politic' (Certeau (1988) pp 139, 142). From birth to mourning after death, the Law takes hold of the body in order to make it its text: the body is transformed into the table of the law, into a living tableau of rules and customs.

The spectacle of the scaffold served as an arena of both catharsis (the individual desire for cruelty) and sacrifice (the social desire for order). But this spectacle, this public arena of cruelty was also, perversely, a site of truth. The punishment, in which the will of the sovereign emerges triumphant, could also determine a relationship of power, not of an object to a knowing subject, but rather an ambiguous, reversible relationship that is the pleasure of being recognised, of becoming an identifiable and legible word in a social language, of being changed into a fragment within an anonymous text, of being inscribed in a symbolic order that has neither owner nor author (Certeau (1988) p 140). Death-by-torture allowed 'the condemned' a momentary saturnalia, where nothing was prohibited or punishable. The condemned became a 'lightning-existence', harshly illuminating the truth of the ambiguity of the justifiable and the outlawed: 'It might be said that all knowledge is linked to the essential forms of cruelty' (Foucault (1976) p 73).

But when cruelty is abolished as public spectacle two transformations occur. The first occurs in the process of the violence of Law. In terms of punishment the effect becomes its inevitability rather than its visible intensity.[3] It is the certainty of being punished and not the horrifying spectacle of public punishment that must discourage the 'crime' of being *other* (*our* violence against *them*) (Foucault (1977b) p 9). It is directed toward representing a common purpose aimed against the anomic savagery lurking just beyond Law's boundaries. The violence which is inside the Law is portrayed by Law as being outside the Law. Elaborate rituals and procedures ('due process') demonstrate the care with which Law now traffics in violence. The procedures and purposes of Law are emphasised while its instrumentalities and wounding effects are kept in the background. While the violence outside the Law is unnecessary, irrational, indiscriminate, gruesome and useless, the finesse of Law's violence is described as rational, purposive and controlled through values, norms and procedures external to violence itself. But as Sarat notes:

> Even when we realise the way law itself often exaggerates the threat of violence outside law, we can never ourselves imagine that law could ever finally conquer and undo force, coercion, and disorder; its promise is a promise to substitute one kind of force – legitimate force – for another (Sarat (1993) p 21).

This force is the perfection of power which renders useless any countervailing exercise of individual power in the determination of identity and existence.

The second transformation in the cruelty of Law involves the reappearance of violence as a shadowy sexual obsession fuelled by phantasies of butchery, death and domination finding expression in a kind of delirious murmuring, increasingly garrulous language. It is a language which discovers in the most murderous impulses both an unlimited fascination and an 'infinite void'. When public cruelty is abolished it reappears as a private event: 'All instincts that do not discharge themselves outwardly *turn inward*' (Nietzsche (1953) p 16). The outlawing of instinct in the postmodern stifles cruel and murderous impulses until the individual becomes 'calculable, regular, necessary'. The internalisation of cruelty and the convergence of pleasure and pain occurs. As Miller notes 'The idea of "self-chosen torture" becomes the key in *The Genealogy of Morals* to interpreting a host of intertwining phenomena: guilt; bad conscience; and above all, the triumph of asceticism in Christianity' (Miller (1990) p 476). The removal of the spectacle of the scaffold through the transfer of Law from action to text engenders a denial of catharsis for the individual and therefore a disruption in the external foundation

3 There is a violence of the visibility of surveillance either through direct incarceration or restriction of movement or through the out-lawing and proscription of particular activities.

of individual identity. This becomes the terrain of the American Psycho and the joyriders and ravers. To avoid this double bind, to escape the lock of paradox, one might say that to be politic is to be tactful, prudent, judicious about how bodies fit into societies, that society might accept tactful, that is, ambiguous, fictitious, imaginary and mythic adjustments (the return of the repressed in the margins of the law).

In the contemporary, the force of Law has determined the regulation of those sexual practices that have emerged as 'shadowy sexual obsessions'. There exists an uneasy balance between capture and counter-capture, allowance and licence, restriction and closure. The removal of the physicality of the Law ushers in an explosion of unorthodox sexualities. As Foucault notes:

> We have not only witnessed a visible explosion of unorthodox sexualities; but … a deployment quite different from law, even if it is locally dependent on procedures of prohibition, has ensured through a network of interconnecting mechanisms, the proliferation of specific pleasures and the multiplication of disparate sexualities (Foucault (1979b) p 49).

But with each recognition there appears a further site of power, a further field of external order and discipline, as the gaze penetrates further. It is a power that reaches the very grain of the individual, touches the body, intrudes into the gesture, the attitude, the discourses, everyday life. There may come a point where the centre cannot hold and the margin becomes the centre. However, in the interim, the imagination deployed in the construction of sexuality continues to be an ordered imagination, restricting the field of play.

How might the cruel and violent banality of the contemporary force of law (administrative and bureaucratic procedures as much as judicial torture or the violence of Lord Lane's sentence) be resisted? How might the violent moment of the with-out law be utilised in confronting the violence of the with-in law? Processes of closure and silencing suggest the inevitability of the implosion of the myth of the internally coherent authority of Law through its perfection of violence-power so that its exercise becomes useless. All that remains is the will to power. It is the implosion of order and the explosion of desire ('the lawless law of the world') that Deleuze and Guattari exploit in their agenda of resistance through the unleashing of the Phantasm along its line of flight from juridic subject to the nomadic.

Foucault urges that 'Phantasms *should* be freed from the restrictions we impose upon them, freed from the dilemmas of truth and falsehood and of being and non-being … ; they must be allowed to conduct their dance even though the results are cruel' (Foucault (1977a) p 170). Or, as Bataille puts it: 'I instantly reenter the night of a lost child, and enter the anguish, in order to prolong rapture with no end other than exhaustion and no exit other than fainting. It is the joy of torture' (Bataille (1988) p 43). The Phantasm, now forced inwards, pursues not the line of flight but the line of resistance in the onslaught of ensuing technological forms of punishment and the rationalisation of the force of law. The desire of the individual – denied the spectacle of the force of Law – becomes enmeshed in the 'tremendous clockwork, composed of ever smaller, ever more subtly "adapted gears" in which there is an ever-growing superficiality of all dominating and commanding events, in which the individual represents minimal force, minimal values' (Nietzsche (1953): (II) 11).[4]

These considerations on the violence of the Law and the nature of the Phantasm provide a useful point of re-engagement regarding an analysis of the relationship between Law and sado-masochism. This line of engagement will be pursued along two avenues. First, regarding the inversion of inscription in which the mark of internal pleasure denies the writing of external authority. Second, regarding the inversion of the violence of Law operating in the sado-masochistic act in which, through ironic reversal, the authority of Law is turned back upon itself and points to sado-masochism as a possible site of transgression in the order of desire through the removal of the authority of symbolic legal order in the form of the phallus.[5]

In both a literal and metaphorical sense the Law continues to inscribe its punishment and writing upon the body, either through direct incarceration or restricted movement, placing the activities of the body under surveillance, or through the out-lawing and proscribing of particular activities (Certeau (1988) p 141). The punishment inscribed upon the individual body by the body politic is no longer corporal or capital but of a control of movement within the gaze which is directly challenged in the sado-masochistic act. In the sado-masochistic act what occurs in terms of inscription is that the very essence of the activity involves the fulfilment of pleasure through the infliction of pain, either the pain that is administered by the sadist or the pain that is received by the masochist. The event is an act of inscribing: not the inscription of words of authority (pain) but the inscription of marks of ecstasy (pleasure). This is an event without writing. And it is an event of suspended inscription in which gratification is obtained through the temporal moment of delayed inscription. The Law possesses its instruments of torture in inscribing; in the sado-masochistic experience these instruments become props. The vast majority of sado-masochistic activities do not involve any real cruelty or physical violence: the game becomes one to tantalise and then satisfy. Playing with the props of torture in a variety of humiliating and degrading scripts, the actors get to savour the illusion of cruelty, of helplessness, of living on the edge. As opposed to Freud's argument that consensual sado-masochism is the 'desire to inflict pain' it is rather the 'social organisation of sexual risk'. Sado-masochism performs the failure of the Enlightenment

4 It will be recalled that Nietzsche's speculations lead him to conclude that within this situation there was 'liberation' for there was nothing more to be afraid of, there was no longer anything left in the self to despise, no longer able to even enjoy the self-infliction of pain. At the end of this path lay 'the last man', the docile denizen of the world.

5 I am aware that in using inversion as a principal device in the establishment of critique it is possible to suggest that at the point of inversion there comes into being merely a further site of (legal) subjectivity. In the process of the identification of the inversion another order of the subject is created: that the inversion itself comes within the gaze. However, it is the purpose of the ensuing analysis to suggest that the process of inversion in the operation sado-masochistic activity, through the ironic nature of the reversal, subverts the mechanism of legal subjectivity. The processes of extension and closure of the external authority of the symbolic legal order subverts the internal maintenance of 'positive' norms of conduct. This is not to deny that sado-masochism, as with other 'limit-experiences', is subject to its own internal 'laws of desire' but that in the utilisation of the figure of the Phantasm these Laws are those of flight along the linear as opposed to the hierarchical and are referential only to the self in the quest for desire as opposed to any form of external order of alienated desire.

idea of individual autonomy, staging the dynamics of power and interdependency for personal pleasure. The activity is a ritual of recognition: the excess of control as spectacle. The 'art' of sado-masochism is theatre, the delicious simulation of harm and high risk:

> Sado-masochism inhabits the anomalous border between the theory of mimesis and the idea of catharsis, neither replicating social power nor finally subverting it, veering between polarities, converting scenes of disempowerment into a staged excess of pleasure, caricaturing social edicts in a sumptuous display of irreverence (McClintock (1993) p 226).

In terms of the significance of the inversion of inscription, the event of writing points to the existence of a separate, distant, despotic law of the body politic (Clastres (1987) p 188). The event of the mark encompasses the memory of the ecstasy of pain as opposed to the fear of pain and suggests an opposition to the body politic in which the body becomes a site/space of the heterotopia, that which is beyond the name, that which is the 'time out of mind' of internal desire as opposed to the time of immemorium of external order. As Clastres suggests:

> The mark on the body, on all bodies alike, declares: You will not have the desire for power; you will not have the desire for submission. And that non-separate law can only have for its inscription a space that is not separate: that space is the body itself (Clastres (1987) p 188).

The sado-masochistic experience operates to prevent the terrifying cruelty of the Law written on the body in the process of the inscription of its external memory of order. The marks acquired in the sado-masochistic relationship and the remembrance of the pain suffered or inflicted in the pursuit of ecstasy are frozen moments of life as opposed to continuous patterns of death. The body becomes a site of opposition and forecloses on the event of writing. The body becomes the site of the mark of its personal history as opposed to the mythical history of authority, order and repression. It is a site of desire and power, not other to Law because of the nature of the mark in opposition to the nature of writing but an event which carries Law away with it. The body is not merely the site of transgression, but the site of the arrival of the 'liberated' Phantasm (the individual imagination of desire/ power). This event is achieved through the operation of the phallus, or rather the arrival of the absent phallus.

The second inversion concerns the structure of reversal of the dynamic of this representation of the sado-masochistic relationship.[6] Deleuze comments that 'Sado-masochism is one of these misbegotten names, a semiological howler' (Deleuze (1989) p 134). Deleuze analysed what appeared to be a common sign linking the activities of sadism and masochism and which could be broken down into irreducibly specific

6 Obviously my consideration of sado-masochism is itself a representation, an image of this alien experience. However, it is an attempt to convey through this partial account the political potential of the experience without opening up the discourse of sado-masochism to overt politicisation since the activity – which is one crucially concerned with the satisfaction of desire – can only be utilised as a transgressive-affirmative activity if it is constructed as an expression of desire, a site of excess, of the heterotopia without determination.

'symptoms' of the one or the other activity. Deleuze identified eleven opposition/differences between the two practices. At some stage in the dynamic, and within an orthodox conception, the two activities are necessarily opposites in the sense of being concerned with discrete bodies: there are two bodies, one to which an action is done, the other from which action takes place. In both activities the role of the phallus as the primary site of pleasure is marginal. This marginalisation is central in the process of inversion in the critique of symbolic law and operates to situate sado-masochism as a 'dangerous' transgressive activity in relation to the external authority of positive law.

'There are very few hard cocks in the orgy room' (Crouch (1990) p 124). In the fulfilment of the desire of the sadist and the masochist the central determinant is the suspension of orgasm (the affirmation of lack). The tools and other props applied in particular sado-masochistic scenarios operate so as to cause to pain to the phallus in its attempt to become erect (for example bondage using cock-rings or the 'English cage'). For the sadist fulfilment-pleasure is achieved through the administration of intense pain in domination. For the masochist fulfilment-pleasure is achieved through the pursual of the intensity of the pain that is inflicted in submission. The 'act' is the achievement of sexual gratification through the displacement of the phallus. The phallus is an instrument to which something 'unnatural' is done, or through its non-participation and its replacement through different tools and devices. The phallus in the very process of the achievement of pleasure is a dormant and repressed entity: not of symbolic law but of absent other. To 'construct' the phallus thus is a fundamental act of disruption.

There is a second level of disruption in operation because of the 'multiplicity' of genders in operation in the sado-masochistic experience. Judicial hetero-centrism may confine the activity for 'political' reasons to homosexuals but the point is that sado-masochism is an activity in which gratification is obtained through exclusive bodies, each fulfilling desire through an individual construction of pain and pleasure. McClintock notes that the outrage of consensual sado-masochism is multiple 'It publicly exposes the possibility that manhood is not *naturally* synonymous with mastery, nor femininity with passivity. Social identity becomes commutable, and the boundaries of gender and class open to invention and transfiguration' (McClintock (1993) p 222). In addition, within the dynamic of the relationship the roles of sadist and masochist, master and slave, may be reversed in the course of the enactment of the scene. Sado-masochism makes explicit the sadistic and masochistic fantasies implicitly at play in all human relationships: 'Sado-masochism is a noun not a molecule' (Stoller (1991) p 21). It can be argued that sexuality as a socially determined and institutionalised condition orders the emotional and intimate life of the individual and that sado-masochism is oppressive because it reinforces patriarchy. But it can also be argued that sado-masochism is egalitarian in that as opposed to the acceptance of inequities in power and hierarchical relationships it enables the adoption of a particular role which expresses a particular sexual need. The key in the sado-masochistic relationship is phantasy: 'The roles, dialogue, fetish and sexual activity are part of a drama or ritual ... The S/M subculture is a theatre in which sexual dramas can be acted out' (Cowie (1990) p 153).

Three points can be ventured regarding the inversion of Law in the sado-masochistic relationship. The first inversion of Law concerns the singularity of the body.

The Law strives to construct docile and alienated bodies. Here the bodies are alienated but not in submission to Law but rather in submission to desire. The desiring body becomes a site of power without external Law in the implementation and satisfaction of desire. The second inversion concerns the construction of what can be considered the 'legal relations' in operation in the sado-masochistic relationship. As identified by Deleuze, sadism is institutional whilst masochism is contractual (Deleuze (1989) p 134). The underlying element is that of trust. The existence of a contract based on trust must be stressed: the activity is consensual. Participating members of a sado-masochistic experience appreciate partners sophisticated enough to play the game within the limits, knowing just when to stretch the limits of pleasure-in-pain and by how much. A promise is entered into that pain will be administered for the benefit of mutual gratification. The levels of inversion in operation can be considered in terms of the body politic.

In being contracted into the body politic as part of being social the payment is repression. In the sado-masochistic experience sociality is exiled in the performance of this private agreement of which trust is of the essence. Law has no role to play. In terms of consent the only role for Law would be as the guarantor of this trust relationship. The violence of Law is disavowed and becomes an order of desire in which the violence of pain becomes the guarantor of pleasure. Rather than succumbing to the violence of the external and symbolic order of Law, in which identity is sacrificed in the formation of the contract that founds the body politic, what occurs is the abandonment of the external referent. This abandoning occurs through the extension of the contract and its ritual enforcement to an absurd logical conclusion. Here desire is fulfilled (liberated) through the satisfaction of imagination without constraint. The participants in this contract-ritual become without-laws. The power of sado-masochism becomes its appropriation from the juridical model of the right-to-punish whilst radically inverting the exercise of this right.

The final inversion concerns the ironic reversal of Law in which sadism and masochism operate as critiques of Law. The sadist, following Sade, follows anarchic human nature, revelling in the exhortation to 'Be Cruel' and transcending the tyranny of Law. Sade mocks the Law by erecting a superior principle of absolute evil that institutes a kind of lawless super-Law (Bogue (1989) pp 45-53). For the masochist, following Masoch, the re-written letter of the Law provides the subversion. By scrupulously applying the Law the masochist demonstrates its absurdity and provokes the disorder that it is intended to prevent. The Law which forbids the satisfaction of desire under threat of subsequent punishment is converted into a Law which demands the punishment first and then orders that the satisfaction of the desire should follow the punishment.

In both inversions the symbol of the phallus remains dormant. In sadism, the phallus becomes a higher principle with the mother as the essential victim. In masochism, the totality of the Law is invested upon the mother, who expels the father from the symbolic realm and the phallus is negated. The masochist's torture purges the inner father and produces via maternal parthenogenesis 'sexless man' (Bogue (1989) p 49).

The satisfaction of this alienated internal desire depends upon innate trust in another and transcends external violence through its form as a particular intimacy between two people and in its form of the physical feelings of pleasure: 'The physical feelings are so intense as to be almost asexual in that most scenes are carried out with neither partner having an erection' (Townsend (1983) p 165). Here we cross the border of sexuality and enter a sphere of intersubjectivity. These are sensations and experience which are unrepresentable, in excess and beyond the name, in which dreams, memories and aspirations take on a new balance against that world we record at any moment through the sense. Sensations which occur when the Phantasm pursues the line of flight. This intensity of pleasure causes the momentary disorganisation of identity, disturbed by sensations of affective processes 'beyond' those connected with psychic organisation. An affirmative disorganisation releases the caged power in which 'self' is discarded:

> There is a creation of anarchy within the body, where its hierarchies, its localisations and designations, its organicity … is in the process of disintegrating … This is something 'unnameable', 'useless', outside of all the programmes of desire. It is the body made totally plastic by pleasure: something that opens itself, that tightens, that throbs, that beats, that gapes (Foucault quoted by Miller (1993) p 274).

Foucault praised sado-masochistic sexual practices for 'inventing new possibilities' in the 'eroticisation of power' (Foucault (1977b) p 34). To go beyond the simple establishment of a particular critique of legal order it is possible to embark upon an emplacement of an analysis regarding repression and resistance. The limit-experience of sado-masochism is a *technology* with which to grapple with otherwise unconscious and unthinkable aspects of negative experience, turning it into something positive, the ability to say 'YES'. As the foundation of a philosophical critique it lays bare the purely negative freedom of the individual. Pain and pleasure experienced as the merging of boundaries becomes a psychological quest, in which all is reversed as guilt becomes joy, pain becomes pleasure, torture becomes ecstasy. This is the site-sight of the Phantasm, the interstice of excess in interruption as a condition of possibility, a political technology and a site of heterotopia. As Bataille writes:

> And it struck me that death was the sole outcome of my erection … the goal of my sexual licentiousness: a geometric incandescence (among other things, the coinciding point of life and death, being and nothingness), perfectly fulgurating (Bataille (1982) p 30).

As Miller states, armed with this Nietzschean knowledge the genealogist of 'suffering-pleasure' might imagine 'new combinations' of impulses and Phantasms, new relationships of power, a new style of life – perhaps even a new 'game' of truth (Miller (1993) p 277). To be invested in the moment of desiring production and to become nomadic.

Through experiments and experiences in and of excess, the arc of transgression transcends the boundary that marks the limit of the internal/external and gives expression to the Phantasm: desire without external Law and imagination without repression. What is at stake is mundane 'social' identity and the possibility to stand revealed in the ecstasy of the act of transgression, what Bataille names 'acts of excess', that rupture the discontinuous individualities that constitute the confined, fragmented condition of human existence. Beyond the moment of recognition but as a constant witness to the unrepresentable. Such an exhortation is dangerous because existence without proscribed limit or boundary is dangerous.[7] But the alternative is the representation of an external order which has become dangerously nomadic which through its decomposition might activate the heterotopic space.

7 There is also the argument that sado-masochism is dangerous because it is an essentially masculine construction of sex and sexuality. In this interpretation sado-masochism operates to enable the acting out of the cruellest and crudest varieties of (masculine) fantasy encompassing violent domination and abject submission in the process of reinforcing (through what a Freudian might described as a 'repetition compulsion') the morbid convergence of sex and death. McKinnon argues for the criminalisation of sex itself until it has been reinvented (McKinnon (1987) pp 3/172). Both the proponents of the experience and the feminist critique of it point to this reinvention of sexuality. The means of achieving this is the dividing point. Either criminalisation (the entrenchment of guilt) or decriminalisation (the exorcism of guilt). Bersani comments:

The relevance of these speculations to the present discussion should be clear: the self which the sexual shatters provides the basis on which sexuality is associated with power. It is possible to think of the sexual as, precisely, moving between a hyperbolic sense of self and a loss of all consciousness of self. But sex as self-hyperbole is perhaps a repression of sex as self-abolition. It inaccurately replicates self-shattering as a self-swelling, a psychic tumescence … *For it is perhaps primarily the degeneration of the sexual into a relationship that condemns sexuality to becoming a struggle for power.* As soon as persons are posited, the war begins (Bersani (1991) p 218).

CHAPTER NINE

CONCLUSION: REORIENTATION

> The pictures which appear in the following pages are photographic by default, meaning that although I *harvested* them with a camera, no photographic skill was involved. I used the cheapest and most automatic apparatus I could lay my hands on and I had nothing to do with either the development or the printing. Apart from the fact that I chose what to see, these images are to all intents and purposes *acheiropoietic*, that is they are what you get if you point a retentive surface in the right direction and leave the rest to chance.
>
> There is nothing scenic or picturesque about these visibilia. On the contrary, most of the stuff was seized from the edge of the officially visible. They are marginal appearances whose normal fate is to be overlooked and undervalued. There are incipient things, not yet ready to be recorded, if ever; or else they are objects no longer fit to be seen and by now in visual disgrace. Negligibles of one sort or another.
>
> They are not mementos since they don't remind me of anything or anyone – in fact I can scarcely remember where and when I got them.
>
> I suspect that what prompted me to take and collect them in the first place was the forlorn hope – anyway by now forlorn – that I might do something *with* them and set them on their feet again ... (Miller (1994)).

The prevailing political tenet of this book has been to follow bell hooks in a quest for a more compassionate sense of justice and a more generous sense of space. This tenet has been expressed through critique as ungovernability in a movement toward an alternative mode of governmentality.

One of the reasons that I framed this book between Sarah Schulman's letter and Jonathan Miller's scrapbook is that they provided an arch which enabled me to investigate aspects of contemporary urban culture and its constituent syndromes of deregulation and disorder with at least a passing reference to a version of reality. The letter and the extract from the scrapbook have provided the polarised references which I have strived to keep foremost in my mind in undertaking the quest. They have also served to crystallise into an affirmative version of reality and meaning some of the more seductive and apocalyptic assumptions of postmodernism regarding politics and ethics. They are an offering conveying something of life as lived in the streets outside my window where the ideas contained in this book might appear to be damagingly insignificant and indulgent in the negotiation of the everyday. In addition the original pretext and the frame of reference have perhaps alerted me to the dangers which lurk within this book. The ambivalence and the excess which I have sought to utilise affirmatively in an analysis of possible strategies of resistance becoming merely variations of individualism, ressentiment and an alternative form of repression and intolerance which I reject. An analysis of the complexity of power relations in the contemporary urban sphere engenders a delicate and precarious balance between crass generalisation-utopian hedonism and obscurantist describing-repressive closure. In avoiding the certainties which modernity afforded it is possible to become lost in an indeterminate space of inexactitude and continual slippage. It is a dilemma which 'Three Stories in Excess' approaches and at this juncture it is necessary to confront some of the issues which arise out of an argument for resistance and emancipation without the Law and premised upon critique as the art of ungovernability and liberation as excess in desire. In this space of reorientation, I attempt to reconcile some of the problems inherent in the ideas of this book and locate my original governing premise concerning justice and community.

In part the philosophical conclusion of 'Three Stories in Excess' can be placed within that strain of social thought that runs from Sade to Bataille and beyond. Foucault incited us to undertake experiments in transgression 'Even though its philosophy is cruel'. This statement encapsulates the ethical dilemma of the paradoxical cruelty of conscience and represents the most severe limitation on a potential affirmative critique of the contemporary based upon an excess in desire. In this analysis of the dilemma the discussion follows Rajchman's reading of late Foucault and will be primarily directed at the constitution of sexual identity, but, as will become clear, there are important consequences regarding the relationship between individual and collective desire, obligation and solidarity beyond this particular psychoanalytic account of ethics.

It can be argued, following Freud and Lacan, that it is our eros which makes us beings of obligation prior to our observance or transgression of any particular obligation; conversely, our eros, our desire, confronts us as an imperative or necessity which we cannot find located in ourselves or in the world of our interests. The reason we cannot find it within or without, the reason for its 'sublime' transcendence to us is that it is structured by repression. 'The Law is repressed desire' declares Lacan (Rajchman (1991) pp 55-61).

Foucault developed this theme in his later work on the history of sexuality: the ethic of the difficult or 'tragic' truth in our libidinal existence that would exceed any knowledge of our Good. Foucault's ethical position is developed not through an interpretation of Freud but through the question of desire as a source of ethics. His genealogy of 'sexuality' and of 'desire' would be a quest for a new image of the passion of thought, a new sense of (erotic) possibility. Foucault expressed the ethical predicament which would accord with the complexities of the everyday as being to rid ourselves of the internalisation through which we construct ourselves as 'subjects of desire' and to set the possibility of an 'erotic subjectivity'. Foucault's ethical question becomes: 'What relations can be established, invented, multiplied, modulated?' Rather than a 'form of desire' an activity such as sado-masochism is taken by Foucault to be ethically desirable as an 'historic occasion to re-open affective and relational virtualities' through the 'diagonal line' it would trace in 'the social fabric' (Foucault (1989) p 207). Foucault returns to his earlier interpretation of the line between law and transgression, the moveable line which opens the possibility of 'carrying away the law' through rupture, discontinuity and displacement. Foucault signals both the condition of possibility in heterotopia and the centrality of multiplicity in the manifestation of (socialised) desire. But he is left with the central political problem of obligation and solidarity.

> To imagine a sexual act that doesn't conform to law or nature is not what disturbs people. But that individuals are beginning to love one another – there's the problem ... Institutional codes can't validate these relations These relations short-circuit and introduce love where there's suppose to be only law, rule, or habit (Foucault (1989) p 205).

The idea of sublimation operates on the precept that our desire is terrible and must be articulated in 'cultural forms' and not through erotic practices. Foucault turns this idea around: it is only the strange conception we have of our 'desire' that induces us to believe that we gratify it in a more fundamental way through the beautiful forms that recreate it than through 'perverse' activities, apparently so much closer to it, which, left to themselves, would end in violence, brutality and death. For Foucault the question is 'What peculiar notion of our desire must we have to think that we must dissociate it from our erotic activities and 'reinvest' it in objects?' Life as art would enable beauty to count as an ethical category in how we might live (Rajchman (1991) pp 108-109).

Foucault sought a new erotic 'after' desire which would restore to eros a sense of improbability, innovation and the beauty of unguided experimentation. Foucault would abandon the tragedy of psychoanalytic 'truth' in a similar vein to Lyotard's abandonment of narrative certainty in preference for the 'pagan'. For Foucault, as for Deleuze and Guattari, 'desire' is not prior to history, but only one of its singular inventions which structures our location as subjects. But history is contingent: it is still possible (perhaps more so now when we have arrived at The End of History and the year 2000 has already happened) to imagine and activate conceptions of community, justice, co-existence through 'speaking truly' of ourselves, practising critique as ungovernability and listening to the little narratives of others.

Foucault's conception of freedom might be attacked as being based on an illusory confidence that arises from defining truth as purely an inward conviction or radical self-creation, a strictly private matter, and to state that any extrapolation into the public sphere would be to repeat the Cartesian error. This criticism is compounded in the work of David Harvey (1989) and Christopher Norris (1990) where Foucault is interpreted as effectively aestheticising issues of politics, morality and social justice, so that terms like 'critique' loses its critical edge. Foucault's subject is one which is reinvented. It is possible to suggest that what this amounts to is anarchy, suggesting as it does a continuous 'standing back from' prior to action without the determination of external values (or in a Baudrillardian reading: a complete determination by external values resulting in the silent majority). But Foucault's promotion of the private realm does not operate without due consideration to truth, values with resultant political consequences. It was Foucault's intention to re-define these values through reference to the private realm and the constitution of governmentality (Miller (1993) p 356-364). Community is central to Foucault's ethic: it was about the bonds we have made with one another, affective and political; it becomes the question of who we are. Foucault did not intend to abandon a social or collective ethic in favour of an individual or private one. Rather, as Rajchman suggests, he wanted to rethink the question of 'community' and the nature of the bond through the passion of our identity:

> To be free is thus to question politics, to question the way power is exercised, disputing its claims to domination. Such questions involve our ethos, our ways of being or becoming who we are. Freedom is thus an 'ethical' matter. 'Freedom', Foucault declares, is 'the ontological condition of ethics; but ethics is the deliberate form assumed by freedom'. If the existence of freedom in history conditions the elaboration of an ethics, that ethics is the attempt to endow this existence with a specific practical form (Rajchman (1991) p 122 incorporating a quotation from Foucault (1987) p 115).

★

> I can't go on, you must go on, I'll go on, you must say words, as long as there are any, until they find me, strange pain, strange sin (Beckett (1965) p 414).

In providing a partial account of the terrain of the contemporary urban sphere through an analysis of the forces of regulation-order and deregulation-disorder it has been possible to demonstrate an approach to the political and ethical dilemmas of freedom and solidarity. I have argued that we are shaped by the act of living in Megalopolis (the biggest of cities, but also a city in ruins, at once endless text always promising meaning but ultimately offering hints and signs of possible and final reality) and that perception is so clouded by everyday consumption and the exposure to technology that it is only possible to live in a vicarious, indirect way as strangers to ourselves and others. Traditional ways of looking at the world have become obsolete. What is at stake (following Certeau (1988) and Olalquiaga (1992)) is our very being – the ways we perceive ourselves and others, and the variety of experience that is available to a population whose sensibilities are mediated by urban exposure. I have attempted to address the benefits as well as the dangers at work in contemporary urban culture – ultimately celebrating the creativity of a popular sensibility that gives beauty and meaning (Miller's scrapbook) to what would otherwise be an unbearable situation (Schulman's letter).

This account of urban culture has been one couched in terms of excess and I am aware of the dangers of hyperbole. In one sense the erosion of depth and the flattening of meaning in the contemporary exiles excess and excludes difference. The point is that the perceived transition from modernity to postmodernity, from modernisation to postmodernisation is the triumph of banality. In this book I have argued that an excess of banality becomes a source of violence. It is an excess identified between the play of forces and powers in the production of counter-forces and counter-powers. A strategy of regulation (of the economic, the cultural, the social and of individual desire) through deregulation has un-determined effects. Order has been maintained through the creation of disorder. The repression of desire through the satiation of consumption in an account of political-economy has resulted in resistance through the refusal of consumption. The repression of desire through lack, in a psychoanalytic account, has resulted in the affirmation of lack. The eradication of difference has resulted in the multiplicity of differences. The struggle for the maintenance of stability has resulted in instability. The processes of the achievement of domination through homogeneity involves the manifestation of heterogeneity. The heightening of the effects of affluence, anomie and alienation as both social and psychological conditions encourages an interpretation of negativity but can become an affirmative condition of possibility. The centre has become the margin, that which is within has become the without.

There is a tendency within much postmodern theory and culture toward 'apocalypticism'. The postmodern city can be excavated as apocalypse, layer upon layer of it. Apocalypticism is increasingly *de rigeur* as we arrive at the *fin de millennium* celebrations couched in a dangerous masculinism. Apocalypticism raises dangers analogous to those of genre blending – there's no way out of an apocalypse – except if the angels come. In mapping the postmodern city as a banal/violent apocalypse (the end of production, the end of the social, the end of history – lost in the post), the territory no longer precedes its mapping. The apocalypticism of masculinist experience can be countered with what feminist theory calls situated knowledge. By explicitly positioning the knowing subject, situated knowledge can puncture the overwhelming subjectlessness of apocalyptic readings of experience, grounding its power grid, enabling entry and the possibility of unravelling the hybridisation of real, unreal, hyperreal and surreal that characterises apocalypse. The monstrous destructivism and relentless and faceless surveillance of all social relations can only be opposed by conscious social agents taking a stand (not standing back from), and knowing when they act, not coherently but in the articulation of incoherence.

Yet, as Katz has noted, apocalypticism captures 'the structured feeling' of our times and places (Katz (1993) p 162), that which is 'darkly unknowable'. Because the contemporary is 'darkly unknowable' regulation and order is absolute but not present in relation to activities which are always happening elsewhere. These activities (stories in excess) suggest the appearance of interstices or cracks from within the grid which might be negotiated and ruptured and that there are accessible spaces of *otherness* within the grid; spaces which can be glimpsed through the unknowing.

The other tendency within postmodern theory is that of insidious fascism which can be explained in terms of the politics of representation. In pursuing a Gramscian analysis of ideology as representation a distinction is maintained between the material sphere of economic production and the ideological sphere of the superstructure. Desire is captured in its representative myths; and it is a desire which, as a collective force, is potentially fascistic. The expression of internal desire coalesces into a series of configurations within external desire which is essentially fascistic in the recognition of lack. However, if desire is social before it is individual then it is not representable. If ideology is both material and force (a flow of desire in Deleuzian terms), it is consequently dissolved as a separate level of ideology or representation. Desire which is unrepresentable cannot be concretised or nominated and therefore is a lack which cannot be signified. It is the movement or flow of desire which is important, a movement of the Phantasm along the line of the limit. There may be a 'phantasy of fascism' but within a nomadic governmentality there is space to encompass such a phantasy which essentially tests the limits of externally imposed obligations and bonds and constantly attests to the surplus nature of lack. In terms of the political economy of desire it is the surplus or potlach, the gift which can never be reciprocated which determines the consistency of an affirmative lack and produces a general as opposed to restrictive economy, an economy of abundance in Bataille's terms (see Bennington

(1995)). A socialisation of desire offers itself to both nomination (fascism) and to alternative realisations (pre-semiotic) which are those of the multiplicity of desire in random configurations and pre-vital flows affording the potential for a non-repressive structuring of desire.

*

I have suggested that such alterations regarding the affirmation-socialisation of desire take place within the existing structures of order and regulation. These alterations utilise the existent dichotomies and inadequacies of the prevailing regime and operate through appropriation and inversion. Hence the importance of the linear as opposed to the hierarchical and the nomadic as opposed to monadic. However, in terms of the articulation of a replacement discourse, I do not abandon the necessity of structure (community) in the organisation of desire (identity) rather I seek through the random, determined and deterritorialised break-flows of counter-hegemonic power a (paradoxical) structure of nomadic governmentality, a structure in the sense of a series of bonds between selves which are non-repressive and represent a justice of otherness (difference and multiplicity) which is 'a compassionate sense of justice'.

The articulation of an ethical position which is relevant to the contemporary and which re-introduces a conception of justice implicating a responsibility to others can be examined through the spatial figure, 'a more generous sense of space'. It is through the conceptualisation of spatial relations that a justice of multiplicity might be realised. Remapping the city as a space of radical openness, a place where, like bell hooks's margin, ties are severed and subjection abounds but also, at the same time, a location for recovery and resistance, a meeting place where new and radical happenings can occur. There are various interpretations and configuration of spaces of otherness which have been approached in the course of this book. bell hooks's 'margins' and Jardine's 'map of new spaces yet to be explored' are both potential spaces in which the feminine is celebrated. Homi Bhaba discusses the '"third space" of the subaltern' in his location of cultural identity. Laclau and Mouffe refer to the importance of spatial relations in the construction of systems of social relations. Virilio, Maffesoli and Certeau each discuss spatial relations relating to their varying conceptions of the contemporary.

What is significant in these variations and evocations of 'other' spaces is, as Soja and Hooper have noted, the insight provided on how fragmentation, ruptures and discontinuities can be politically transformed from liability and weakness to opportunity and strength (Soja and Hooper (1993) p 193). Throughout this book I have used Foucault's identification of the space of heterotopia as a marker of potentiality. Heterotopia as a counter-site, a kind of enacted utopia in which the real sites, all the other real sites that can be found within urban culture, are simultaneously represented, contested and inverted. Heterotopias, combining the real and the imagined (following Lefebvre), are the spaces in which we live and which draw us out of ourselves. They are the spaces in which the erosion of our lives, our time and our history occurs and the space that claws and gnaws at us (Foucault (1986a)). The importance of Foucault's conceptualisation of heterotopia is that it is a fluid space as opposed to the static and located spaces of feminism and race. Heterotopia is a space of multiplicity, ambivalence and intersubjectivity, both a repository for the detritus (refuse) of the urban and a deterritorialised space occurring within the urban as an interstice. It can be analysed in a sociological interpretation as a 'wild zone' (even nominated-represented as a deregulated space) of disruption and discontinuity (a space of the Phantasm as the *mis-en-scène* of a non-repressed desire) which ultimately defeats the processes of nomination and representation.

This 'structured counter-space' provides a possible site in the articulation of a humanistically orientated replacement discourse. It is not a space-site which is 'out-there' but rather of the existent of the 'within' of the urban; it is a shifting space of nomadology and slippage. There is the paradoxical image of a situated fluidity ('an organised system of differences' marked by ambiguity: Laclau and Mouffe (1985) p 135; see also the analysis by Milovanovic (1992) pp 236-240). The continuum of movement within the urban is an important element in becoming. As I have previously noted the affirmatively nomadic is matched by the dangerously nomadic of a moveable law, the external gaze which has been dislodged to become even more terrifyingly encompassing. But Megalopolis has become too extreme to be consistently surveilled and subjected. Governmentality has become a series of rapprochements and negotiations between transiently coalescing-coercive hegemonic groupings. The affirmatively nomadic escapes the gaze of external objectivity in a movement of capture and counter-capture.

But movement here is also related to the idea of critique (the art of becoming ungovernable) in that, as opposed to the static certainty of the external, the practice of critique constantly questions and challenges. Therefore, as opposed to the process of suture and interpellation utilised as a strategy in the universalisation of discourses, critique here becomes a strategy of rupture (violence), puncturing through the 'seamless wall' and allowing the retrieval and activation of discourses of dissensus. But it is not a rupture in the recognition of the other (immediate nomination and subjection – the witness as traitor) but rather a constant and itinerant interrogation at the limit which serves to 'carry away the law'. By always calling into question and challenging the authority of Law through fulfilling its desire for transgression and always denying its power by manifesting the lack of the desire of Law and affirming the excitement involved in the ever failing satiation of desire (thus acting in a political economy of transgression as desire-capital always circulating as a line of flight) desire is conceived as

> [A] forward movement, a flight towards an object which always eludes our grasp, the attempt, never successful but never frustrating, to reach the unattainable by exploring the paths of the possible (Lecercle (1985) p 116).

The space of this alternative replacement discourse (encompassing freedom-identity, bond-obligation, community-solidarity) has been discussed by Milovanovic (1992) and Laclau and Mouffe (1985) in terms of arrival through organic crises periodically erupting 'as a result of an overdetermination of circumstances' (Laclau and Mouffe (1985) p 136). These produce crises in identities, a proliferation of contrarieties and floating signifiers (Milovanovic (1992) p 239) opening up as the desiring-machine breaks down (following Deleuze and Guattari) enabling a multiplicity of discursive subject-positions in which value is created by an active affirmation. Here momentary residence can be assumed without these positions unilaterally dominating and subjecting experience to premature closure. As Milovanovic suggests:

> Most important with these suggestions by post-modernist theorists is that ambivalence, irregularities, contrarities, differences and paradoxes are not necessarily sources of pathology; rather they are the beginning points for alternative articulations and the occasion for the possible development of a multifaceted replacement discourse that would offer less structured discursive subject-positions within which a subject may take up residence. A replacement discourse would be much like a dissipative structure in form, responding to changes in the environment while offering a degree of stability within some form of an ideal speech situation (Milovanovic (1992) p 257).

★

I conclude with Jonathan Miller's note accompanying his scrapbook of photographs. These are personal ephemera, random images representing the detritus of the contemporary, on the edge of the 'officially visible' and collected with the forlorn hope that the photographer 'might do something with them and set them on their feet again'. There is as an honesty here as in Sarah Schulman's letter. Schulman identifies the horror, Miller points to the beauty. For Miller, his photographs of 'incipient things', are affirmations of lack, neglect, detritus and refuse. These are pictures from within but which are without. They are without-law but still they challenge conceptions of meaning and reality and provide, for Miller, moments and spaces of possibility. In the sense that they are random and undetermined, irregular and disordered, they are ungovernable in the sense of a 'law of looking'. They represent, in the context of this excursion, the space of heterotopia, out-with the law in an alternative economy of abundance, a margin where we might encounter the possibility of a more generous sense of space and a more compassionate sense of justice. In moving towards this shifting space only a partial and fragmentary account has been ventured. There is an abundance of un-working left to be done.

BIBLIOGRAPHY

Aglietta, M A, *Theory of Capitalist Regulation* (London: New Left Books, 1979).

Althusser, L, *For Marx* (London: Allen Lane, 1969).

Althusser, L, *Lenin and Philosophy* (London: New Left Books, 1971).

Althusser, L and Balibar, E, *Reading Capital* (London: New Left Books, 1968).

Amar, A, 'A Psychoanalytic Study of Money' (1976) in *The Psychoanalysis of Money* (Borneman, E, ed; New York: Urizen Books).

Arendt, H, *Eichmann in Jerusalem: A Report on the Banality of Evil* (Harmondsworth: Penguin, 1977).

Artaud, A, 'To Have Done With The Judgement of God' (1988) in *Antonin Artaud: Selected Writings* (Sontag, S, ed; Berkeley, CA: University of California Press).

Barron, A, 'Lyotard and the Problem of Judgement' (1992) in *Judging Lyotard* (Benjamin, A, ed; London: Routledge).

Barthes, R, *S/Z* (New York: Hill and Wang, 1974).

Bataille, G, *The Story of the Eye* (Harmondsworth: Penguin, 1982).

Bataille, G, *Inner Experience* (Albany, NY: State University New York Press, 1988).

Baudrillard, J, *Les Systèmes des Objets* (Paris: Denoel, 1968).

Baudrillard, J, 'Le Ludique et le policier' (1969a) *Utopie* no 2–3 pp 147–155.

Baudrillard, J, 'La practique sociale de la technique' (1969b) *Utopie* no 2–3 pp 147–155.

Baudrillard, J, *La Société de Consommation* (Paris: Gallimard, 1970).

Baudrillard, J, *The Mirror of Production* (St Louis, MIS: Telos, 1975).

Baudrillard, J, *For A Critique of the Political Economy of the Sign* (St Louis, MIS: Telos, 1981).

Baudrillard, J, 'The Beaubourg Effect: Implosion and Deterrence' (1982) *October* vol 20 Spring pp 3–13.

Baudrillard, J, *Simulations* (New York: Semiotext(e), 1983a).

Baudrillard, J, *In The Shadow of the Silent Majorities* (New York: Semiotext(e), 1983b).

Baudrillard, J, *The Evil Demon of Images* (Annandale, Sydney: Power Institute, 1987).

Baudrillard, J, 'Consumer Society' (1988) in *Jean Baudrillard: Selected Writings* (Poster, M, ed; London: Polity).

Baudrillard, J, 'The End of Production' (1989) *Polygraph* vol 2 no 3 pp 5–26.

Baudrillard, J, *Fatal Strategies* (London: Pluto, 1990).

Baudrillard, J, 'Transpolitics, Transsexuality, Transaesthetics' (1992) in *Jean Baudrillard: The Disappearance of Art and Politics* (Stearns, W and Chaloupka, W, eds; Basingstoke: MacMillan).

Baudrillard, J, *Symbolic Exchange and Death* (London: Sage, 1993a).

Baudrillard, J, *The Transparency of Evil* (London: Verso, 1993b).

Beckett, S, *Krapp's Last Tape* (London: Faber, 1959).

Beckett, S, 'The Unnameable' (1965) in *Three Novels* (New York: Calder and Bowers).

Bell, D, *The Cultural Contradictions of Capitalism* (London: Heinemann, 1976).

Bennington, G, 'Introduction to Economics 1: Because the World is Round' (1995) in *Bataille: Writing the Sacred* (Bailey Gill, C, ed; London: Routledge).

Berger, J, *And Our Faces, My Heart, Brief as Photos* (London: Penguin Books, 1984).

Berman, H, *Law and Revolution* (Cambridge MA: Harvard University Press, 1983).

Bersani, L, 'Is the Rectum a Grave?' (1988) in *AIDS: Cultural Analysis and Cultural Activism* (Crimp, D, ed; Cambridge, MA: MIT Press).

Bhaba, H, '"Caliban Speaks to Prospero": Cultural Identity and the Crisis of Representation' (conference presentation) (1991) in *Critical Fictions* (Mariani, P, ed; Seattle, WS: Bay Press).

Black, J, *The Aesthetics of Murder: A Study in Romantic Literature and Contemporary Culture* (Baltimore: Johns Hopkins University Press, 1991).

Blackstone, W, *Commentaries on the Laws of England* (31 BL COM (17th edn), 1830).

Blue Arrow *Inspectors' Report on County NatWest Limited and County NatWest Securities Ltd* (London: HMSO, 1989).

Bogue, R, *Deleuze and Guattari* (London: Routledge, 1989).

Borsch-Jacobsen, M, 'The Law of Psychoanalysis' (1985) *Diacritics* vol 15 pp 26–37.

Bosworth-Davies, R, 'An analysis of compliance officers: Attitudes towards insider dealing' (1993) *Crime, Law and Social Change* vol 20 pp 339–357.

Bourdieu, P, 'Intellectual Field and Creative Project' (1971) in *Knowledge and Control* (Young, M, ed; London: Collier-Macmillan).

Bourdieu, P, *Outline of a Theory of Practice* (Cambridge: Cambridge University Press, 1977).

Bourdieu, P, 'The Production of Belief: Contribution to the Construction of an Economy of Symbolic Goods' in *Media, Culture and Society* vol 2 no 3 1979 pp 261–293.

Bourdieu, P, *Distinction: A Social Critique of the Judgement of Taste* (London: Routledge, 1984).

Bourdieu, P, *In Other Worlds* (Cambridge: Polity, 1990).

Box, S, *Power, Crime and Mystification* (London: Tavistock, 1983).

Bracewell, M and Evans, J, 'Anti-hero for a barbed wire future' (1993) *The Guardian* 16 October.

Braudel, F, *Afterthoghts on Material Civilisation and Capitalism* (Baltimore: The Johns Hopkins University Press, 1977).

Brooks, P, *Body Work: Objects of Desire in Modern Narrative* (Cambridge, MA: Harvard University Press, 1993).

Butler, J, *Gender Trouble: Feminism and the Subversion of Identity* (London: Routledge, 1990).

Castel, R, 'From Dangerousness to Risk' (1991) in *The Foucault Effect: Studies in Governmentality* (Burchell, G, Gordon, C, Miller, P, eds; London: Harvester Wheatsheaf).

Castells, M, *The Urban Question* (London: Edward Arnold, 1977).

Certeau de, M, *The Practice of Everyday Life* (Berkeley, CA: University of California Press, 1988).

Chambers, I, *Border Dialogues: Journeys in Postmodernity* (London: Routledge, 1990).

Chambers, I, 'Cities Without Maps' (1993) in *Mapping the Futures: Local Cultures, Global Change* (Bird, J, Curtis, B, Putman, T, Robertson, G, Tickner, L, eds; Routledge: London).

Chambers, I, *Migrancy, Culture, Identity* (London: Routledge, 1994).

Chen, K-H, 'Post-Marxism: Between/beyond critical postmodernism and cultural studies' (1991) *Media, Culture and Society* vol 1 no 13 pp 35–51.

Churchill, C, *Serious Money* (London: Samuel French, 1987).

Clastres, P, *Society Against the State* (New York: Zone Books, 1987).

Coakley, J, 'London as an International Financial Centre' in *Global Finance and Urban Living: A Study in Metropolitan Change* (Budd, L and Whimster, S, eds; London: Routledge, 1992).

Cooke, P, 'Modernity, Postmodernity and the City' (1988) *Theory, Culture and Society* vol 5 no 2–3 pp 475–493.

Cornell, D, 'From the Lighthouse: The Promise of Redemption and the Possibility of Legal Interpretation' (1990) *Cardozo Law Review* vol 11 p 1689.

Cowie, E, 'Fantasia' (1990) in *The Woman in Question: m/f* (Adams, P and Cowie, E, eds; London: Verso).

Cover, R, 'Violence and the Word' (1986) *Yale Law Journal* vol 95 p 1601

Crook, S, Pakulski, J, Waters, M, *Postmodernization: Change in Advanced Society* (London: Sage, 1992).

Crouch, S, *Notes of a Hanging Judge* (New York: Free Press, 1990).

Davis, M, 'Urban Renaissance and the Spirit of Postmodernism' (1985) *New Left Review* no 151 pp 106–115.

Davis, M, *City of Quartz: Excavating the Future in Los Angeles* (London: Verso, 1990).

Deleuze, G and Guattari, F, *Anti-Oedipus: Capitalism and Schizophrenia* (Preface by Foucault M) (New York: Viking, 1977).

Deleuze, G and Guattari, F, 'Rhizome: Introduction' (1981) *Ideology and Consciousness* no 8 pp 49–71.

Deleuze, G and Guattari, F, *On the Line* (New York: Semiotext(e), 1983).

Deleuze, G and Guattari, F, *Nomadology: The War Machine* (New York: Semiotext(e), 1986).

Deleuze, G and Guattari, F, *A Thousand Plateaus: Capitalism and Schizophrenia* (Minneapolis, MIN: University of Minnesota Press, 1987).

Deleuze, G, *Nietzsche and Philosophy* (London: Athlone Press, 1983).

Deleuze, G, 'Coldness and Cruelty' (1989) in *Masochism* (Deleuze, G and Sacher-Masoch, L; New York: Zone Books).

Deleuze, G, *The Logic of Sense* (New York: Columbia University Press, 1990).

Denzin, N, *Images of Postmodern Society* (London: Sage, 1991).

Derrida, J, 'Sending: On Representation' (1982) *Social Research* vol 2 Summer pp 294–326.

Derrida, J, 'Force of Law: The "Mystical Foundation of Authority"' (1992) in *Deconstruction and the Possibility of Justice* (Cornell, D, Rosenfeld, M, Gray Carlson, D, eds; New York: Routledge).

Dostoevsky, F, *Notes from Underground* (London: Vintage, 1864/1993).

Douzinas, C, Warrington, R with McVeigh, R, *Postmodern Jurisprudence: The Law of the Text in the Texts of the Law* (London: Routledge, 1991).

Douzinas, C and Warrington, R, 'A Well-Founded Fear of Justice' (1991) *Law and Critique* vol II no 2 pp 115–147.

Durkheim, E, *Suicide* (New York: Free Press, 1898/1951).

Dyer, G, 'Review of "The James Bulger Case" by David James Smith' (1994) *The Guardian* 12 February.

Edelman, M, 'The Construction and Uses of Social Problems' (1992) in *Jean Baudrillard: The Disappearance of Art and Politics* (Stearns, W and Chaloupka, W, eds; New York: MacMillan).

Easton Ellis, B, *American Psycho* (London: Picador, 1991).

Featherstone, M, 'Consumer Culture: An Introduction' (1983) *Theory, Culture and Society* vol 1 no 3 pp 4–9.

Featherstone, M, *Consumer Culture and Postmodernism* (London: Sage, 1991).

Fish, A, 'The Law Wishes to Have a Formal Existence' (1991) in *The Fate of Law* (Sarat, A and Kearns, T, eds; Ann Arbor: University of Michigan Press).

Foucault, M, '*Un si cruel savoir*' (1962) *Critique* no 102 p 606.

Foucault, M, *The Order of Things: An Archaeology of the Human Sciences* (London: Tavistock, 1970).

Foucault, M, *The Archaeology of Knowledge* (New York: Vintage Press, 1973).

Foucault, M, *Mental Illness and Psychology* (London: Tavistock, 1976).

Foucault, M, 'A Preface to Transgression/*Theatrum Philosophicum*' (1977a) in *Language, Counter-Memory, Practice: Selected Interviews with Michel Foucault* (Bouchard, D, ed; New York: Cornell University Press).

Foucault, M, *Discipline and Punish* (London: Allen Lane, 1977b).

Foucault, M, 'Governmentality' (1979a) *Ideology and Consciousness* vol 6 no 5 pp 5–21.

Foucault, M, *The History of Sexuality: Volume 1* (London: Allen Lane, 1979b).

Foucault, M, 'Conversation with Michel Foucault' (1980a) *Threepenny Review* vol 1 Winter-Spring pp 4–5.

Foucault, M, *Power/Knowledge: Selected Interviews and Other Writings 1972–1977* (Gordon, C, ed; Brighton: Harvester Wheatsheaf, 1980b).

Foucault, M (ed), *I, Pierre Rivière, having slaughtered my mother, my sister, my brother: A Case of Parricide in the 19th Century* (Lincoln, NA: University of Nebraska Press, 1982).

Foucault, M, 'The subject and power' (1983) in *Michel Foucault: Beyond Structuralism and Hermeneutics* (Dreyfus, H and Rabinow, P, eds; Chicago: University of Chicago Press).

Foucault, M, 'What Is Enlightenment?' (1984) in *The Foucault Reader* (Rabinow, P, ed; New York: Pantheon Books).

Foucault, M, 'Of Other Spaces' (1986a) *Diacritics* vol 16 pp 22–27.

Foucault, M, *Death and the Labyrinth: The World of Raymond Roussel* (Berkeley: University of California Press, 1986b).

Foucault, M, *Technologies of Self: A Seminar with Michel Foucault* (Martin, L, Gutman, H, Hutton, P, eds; London: Tavistock, 1988).

Foucault, M, *Foucault Live* (Lotringer, S, ed; New York: Semiotext(e), 1989).

Foucault, M, '*Qu'est-ce que la critique?*' (1990) *Bulletin de la Société française de philosophie* 84th year no 2 (a transcription of a lecture delivered on 27 May 1978, at the Sorbonne).

Foucault, M, 'Politics and the Study of Discourse/Questions of Methods' (1991) in *The Foucault Effect: Studies in Governmentality* (Burchell, G, Gordon, C, Miller, P, eds; London: Harvester Wheatsheaf).

Fraser, N, 'Rethinking the Public Sphere' (1991) *Social Text* vol 8(13) no 9(1) pp 56–80.

Frisby, D, *Sociological Impressionism: A Reassessment of Georg Simmel's Social Theory* (London: Heinemann, 1985).

Freud, S, *Civilisation and its Discontents* (London: Hogarth, 1953).

Fromm, E, *The Sane Society* (New York: Rinehart, 1955).

Gamble, A, 'Privatization, Thatcherism and the British State' (1989) in *Thatcher's Law* (Gamble, A and Wells, C, eds; Cardiff: GPC Books).

Gane, M (Ed), *Ideological Representation and Power in Social Relations* (London: Routledge 1989).

Gane, M, *Baudrillard's Bestiary: Baudrillard and Culture* (London: Routledge, 1991).

Giddens, A, *The Social Structure of Advanced Societies* (London: Macmillan, 1980).

Giddens, A, *The Nation State and Violence* (Cambridge: Polity, 1985).

Girard, R, *Violence and the Sacred* (Baltimore: Johns Hopkins University Press, 1977).

Goodrich, P, *Languages of Law: From Logics of Memory to Nomadic Masks* (London: Wiedenfeld, 1990).

Goodrich, P, 'Sleeping with the Enemy: An Essay on the Politics of Critical Legal Studies in America' (1993) *New York University Law Review* vol 68 no 2 pp 389–425.

Gordon, C, 'The Soul of the Citizen: Max Weber and Michel Foucault on rationality and government' (1987) in *Max Weber, Rationality and Modernity* (Whimster, S and Lash, S, eds; London: Allen and Unwin).

Gordon, C, 'Governmental Rationality: An Introduction' (1991) in *The Foucault Effect: Studies in Governmentality* (Burchell, G, Gordon, C, Miller, P, eds; London: Harvester Wheatsheaf).

Gottman, J, *Megalopolis* (New York: Free Press, 1961).

Gower, L, *Review of Investor Protection (A Discussion Document)* (London: HMSO, 1982).

Grace, H, 'Business, Pleasure, Narrative: The folktale in our times' (1991) in *Cartographies: Poststructuralism and the Mapping of Bodies and Spaces* (Diprose, R and Ferrell, R, eds; London: Allen and Unwin).

Gramsci, A, *Selections from the Prison Notebooks* (London: Lawrence and Wishart, 1973).

Gramsci, A, *Selections from the Cultural Writings* (London: Cambridge, MA: Harvard University Press, 1985).

Habermas, J, *Legitimation Crisis* (Boston, MA: Beacon Hill, 1975).

Habermas, J, *The Philosophical Discourse of Modernity* (Cambridge: Polity, 1987).

Hachomovitch, Y, 'One Law on the Other' (1990) *International Journal for the Semiotics of Law* vol III no 8 pp 187–200.

Hall, S, 'Brave New World' (1988a) *Marxism Today* October pp 24–33.

Hall, S, *The Hard Road to Renewal: Thatcherism and the Crisis of the Left* (London: Verso, 1988b).

Harvey, D, *The Urban Experience* (Oxford: Blackwell, 1988).

Harvey, D, *The Condition of Postmodernity: An Enquiry Into the Origins of Cultural Change* (Oxford: Blackwell, 1989).

Hebdige, D, *Subculture: The Meaning of Style* (London: Routledge, 1979).

Hebdige, D, *Hiding in the Light* (London: Comedia/Routledge, 1988).

Heidegger, M, 'Building, Dwelling, Thinking' (1971) in *Poetry, Language, Thought* (New York: Harper Colophon).

Henry, S and Milovanovic, D, 'Constitutive Criminology' (1991) *Criminology* vol 29 pp 293–315.

Hewison, R, 'News From Somewhere' (1993) in *Mapping the Futures: Local Cultures, Global Change* (Bird, J, Curtis, B, Robertson, G, Tickner, L, eds; London: Routledge).

Hobbs, D, *Doing the Business: Entrepreneurship, the Working Class and Detectives in the East End of London* (Oxford: Oxford University Press, 1989).

Hodgson, G, 'Hatred and the Establishment' (1990) *The Independent* 28 February.

Holmes, R and de Burger, J, *Serial Murder* (New York: Sage, 1988).

hooks, b, *Yearnings: Race, Gender and Cultural Politics* (London: Turnaround, 1991).

Horney, K, *Our Inner Conflicts* (London: Routledge, 1946).

Hutcheon, L, *The Politics of Postmodernism* (London: Routledge, 1989).

Ingham, G, *Capitalism Divided? The City and Industry in British Social Development* (London: MacMillan, 1984).

Jackson, P, *Maps of Meaning* (London: Allen and Unwin, 1989).

Jameson, F, 'Postmodernism: Or The Cultural Logic of Late Capitalism' (1984) *New Left Review* no 146 pp 53–92.

Jameson, F, 'Reification and Utopia in Mass Culture' (1985) *Social Text* vol 1 no 1.

Jameson, F, *Postmodernism, Or The Cultural Logic of Late Capitalism* (London: Verso, 1991).

Jardine, A, *Gynesis: Configurations of Women and Modernity* (New York: Cornell University Press, 1985).

Jessop, B, 'Regulation theories in retrospect and prospect' (1990) *Economy and Society* vol 19 May pp 153–216.

Jessop, B and Stones, R, 'Old City and New Times: Economic and Political Aspects of Deregulation' (1992) in *Global Finance and Urban Living: A Study in Metropolitan Change* (Budd, L and Whimster, S, eds; London: Routledge).

Kafka, F, 'In the Penal Colony' (1919/1961) from *In The Penal Colony: Stories and Short Pieces* (New York: Schocken Books).

Kant, I, 'What is Enlightenment?' (1963) in *On History* (Indianapolis, IND: Indiana University Press).

Kantorowicz, E, *The King's Two Bodies* (New Jersey: Princeton University Press, 1957).

Katz, J, *Seductions of Crime* (New York: Basic Books, 1989).

Kearney, R, *Poetics of Imagining* (London: Harper Collins, 1991).

Keat, R, 'Introduction: Starship Britain or Universal Enterprise?' (1990) in *Enterprise Culture* (Keat, R and Abercrombie, N, eds; London: Routledge).

Keat, R and Abercrombie, R (eds), *Enterprise Culture* (London: Routledge, 1990).

Keith, M and Pile, S (eds), *Place and the Politics of Identity* (London: Routledge, 1993).

Kershaw, A, 'A Spanner in the Works' (1992) *The Guardian* 8–9 February.

Kmetyk, T, 'When Killing is too Ghastly for Words' (1991) *The Guardian* 15 January.

Kristeva, J, *Revolution in Poetic Language* (New York: Columbia University Press, 1984).

Kroker, A and Cook, D, *The Postmodern Scene: Excremental Culture and Hyper-Aesthetics* (London: MacMillan, 1988).

Lacan, J, 'The Mirror stage as formative of the function of the I as revealed in psychoanalytic experience' (1977) in *Ecrits: A Selection* (Sheridan, A, ed; London: Tavistock).

Laclau, E and Mouffe, C, *Hegemony and Socialist Strategy* (London: Verso, 1985).

Laplanche, J and Pontalis, J-B, *The Language of Psycho-Analysis* (London: Hogarth Press/Institute of Psycho-Analysis, 1980).

Lash, S, 'Discourse or Figure? Postmodernism as a Regime of Signification' (1988) *Theory, Culture and Society* vol 5 no 2–3 pp 311–337.

Lash, S, *The Sociology of Postmodernism* (London: Routledge, 1990).

Lash, S and Urry *The Economies of Signs and Space* (London: Routledge,1993).

Lazar, D, *Markets and Ideology in the City of London* (Basingstoke: MacMillan, 1990).

Lecercle, J-J, *Philosophy Through the Looking Glass: Language, Nonsense, Desire* (London: Hutchinson, 1985).

Lefebvre, H, *Le Manifeste Differentialiste* (Paris: Editions Gallimard, 1970).

Lefebvre, H, *Everyday Life in the Modern World* (London: Allen Lane, 1972).

Lemert, C and Gillan, G, *Michel Foucault: Social Theory as Transgression* (New York: Columbia University Press, 1982).

Lewis, M, *Liar's Poker* (London: Hodder and Stoughton, 1989).

Lipietz, A, 'New Tendencies in the International Division of Labour: Regimes of Accumulation and Modes of Regulation' (1986) in *Production Work, Territory: The Geographical Anatomy of Industrial Capitalism* (Scott, A and Storper, M, eds; London: Allen and Unwin).

Lloyd, A, 'Death of the Honourable Englishman' (1988) *GQ* December pp 152–155.

Lukes, S, *Essays in Social Theory* (London: MacMillan, 1977).

Lyotard, J-F, *The Postmodern Condition: A Report on Knowledge* (Manchester: Manchester University Press, 1984).

Lyotard, J-F, *Just Gaming* (Manchester: Manchester University Press, 1985).

Lyotard, J-F, *The Differend: Phrases in Dispute* (Minneapolis, MA: University of Minnesota Press, 1988).

Lyotard, J-F, *Heidegger and 'the jews'* (Minneapolis: University of Minnesota Press, 1990).

Lyotard, J-F, *The Inhuman* (Cambridge: Polity, 1991).

Lyotard, J-F, *The Postmodern Explained to Children: Correspondence 1982–1985* (London: Turnaround, 1992).

McClintock, A, 'Maid to Order: Commercial S/M and Gender Power' (1993) in *Dirty Looks: Women, Pornography, Power* (Church, P and Gibson, R, eds; London: British Film Institute).

McKinnon, C, *Feminism Unmodified: Discourses on Life and Law* (Cambridge, MA: Harvard University Press, 1987).

McRobbie, A, *Zoot Suits and Second Hand Dress* (London: Routledge, 1989).

Maffesoli, M, 'La Paradigme esthetique' (1986) in *Georg Simmel: la sociologie et l'expérience du monde moderne* (Paris: Meridiens Klincksieck) pp 103–119.

Maffesoli, M, 'The Imaginary and the Everyday' (1992) in *Jean Baudrillard: The Disappearance of Art and Politics* (Stearns, W and Chaloupka, W, eds; Basingstoke: MacMillan).

Marcuse, H, *Eros and Civilisation* (Boston, MA: Beacon Hill, 1955).

Matza, D, *Becoming Deviant* (New Jersey: Prentice-Hall, 1969).

Marx, K, *Economic and Philosophical Manuscripts of 1844* (London: Lawrence and Wishart, 1959).

Marx, K, *A Contribution to the Critique of the Political Economy* (London: Lawrence and Wishart, 1971).

Marx, K, *Grundrisse* (Harmondsworth: Penguin, 1973).

Mazzoleni, M, 'The City and the Imaginary' (1993) in *Space and Place: Theories of Identity and Location* (Carter, E, Donald, J, Squires, J, eds; London: Lawrence and Wishart/New Formations).

Merton, R, 'Social Structure and Anomie' (1938) *American Sociological Review* vol 3 October pp 672–82.

Merton, R, *Social Structure and Social Theory* (New York: Free Press, 1957 2nd edn).

Mestrovic, S, *The Coming Fin de Siècle* (London: Routledge, 1991).

Miller, J, 'Jonathan Miller's Scrapbook' (1994) *The Observer* (Magazine) 20 March.

Miller, J 'Carnivals of Atrocity: Foucault, Nietzsche, Cruelty' (1990) *Political Theory* vol 18 no 3 pp 470–491.

Miller, J, *The Passion of Michel Foucault* (New York: Simon and Schuster, 1993).

Miller, P and Rose, N, 'Governing Economic Life' (1990) *Economy and Society* vol 19 February pp 1–31.

Milovanovic, D, *Postmodern Law and Disorder: Psychoanalytic Semiotics, Chaos and Juridic Exegeses* (Liverpool: Deborah Charles, 1992).

Minson, J, *Genealogies of Morals: Foucault, Donzelot and the Eccentricity of Ethics* (London: MacMillan, 1985).

Morris, M, 'Room 101 Or A few of the Worst Things in the World' (1988) in *Seduced and Abandoned* (Frankovits, A, ed; Sydney: Stonemoss).

Morris, M, 'The Man in the Mirror: David Harvey's 'Condition of Postmodernity'' (1992) in *Cultural Theory and Cultural Change* (Featherstone, M, ed; London: Sage).

Morris, M, 'Future Fear' (1993) in *Mapping the Futures: Local Cultures, Global Change* (Bird, J, Curtis, B, Putman, T, Roberston, G, Tickner, L, eds; London: Routledge).

Mouffe, C, 'Radical Democracy: modern or postmodern?' (1988) in *Universal Abandon* (Ross, A, ed; Minneapolis, MA: University of Minnesota Press).

Murray, R, 'Life After Henry (Ford)' (1988) *Marxism Today* October pp 8–13.

Nietzsche, F, *Ecce Homo* (Edinburgh: Foulis, 1911).

Nietzsche, F, *The Birth of Tragedy/The Genealogy of Morals* (New York: Anchor Books/Doubleday, 1953).

Nietzsche, F, *The Gay Science* (New York: Vintage, 1974).

Norris, C, *What's Wrong With Postmodernism: Critical Theory and the end of Philosophy* (London: Harvester Wheatsheaf, 1990).

Olalquiaga, C, *Megalopolis* (Minneapolis MIN: University of Minnesota Press, 1992).

Parkin, F, *Marxism and Class Theory: A Bourgeois Critique* (London: Tavistock, 1990).

Perez, R, *On (An)Archy and Schizoanalysis* (New York: Autonomedia, 1990).

Perkin, H, *The Rise of Professional Society: England Since 1880* (London: Routledge, 1989).

Perkin, H, 'The enterprise culture in historical perspective: birth, life, death – and resurrection?' (1992) in *The Values of the Enterprise Culture* (Heelas, P and Morris, P, eds; London: Routledge).

Pevear, R and Volokhonsky, L, 'Foreword' (1993) in *Notes From Underground* (Dostoevsky, F; London: Vintage).

Pfohl, S, *Death at the Parasite Cafe: Social Science (Fictions) and the Postmodern* (Basingstoke: MacMillan, 1992).

Presdee, M, 'British Sociological Association Conference' (1992) Unpublished Paper 6–9 April.

Pryke, M, 'An international city going 'Global': spatial change in the City of London' (1991) *Environment and Planning D: Society and Space* 9 pp 197–222.

Pynchon, T, *The Crying of Lot 49* (Harmondsworth: Penguin, 1967).

Rajchman, J, *Truth and Eros: Foucault, Lacan and the Question of Ethics* (London: Routledge, 1991).

Redhead, S, *The End of the Century Party: Youth and Pop Towards 2000* (Manchester: Manchester University Press, 1990).

Redhead, S, 'Rave Off: Youth Subcultures and the Law' (1991) *Social Studies Review* vol 6 no 3.

Redhead, S (ed), *Rave Off: Politics and Deviance in Contemporary Youth Culture* (Aldershot: Avebury, 1993).

Redhead, S, *Unpopular Cultures: The Birth of Law and Popular Culture* (Manchester: Manchester University Press, 1995).

Rider, B, Chaikin, D, Abrams, C, *Guide to the Financial Services Act 1986* (London: CCH Editions, 1987).

Rhodes, C and Nabi, N, 'Brick Lane: A Village Economy in the Shadow of the City?' (1992) in *Global Finance and Urban Living: A Study of Metropolitan Change* (Budd, L and Whimster, S, eds; London: Routledge).

Ronnell, A, *Crack Wars: Literature, Addiction and Mania* (Lincoln, NA: University of Nebraska Press, 1992).

Rorty, R, 'Habermas and Lyotard on Postmodernity' (1992) in *Habermas and Modernity* (Bernstein, R, ed; Cambridge: Polity).

Rose, G, *The Dialectic of Nihilism: Post-Structuralism and Law* (Oxford: Blackwell, 1984).

Rose, N, *Governing the Soul: The Shaping of the Private Self* (London: Routledge, 1987).

Rothman, B, *Signifying Nothing: The Semiotics of Zero* (Basingstoke: MacMillan, 1987).

Rousseau, J-J, *The Social Contract* (Harmondsworth: Penguin, 1968).

Rushbridger, A, 'Gentlemen and Players' (1990) *The Guardian* 1 February.

Ryan, M, *Politics and Culture* (Basingstoke: MacMillan, 1989).

Saled, R, 'Crime as a Mode of Subjectivization: Lacan and the Law' (1993) *Law and Critique* vol IV no 1 pp 3–20.

Sarat, A, 'Speaking of Death: Narratives of Violence in Capital Trials' (1993) *Law and Society Review* vol 27 no 1 pp 19–58.

Sarat, A and Kearns, T, 'A Journey through Forgetting' (1991) in *The Fate of Law* (Sarat, A and Kearns, T, eds; Ann Arbor, MIC: University of Michigan Press).

Scarry, E, *The Body in Pain: The Making and Unmaking of the World* (New York: Oxford University Press, 1985).

Schulman, S, 'Letter of June 19th 1991' (1991) *ICA Postcard* (Norfolk: Coracle Docking).

Scott, J, *The Upper Classes: Property and Privilege in Britain* (Basingstoke: MacMillan, 1982).

Scott, J, *Corporations, Classes and Capitalism* (Basingstoke: MacMillan, 1985, 2nd ed).

Shapiro, M, *Reading the Postmodern Polity* (Minneapolis, MIN: University of Minneapolis Press, 1992).

Shapiro, S, *Passion and Excess: Blanchot, Bataille and Literary Theory* (Tallahassie, FL: Florida State University Press, 1990).

Shields, R, 'Introduction to "The Ethics of Aesthetics"' (1991a) *Theory, Culture and Society* vol 3 no 1 pp 1–7.

Shields, R, 'A truant proximity: presence and absence in the space of modernity' (1991b) *Environment and Planning D: Society and Space* no 10 pp 181–198.

Shklar, J, *Ordinary Vices* (Cambridge, MA: Harvard University Press, 1984).

Simmel, G, 'The Metropolis and Mental Life' (1971) in *Georg Simmel: On Individuality and Social Forms* (Levine, N, ed; Chicago: University of Chicago Press).

Simon, S and Gagnon, J, 'The Anomie of Affluence: A Post-Mertonian Conception' (1976) *American Journal of Sociology* no 82 pp 356–378.

Soja, E, *Postmodern Geographies: The Reassertion of Space in Critical Social Theory* (London: Verso, 1989).

Soja, E and Hooper, B, 'The Spaces That Difference Makes: Some Notes on the Geographical Margins of the New Cultural Politics' (1993) in *Place and the Politics of Identity* (Keith, M and Pile, S, eds; London: Routledge).

Stafford, L, 'London's Financial Markets: Perspectives and Prospects' (1992) in *Global Finance and Urban Living: A Study in Metropolitan Change* (Budd, L and Whimster, S, eds; London: Routledge).

Stallybrass, P and Whyte, A, *The Politics and Poetics of Transgression* (London: Methuen, 1986).

Stanley, C, 'Cultural Contradictions in the Legitimation of Market Practice: Paradox in the Regulation of the City' (1992a) in *Global Finance and Urban Living: A Study of Metropolitan Change* (Budd, L and Whimster, S, eds; London: Routledge).

Stanley, C, 'Serious Money: Legitimation of Deviancy in the Financial Markets' (1992b) *International Journal of the Sociology of Law* vol 20 pp 43–60.

Stanley, C, 'Sins and Passions' (1993) *Law and Critique* vol IV no 2 pp 207–226.

Stanley, C, 'Speculators: Culture, Economy and the Legitimation of Deviance' (1994a) *Crime, Law and Social Change* vol 21 pp 229–251.

Stanley, C, 'Mavericks at the Casino: Legal and Ethical Indeterminacy in the Financial Markets' (1994b) *Asset Protection and Financial Crime* vol 2 no 2 pp 137–150.

Stanley, C, 'Teenage Kicks: Urban Narratives of Dissent Not Deviance' (1995) *Crime, Law and Social Change* vol 22 pp 91–119.

Strange, S, *Casino Capitalism* (Oxford: Blackwell, 1986).

Steureman, E, 'Habermas vs Lyotard: Modernity vs Postmodernity?' (1992) in *Judging Lyotard* (Benjamin, A, ed; London: Routledge).

Stoller, R, *Pain and Passion: A Psychoanalyst Explores the World of S/M* (New York: Free Press, 1991).

Taylor, B, 'Reason and Happiness: Some Psychoanalytic Themes in Critical Theory' (1985) in *Habermass and Modernity* (Bernstein, R, ed; Cambridge: Polity).

Taylor, I (ed), *The Social Effects of Free Market Policies* (London: Harvester Wheatsheaf, 1990).

Taylor, M, *Erring: A Postmodern A/Theology* (Chicago: University of Chicago Press, 1987).

Taylor, M, 'Desire of Law Law of Desire' (1990) *Cardozo Law Review* no 11 pp 1269–1274.

Taylor, W, 'Crime? Greed? Big Ideas? What were the '80s About?' (1992) *Harvard Business Review* January-February pp 32–45.

Teubner, G, 'Regulatory Law: Chronicle of a Death Foretold' (1992) *Social and Legal Studies* vol I no 2 pp 451–475.

Thrift, N and Leyshon, A, 'In the Wake of Money: The City and the Accumulation of Value' (1992) in *Global Finance and Urban Living: A Study in Metropolitan Change* (Budd, L and Whimster, S, eds; London: Routledge).

Townsend L, *The Leatherman's Handbook II* (San Francisco, CA: Bay Press, 1983).

Ulmer, G, *Applied Grammatology* (Baltimore: John Hopkins University Press, 1989).

Urry, J, *The Anatomy of Capitalist Societies* (London: MacMillan, 1981).

Urry, J, 'Social Relations, Space and Time' (1985) in *Social Relations and Spatial Structures* (Gregory, D and Urry, J, eds; London: MacMillan).

Urry, J, 'Disorganised Capitalism' (1988) *Marxism Today* October.

Urry, J and Lash, S, *The End of Organised Capitalism* (London: Polity, 1987).

Veljanovski, C, 'Introduction' (1988) in *Financial Regulation – Or Over-Regulation?* (Seldon, A, ed; London: Institute of Economic Affairs).

Virilio, P, *Speed and Politics* (New York: Semiotext(e), 1986).

Wakefield, N, *Postmodernism: Twilight of the Real* (London: Pluto Press, 1990).

Weait, M, 'Swans Reflecting Elephants: Imagery and the Law' (1992) *Law and Critique* vol III no 1 pp 51–67.

Weiner, M, *English Culture and the Decline of the Industrial Spirit 1850–1980* (Harmondsworth: Penguin, 1985).

Weinstein, D and Weinstein, A, *Postmodern(ized) Simmel* (London: Routledge, 1993).

Whimster, S and Budd, L, 'Introduction' (1992) in *Global Finance and Urban Living: A Study in Metropolitan Change* (London: Routledge).

Whimster, S, 'Yuppies: A Keyword of the 1980s' (1992) in *Global Finance and Urban Living: A Study in Metropolitan Change* (London: Routledge).

Willems-Braun, B, 'Situating cultural politics: fringe festivals and the production of spaces of intersubjectivity' (1994) *Economy and Planning D: Society and Space* no 12 pp 74–104.

Winder, R, 'When Murder Is Not Enough' (1991) *The Guardian* 27 April.

Winterson, J, *Sexing the Cherry* (London: Vintage, 1989).

Wolfe, T, *The Bonfire of the Vanities* (London: Picador, 1987).

Wyschogrod, E, *Saints and Postmodernism* (Chicago: University of Chicago Press, 1990).

Young, E, 'Children of the Revolution: Fiction takes to the Streets/The Beast in the Jungle, the Figure in the Carpet' (1992) in *Shopping in Space: Essays on American 'Blank Generation' Fiction* (Young, E and Caveney, G, eds; London: Serpent's Tail).

Zizek, S, *Enjoy Your Symptom! Jacques Lacan in Hollywood and out* (London: Routledge, 1992).

Zukin, S, 'The Postmodern Debate Over Urban Form' (1988) *Theory, Culture and Society* vol 5 no 2–3 pp 431–477.

Zukin, S, 'Postmodern Urban Landscapes: Mapping Culture and Power' (1992) in *Modernity and Identity* (Lash, S and Friedman, J, eds; Oxford: Blackwell).

INDEX

A

accelerated sclerosis............42, 59–61, 148

accumulation 47–48, 51, 52, 54, 57, 70, 81, 101
 capital...10, 30
 flexible 2, 29, 46

aesthetics 4, 29, 32, 67, 106, 130, 193
 of violence.......................136–138, 141

affirmation .....xi, xii, xiii, 10, 51, 107, 112, 122, 144–145, 148–150
 of lack 11, 55, 154–155, 187, 194
 and transgression [*see* transgression, affirmative]

affluence..........ix, x, xii, 10, 23, 25, 27, 29, 32, 33, 45–48, 49, 50, 52, 54,61,80, 88, 99, 160, 194
 and anomie [*see* anomie of affluence]
 excess of....................................45, 104
 absence of................45, 72, 80, 99, 104, 158, 162

agency..................iii, 37, 87, 147, 151, 159

alienation ....ix, x, 9, 10, 23, 25, 27, 29, 32, 33, 45, 49, 52, 59–61, 69, 131, 155, 160, 163, 194
 of desire [*see* desire, alienation of]
 hyper- 59–61, 143

alterity 1, 2
 [*see also* otherness]
 and justice [*see* justice and alterity]

Althusser, L 38–39, 42

ambivalence...................3, 7, 13, 154–155, 158, 162
 anomie.............ix, x, 10, 23, 25, 27, 29, 32, 33, 45, 49, 52, 58, 69, 88–89, 101, 155, 160, 194
 of affluence............................50, 51, 97
 and opposition 54
 of scarcity 49–50, 97

architecture
 postmodern.................................75–76

Arendt, H 16, 143

association......................................iii, 110

authority.................45, 52, 54, 61, 71, 94, 96, 113–114, 126, 141, 142, 187
 and deregulation [*see* deregulation and authority]
 and regulation [*see* regulation and authority]

B

Bataille, G 118–119, 120, 137, 140, 184, 189, 190, 195

Baudrillard, J...............9–10, 26n 7, 32, 53, 57n 3, 58, 79, 84, 104, 111, 119, 142, 166
 [*see also* conformity, hyper-, reality, hyper-, implosion, seduction, simulation, politics, trans-]
 'The Beaubourg Effect'......................72
 Simulations 17, 27, 27n 8, 29, 31, 47, 65, 127, 134
 In the Shadow of the Silent Majorities......66
 The Evil Demon of Images................23n 3
 'Consumer Society' 46, 52, 135, 167
 The End of Production.........28, 69, 76–77
 Fatal Strategies 54, 108
 'Transpolitics, Transsexuality, Trans-ethics'............................45–46
 Symbolic Exchange and Death.........28, 33, 60, 76–77, 143

belonging................................v, 6, 31, 32
 space of.....................................31, 106

Blanchot, M................................121, 141
 [*see also* law and transgression]

Blue Arrow affair 90–93

body ....xi, 19, 31, 112–114, 115, 125, 126, 148, 173, 186
 and desire...............xi, 18, 116, 169, 179
 disordered ....xii, 171
 individual......................xi, 18, 113, 114, 116, 169, 182
 of law..............xi, 12–13, 169, 179–180
 politic ....xi, 113–116, 148, 171, 179–180, 182, 188
 and power [*see* power, bio-]
 regulated..............................v, 113, 123
 and transgression 112
 without-organs..............xi, 41, 60, 108, 112–116, 120, 125, 126

Bogue, R....................41, 60, 120n 5, 123, 188, 189

borders..14, 107
[*see also* boundaries, limits]

boundaries............................7, 39, 87, 165
[*see also* borders, limits]

Bourdieu, P 31, 32, 40, 79, 80n 4, 160
[*see also* habitus]

Brown ....xiii, 169–190
[*see also* Operation Spanner, sado-masochism]
and consent.......172, 174, 176–177, 188
and excess................................171, 190

C

capital ....iv, vii, ix, x, 12, 23, 30, 24, 42, 63, 67, 70
[*see also* capitalism]
accumulation [*see* accumulation, capital]
flight 42, 65
multinational.....................................46
and symbolic laws [*see* symbolic laws of capital]

capitalism......................ix, 3, 5, 23, 30, 34, 42, 57–58, 69, 72, 129, 137, 152
and crisis [*see* crisis of capitalism]
disorganised 159
global 30, 46, 64, 69, 70, 74, 77, 78
late.................................22, 27, 46, 101
postmodern 28, 38, 45–46, 57
and regulation [*see* regulation and capitalism]
and schizophrenia..............................60
urban 41

Certeau de, M 4, 5, 23, 25, 41–42, 146, 182, 183, 194, 196

Chambers, I..................6–7, 9, 16, 23, 33, 34, 62, 64, 158

chaos.......................................xiii, 2, 102

Churchill, C
Serious Money 73–74, 75, 78, 80, 81, 86, 92n 9, 99

city ....iii, iv, v, vii, ix, 6, 33, 42, 104, 105, 110, 116
[*see also* The City of London, Megalopolis, urban]
and community [*see* community and city]
global v inner 99–103
[*see also* London, East End]
and law [*see* law and city]
postmodern.........iv, v, vi, viii, xi, 5, 152
and space [*see* space of city]

colonisation 5, 7, 8, 12, 15, 16, 31, 35, 42, 60, 105, 106–107, 146, 149

commodification ....iv, 30, 45–48, 57, 59, 85, 108, 129, 162
of desire [*see* desire as commodity]
and fetishism [*see* fetishism, commodity]
hyper- 49, 50, 58

communication 30, 32, 61, 153

community ....iii, vi, xi, xiii, 65–66, 78, 79, 100, 103, 114, 146, 155, 193
and city ....v, 100
and desire [*see* desire, communal]
of difference........................20, 155, 162
interpretive 21
and justice..............vii, xi, xiii, 101, 192
local v
of others ....iii, 100, 149

conformity 89, 123
hyper- 53–54, 121

consumption.............iv, ix, xii, 10, 15, 22, 27, 30, 31, 34, 35, 45–48, 50, 52, 53, 59, 61, 64, 65, 67, 76, 79, 84, 85, 118, 131, 141, 146, 194
and *American Psycho* [*see American Psycho* and consumption]
absence of ....xiii, 47
culture of [*see* culture of consumption]
economy of [*see* economy of consumption]
excess of [*see* excess of consumption]
hyper- 59, 162–163
order of.......................................32, 33
politics of 108
self- 51, 55
and society [*see* social/society, consumer]
violence of [*see* violence of consumption]

'the contemporary' 8, 14, 32, 55, 159, 167, 196
[*see also* postmodernity]

crime....139–140
City....70, 86, 87, 90, 93, 97, 100
state....71–72, 86

criminology....vii, xii, 64n 5, 103, 149, 156, 158

crisis
of capitalism....84
of metaphysics....37
of legitimation....xiii, 27, 29, 33, 35, 80
of politics....iv, xiii
of regulation....ix

cruelty....140, 169, 181–183, 192
[*see also* violence]

cultural theory....iii, x, 4, 158

culture....iv, vii, ix, 30, 88, 103
as conflictual....38–40
of consumption....xii, ix, 76, 89, 145, 163
disciplinary....31
enterprise....x, 52, 70, 74, 84, 85, 89, 97, 102
of excess....42
global....26, 30
and order [*see* order and culture]
signifying....46, 55
sub-....xii, 38, 103, 156, 158, 159–160, 161
urban [*see* urban culture]
visual....127–128,
youth....xii, 156, 158

cyberspace....vi, 164

D

Davis, M....9, 14

decolonisation....v, ix, 8, 9, 12, 14, 42, 112, 149

deconstruction....iii, 43

Deleuze, G....v, 9, 65, 118–119, 120n 5, 147
[*see also* Phantasm]
Nietzsche and Philosophy....11, 61, 180
'Coldness and Cruelty'....133, 186–187, 188
The Logic of Sense....61, 123–124
and Guattari, F....32, 38, 42, 119, 184, 193, 197
[*see also* body-without-organs, desiring machines, deterritorialisation, nomadism/nomadology, rhizome, schizophrenia]
Anti-Oedipus: Capitalism and Schizophrenia....26n 7, 33, 41, 55, 60, 114, 115–116, 143
'Rhizome: Introduction'....55
On the Line....59, 115
Nomadology: The War Machine....4, 23n 3
A Thousand Plateaus: Capitalism and Schizophrenia....60, 122, 125, 175

deregulation....iv, v, vii, ix, 9, 24, 42, 45, 53, 54, 79, 108, 147
and authority....52
of desire....xi, 31, 124, 143, 145
and disorder....vii, ix, 101
financial....x, 100–106
and space....ix, xii, 8, 165
urban....x, 100–101, 105–106, 148

Derrida, J....15n 5, 150, 181n 2

desire....iv, v, vii, xi, xii, 17, 29, 42, 47, 58, 144, 184, 193
alienation of....ix, 55, 185n 5
and *American Psycho* [*see American Psycho* and desire]
and body [*see* body and desire]
as commodity....65, 110, 121,
communal....20, 117, 121, 126, 153, 192
deregulation of [*see* deregulation of desire]
emancipation of....34, 52, 59, 121, 167, 171, 188, 196
and excess....55, 141, 192
exhaustion of....55
and identity [*see* identity and desire]
individual....16, 18, 22, 31, 32, 52, 55, 84, 104, 106, 153, 171, 185, 192
and lack....47, 55, 118, 119, 125, 153, 162, 165, 167, 194
and language....122, 143, 195
and law [*see* law and desire]
movement of....18, 55, 88, 121, 148
of/for other....32, 41
production of....xii, 16, 38, 48, 88, 121–122, 126, 147, 156, 163
and refusal....60
regulation of [*see* regulation of desire]

representation of [*see* representation of desire and]
repressed 32, 59, 122, 167, 194
satiation of 32, 54, 55, 66, 88, 89, 119, 160
and sexuality 171
socialisation of 28, 122, 195
space of [*see* space of desire]

desiring-machines 41, 60, 116, 120, 145

desublimation..................................52, 59

deterritorialisation ....v, 16, 32, 38, 42, 45, 60, 104, 116, 119, 122, 125, 146, 148, 196

deviance...............x, xii, 26, 43, 50, 70, 86, 87, 88–89, 97, 100, 140, 149, 152, 158, 162, 170

difference....................iii, 12, 15, 111, 126, 151, 162, 194
[*see also* alterity, otherness]
community of [*see* community of difference]
politics of [*see* politics of difference]

discipline 18, 22, 24, 25, 31, 32, 64, 103, 105, 117, 143, 148, 151, 169–170

discourse 40–41, 151
and space [*see* space, discursive]

disorder..................iv, v, ix, xi, xii, 5, 7, 9, 11, 17, 44, 49, 60, 167, 194
in city...................6, 105, 106, 132, 155
and deregulation [*see* deregulation and disorder]

disorientation ....iv, vii, 1, 9

Dostoevsky, F 130–131, 142, 143

Douzinas, C, Warrington, R, with McVeigh, S 15n 6, 22, 181

Durkheim, E 48–55, 57–61, 88–90, 141n 8
[*see also* anomie, solidarity]

E

Easton-Ellis, B
American Psycho ....xii, 74n 2, 127–144, 154n 6, 159, 163
and consumption......................133, 136
and desire 132, 134
and excess.........................132, 134, 136
and psychoanalysis 139–140
and serial killing........................128, 135
and transgression 128, 133, 140, 142
and violence.....129, 130–131, 132–133, 136–138, 142

economy...30, 77
of consumption 30, 129
of desire...................................108, 119
of excess......................78, 120, 128, 137
of images..11
political ....iv, v, vii, viii, ix, 11, 15, 21, 30, 47, 108
of simulations 27, 28, 29
symbolic ....xi, 10, 40, 45, 48
of transgression 45, 47–48, 57, 59, 61, 69, 112, 120, 146, 162, 197

emancipation 23, 28, 34, 37, 47, 52, 53, 58, 65, 117, 146
of desire [*see* desire, emancipation of]

ethics ....iii, v, viii, 8, 11, 15, 20, 67, 78, 106, 117, 121, 191, 192, 196
of affluence..................................45, 48
business 80, 87, 88
of excess..17
schizophrenic 38, 42
and space [*see* space and ethics]

'the everyday' ....iii, v, viii, 8, 11, 15, 20, 31, 109, 136, 150, 162, 163

excess.......................iv, v, x, 18n 8, 23, 51, 52, 66, 79, 105, 107, 111, 155, 167, 194
aesthetics of.................................17, 67
of affluence [*see* affluence, excess of]
of alienation 57
and *American Psycho* [*see American Psycho* and excess]
and *Brown* [*see Brown* and excess]
of consumption 47, 49
culture of [*see* culture of excess]
and desire [*see* desire and excess]
economy of [*see* economy of excess]
ethics of [*see* ethics of excess]
as force...17
and law [*see* law and excess]
of regulation ....vii, 126, 152
of representation.........................19, 124

of reproduction 45
and resistance ....x, xiii
and transgression 19, 142–144
urban ....ix, xi, xii, xiii, 64, 105, 146

exchange 27, 78, 83, 120
[*see also* economy, market]

F

fantasy 50–56
[*see also* phantasy]

Featherstone, M....27, 28, 50, 108

fetishism....47
commodity 46

finance/financial....ix, 72–73, 76
deregulation [*see* deregulation, financial]
global....75, 77, 80, 89
market [*see* market, financial]
regulation [*see* regulation, financial]

Foucault, M....xiii, 16n 7, 30, 32, 44, 171, 194
[*see also* discipline, governmentality, heterotopia]
The Order of Things 123
Mental Illness and Psychology....183
'A Preface to Transgression' 18–19, 118, 119, 123
Discipline and Punish 31, 64, 103–104, 114, 123, 148n 2, 181, 183, 189
'On Governmentality' 24, 43, 119
The History of Sexuality: Vol 1 ....115n 4, 70, 184
Power/Knowledge....43, 153
'Of Other Spaces' ....iv, vi, 4, 147, 196
Death and the Labyrinth....133
Technologies of Self....108n 1
Foucault Live 192–193
'Qu'est-ce que la critique?' 10
'Politics and the Study of Discourse' 24

fragmentation....v, 5, 6, 11, 21, 22, 26, 28, 31, 33, 38, 40, 41, 45, 49, 55, 69, 72, 79, 88, 107, 115, 149, 153, 196

Freud, S ....v, 51, 56, 122, 122n 6, 139
[*see also* Phantasy]

G

Gane, M 51, 52, 57n 3, 58, 59

gaze 18, 23, 31, 63, 67, 117, 128, 148, 162, 167, 197

globalisation....6, 15, 28, 30, 36, 51, 82
of capitalism [*see* capitalism, global]
and city [*see* city, global]
of culture [*see* culture, global]
of finance [*see* finance, global]

Goodrich, P....viii, 8n 2, 11–16, 32, 61, 109n 2, 113n 3, 114, 166, 170, 179, 180
[*see also* accelerated sclerosis]

governmentality....iv, viii, x, xi, xii, xiii, 8, 12, 17, 18, 24, 30, 32, 42, 43, 60, 83–84, 105, 147, 152, 153, 193, 197
nomadic....42, 67, 101, 104, 126, 144, 154, 166, 195, 196

Gramsci, A 39, 66, 159–160
[*see also* hegemony]

gratification....51, 52–53, 55, 65, 71, 89

H

Habermas, J 53–54, 66, 79, 155n 7

habitus....v, 32, 80, 80n 4

hacking....xii, 144, 149, 153, 155, 156, 157, 161, 164, 166–167

Harvey, D....iv, vii–viii, 1–4, 12, 15n 5, 22n 2, 24, 25n 5, 27, 31, 33–34, 65, 193

Hebdige, D 84, 127n 1, 158, 159–160, 162

hegemony 8, 38–40, 151, 159–160, 162

Heidegger, M....7, 8, 107

Henry, S and Milanovic, D 151–152

heterotopia ....vi, vii, xiii, 4, 7, 9, 32, 44, 80, 104, 105, 107, 108, 112, 146, 147, 186, 189, 190, 192, 196, 198

hierarchy....7, 17, 34, 38, 40, 41, 43, 196
[*see also* power relations]
material....72, 73, 78, 102

hooks, b ....iii, vi, 4, 9, 16, 191, 196

hyperinflation........18, 24, 35, 44, 106, 145

I

identification...............16, 17, 32, 107, 151

identity ....iii, v, xi, xii, 6, 15, 30, 32, 33, 65, 79, 116
- desire and...........xiii, 154–155, 160, 162
- fractured.....................................xii, 100
- and place..3
- plural...16, 109
- and power [*see* power and identity]
- production of ....ix, 15, 18, 34, 38, 45, 50, 153, 167, 170, 183
- and space..xiii

ideology ....iv, v, xi, 28, 52, 82, 109, 195 [*see also* hegemony]

images 3, 12, 17, 46
- and culture [*see* culture, visual]
- and economy [*see* economy of images]
- and law [*see* law, images of]

Imaginary................7, 34, 65, 75, 110, 162

implosion.................vi, 12, 24, 30, 55, 61, 77, 78, 108, 109, 127, 149, 152, 155, 167, 184

individual.................30, 31, 33, 35, 38, 52, 65, 85, 101,152 [*see also* subjectivity]

individualisation.............31, 43, 51, 84, 97, 101, 163

interstices ....vi, xii, 4, 5, 14, 37, 42, 105, 106, 107, 118, 119, 143, 167

intersubjectivity 7, 40, 107, 112, 152, 154–155, 158, 160, 164, 189, 196

intolerance 10, 191

J

Jameson, F..........................viii, 18, 27, 28, 34, 35, 38, 45

joyriding ....xii, 149, 153, 155–158, 161, 164, 165, 166

justice ....iii, v, vi, xi, 5, 11, 15n 6, 24n 4, 28, 34, 65, 198
- and alterity...........................viii, 67, 196
- aporia of...111
- and community [*see* community and justice]
- and resistance...........................110, 112

K

Kant, I 10, 16n 7, 37, 106, 116, 138, 140

Kristeva, J..9, 124

L

labelling 26, 152

Lacan, J ....119, 125n 8, 140, 192 [*see also* Imaginary, Real, Symbolic]

lack ....xi, xiii, 195
- affirmation of [*see* affirmation of lack]
- and desire [*see* desire and lack]
- of/in law....................xii, 125, 155, 197

Laclau, E and Mouffe, C....15–16, 40, 161, 196, 197

Lash, S and Urry, J ....vi, 29 [*see also* tamezones, wildzones]

law.......................iii, v, 170–171, 178, 179
- art of...11
- body of [*see* body of law]
- and city v
- and desire..............xi, xiii, 23, 105, 108, 116, 117–118, 120, 142, 155, 165, 169–170, 179, 197
- and excess 23
- images of............................11–12, 170
- and lack [*see* lack, of/in law]
- and language....................112, 127, 170
- limits of...............................54, 61, 119
- as metanarrative................................23
- narratives of [*see* narratives of law]
- nomadic ....xii, 12, 23, 147, 148–149, 166, 180, 197
- and order.................................24, 170
- of other 22, 170
- out-(with/out)-law.......vi, vii, x, xii, 11, 14, 16–20, 65, 69, 104, 106, 113, 115, 118, 126, 146n 1, 148, 155, 159, 171, 182, 198

paternal 139
postmodern 12, 13, 23, 25
and rationality 44
of representation [see representation, law of]
and sado-masochism 185–188
sociology of.................................. iii, vii
and space .... iv, viii, 104, 115
and subject [see subjectivity, legal]
and/of symbolic 13, 170, 180–181, 187
and transgression ....vi, xi, 116, 117–121, 126, 142, 149, 185, 192, 197
and violence......xiii, 114, 119, 171, 180, 181–185, 188

Lefebvre, H 18, 25, 30, 46

legitimation ....iv, viii, ix, 19, 25, 30, 32, 33, 35, 36, 37, 38, 40, 42, 44, 51, 59, 70, 74, 84, 89, 93, 103, 104, 105, 106, 112, 150–151, 164
[*see also* authority, meta-narratives]
crisis [*see* crisis of legitimation]
and order [*see* order and legitimation]

limits .... xi, 37, 107, 126
[*see also* borders, boundaries]
of language 112, 113
[*see also* unrepresentability]
of law [*see* law, limits of]
and transgression .....xi, 18–19, 112, 117, 118, 120, 141, 155

linearity 6, 7, 17, 40, 41, 43, 121, 126
[*see also* narrative]

London
the City .... x, 69–70, 73–76, 80–82, 85–86, 87–100, 152
and crime [*see* crime, City]
East End................ x, 72, 73n 1, 99–103
Stoke Newington 8

local................................. 16, 41, 110, 153
[*see also* place]
community [*see* community, local]
resistance [*see* resistance, local]

Lyotard, J-F ....iv, 15n 5, 16, 28, 35, 41, 66, 152, 193
[*see also* metanarratives]
The Postmodern Condition.....vii–viii, 2–3, 22n 2, 27, 29, 36–37, 110
The Differend 10, 110–111
Heidegger and 'the jews' 105
The Inhuman 8, 26
The Postmodern Explained to Children.................... 22n 2, 25, 53n 2

M

Maffesoli, M 4, 109–110, 111, 196

mapping 6, 19, 22, 147

marginality 3, 5, 9, 33, 37, 42, 43, 45, 49, 55, 60, 104, 107, 160, 198
and space 12, 106

market 15, 27, 28, 46, 49, 51, 54, 55, 57–58, 94, 96
[*see also* economy, exchange]
commodity 77, 78
financial 69–70, 72, 73, 74, 77, 81–82, 87
[*see also*, London, the City]
free.. xiii, 69
and regulation 54

Marx, K........................... 2–3, 10, 45, 130
[*see also* alienation, commodification, production]

Mazzolini, M......................... 66, 107, 148

meaning......................... 9, 11, 40–41, 126
[*see also* signification]
absence of......................... ix, x, 28, 108
production of....151–152, 155, 159, 176

Megalopolis ....iv, viii, x, xii, 5, 20, 26, 30–34, 61–67, 145, 146, 148, 163, 194, 197
[*see also* city]

metanarrative................. viii, ix, xi, 2–3, 5, 15n 6, 16, 22, 24, 26, 27, 33, 36, 37, 51, 52, 55, 111, 115, 152
[*see also* legitimation]
and law [*see* law as metanarrative]

metaphor.................................. 50–51, 55
collective 55, 89

Miller, J .... vi, xiii, 191, 198

modernity ....iv, viii, 2, 6, 8, 41, 53, 192
modernisation ...v, 50, 57, 80, 82, 84, 89
[*see also* rationalisation]

money.........71, 73, 74, 76–78, 129–130
panic [*see* panic money]

Morris, M ....vii, 2, 64

Mouffe, C.....................................34, 145
and Laclau, E [*see* Laclau, E and Mouffe, C]

N

narratives.......................................37, 160
of dissensus......x, 8, 12, 15n 6, 126, 145, 146, 152, 156, 159, 160, 167, 170
of law......................................173, 181
meta- [*see* metanarratives]
of otherness.................................9, 106
plural...15, 23

neoliberalism 36, 43, 70, 84, 89, 103, 104, 165

Nietzsche, F..................10, 16, 16n 7, 106, 138–139, 140, 182, 183, 185
[*see also* ressentiment]

nomadism/nomadology ....x, xi, 6, 9, 23, 23n 3, 32, 42, 44, 59, 67, 101, 148, 189, 190
and governmentality [*see* governmentality, nomadic]
and law [*see* law, nomadic]
and space [*see* space, nomadic]
and subjectivity [*see* subjectivity, nomadic]

nostalgia.................14, 32, 46, 52, 84, 162

O

obligation ....iii, 14, 49, 106, 113, 117, 155, 192
[*see also* responsibility]

Operation Spanner......................171–174

opposition 30, 34, 47, 56, 64, 108, 141, 152, 155, 171
[*see also* refusal, resistance]
anomie and [*see* anomie and opposition]

order.........................iv, v, vii, ix, xiii, 7, 9, 15, 16, 17, 24, 26, 29, 32, 33, 43, 44, 49, 60, 115, 132, 152, 167, 184, 194
of consumption [*see* consumption, order of]
and culture 38–42
and law [*see* law and order]
and legitimation 35–37
and regulation...............42–44, 151, 167
and signification 17–18
urban...14, 105

origins...14, 150

otherness........iii, xii, 4, 8, 10, 15, 122, 124
[*see also* alterity]
community of [*see* community of others]
and law [*see* law of other, out-(with/out)-law]
narratives of [*see* narratives of otherness]
space of [*see* space of otherness]

P

panic..46
money 84
moral 158

Pfohl, S 25n 5, 26n 6, 53

phantasm.................xi, 108, 112, 115, 121, 126, 184, 185, 189, 190

phantasy ....xi, 106, 187
[*see also* fantasy]

place..................................3, 37, 105, 106
[*see also* local, space]
and identity [*see* identity and place]

politics ....iii, 11, 14, 15, 28, 71, 83, 101, 155, 158
[*see also* governmentality, neo-liberalism]
body [*see* body politic]
of consumption [*see* consumption, politics of]
crisis of [*see* crisis of politics]
of difference viii
economy [*see* economy, political]
of place [*see* place, politics of]
of postmodernity ....iii, xi, 191
of representation ......iii, xi, 64, 108–109, 112, 121, 155
of space 32
trans- 23, 42, 44, 59, 62
of transgression 136, 138

post 10, 12, 14, 27

postindustrialism..................27, 29–30, 46

postmodernism 5, 8, 11, 12, 14, 21, 23, 25–27, 50, 61, 137
[*see also* postmodernity]
architecture [*see* architecture, postmodern]
capitalism [*see* capitalism, postmodern]
city [*see* city, postmodern]
jurisprudence iv
law [*see* law, postmodern]
poetics of xi
space [*see* postmodern space]
theory..............................vii, viii, 26
and uncertainty...................21, 108, 162

postmodernisation ....iii, iv, v, vi, vii, ix, 28, 57–58, 69, 80, 82–83, 84, 89, 103, 162, 194

postmodernity ....iv, vii, ix, 1–2, 7, 27–28, 32, 45, 49, 66, 162, 163, 194
[*see also* the contemporary, postmodernism]
politics of, [*see* politics of postmodernity]

power............................5, 11, 18, 22, 30, 86, 109, 114, 121, 147
[*see also* discipline, governmentality, hegemony]
bio- 44, 114, 169
and identity 43, 153
relations.........................x, xi, 2, 18, 24, 30–31, 38–41, 87, 103, 105, 106, 111, 119, 122, 158, 160
[*see also* hierarchy]
and space [*see* space and power]

production 52, 73, 78, 80, 119–120
of desire [*see* desire, production of]
end of.............................45–46, 58, 64
of identity [*see* identity, production of]
of meaning [*see* meaning, production of]
mode of ....viii, ix, 3, 27, 76, 83, 151
of reality [*see* reality, production of]
space of 30–31

psychoanalysis ....vi, x, 117, 122, 141
[*see also* Freud, S, Lacan, J]
and *American Psycho* [*see American Psycho* and psychoanalysis]

punishment......xi, 170, 182–183, 184, 188

R

Rajchman, J..................xiii, 192, 193, 194

rationality 25, 30, 110, 150
and law [*see* law and rationality]

rationalisation 30, 49, 57, 104
[*see also* modernisation]

raving............xii, 144, 149, 153, 155–159, 161, 164, 165–166

Real...7, 27

reality
hyper- 59, 108, 109
production of....107, 150–151, 152, 159

Redhead, S 158

reflexivity..29

refusal ....ix, x, xi, xii, 8, 11, 15, 18, 47, 61, 62, 63, 107, 149, 155, 171
[*see also* opposition, resistance]
and desire [*see* desire and refusal]
space of [*see* space of refusal]

regulation ....iii, iv, v, vi, vii, ix, 9, 11, 16, 24, 25, 35, 41, 43–44, 51, 55, 60, 61, 84, 137, 151
[*see also* deregulation, governmentality]
and authority...............................52, 70
and body [*see* body, regulated]
and capitalism..............................22, 69
collapse of....................52, 63, 104, 143
of conduct..................................39, 96
crisis of [*see* crisis of regulation]
of desire..............................xii, 48, 196
excess of [*see* excess of regulation]
financial 87–88, 93–96, 98–99
and market [*see* market and regulation]
and order [*see* order and regulation]
post-.......................................x, 43, 57
of sexuality [*see* sexuality, regulation of]
urban ....viii, xii, 14, 21, 38, 148

representation 3, 16, 17, 76, 109, 110, 112, 126, 121, 150
[*see also* signification, unrepresentability]
denial of..iii
of desire xi
[*see also* desire and language]
excess of [*see* excess of representation]
law of..iii

politics of [*see* politics of representation]
of power.................................106, 109
and space [*see* space and representation]

repression.................vi, xi, 7, 8, 15, 18, 19, 20, 23, 24, 25, 31, 32, 58, 104, 106, 117, 122, 132, 145, 146, 148, 152, 169, 171, 191, 192
and desire [*see* desire, repressed]

reproduction.............iv, 29, 30, 35, 38, 42, 45–47, 55, 58, 73, 76, 80
excess of [*see* excess of reproduction]
mode of............................viii, ix, 27, 48

resistance...................ix, x, 7, 8, 11, 12, 15, 16, 17, 18, 23, 31, 32, 33, 40, 41, 42, 44, 53, 54, 60, 61, 63, 104, 106, 111, 121, 122, 146, 161, 184
[*see also* opposition, refusal]
and excess [*see* excess and resistance]
and justice [*see* justice and resistance]
local..16
and transgression 19
urban [*see* urban resistance]

responsibility.................xiii, 10, 11, 20, 33, 43, 65, 85, 106, 113, 196
[*see also* obligation]

ressentiment...................................xii, 132

rhizome..........................x, 55, 59, 61, 104

risk.....................................43, 69, 98, 105

Rose, G...................................23, 38, 116

Rousseau, J-J 12–14, 113, 113n 3, 182

rupture 5, 27, 35, 61, 104, 106, 107, 115, 120,196

S

sacrifice 114, 135, 136, 140, 171, 182

sado-masochism......vii, xiii, 144, 169–177, 181, 185–187, 190n 7
[*see also* cases, *Brown*]
and law [*see* law and sado-masochism]
and violence [*see* violence and sado-masochism]

schizophrenia 33, 41, 56, 121, 126, 162
and capitalism [*see* capitalism and schizophrenia]
and ethics [*see* ethics, schizophrenic]
and space [*see* space, schizophrenic]
subjectivity [*see* subjectivity, schizophrenic]

Schulman, S..................vi, vii, 1, 9, 10, 14, 19–20, 62–63, 65, 127, 191, 198

seduction ....v, 17, 34, 52, 58, 109, 134, 142, 162
auto-...51

sexuality..........................xii, 182, 184, 189
[*see also* sado-masochism]
and desire [*see* desire and sexuality]
regulation of, ...xiii, 184

signification ....ix, 17, 19, 30, 38–40, 47, 59, 109, 110, 121
[*see also* Symbolic]
and culture [*see* culture, signifying]
and order [*see* order and signification]
regime of, ...42, 54, 108, 109, 112, 122

Simon, S and Gagnon, J.........50, 50n 1, 89

simulation .....iv, 17, 34, 59, 65, 76, 79, 84, 108, 142
economy of [*see* economy of simulation]

Simmel, G...........v, 9, 27, 67, 155–156n 7

social/society.............................22, 30, 66
contract.................11, 12, 179, 182, 188
[*see also* Rousseau, Walliker]
control 53, 55
consumer........................xiii, 30, 47, 52, 54, 70, 129, 143
end of 46

sociology...4, 158

Soja, E 99–100, 147, 196

solidarity 7, 15, 49, 51, 60, 88, 119, 161, 192
[*see also* community]

sovereignty..............................ix, 24, 113,

space ....iii, iv, 3, 5, 11–12, 16, 32, 106, 146, 196, 198
[*see also* interstices, place, spatiality]
of belonging [*see* belonging, space of]
of city 6, 7, 103, 105, 146

conflictual 8, 152
and deregulation [*see* deregulation and space]
of desire 18, 106, 126, 169
discursive....8, 24, 153
disordered....vi, 102–103, 105, 146, 147, 163
governance of....24, 169–170
and ethics....iii
and identity [*see* identity and space]
and law [*see* law and space]
and marginality [*see* marginality and space]
nomadic....154
of otherness...iii, 3–4, 5, 9, 32, 105, 107, 121, 126, 143, 154, 155, 195
politics of [*see* politics of space]
postmodern....3
and power....7
of production [*see* production, space of]
of refusal....x, 32, 104
and representation....46
schizophrenic....28
of transgression....19

spatiality....iv, vi, 4, 5, 18, 30, 155
[*see also* space]

spectacle....66, 123, 140, 182, 184, 185

state....iii, 11–12, 24, 67, 70, 80, 94
and crime [*see* crime, state]

stranger....iii, 9, 155–156n 7

subjectivity ....iii, 6, 8, 11, 18, 28, 37, 44, 66, 84, 87, 123, 143, 148, 155
[*see also* individual]
legal....iii, 123, 124, 152, 184
nomadic....41, 42, 60, 115, 116, 120, 124–125, 184
schizophrenic....41

sublime....37

surveillance....v, 24, 31, 95, 105, 145, 146, 147, 148, 166, 171

Symbolic 6, 27, 31, 112, 155
[*see also* signification]
economy [*see* economy, symbolic]
law and/of [*see* law and/of symbolic]
laws of capital ....ix, 32, 42, 70, 72–86, 104, 135, 142
violence [*see* symbolic violence]

T

tamezones....x, 99, 101, 145, 167

Taylor, I....v, 25n 5

Taylor, M....117–118, 120

temporality ....iv, 2, 4, 5, 32, 84, 107
governance of....24, 84

territorialisation ....vi, 14, 105, 107, 117, 148

totalisation....54, 59, 60, 110

transgression ....vi, x, xi, 18, 18n 8, 19, 22, 26, 32, 33, 34, 54, 55, 57, 58, 60, 61, 64, 69, 87, 112, 141, 158, 163, 171, 186, 190
affirmative....xii, 108, 116–121, 126, 132, 144, 148–149, 154
and *American Psycho* [*see American Psycho* and transgression]
and body [*see* body and transgression]
economy of [*see* economy of transgression]
and excess [*see* excess and transgression]
and law [*see* law and transgression]
and limits [*see* limits and transgression]
politics of [*see* politics of transgression]
space of [*see* space of transgression]

U

ungovernability 11, 106, 107, 108, 138, 155, 192

unrepresentability ....iii, xi, 2, 8, 16, 17, 18, 66, 108–112, 124, 141, 145, 190, 195
[*see also* limits of language]

urban ....iv, v, vi, viii, 5, 6, 14, 33, 38, 148, 196–197
[*see also* city, Megalopolis]
capitalism [*see* capitalism, urban]
culture ....viii, ix, x, xii, 10, 21, 24, 25, 26, 27, 28, 31, 35, 37, 45–47, 48, 50, 56, 60, 64, 100, 134, 136, 155, 191, 194
deprivation....72, 101
deregulation [*see* deregulation, urban]
excess [*see* excess, urban]
order [*see* order, urban]

regulation [*see* regulation, urban]
resistance..32
studies..28

urbanisation ....v, vii, 21, 28, 29, 42, 66, 147, 148
[*see also* urban]
hyper-..26

U

Urry, J 39
and Lash, S [*see* Lash, S and Urry, J]

utopianism......................4, 13, 33, 37, 107

V

value 10, 11, 70, 78, 106, 109
absence of.......................................ix, x
exchange 108, 119
use..69, 108

violence 10, 13, 15, 42, 63, 72, 100, 103, 117, 140, 143
aesthetics of [*see* aesthetics of violence]
and *American Psycho* [*see* *American Psycho* and violence]
of consumption 152, 161, 163
and law [*see* law and violence]
and sado-masochism................169, 176
symbolic 72, 123, 134

Virilio, P 11–12, 32, 65, 166, 196

W

Walliker, D
The Contract ....viii, 12–13, 113n 3

Whimster, S...86
and Budd, L 73n 1

Whiteread, R
House..vi, 101

wildzones ....x, 99, 100–101, 104, 105, 106–107, 108, 146, 148–149, 167, 196

wrecking...156

Y

yuppies 73n 2, 86, 128, 131, 132